EDWARD THE CONFESSOR

The Yale English Monarchs Series

* Available in the U.S. from University of California Press

EDWARD THE CONFESSOR

Last of the Royal Blood

Tom Licence

YALE UNIVERSITY PRESS
NEW HAVEN AND LONDON

For information about this and other Yale University Press publications, please contact:
U.S. Office: sales.press@yale.edu   yalebooks.com
Europe Office: sales@yaleup.co.uk   yalebooks.co.uk

Set in Baskerville by IDSUK (DataConnection) Ltd
Printed in Great Britain by CPI Group (UK) Ltd, Croydon CR0 4YY

Library of Congress Control Number: 2020938190

ISBN 978-0-300-21154-2

A catalogue record for this book is available from the British Library.

10 9 8 7 6 5 4 3 2

For Ben

CONTENTS

PLATES

1. Emma with her children Edward and Alfred, as depicted in an illustrated Anglo-Norman verse *Life* of St Edward the Confessor. Cambridge University Library, MS Ee.3.59, fol. 4r (England, c. 1250–60). © Cambridge University Library/CC BY-NC 3.0.
2. Emma presenting her children to Duke Richard II of Normandy, as depicted in an illustrated verse *Life* of St Edward the Confessor: Cambridge University Library, MS Ee.3.59, fol. 4v (England, c. 1250–60). © Cambridge University Library/CC BY-NC 3.0.
3. *Encomium Emma Reginae*, prefatory image. London, British Library, MS Additional 33241, fol. 1v. © British Library Board. All Rights Reserved/Bridgeman Images.
4. Wisdom enthroned in her temple, from a Canterbury manuscript of *Psychomachia* by Prudentius. London, British Library, MS Cotton Cleopatra C. VIII, fol. 36r (late tenth/early eleventh century). © British Library Board. All Rights Reserved/Bridgeman Images.
5. Detail of a page from the Book of Life of New Minster abbey, Winchester. London, British Library, MS Stowe 944, fol. 29r (this entry 1050s/60s). © British Library Board. All Rights Reserved/Bridgeman Images.
6. The king in his court. From Bodleian Library MS Junius 11, p. 57 (England, c. 1000). © Bodleian Libraries, University of Oxford.
7. Edward, penny, *Pacx*, c. 1042–4; moneyer: Swart, Stamford mint. Arthur Bryant Coins Limited.
8. Edward, penny, *Sovereign Eagles*, c. 1056–9; moneyer: Swertic, Wilton mint. Arthur Bryant Coins Limited.
9. Edward, penny, *Facing Bust*, c. 1062–5; moneyer: Burewine, Wallingford mint. Arthur Bryant Coins Limited.
10. Edward, penny, *Pyramids*, c. 1065–6; moneyer: Aelmer, Lincoln mint. Arthur Bryant Coins Limited.
11. Harold, penny, *Pax*, 1066; moneyer: Aelmer, Lincoln mint. Bryant Coins Limited.
12. 341 Edward *Pacx* pennies, from a hoard of about 2,300 coins, buried at Leziate in Norfolk, c. 1043. Photo: Liam Draycott, reproduced with permission of Norfolk Historic Environment.

The Central Zone of Action

0   100 miles
0   100 km

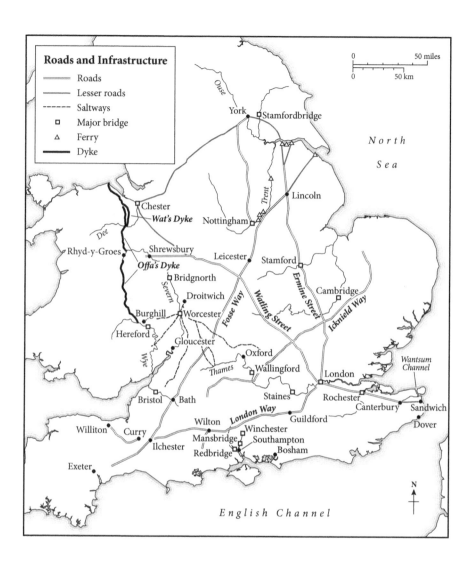

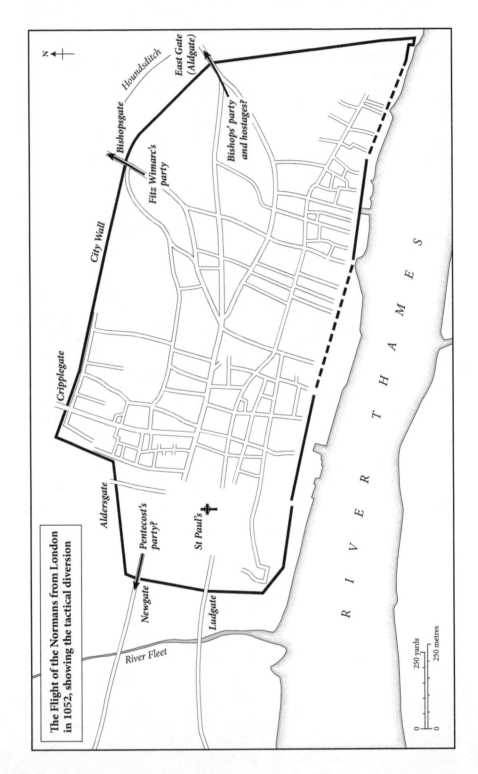

The Flight of the Normans from London in 1052, showing the tactical diversion

N

East Gate (Aldgate)

Houndsditch

Bishopsgate

Bishops' party and hostages?

Fitz Wimarc's party

City Wall

Cripplegate

Aldergate

Pentecost's party?

Newgate

St Paul's

Ludgate

River Fleet

R I V E R   T H A M E S

250 yards

0

250 metres

0

PREFACE

On Saturday 14 October 2017, on the grassy slopes beneath Battle abbey, I sat with one of my students, red and white flag in one hand, pint of cider in the other, as a host of Norman cavalry charged the English on the hill. No one dared believe history would be re-written that day, but most of us cheered Harold and booed the Norman duke, while a few waved flags for the latter, happy with the tide of events. Prior to the action, Harold and William had each put his case to the crowd. Edward the Confessor had croaked out his last words in a fit of hammy wheezing. Once more the stage was set for the re-enactment of the drama – a drama inviting us to choose sides in a battle for English identity. It is a drama that reverberates to this day.

I was less familiar with Edward the Confessor in 2005 when I heard a recreation of music from his reign being performed in Westminster abbey. Music transports us back into the past. It frees a spirit long contained, like incense from a tomb. Arriving at the University of East Anglia in 2009, I started teaching the special subject on the Norman Conquest. Plans for a new Yale biography of Edward were hatched in the summer of 2013; and I began early drafts two years later during a period of study leave in Berlin. Another spell of leave in 2018 allowed me to prepare a final draft, but the rewriting and polishing ran into 2020.

Edward has not been attractive to historian-biographers. E. A. Freeman admired him as a saint but rejected him as a king. Frank Barlow, who wrote the previous biography of the Confessor in this series, in 1970, hardly warmed to him, though he did deem him competent. My sense was that the man and the reign were poorly understood; that over the years Edward had acquired too much baggage and become so entangled with an emotive national story about the downfall of Anglo-Saxon England that it was difficult for historians to approach him with an open mind.

In the fifty years since Barlow's Edward took shape, scholars studying the Conquest era have made many important discoveries and filled a few holes. They have come at tough problems from new angles and chipped away old defences. I am greatly indebted to the late Frank Barlow, whose interests foreshadowed my own, and to the work of others, particularly David Bates, Pierre Bauduin, Stephen Baxter, Katherine Keats-Rohan, Simon Keynes, Levi Roach, Pauline Stafford, Liesbeth van Houts, and Ann Williams. They and many others have been putting together sections of the jigsaw, enabling me better to see and imagine a credible configuration.

Sarah Foot and Judith Green assisted at an early stage by sharing their experience on writing biography. Katherine Keats-Rohan has been attentive on Brittany and on the Bayeux Tapestry. Stephen Baxter has kindly shared his thoughts on the chroniclers, Domesday Book and the earls. Charles Insley, Chris Lewis, Simon Keynes, Richard Sharpe †, Nicholas Vincent and David Woodman have assisted with charters, and Susan Kelly refined my arguments for Appendix 2 (where any errors are mine). Rory Naismith, Hugh Pagan, Jo Porter and Gareth Williams addressed numismatic enquiries, and Jo and Rebecca Pinner supplied photos of the face I forgot to photograph in Copenhagen. Rosalind Love and Elizabeth Tyler have, for the past ten years, shared their thoughts on the *Vita Ædwardi regis* (*The Life of King Edward*). Levi Roach and Katy Cubitt have endured interrogations on the character of Edward's father, and I thank for their help Mark Bailey, Wendy Davies, Hugh Doherty, Veronique Gazeau, Robert Liddiard, Ben Pohl, Ben Savill, Francesca Tinti, Emily Ward, and Emily Winkler.

The lead acknowledgements remain. First, I am most grateful to Robert Baldock for commissioning the biography, and to Heather McCallum and her team for seeing it through to the shelf. I'm also grateful to the few who have given me more scholarly assistance than anyone else. They are David Bates, who encouraged me to take on Edward; Simon Keynes, Liesbeth van Houts, and my PhD student Liam Draycott. Mistakes and oversights are mine. The five people who read drafts and helped improve the book were my husband, Ben Ross, David Bates, Stephen Church, Liesbeth van Houts, and Ann Williams, and it was Ben who got me thinking about character and plot and how to craft a good story. Like the re-enactors, I could not rewrite the ending, but I have at least shifted the light so that its shadow falls elsewhere.

ABBREVIATIONS

AB	*Analecta Bollandiana*
Acta SS.	*Acta Sanctorum*, ed. J. Bolland et al., 67 vols (Antwerp and Brussels, 1643–)
Ælfric, CH: FS	Ælfric, *Catholic Homilies: The First Series*, ed. P. Clemoes, EETS s.s. 17 (Oxford, 1997)
ANS	*Anglo-Norman Studies: Proceedings of the Battle Conference*
ASC	Anglo-Saxon Chronicle, cited by manuscript and year (corrected in square brackets if necessary); unless otherwise stated, from the following editions: *The Anglo-Saxon Chronicle, a Collaborative Edition*, vol. 5: *MS C, a Semi-diplomatic Edition with Introduction and Indices*, ed. K. O'Brien O'Keeffe (Cambridge, 2001); vol. 6: *MS D, a Semi-diplomatic Edition with Introduction and Indices*, ed. G. P. Cubbin (Cambridge, 1996); vol. 7: *MS E, a Semi-diplomatic Edition with Introduction and Indices*, ed. S. Irvine (Cambridge, 2004). Translations are supplied from *The Anglo-Saxon Chronicles*, ed. and tr. M. Swanton, rev. edn (London, 2000); and *The Anglo-Saxon Chronicle: A Revised Translation*, ed. and tr. D. Whitelock, D. C. Douglas and S. I. Tucker (London, 1961). Where stated, translations are my own.
ASE	*Anglo-Saxon England*
BAA	British Archaeological Association
BAR	British Archaeological Reports
Barlow, *Edward*	F. Barlow, *Edward the Confessor* (London, 1970; new edn, 1997)
BHL	*Bibliotheca Hagiographica Latina*, prepared by the Bollandists, 2 vols (Brussels, 1899–1901, with supplements, 1911, 1986). Cited by number.
BL	British Library
BT	*The Bayeux Tapestry: The Complete Tapestry in Colour*, ed. D. M. Wilson (London, 1985), cited by plate number.
Carmen	*The Carmen de Hastingae Proelio of Guy, Bishop of Amiens*, ed. C. Morton and H. Muntz, OMT (Oxford, 1972); alternatively (where stated) *The*

	Carmen de Hastingae Proelio of Guy Bishop of Amiens, ed. and tr. F. Barlow, OMT (Oxford, 1999).
CCCM	Corpus Christianorum Continuatio Mediaevalis
EER	*Encomium Emmae Reginae*, ed. A. Campbell, Camden 3rd ser. 72 (London, 1949), Camden Classic Reprints 4 (Cambridge, 1998), with a supplementary introduction by S. Keynes.
EETS	Early English Text Society
EHR	*English Historical Review*
EME	*Early Medieval Europe*
Freeman, *NC*	E. A. Freeman, *The History of the Norman Conquest of England*, 6 vols (i–ii, 3rd edn, Oxford, 1877; iii–iv, 2nd edn, Oxford, 1875; v–vi, 1st edn, Oxford, 1876–9)
GDB	*Great Domesday Book: Library Edition*, ed. A. Williams and R. W. H. Erskine (London, 1986–92), cited by folio number and column letter.
GG	*The Gesta Guillelmi of William of Poitiers*, ed. and tr. R. H. C. Davis and M. Chibnall, OMT (Oxford, 1998)
GHEP	Adam of Bremen, *Gesta Hammaburgensis ecclesiae pontificum*, ed. B. Schmeidler, MGH Scriptores (Hanover and Leipzig, 1917)
GND	*The Gesta Normannorum Ducum of William of Jumièges, Orderic Vitalis, and Robert of Torigni*, ed. and tr. E. M. C. van Houts, OMT, 2 vols (Oxford, 1992–5)
GR	William of Malmesbury, *Gesta regum Anglorum: The History of the English Kings*, ed. and tr. R. A. B. Mynors, M. Winterbottom, and R. M. Thomson, OMT, 2 vols (Oxford, 1998–9)
HN	Eadmer, *Historia nouorum in Anglia*, ed. M. Rule, RS 81 (London, 1884)
HSJ	*Haskins Society Journal*
JEH	*Journal of Ecclesiastical History*
JL	*Regesta pontificum Romanorum*, ed. P. Jaffé; 2nd edn under G. Wattenbach, corrected and amplified by S. Loewenfeld, F. Kaltenbrunner, and P. Ewald, 2 vols (Leipzig, 1885–8)
JW	*The Chronicle of John of Worcester*, ed. R. R. Darlington and P. McGurk, OMT, 2 vols (vols ii and iii) (Oxford, 1995–8)
Laws	*The Laws of the Kings of England from Edmund to Henry I*, ed. and tr. A. J. Robertson (Cambridge, 1925)
LE	*Liber Eliensis*, ed. E. O. Blake (Camden 3rd ser., xcii; London, 1962)

MGH	Monumenta Germaniae Historica
MSE	Herman the Archdeacon and Goscelin of Saint-Bertin, *Miracles of St Edmund*, ed. and tr. T. Licence, with the assistance of L. Lockyer, OMT (Oxford, 2014)
MSHAB	*Mémoires de la Société d'Histoire et d'Archéologie de Bretagne*
ODNB	*Oxford Dictionary of National Biography*, ed. H. C. G. Matthew and B. Harrison, 60 vols (Oxford, 2004) (http://www.oxforddnb.com/view/article/)
OMT	Oxford Medieval Texts
OV	*The Ecclesiastical History of Orderic Vitalis*, ed. and tr. M. Chibnall, OMT, 6 vols (Oxford, 1969–80)
PL	Patrologia cursus completus. Series Latina, ed. J.-P. Migne, 221 vols (Paris, 1844–64)
P&P	*Past & Present*
Psy.	Prudentius, *Psychomachia*: H. J. Thompson, tr., *Prudentius, with an English Translation*, Loeb Classical Library 387, 2 vols (London, 1949–53), I, 274–343, cited by line number.
RADN	*Recueil des actes des ducs de Normandie de 911 à 1066*, ed. M. Fauroux, Mémoires de la Société des Antiquaires de Normandie, vol. xxxvi (Caen, 1961)
Regesta	*Regesta Regum Anglo-Normannorum: The Acta of William I (1066–1087)*, ed. D. Bates (Oxford, 1998)
RS	Rolls Series
S	P. H. Sawyer, *Anglo-Saxon Charters: An Annotated List and Bibliography*, rev. S. E. Kelly and R. Rushforth (http://www.esawyer.org.uk), cited by number.
SHR	*Scottish Historical Review*
TRHS	*Transactions of the Royal Historical Society*
Vita	*The Life of King Edward who rests at Westminster*, attributed to a monk of Saint-Bertin, ed. and tr. F. Barlow, OMT (Oxford, 2nd edn, 1992)
Writs, ed. Harmer	*Anglo-Saxon Writs*, ed. F. E. Harmer (Manchester, 1952; new edn, 1989)

INTRODUCTION

In 1685, workmen in Westminster abbey broke into the tomb of Edward the Confessor. They found his skeleton robed in Byzantine silk which threatened to come apart at the touch. A golden relic-holder for a piece of the True Cross hung around his neck.[1] More tenacious was the narrative that had been spun around the man himself. Legend declared that Edward had been holy, pure, untainted; blameless in the eyes of God. Historians had sometimes even wondered whether a person so honest and plain-dealing was suited to being king at all. That his reign was followed by the Norman Conquest intensified the spotlight on his performance. Was he, as some argued, a weak king who doomed England by promising it first to William, then Harold? Or was he in fact not the unworldly innocent legend would have us believe?

We can start with the bare bones. Edward obtained the throne in ruthless times and held it almost twenty-four years (1042–66). The question is whether his survival was due more to luck or judgement; whether he merely occupied the throne or made his reign a success. In his era, a king was regarded as successful if he ruled justly enough not to be called a tyrant, held his kingdom in relative peace, and passed it safely to an heir. Peacemaking and justice were values he could enshrine in his conduct, but peace itself and the provision of heirs were blessings only God could provide.[2] Frequently sought in prayer, they were believed to come as rewards of righteous kingship, just as discord and loss of heirs denoted God's displeasure.[3] No king in the eleventh century ticked all three boxes – escaping charges of tyranny, keeping the peace, and preparing the way to an undisputed succession. The fact that all kings in some way fell short shows that kingship had become an impossible ideal. It had been from the start, for the Bible told that even King David had sinned, and he was the

---

[1] C. Taylour [Henry Keepe], *A true and perfect narrative of the strange and unexpected finding the crucifix & gold-chain of that most pious prince, St Edward the Confessor* [etc.] (London, 1688), pp. 6, 12–14.

[2] P. J. E. Kershaw, *Peaceful Kings: Peace, Power, and the Early Medieval Political Imagination* (Oxford, 2011), p. 14; R. Meens, 'Politics, Mirrors of Princes and the Bible: Sins, Kings and the Well-being of the Realm', *EME* 7 (1998), 345–57, at p. 351.

[3] Hincmar of Rheims, *De regis persona et regio ministerio, ad Carolum Calvum regem*, PL 125, cols 833–56, at col. 836.

Anointed One, chosen by God.[4] The biography of a king, however, cannot be a study of kingship, and it should be more than the history of a reign. It is quite simply the story of a man who became king, and of how the office became him. And since 'no man is an island' – particularly no king – it is the story of those around him: mother and father, wife and in-laws, those who helped and those who resisted him.

Edward's story lays claim to our attention. For 950 years he has been cast as the ruler who promised the throne to William or Harold or both. Without the answer to that mystery, we can hardly explain the Norman Conquest, which is still the most famous event – and one of the most contentious – in English history. Edward is also a saint of the Catholic Church. Unlike mere heroes who conquered others, he was deemed to have triumphed in the harder struggle of conquering himself. To study Edward is to examine the attainability of not one ideal but two: whether a person could become king and a saint in addition. Could he enjoy power and exercise self-control? Forced into exile in boyhood, he spent twenty-four years abroad before returning to England, attaining the throne, and reigning another twenty-four. Three kings in that century gained the throne by war. Edward acceded without bloodshed, and his reign would become an interval of peace and prosperity between periods of strife.[5] That it led to 1066 upset the belief that a well-ruled kingdom was safe in God's hands. We might think that the tradition of interpreting catastrophe as proof of God's disfavour would have worked to Edward's disadvantage, just as opinion turned against his father, Æthelred 'the Unready', after the Danish conquest of 1016. Remarkably, however, no writer that we know of blamed Edward for the Norman Conquest. On the contrary, contemporaries soon began laying the blame elsewhere.

Finishing his work soon after the bloodshed of 1066, Edward's biographer blamed the disaster on the leading men of the kingdom. He did so by recounting a prophecy supposedly communicated to Edward on his deathbed, when two long-dead monks whom he had known in his youth in Normandy appeared to him and announced that within a year and a day of his death God would hand the kingdom over to devils – that is, the army of William the Conqueror – because the earls, bishops, abbots, and clergy of England all served the devil.[6] The reason for including such a prophecy, presumably, was to quell any suspicion that the Conquest was a punishment for Edward's own sins, or those of his queen, Edith, whom the author wished to please. We can only guess the retort that would have followed – that Edward had appointed his ministers and was accountable for their conduct. A defence against that line of argument becomes visible c. 1074, when Adam of Bremen, an admirer of Edward, wrote that Edith's

---

[4] 2 Kgs (2 Sam.) 2:4.
[5] *Vita*, p. 19; *MSE*, p. 45.
[6] *Vita*, pp. 117–19.

brothers had controlled England with Edward as their puppet.[7] He may echo the opinions of the Danish king Sven Estrithsson, or of English exiles at the Danish court. Wherever the belief came from, it reinforces the impression that contemporaries blamed Edward's inner circle.

By the 1120s, when the historian William of Malmesbury wrote his *Deeds of the Kings of the English*, a more developed defence was in circulation. Edward's supporters were now arguing that the destruction of monasteries and corruption of law courts, which critics laid at his door, 'came about without his knowledge through the violence of Earl Godwine and his sons, who laughed at the king's gentleness, and that later when it was reported to him he punished them severely and exiled the culprits'.[8] Claims like this were merely a permutation of the view espoused fifty years earlier by Adam of Bremen. They did, however, mean that Edward's supporters had two lines of defence. Either the king had been powerless to control his over-mighty in-laws, including his father-in-law Earl Godwine, or he was unaware that in promoting them he had appointed servants of the devil.

Another idea that emerged as a prop to their defence held Edward to be a simple man, easily taken advantage of. In Malmesbury's day, his supporters employed the idea to blame Godwine's family – Edward's in-laws – for dominating the king, mocking his simple ways, and making jokes about him.[9] Those themes had a pedigree, since the belief that Godwine and his son Harold had abused their position to amass land and riches, and ultimately seize the kingdom, was current in 1066.[10] Edward was not regarded as a simpleton then, neither by a monk at Bury St Edmunds in c. 1070, nor by Adam of Bremen c. 1074, nor by the different chroniclers writing in the eleventh century whose collected works we refer to as the Anglo-Saxon Chronicle, nor by the historian Eadmer in the years around 1100.[11] In Malmesbury's era, however, there was a burst of historical activity, and it was, so it seems, in that context that new excuses were made for Edward; indeed, Malmesbury is the first to refer to him as 'Edward the Simple'.[12] By this he meant something like 'innocent

---

[7] *GHEP*, p. 155: 'Et tenuerunt Angliam in ditione sua, Edwardo tantum uita et inani regis nomine contento' ('They held England under their thumb, Edward being content to live as king in name only'). Adam expresses his approval of Edward at pp. 136, 152.

[8] *GR*, I, §196 (p. 351). There is little evidence of the destruction of monasteries in Edward's reign.

[9] Ibid., §197 (p. 355).

[10] A. Williams, 'Land and Power in the Eleventh Century: The Estates of Harold Godwineson', *ANS* 3 (1981), 170–87, at pp. 181–2.

[11] ASC C, 1065 [1066]: 'the princely Edward defended homeland, country, and nation'; *MSE*, p. 47: 'a champion of justice'; *GHEP*, p. 136: 'a holy man who feared God' ('uir sanctus et timens Deum'); p. 152: 'a most holy king ['sanctissimus rex'] who ruled the kingdom with justice'.

[12] Among the historians rewriting the past were Malmesbury, John of Worcester, Orderic Vitalis, Henry of Huntingdon, and Simeon of Durham. For 'Eduardus simplex', see *GR*, I, § 259 (p. 478); I, § 300 (p. 534).

of deceit', a man who was uncomplicated and plain-dealing – though he admits such a virtue was undesirable in a king.[13]

How the idea may have developed is easy to see. Almost from the moment Edward was dead, if not before, opportunists began claiming he had granted them all sorts of things – lands, honours, even his kingdom – and it may have been this wolfish response to the demise of the dynasty which led people in hindsight to imagine Edward as a lamb, yielding to every predator.[14] The realm had grown more prosperous than ever before. It is an indication of the general interest in grabbing a piece of England's wealth that in February 1068, when the abbot of Saint-Riquier in Ponthieu, hoping to claim estates in England, arrived at Wissant to cross the English Channel, he found that a crowd of more than a hundred monks and abbots and a host of soldiers and merchants all seeking the same thing had accumulated in the two weeks in which bad weather had prevented a crossing.[15]

While historians such as Malmesbury were trying to make sense of Edward's place in the scheme of things, the theme of his dove-like innocence attracted hagiographers who were interested in the image of a saint and miracle worker created by his earliest biographer. Osbert of Clare, a monk of Westminster, compiled a new, exclusively hagiographical biography, in a bid to obtain papal canonization of the monarch entombed in his abbey.[16] Though Osbert's 1138 campaign failed, a fresh initiative in altered political circumstances achieved the desired result in 1161, and, with his papal canonization, Edward became a confessor – a saint who displayed (or 'confessed') his virtues by his holy life.[17] Reports of his faithfulness to Edith were morphing into a flattering belief that the couple had abstained from sex on account of their love of God.[18] Within a few years of 1161, a friend of the abbot of Westminster, Ailred of Rievaulx, rewrote Osbert's *Life of St Edward*, producing what became the standard Latin study of the king.[19] He embellished the image of the chaste and guileless Edward often seemingly at the mercy of his scheming, ambitious in-laws, and he reinforced the myth that Edward was an unworldly man, better suited to a religious life. There was a slight suggestion of this in the earliest

---

[13] Ibid. § 196 (p. 349).

[14] Cf. ibid., § 197 (p. 353): 'In the need of the moment there was nothing Edward would not promise.'

[15] Hariulf, *Chronique de l'abbaye de Saint-Riquier (Ve siècle–1104)*, ed. F. Lot (Paris, 1894), p. 241.

[16] 'La vie de s. Édouard le Confesseur par Osbert de Clare', ed. M. Bloch, *AB* 41 (1923), 5–131.

[17] Barlow, *Edward*, Appendix D, pp. 309–27; E. Bozóky, 'The Sanctity and Canonisation of Edward the Confessor', in R. Mortimer, ed., *Edward the Confessor: The Man and the Legend* (Woodbridge, 2009), 173–86.

[18] Freeman, *NC*, II, pp. 539–44.

[19] Ailred of Rievaulx, *Vita s. Edwardi regis*, PL 195, cols 737–90.

biographer's remark that he 'lived among men as an angel', and more than a whiff of it in Malmesbury's comment that 'the simplicity of his character made him hardly fit to govern'.[20] Both, however, were trying to pour cold water on the idea that a man they regarded as godly might have warmed to earthly power.

During England's Catholic centuries this all remained to Edward's credit, but with the advent of Protestant modernity and Victorian admiration for muscular, patriotic leadership, myths once spun around Edward in his defence made him unattractive to advocates of a new masculinity.[21] E. A. Freeman was the first to write a history of the reign, though he admitted as early as p. 37 that it centred on Harold; and while acknowledging Edward's saintliness, he deplored it in a king. To Freeman, Edward was a monkish foreigner, lacking the paternal qualities of leadership, love of country, and military command. Nowhere is his view clearer than in the comparison between Earl Godwine, 'the stout Englishman . . . the chieftain great alike in battle and counsel', and Edward, 'the timid devotee who shrank from the toils and responsibilities of an earthly kingdom'; he also tells us that Edward was 'utterly lacking . . . in all kingly qualities', 'unworthy' of his 'glorious forefathers', a 'weak king', a 'feeble king', a 'wayward and half-foreign king', and much else in this vein.[22] As a cheerleader for Harold and an admirer of William, Freeman blamed the Conquest on Edward without making the point so plainly as to offend Edward's admirers (who were still allowed to admire Edward, but as a saint, not a king). In Freeman's eyes, the Conquest began with Edward's indulgence of Norman favourites. The consequent struggle between 'natives and foreigners' reached the moment where bloodshed became inevitable once Edward promised the throne to the duke of Normandy.[23] Lionizing Harold as the man self-tasked with standing up for England, Freeman presented him as 'the hero and the martyr of our native freedom'.[24] He knew, of course, that martyrs outrank confessors in the halls of the blessed. Not only was he turning Edward's reign into Harold's story, he was overwriting Edward's cult with a hero-cult of Harold.

Even before this trend was approved by the Oxford professor, it was manifesting in novels such as Bulwer-Lytton's *Harold*. Here we read of

---

[20] *Vita*, p. 63; *GR*, I, § 196 (p. 349).

[21] Cf. R. Lavelle, *Aethelred II, King of the English 987–1016* (Stroud, 2002), p. 9: '[modern] judgements on pre-industrial history favour active rulers'. See J. Tosh, 'Masculinities in an Industrializing Society: Britain, 1800–1914', *Journal of British Studies* 41 (2005), 330–42, at p. 335, on 'manliness': 'Its core attributes were physical vigour, energy and resolution, courage and straightforwardness. Its public face . . . the capacity to make one's own way in the world and to be one's own master.' Freeman believed that Edward lacked such qualities.

[22] Freeman, *NC*, II, pp. 15, 23, 300, 319, 160, 390, 40.

[23] Ibid., pp. 29–31, 300–9, 430–2.

[24] Ibid., p. 37.

Edward's 'infantine simplicity' and 'listlessness'; of a king 'morally wavering and irresolute', 'often weak to childishness'; 'an irresolute prince who never seemed three days or three minutes together in the same mind'.[25] Bulwer-Lytton extended the slurring to Edward's heir, Edgar Ætheling, 'a boy feeble in mind as body, and half-foreign'; and he evidently shared Freeman's belief that the Conquest began before 1066, for when William leaves Edward's company in 1051, after being promised the throne, he remarks, 'Is not England part of Normandy already?'[26] Dickens, writing *A Child's History of England* about the same time, applauded 'the brave Harold' but had little time for 'the dreary old Confessor'.[27] Though the popular image of Edward had improved enough a century later for Alfred Duggan to publish his sympathetic novel *The Cunning of the Dove*, its thraldom to ideas introduced by Malmesbury is plain in the mumblings of its protagonist: 'I am not a very effective King, and I am not very interested in Kingdoms. What matters to me most . . . is that I should scrape to Heaven after I am dead.'[28]

Frank Barlow, who finished the previous biography of Edward in this series in 1970, was an inheritor of those traditions and the unconscious bias they imparted. Born in 1911 he was also an inheritor of Victorian ideals of masculinity. As an admirer of active, patriarchal, military men, he was disappointed not to find in Edward the adventurous fighting spirit he discerned in contemporary Scandinavian kings, and by Edward's attitude to women, which seemed unchivalrous.[29] After exiling her father Godwine and her brothers, Edward had sent his wife, Edith, to a nunnery. Dickens was outraged, remarking that 'Edward the Confessor, with the true meanness of a mean spirit, visited his dislike [of Godwine and his sons] upon the helpless daughter and sister'; his opinion echoes eerily in Barlow's reference to Edward's 'dislike of Godwine' and his statement, several lines later, that Edward was 'the sort of man who could have taken it out on his wife'.[30] Something Dickensian seems to have lodged in the mind of Barlow the schoolboy. On the same page, he says that Godwine, in comparison, 'was a patient man and in the true interests of his family was remarkably long-suffering'.[31] Like Freeman, Barlow juxtaposes Edward's unattractiveness and Godwine's wholesome paternalism.[32]

---

[25] E. Bulwer-Lytton, *Harold* (3rd edn, London, 1853), pp. 44, 91, 94, 107, 42.

[26] Ibid., pp. 251, 42.

[27] Charles Dickens, *A Child's History of England* (London, 1870), pp. 37, 32. The *History* originally appeared in his *Household Words* weekly magazine (Jan. 1851–Dec. 1853).

[28] A. Duggan, *The Cunning of the Dove* (London, 1960), p. 176.

[29] Barlow, *Edward*, pp. 19, 90.

[30] Dickens, *Child's History*, p. 30; Barlow, *Edward*, p. 90.

[31] Barlow, *Edward*, p. 90.

[32] Barlow's contrast between the family man and the implicit wife-beater corresponds to Freeman's contrast between the 'stout Englishman' and 'timid devotee', but it impugns the latter's saintliness in a way Freeman never did: Freeman, *NC*, II, p. 15.

Aware that pious enthusiasm for Edward was growing as he wrote, Barlow – a sceptic and a conscientious iconoclast – felt duty-bound to uncover his subject's human failings. Suspecting flaws in Edward's character, he chipped away at his saintliness, which Freeman had left intact. Freeman had written that 'of his many personal virtues, his earnest piety, his good intentions in every way, his sincere desire for the welfare of his people, there can be no doubt'.[33] Barlow begged to differ, and he did so by peppering the articles preparatory to his biography with critical asides. In an article of 1965 on Edward's 'early life, character and attitudes', he cast him as a man who 'used other people', who 'sacrificed some of his dearest friends . . . to keep his position', who 'bought peace at almost any price', who apparently never 'searched for work', whose attitude to his wife was 'calculating and casual', even leading to 'bad behaviour', and whose treatment of the Church was 'careless'.[34] On Edward's decision to negotiate with William when the latter was out of favour with the pope, he remarks, 'such a disregard of principles can, of course, be considered typical of Edward'.[35] The verdict he arrives at 'is not a view which makes of Edward a noble or even a likeable man. It does not endow him with qualities predestined to earn him sanctity. But,' he assures us, 'there is no evidence that Edward was ever much loved.'[36] Though less mordant, his biography applauds its subject with faint praise. 'Although he was neither a wise statesman nor a convincing soldier,' we read, 'he was both belligerent and worldly wise.'[37]

Barlow's sideswipes should put us on guard, for just as Freeman's mission to proclaim Harold an English martyr necessitated trampling upon the Confessor (who was already well trodden on by that point), Barlow's desire to confront the pious with the failings of their saint is detectable in the levity of his really quite damning asides. Later he would warm to William Rufus, a monarch – in contrast to Edward – much maligned by the Church, whom Barlow fondly rehabilitated as a model of chivalry in a biography for the present series. Neither Freeman nor Barlow meant to be unfair to Edward. Both simply served what they considered to be greater causes than doing justice to a man who had been praised for many centuries. Judging him by the standards of Victorian masculinity and – in Barlow's case – by the Scandinavian warrior ethos, they laid too little emphasis on Frankish and English models of kingship, which valued peacemaking, just rule, and delegation of command.

---

[33] Freeman, NC, II, p. 23.

[34] F. Barlow, 'Edward the Confessor's Early Life, Character and Attitudes', EHR 80 (1965), 225–51; repr. in idem, The Norman Conquest and Beyond (London, 1983), 57–83, at pp. 67, 69, 68, 69.

[35] Ibid., p. 81.

[36] Ibid., p. 83.

[37] Barlow, Edward, p. 72.

Whether as a consequence of their lack of love for Edward, or of an opinion, among advocates of a structuralist approach, that 'the puzzle of Edward's reign is unlikely to be resolved with another careful examination of the well-worn narrative sources', no one until now has been inspired to rewrite his biography.[38]

The paradox is that most of the alleged attributes criticized in Edward since Victorian times were first mooted after the Conquest as defences of his character. This merely shows that what one age admires another learns to despise. Exposure to relentless criticism of Edward builds our immune system. It reveals sources of unconscious bias and dissolves preconceptions that prevent us from approaching the subject with an open mind. In the same category are a few well-established ideas about Edward which relate to old preconceptions. Whether they are sound or unsound, it is useful to have them on the table. The first is that Edward never strived for the throne and was content to leave the government to others. In Freeman's opinion, Edward took the crown 'with a good deal of unwillingness'.[39] Barlow maintained that Edward was 'rootless, discontented, mean and irascible' – a 'disillusioned exile, living by his wits, hoping for something to turn up', and that Edward, 'disillusioned, cynical, without great hopes or great ambition, was prepared to accept whatever fate had in store'. Though he believed such traits discernible in his subject, his inspiration may have been George Duby's model of landless younger sons, left behind by the feudal system.[40]

The second belief is that Edward was ruled by his in-laws (the Godwines), and that the latter half of his reign was in reality 'the reign of Harold'.[41] This idea was emerging by the mid-1070s, as we have seen, though the claim that it was specifically Harold who ruled the king is Freeman's token contribution. The D text of the Chronicle observes that, before his exile of 1051–2, Godwine seemed to rule the king and all England. But its manifest point is that he was swiftly undone.[42] After 1053, the English began defeating the Welsh and Scots. Edward's earliest biographer had his own motives for crediting the victories to Harold and Tostig. Freeman, believing that no one except Harold could possibly have run the country so well, noted that 'the policy of Edward's reign is from

[38] The quote is from R. Fleming, *Kings and Lords in Conquest England* (Cambridge, 1991), p. 54.

[39] Freeman, *NC*, II, p. 306.

[40] F. Barlow, 'Edward the Confessor and the Norman Conquest', Hastings and Bexhill Branch of the Historical Association Pamphlet, 1971; repr. in idem, *Norman Conquest and Beyond*, 99–111, at p. 105; idem, *Edward*, pp. 71, 42; cf. G. Duby, 'Dans la France du nord-ouest au XIIe siècle: les "jeunes" dans la société aristocratique', *Annales. Économies, Sociétés, Civilisations* 19 (1964), 835–46.

[41] Freeman, *NC*, II, p. 29.

[42] ASC D, 1052 [1051]; cf. Barlow, *Edward*, p. 109: 'The earl was out of favour, was not listened to . . .'.

henceforth a policy thoroughly English. In other words, it is the policy of Harold.'[43] The idea took hold, causing historians to regard Harold as the mastermind of projects such as the mission to bring Edward the Exile back to England in 1054–7 and a possible mission to Normandy to recover hostages from William.[44] The same long-standing perception of a vacuum at the centre of government lingers with the recent verdict that Edward 'is curiously absent . . . at crucial moments even when it is clear that he was the principal actor'.[45]

The last of the ideas that need to be set on the table is the belief that Edward offered the throne to multiple contenders. After 1066, when Harold, William, Edgar the aetheling, and Sven Estrithsson of Denmark all claimed that Edward had offered it to them, it was an easy conclusion to reach, especially in an age when formal argument advanced by reconciling the claims of competing authorities. Such was the gist of Malmesbury's remark, that 'in the need of the moment there was nothing Edward would not promise – he pledged loyalty to both sides in an argument' – a nod from Malmesbury to the claims of both Harold and William.[46] As Freeman put it, 'in a weak prince like Edward changes of purpose of this kind are in no way wonderful [i.e. surprising]'.[47] Taking Freeman's lead, historians imagined that Edward could have vacillated between as many as nine or ten 'candidates' in the course of his reign, including the son he never had, William of Normandy, his nephews Ralph of Hereford and Walter of Mantes, Sven Estrithsson, Edward the Exile, his son Edgar Ætheling, Eustace of Boulogne, Tostig, and Harold.[48] This would have been news to William of Malmesbury.

It emerges from all the foregoing discussion that there is a fundamental question to be answered about Edward's character. Was he a weak and vacillating prince, or Barlow's wily and unprincipled one, or was he a conscientious, competent ruler who demonstrated princely virtues? The Anglo-Saxons liked a good riddle. Tackling this one is the only response to the myths now open to scrutiny. Pauline Stafford has said that 'in this

[43] Freeman, *NC*, II, p. 366; cf. p. 367: 'that Harold ruled Edward there is no doubt'.

[44] E.g. T. J. Oleson, *The Witenagemot in the Reign of Edward the Confessor: A Study in the Constitutional History of Eleventh-century England* (Oxford, 1955), p. 3: 'From 1052 until the end of the reign of Edward the government was dominated by Harold, and the king apparently resigned himself to a secondary position.' Cf. E. John, 'Edward the Confessor and the Norman Succession', *EHR* 94 (1979), 241–67, at p. 257.

[45] R. Mortimer, 'Edward the Confessor: The Man and the Legend', in idem, ed., *Edward*, 1–40, at p. 12. Cf. Barlow, *Edward*, p. 286: 'a weak but persistent ruler'.

[46] Malmesbury was, however, carefully speaking in general terms: *GR*, I, § 197 (p. 353).

[47] Freeman, *NC*, II, p. 306.

[48] E.g. Barlow, *Edward*, p. 219 (where eight or nine 'candidates' are named); cf. p. 228, where Barlow refers to Edward's 'policy of playing off the claimants against each other' and detects 'cruel humour'. Cf. H. J. Tanner, *Families, Friends and Allies: Boulogne and Politics in Northern France and England, c. 879–1160* (Leiden and Boston, 2004), p. 92: 'Edward had several candidates to choose from.'

period ... character cannot be known'; and there's no denying that thought processes are concealed from the historian.[49] Thoughts, however, only matter when they lead to action, and action – especially persistent, habitual action – is as close to character as anyone can hope to get. 'By their fruits you shall know them.'[50] The challenging part lies in interpreting the action in its proper context, given what little detail we have to go on. Another challenge is the need to examine character from an eleventh-century perspective. People then were not encouraged to ground their sense of self in studied individuality. Rather, they were taught to conform to one or more types (king, mother, queen, Christian); to embrace those roles and find fulfilment within a socio-celestial order.[51] If Edward the individual is unapparent, it may be because he became the type of his sacred persona. To be a king – another Solomon – he first had to empty himself and become God's vessel. Perhaps his character abided in the projection of the king sat upon the throne.

The fifty years since Barlow wrote the first Yale biography of Edward have brought forth new studies and new perspectives. We happen to be standing on the uppermost of a sequence of scaffolded platforms erected on the shoulders of giants! So many of our beliefs go back to Freeman, and beyond to William of Malmesbury, but at least from our wobbly vantage point we can assess the state of the foundations and look to rebuild them from the ground up. That means returning to the 'well-worn' narrative sources, equipped with refined insights, literary approaches to the texts, and a conscious immunity to the baggage of Victorian masculinities and counter-devotional attitudes that worked against Edward in the past. Such are the initial steps of revisionist biography. Whether Edward comes out differently remains to be seen. A relativist might say that the Edward in this book could only ever be my Edward, but since I am accountable to the sources, he must be a convincing Edward, or he is no Edward at all.

THE SOURCES

Near the end of Edward's life, an anonymous author began an account of the reign, which he completed after William's coronation, possibly in 1067.[52] Since the extant copy survives in a manuscript of *c.* 1100, under the title *The Life of King Edward who rests at Westminster*, it may have been revised

---

[49] P. Stafford, *Unification and Conquest: A Political and Social History of England in the Tenth and Eleventh Centuries* (London, 1989), p. 59.

[50] Matt. 7:16. A. Sheppard, *Families of the King: Writing Identity in the Anglo-Saxon Chronicle* (Toronto and London, 2004), p. 22, notes the early medieval view that interior moral qualities were made visible by action.

[51] P. Stafford, *Queen Emma and Queen Edith: Queenship and Women's Power in Eleventh-century England* (Oxford, 1997), p. 55.

[52] *Vita*, passim; T. Licence, 'The Date and Authorship of the *Vita Ædwardi regis*', ASE 44 (2016), 259–85.

in the interval, though later writers who used it show no signs of having seen a different version.[53] The author's identity, long a matter of debate, has lately been established. He was the Flemish monk Folcard of Saint-Bertin, resident in England by the 1060s.[54] During that time, Queen Edith sent him to Archbishop Ealdred of York (1060–9), for whom he composed offices in honour of St John of Beverley, Ealdred's remote predecessor. Folcard possibly began *The Life of Edward* (hereafter the *Vita*) during the crisis of the northern rebellion in early October 1065. Writing when Edward was at his weakest, he looked to an earlier crisis of 1051–2 in the hope of auguring a happy ending to the current one. He thereby inadvertently emphasized the two moments when Edward was disempowered, an accident that fed the myth of Edward's incapacity. As events unfolded – first Edward's death, then Harold's coronation, then the mustering of enemies bent upon invasion – Folcard tried to adapt his story. He may have abandoned the work for several months until the climax of the year 1066 forced him to change course.

Notwithstanding the title it acquired, the work is no straightforward biography. And it does not claim to be. A prosimetrum (alternating poems and prose), it is cast as a 'song' of blessed progeny: children of noble, royal, and divine descent. Folcard reveals his desire to sing about Edward, his queen Edith, Godwine her father, and Godwine's sons.[55] He means specifically Harold and Tostig, for we hear nothing of the eldest son Swegn (d. 1052) and hardly anything of the younger brothers Gyrth and Leofwine. Whether he first intended to write a simple encomium of the dynasty, Folcard adapted his design to reflect the struggle going on in the kingdom, mirroring the struggle of the soul. Drawing upon the late antique poem *Psychomachia* by Prudentius (*fl.* 400), he created a drama as follows. Edward, Edith, Godwine, Harold, and Tostig struggle to preserve the peace of the kingdom. Their success depends on the contest between Virtues and Vices for their souls. Edward, from an ancient royal line – a king chosen by God for the good of His people – is led astray by evil advice. Godwine, a father to the same people and the other protagonists, is wrongfully driven into exile but returns. Although he has the chance to punish the errant king, the Virtues prevail, and peace is restored. After his death, the peace is inherited by his sons Harold and Tostig, who jointly uphold it. As long as they triumph against the Vices, they triumph over earthly enemies – the Welsh and the Scots – and preserve the unity of the realm which mirrors the undivided soul. Edward, signifying the peaceable king Solomon, and Edith, who signifies Mary, the queen of heaven, each

---

[53] H. Summerson, 'Tudor Antiquaries and the *Vita Ædwardi regis*', *ASE* 38 (2009), 157–84.

[54] Licence, 'Date and Authorship'; idem, 'A New Source for the *Vita Ædwardi regis*', *Journal of Medieval Latin* 29 (2019), 1–19; and below, Appendix 3.

[55] *Vita*, pp. 7–9: 'You'll tell, but one by one, of their great worth' (p. 9); cf. p. 85: 'We thought . . . to tell of blessed progeny.'

build a temple (Westminster abbey and Wilton nunnery), denoting the temple of the soul that triumphs over the Vices. The brothers, however, come under attack. Envy assails them before morphing into Discord, then Sin. A rebellion arises, the brothers quarrel, and Tostig is forced into exile.

Addressed to Edith, the *Vita* captures her ambivalence towards her brothers Harold and Tostig. Her positive feelings regarding them are indicated in the prose, but the poems which alternate with the prose are awash with fears. They often erupt from the storyworld of pagan history which furnishes dark tales of brothers murdering brothers; of parents devouring their offspring (or children devouring their parents), and of a monstrous people destined for death. In one poem, the quarrel between Harold and Tostig is personified as Discord, whose worst crime – of seven crimes, according to the Book of Proverbs – is stirring up discords between brothers.[56] This is the crime that destroys that love which alone dissolves all sins. The 'love' Folcard refers to is the divine bond that binds together the cosmos.[57] Personified as Concord, it stands, in the microcosm, for the love of family, and for Edith herself, who upholds it. For she is that bond. The quarrel between her brothers is tearing apart the kingdom and her soul. The *Vita*, as though in sympathy with the cosmic dissolution, is torn between hope and fear, light and darkness, prose and poetry. It is both text and un-text: the unravelling of Edith the peaceweaver.

It may be that Edward was to have played a greater part in the story. Folcard, however, soon became preoccupied with the brothers' quarrel and so with their father's more positive precedent, for Godwine had defused a quarrel with the king. By winter 1065, Edward was no longer at the forefront of the tragedy that was unfolding; indeed, all the characters in the *Vita* eventually fall prey to forces beyond human control. Chaos, Envy, and Discord prowl around in the narrative, seeking whom they may devour. Even the author must obey the muse of history as she guides him down darker and ever more tortuous paths into hellish antiquity and the terrors of Edith's mind. Yet Edith remains his Pole Star.[58] The second half of the work presents a dream-like past in which the dead king's saintliness redeems the unbearable reality his character is made to foretell. He is redeemed too, having triumphed over the Vices and joined the saints in heaven. Redemption for Edith can come only in the spiritual realm and by reading and re-reading the unravelling text, in search of understanding and healing.[59]

From the *Vita*, we turn to the Anglo-Saxon Chronicle, which is a different kind of source. Written in the vernacular (Old English) rather

---

[56] *Vita*, p. 59; cf. Prov. 6:16–19; see also Appendix 3.

[57] M. Lapidge, 'A Stoic Metaphor in Late Latin Poetry: The Binding of the Cosmos', *Latomus* 39 (1980), 817–37.

[58] Cf. *Vita*, p. 5.

[59] Ibid., p. 91.

than in Latin, the several separate chronicles, known collectively in the singular as the Anglo-Saxon Chronicle, record events against each year in entries known as annals. Not every year received an entry, and notices vary in length and detail, though the subject matter is broadly consistent and consistent with the interests of continental chroniclers in deaths and appointments, wars and weather phenomena, and turns of events affecting the kingdom. The project of compiling an 'official' chronicle began at the court of Edward's ancestor King Alfred (871–99), but, by copying and continuation, one text ramified into many. In Edward's reign the chronicles become more detailed, for reasons that remain unclear. The ones which interest us are C, D, and E. To summarize the arguments of Appendix 1: E's section for the years covering most of Edward's reign (i.e. 1042–63, in that instance) was compiled by a partisan of Archbishop Stigand of Canterbury at one of the two monasteries there – either Christ Church cathedral priory or St Augustine's abbey. Work on that section began in or after 1052 and finished by 1070, apart from the few additions made when the text was later at Peterborough. My interpretation differs slightly from the old idea that E was produced at St Augustine's by a supporter of Earl Godwine – not that I claim the chronicler was unfriendly to the earl.

D is thought to have been written by a cleric close to Archbishop Ealdred of York, who was one of Folcard's patrons.[60] Such an interpretation works for the years 1042–67, so I take it to be correct. C appears to have been written by a cleric whose distinguishing interest is his disapproval of impropriety. Yet he reserves his disapproval for Earl Godwine and his kin while excusing the misbehaviour of Earl Ælfgar of Mercia. His horizons encompass a broad spread of events, geographically speaking, though perhaps a 'Mercian' – that is, north-west of London – emphasis is detectable.[61] If D and E are linked to the two archbishops, C may emanate from the bishopric of London. It was apparently compiled during Edward's reign, at least up to the annal for 1065. D and E both drew on C or a version of it and were finished – and maybe edited – after the Conquest. The chroniclers had a chance to compare their accounts, for the elites were in constant contact. Decisions could therefore have been made by regime figures such as the two archbishops about what to suppress, including annals for 1062 and 1063, which all versions lack, though events of 1064 are ascribed to the latter year.

Another kind of source is the royal charter, which recorded the recipient's title to lands and privileges. Two types of charter were issued by King Edward: the diploma and the writ. Diplomas were solemn, Latin

---

[60] E.g. P. Wormald, 'How Do We Know So Much about Anglo-Saxon Deerhurst?', in idem, *The Times of Bede: Studies in Early English Christian Society and its Historian*, ed. S. Baxter (Oxford, 2006), 229–48, at pp. 238–9. For more detailed discussion, see Appendix 1.
[61] Appendix 1, pp. 261–2.

instruments beginning with an invocation of divine authority, proceeding to outline religious reasons for the granting of the gift (in a section known as the proem), before describing the estates and privileges handed over. The bounds of the estates were then set out in the vernacular so that anyone might read them. Typically, there was an anathema clause, invoking divine wrath on persons who infringed the terms of the grant, and sometimes there was a dating clause. Here concluded the substantive part of the diploma, to be followed by the witness list, which the king headed, above the queen and two archbishops. Then came the bishops, earls, sometimes abbots or chaplains, and thegns. Scholars have long been unsure who was responsible for diploma production and of the circumstances in which such charters were issued. When Barlow wrote his biography, he shared the opinion of the charter expert Pierre Chaplais that diplomas were drawn up after the royal assembly where the grant was made. He therefore did not consider them reliable evidence of who attended assemblies, or of hierarchies that may be discerned in the ordering of witnesses. There is a debate too between proponents of curial production and beneficiary production – between scholars who argue for the existence of a central writing office and others who argue that diploma production was delegated to the beneficiaries. Arguments have also been made for the use of both systems side by side. Appendix 2 argues that in Edward's reign the task of overseeing diploma production fell to the bishop of the diocese in which the land grant lay; and I build on the premise that witness lists reveal which potentates attended assemblies. There are, however, many shades of forgeries that were created to 'improve' legal title.

Writ-charters (which for ease I call writs, though writs are a broader category) typically took the form of letters addressed to officers of the shire courts – the earl, bishop, and sheriff – notifying them of a grant the king had made and ordering that it be upheld. Written in the vernacular, they were read aloud in the shire courts as notices of royal decisions. Writs seem to have been little used before Edward's reign when they became an important instrument of central government, enabling the king to issue orders quickly and directly to his ministers in the shires. It is in Edward's reign that we see the first use of the double-sided pendent seal to authenticate writs, to guard against forgery. Authentic writs provide contemporary evidence for the king's decisions and actions, and they identify the officers who presided over regional power structures such as earldoms, bishoprics, and shire courts at the time of issue. In certain instances they may provide glimpses into the king's mind. The same is true of diplomas.

Among miscellaneous other sources that help us piece together the picture, the so-called *Encomium Emmae reginae* (Encomium of Queen Emma: a title from the seventeenth century)[62] is a courtly work propagating

---

[62] *EER*, p. xviii.

a narrative that is friendly to Edward's Norman mother Emma. Its main design is to honour her and the Danish dynasty into which she remarried after the death of Edward's father. Written by a Flemish cleric in the reign of King Harthacnut (1040–2), it bends the truth in multiple ways to Emma's advantage – and Edward's disadvantage – for political and personal reasons. As a source written in the thick of great intrigue, it is not alone in doing so. The *Vita*, and sometimes the chronicles, provide distorted accounts too; and once Edward was dead – if not before – the desire for a neutral, objective account was seldom the motive that animated commentators on his reign. When Edward came to the throne in 1042, the anonymous author of the *Encomium* rewrote the ending, to give the impression that he had anticipated Edward's succession all along.[63] Folcard, writing the *Vita* more than twenty years later, resumed the model of praising a queen through her male kin, though, like the encomiast, he was overtaken by regime change, in 1066, and forced to change the ending.

The Bayeux Tapestry – technically an embroidery – also weaves a story of the turnaround of kings but, in its case, from hindsight. More will be said about it in the proper place, but I would encourage us to read it as a narrative emanating from the years when Archbishop Stigand of Canterbury and Bishop Odo of Bayeux, as earl of Kent, were players in politics, negotiating around each other – that is to say, the years between 1066 and 1070. We could read it as the saga of Harold and William, with morals in the margins, and treating Stigand and Odo as power brokers for the rival protagonists.[64] The E text of the Chronicle, which I link to Stigand too, shares the Tapestry's interest in placing the archbishop centre-stage. It reminds us that the archbishops – both of them, Stigand and Ealdred of York – led the way in crafting the 'official story'. That is to say Ealdred can be linked to the D text and the *Vita*, while Stigand can be linked to the E text and the Tapestry.

Two Norman writers worth mentioning at the outset are the monk William of Jumièges and the ducal chaplain William of Poitiers. Jumièges wrote most of his *Deeds of the Norman Dukes* up to 1063, as I argue in Appendix 4. He returned to it after the Conquest, in *c.* 1069, to bring it up to date. Poitiers, compiling the *Deeds of Duke William* in the mid-1070s, used Jumièges as a source text to rewrite and embellish. An apologist for William, he defends the duke's every action, presenting him as a man who

---

[63] Ibid. For the revised ending, see T. Bolton, 'A Newly Emergent Mediaeval Manuscript Containing *Encomium Emmae Reginae* with the Only Known Complete Text of the Recension Prepared for King Edward the Confessor', *Mediaeval Studies* 19 (2009), 205–12, and S. Keynes and R. Love, 'Earl Godwine's Ship', *ASE* 38 (2009), 185–223, at pp. 193–9.

[64] I align here with K. S. B. Keats-Rohan, 'Through the Eye of the Needle: Stigand, the Bayeux Tapestry and the Beginning of the *Historia Anglorum*', in D. Roffe, ed., *The English and their Legacy, 900–1200: Essays in Honour of Ann Williams* (Woodbridge, 2012), pp. 159–74.

could do no wrong. This was maybe how the duke saw himself, at least by his middle years.[65] It would be too crude to apply a system of warning lights to the sources – amber for everything written after 1066; red for anything later than 1070 (when claims and counter-claims were mounting). Still, the narratives devised by the human brain are faulty at the best of times, and when the legitimacy of an invasion is at stake, we must expect our writers to lie. Everything involves deceit.[66] Courtly apologists dished up lies on a gilded platter and force-fed them to anyone who dared to remember the truth.[67] Readiness to swallow the official version of events was an affirmation of loyalty to the regime.

If sources closest to the affairs that interest us are the most likely to conceal and distort, those farthest in space or time are the most ill-informed. Rumours spring up as weeds upon every court intrigue. Surmise piles upon surmise; defence upon allegation, until the version put about by even an informed contemporary is a murky reflection of what occurred. Events are complex. Narrative simplifies, selects, reshapes. We historians are readily impressed by things written down long ago; we impute honesty and authority to the author, and the fewer details we have about the events that interest us, the more we try to rehabilitate sources that purport to offer something extra. Peckish for more, we bite at lies and rumours confected by crafty writers under the imprimatur of text. Handling their claims, we perpetuate fictions. If seeking affirmation, we affirm interpretations that serve presentist agendas. We align with characters whose stories, attributes or qualities reflect what we like to see in ourselves.

The more we study the past, the more we find our way in a maze of stories and mirrors. The sources, however, will only deceive us if we let ourselves be deceived. Sometimes the exposure of a lie is the most telling breakthrough, because it lays bare a deceiver's motive, and, by exposing our own preconceptions at the outset, we remain alert to assumptions that may cause us to read into the sources what we think should be there. Truths can always be found by comparing different accounts; in silences and omissions; or in eliciting a refutation. They are rarely stated, for nothing is written down because it is true. We must ask of each detail, why is the author telling us this? *Cui bono?* Whom does it serve?

---

[65] 'The characteristic strikingly present almost from the beginning of William's life is his sense of entitlement': D. Bates, *William the Conqueror* (New Haven and London, 2016), p. 517.

[66] E.g. *Vita*, p. 51; *Carmen*, p. 47, on deceit as a normal component of politics.

[67] E. M. Tyler, 'Talking about History in Eleventh-century England: The *Encomium Emmae Reginae* and the Court of Harthacnut', *EME* 13 (2005), 359–83; and Tyler, 'Fictions of Family: The *Encomium Emmae Reginae* and Virgil's *Æneid*', *Viator* 36 (2008), 149–79.

Chapter 1

CHILDHOOD

Condicionem principum miserrimam aiebat, quibus de coniuratione comperta non crederentur nisi occisis

(He used to say that the lot of princes was most unhappy, since when they discovered a conspiracy, no one believed them unless they had been killed)[1]

FATHER

Once upon a time the emperor Domitian, 'becoming more anxious every day', lined the walls of his colonnades with mirrors, so he could watch for assassins who might be lurking behind him.[2] There he walked with his fears until they came true. Nine hundred years later Æthelred too was becoming a fearful man. His worries were a belief he had incurred a curse and a haunting sense that men were plotting against him. As a boy of ten or twelve in 978 he had come to the throne after his half-brother, King Edward, had been murdered. Æthelred's faction were the beneficiaries of the crime, whose perpetrators are now unknown. Barring a plot in 985 and a resurgence of minor viking raids, his first decade wearing the crown had been peaceful. God was favouring his marriage with sons and daughters. On the Robertian displacement of the Carolingian line in France in 987, his dynasty – the House of Cerdic – could claim to be the oldest and most distinguished in Europe. All had seemed well – his dynasty secure – in God's providential scheme.

In summer 991 the Norwegian warlord Olaf Tryggvason arrived at Folkestone with ninety-three ships, an attack force of an altogether different order to the seven ships that raided Southampton in 981, or the three that attacked Dorset in 982. When troops gathered by Ealdorman Byrhtnoth went to fight them near Maldon, the invaders defeated them and killed the ealdorman. Few of the senior statesmen now remained of those Æthelred had inherited from his father. His tutor, Bishop Æthelwold, had died in 984, Archbishop Dunstan of Canterbury in 988, and now the esteemed Byrhtnoth. The following year saw the deaths of Archbishop

---

[1] Suetonius, *Lives of the Caesars*, vol. II, tr. J. C. Rolfe, Loeb Classical Library 38 (Cambridge, MA, 1914), pp. 364/5 (quoting Domitian).

[2] Ibid., p. 355.

Oswald of York and Ealdorman Æthelwine, the last of his father's chief advisors. They left the young king facing a viking army ten times the size of any he had faced and lacking the support of the two senior ealdormen and three senior bishops of his youth.

No diplomas survive for the years 991 and 992. When the sequence recommences in 993, we find indications of the fears that were growing in Æthelred's mind. A diploma issued that summer for Abingdon abbey contains a uniquely personal preamble in which the draftsman, adopting the king's persona (as per usual), explains that Æthelred's thoughts had been racing, working to understand what had gone wrong. He had traced the trials that had befallen him and his nation back to the death of Bishop Æthelwold in the seventh year of his reign, and he lovingly recalled the bishop as one who had cared for him and the realm. At last divine grace had pricked his conscience by drawing him back to a memory from his youth, when he had done things in ignorance and had reduced the abbey of Abingdon – once Æthelwold's own monastery – into servitude, by selling the abbot's office to the brother of Ealdorman Ælfric of Hampshire. He had done this on the advice of avaricious men, including Ælfric himself. As soon as he had realized this, he had arranged for a council and synod to be convened at Winchester, 'in order to be free of the terrible curse as quickly as possible'.[3] This peculiar statement exposed the king's belief he had incurred a curse. Perhaps it was a malediction of the kind Bishop Æthelwold – now gaining power as a saint entombed at Winchester – would have invoked against anybody infringing Abingdon's immunities.[4]

Details in the charter give the impression the king was pulling through a severe bout of anxiety. There is the intense rumination and introspection, the overtly emotional memories attached to Æthelwold, the extraordinary candour of the monologue, the desire to apportion blame; invasive fears about a curse, the mental re-ordering of events into a narrative of resolution, and the gathering of family around him. For this was the first diploma since the year of Æthelwold's death to be witnessed by Ælfthryth, the king's mother, and the first that is attested by any of his sons, Athelstan, Ecgberht, Eadred, and Edmund. It was in 993 or 994 that Archbishop Sigeric of Canterbury persuaded Æthelred to found a monastery at Cholsey in honour of his murdered predecessor, who was said to be working miracles.[5] Appeasing the numen of his half-brother King Edward went hand in hand with appeasing the ghostly Æthelwold. Æthelred's diploma for Abingdon, of 993, ushered in a mood of penitence

[3] S 876.

[4] On his cult, see Wulfstan of Winchester, *Life of St. Æthelwold*, ed. and tr. M. Lapidge and M. Winterbottom, OMT (Oxford, 1991), pp. cxii–cxliii.

[5] S. Keynes, 'The Cult of King Edward the Martyr During the Reign of King Æthelred the Unready', in J. L. Nelson, S. Reynolds, and S. M. Johns, ed., *Gender and Historiography: Studies in the Earlier Middle Ages in Honour of Pauline Stafford* (London, 2012), 115–25, at p. 119.

that coloured the remainder of the reign. Though the king admitted past errors, it shows him shifting blame onto his former self and others he believed had led him astray. Ealdorman Ælfric had to accept the charges of avarice and a loss of influence over Abingdon, and in the same year Æthelred ordered the ealdorman's son's eyes to be put out for a crime unspecified in the sources.

The story coalescing in Æthelred's mind revolved around fears of a curse and fears of evil men. Rather like the serpents of Anglo-Saxon art, those fears were entwined, chasing each other. Æthelred traced his trials back to the year 984–5, the year he sold Æthelwold's monastery to Ælfric's brother and the year another Ealdorman Ælfric – the ealdorman of Mercia – was driven from the realm for treason. The curse and plots thus began to work their evil simultaneously – the two were interlinked from the start. As sea-borne raids continued through the 990s sometimes under Olaf, sometimes King Sven of Denmark, and as Æthelred made further efforts to rid himself of the evils befalling him, terrors continued to lurk in the periphery of his vision. In a diploma of 997 he restored 100 hides to Winchester, admitting he had taken the land unjustly in his youth and that he feared incurring God's wrath and the 'apostolic rage' of the monastery's saints Peter and Paul.[6] Another diploma assigned land to Abingdon in compensation for estates alienated by his predecessor which their father King Edgar had given for the benefit of his soul. Æthelred feared that by retaining them he would incur his father's curse (maledictum).[7] His earlier fear of having incurred a curse was spawning anxieties about multiple curses.

Part of the land he granted to Abingdon in compensation had been forfeited by Ealdorman Ælfric of Mercia on his expulsion in 985. The diploma identifies his crime as treason (maiestatis reum), and despite the passage of many years a strength of feeling is evoked in Æthelred's assertion that he was 'a traitor to me and all my people'.[8] In 995 and 998 the king restored land to Rochester as part of the programme of righting the wrongs of his youth.[9] Though it was the king who laid waste the bishopric there in 986 for unrecorded reasons, the second diploma focuses on the Kentish thegn Æthelsige, 'a wretched enemy of Almighty God and the whole nation', whose crimes declared him to be 'a public enemy'.[10] He had forfeited land to the king, who now restored it to Rochester. About the same date, when the widow of an Essex thegn brought his death-duty (heriot) to the king at Cookham, the king renewed old charges against her husband, accusing him of aiding a plot to receive King Sven several years

[6] S 891: 'et supernum metuens examen, furoremque apostolicum incurrere'.
[7] S 937 (990 × 1000, perhaps 999).
[8] Ibid.: 'contra me et contra omnem gentem meam reus'.
[9] S 885, S 993.
[10] S 993: 'infelice dei omnipotentis ac totius populi inimico' and 'publicus hostis'.

earlier. His widow was obliged to surrender her morning gift to Christ Church, Canterbury, before the king was prepared to validate his will.[11]

The fixation on Ælfric's treachery a decade after his banishment, and the reopening of charges against a dead man, show that their offences were still raw – that Æthelred scratched at wounds and kept them open. His fears that thegns in Kent and Essex were collaborating with his enemies were not groundless. The Chronicle lays the same charge against Ealdorman Ælfric of Hampshire, who supposedly warned the vikings of an attack by the royal fleet, allowing them to escape.[12] That was in 992, and the allegations around Ælfric could account for Æthelred's decision to have his son blinded in 993.[13] The king meanwhile continued his shows of remorse, restoring land to monasteries to compensate for youthful misdemeanours and perpetuating the idea that his misconduct lay in the past. Though borne of inner turmoil, the narrative was as much a device for disarming anyone critical of his adult self. That he had critics is shown by the fact that nobles whose interests should have aligned with his were lending support to his enemies. Even a rumour of a plot to receive Sven implies awareness that loyalty to Æthelred was not always politic. Finding his deputies unpredictable, the king turned to mercenaries; but in 1001 a viking named Pallig, whom he had purchased with land and treasure, met the raiders off the Hampshire coast and joined their attack on Dorset.[14]

Æthelred was fighting on too many fronts to be constantly glancing over his shoulder. In 991 he had secured one of them by agreeing a peace treaty with Richard I of Normandy, which sought to exclude pirates from havens in the English Channel; and it was time to consolidate the Norman alliance.[15] After bearing him six sons and two daughters, Æthelred's wife had died or served her purpose – we do not know what became of her. Either way, the king arranged to marry Emma, the sister of Duke Richard II (996–1026). His choice of bride reveals the importance he attached to the Norman alliance, because kings normally married into the English nobility, though Æthelred may have been distrustful of the latter. Since the Normans were seafarers of viking extraction themselves, he probably hoped they would lend support against his enemies. Emma arrived to celebrate her marriage in the spring of 1002.[16] That same year the king heard of a plot among the Danes in his realm to murder him and his advisors, so he sent out secret orders that all Danish men in England should be killed on St Brice's Day (13 November). Whether the mandate applied only to men like Pallig who had settled with Æthelred's permission

---

[11] S 939 (996 × 999).
[12] ASC E, 992.
[13] Ibid., 993.
[14] ASC A, 1001.
[15] A. Williams, *Æthelred the Unready: The Ill-counselled King* (London, 2003), pp. 43–4.
[16] ASC E, 1002.

or to a larger immigrant population, it could hardly have included everyone of Danish ancestry. Even so, the raids of the previous decade must have engendered a hatred of Danes, and whoever executed the decree may not have been fussy.

In Oxford the frightened victims sought refuge in a church. Their action was a desperate appeal to Æthelred's own laws, which allowed people who were accused of crimes to delay reprisals by seeking sanctuary.[17] The townsfolk burnt it down with the people inside. It was not the reaction of agents of the state carefully separating a category of Danes to be slaughtered. Two years later Æthelred paid for the church's restoration, acknowledging the damage had been done in following his orders 'to separate the cockles from the wheat'.[18] He was referring to Christ's parable about the cleansing of God's harvest of souls from evildoers sprung up among them.[19] When cockles – that is, weeds – begin to grow, it is hard to separate them from the crop, but at the harvest, which foretokened Judgment Day, the weeds would be identified and burnt. Perhaps the Danes had seemed to behave like Christians by fleeing to a place of sanctuary. The grim jest was a reminder their fate was deserved. Though the king of the Danes and many of his people were Christian, Æthelred's diplomas, and masses sung in his reign, equated 'Dane' with 'pagan' and 'heathen':[20] a form of elision which made it easier to slaughter that people without qualms. An East Anglian source claims that the order went out through the king's general Ulfcytel, and that men and women were massacred in Thetford, the administrative centre of the region.[21] Though these details were written down c. 1100, they may represent second-generation testimony.

If the king's shows of remorse were theatre to disarm his critics, the massacre was an attempt to win public approval by appealing to anti-Danish sentiment. That it was a cynical ploy cannot be ruled out, given that the king granted land to a Dane only a few years later.[22] Yet Pallig's treachery in 1001 and rumours of a plot which followed were enough to energize a suspicious mind. Part of the madness of the massacre was the foreseeable strain it placed on the diplomacy underpinning the Anglo-Norman alliance. The biographer of Norman dukes, William of Jumièges, writing up to sixty years later, provides plausible detail, claiming Sven of Denmark responded to the massacre by approaching Duke Richard II and agreeing a peace treaty which allowed the Danes to sell their booty in

---

[17] VI Æthelred 14 (*Laws*, p. 96).

[18] S 909.

[19] Matt. 13:25–30.

[20] E.g. S 911, S 925, S 931; for the Mass *Contra paganos*, L. Roach, *Æthelred the Unready* (New Haven and London, 2016), pp. 157–8, 190, 269, and see also p. 265.

[21] *MSE*, p. 159.

[22] Roach, *Æthelred*, p. 192.

Norman harbours. Though he telescopes events, associating the overture with Sven's plan to invade England in 1013, it would not have taken Sven a decade to respond, and it is reasonable to date his treaty with Richard to 1003.[23] Respect for the new alliance could explain why Emma's Norman reeve in Exeter opened the gates to Sven's army when it arrived there that summer.[24]

Jumièges provides another detail which fits well in this context. He claims that after Emma's marriage, dissension arose between the king and the duke, provoking an English attack on Val-de-Saire, the north-eastern tip of the Cotentin.[25] The peninsula was a suitable place for Channel pirates to offload booty. If the attack occurred in 1003, Æthelred's fleet might have pursued Sven's forces, which had been ransacking Wessex, to where they sold the plunder in Normandy, either to strike against their abettors or recover some of the 'great war booty' they had taken.[26] Having secured an alliance to prevent such a thing, Æthelred had jeopardized it already by ordering a massacre which united Normans and Danes against him. Judging by the tenor of the stories Jumièges picked up later, Norman perceptions of Æthelred soured. Approving of Sven, he condemns Æthelred for the St Brice's day atrocities. The king, he claims, arranged for mastiffs to tear off women's breasts, and for infants to be crushed against doorposts. Our East Anglian source of c. 1100 airs an independent tradition alleging reprisals pitched at the same level. Though again the writer muddles the chronology, he claims that when the Danes sought vengeance in East Anglia, in each town they came to, they stuck clumps of spears in the street and flung little boys on top, where they hung bleeding and twitching.[27] Sven's forces attacked East Anglia in 1004, fought Ulfcytel, and burned Norwich and Thetford. Whatever was done on both sides – and atrocities are perpetrated in war – a viciousness was descending which left its mark in the imagination.

In the spring of 1002 ahead of this bloody tide, Emma of Normandy sailed to England, leaving her kin, country and people; she took a new name and family; she entered a strange land. Her father Richard I had been neither a fully fledged viking nor a model French count. Six years had passed since his Christian burial on the heights above Fécamp harbour, in the guise of a viking warrior, uniting old ways and the new.[28] Her Danish-born mother Gunnor linked her to the culture and storyworld of the Danish people, yet Emma arrived in a realm where vikings and

---

[23] *GND*, II, pp. 17–19; Williams, *Æthelred*, p. 55.

[24] ASC E, 1003.

[25] *GND*, II, pp. 11–13.

[26] ASC E, 1003.

[27] *GND*, II, pp. 15–17. *MSE*, p. 161. Both writers place the reprisals for the massacre later than is credible.

[28] Stafford, *Emma and Edith*, p. 210.

Danes were massacred as public enemies. To her new stepsons, perhaps her equals in age, she was a figure difficult to imagine into the gap left by their mother and the grandmother who had brought them up.[29] Emma herself had to overcome the language barrier, while the worsening of relations between her husband and brother, along with the treacherous behaviour of her reeve in inviting the attack on what was her dower at Exeter, compounded her vulnerability. Her husband was a man who looked for someone to punish when things went wrong. The work written to please her suppresses his existence, writing him out of her life. She could not write him out of her life in 1002. Maybe still only in her teens, she had to get into bed with him.

MOTHER

Æthelred's marriage to Emma reminds us how little we know. Was there an expectation her sons might supplant their older half-brothers? Was Æthelred's first wife a consecrated queen as Emma would soon be? If not, did it harm the prospects of the sons of that marriage? Duke Richard II must have wanted a nephew who might inherit the English throne, but the dissent that arose between him and Æthelred may, for all we know, have damaged a mutual understanding. Questions aside, Æthelred's sons had cause to feel threatened by Emma's arrival, whatever assurances they received. Queens could aspire to guide the king's counsel and oversee the transition from one reign to the next. As mothers, they favoured their own offspring. Such fears were enough to fuel any anxious tendencies the boys were deriving from their father. Emma took the English name of their mother Ælfgifu, perpetuating yet overwriting her memory. Her first child took a name as regal as theirs, a name meaning 'wealthy guardian'. It was a name borne by two kings of Cerdic's bloodline, Edward the Elder (899–924) and Æthelred's half-brother, Edward the Martyr (975–8).

Edward was born at Islip near Oxford, a place his mother gave him as a birthday gift.[30] The earliest he could have been born is December 1002, the latest 1005 when he attests a diploma.[31] No charters survive from the year 1003. Three survive from 1004. One, granting land to Westminster, is witnessed by the six sons of Æthelred's first marriage but not by Emma and not by Edward. Emma is also absent from the witness list of the second, which records a gift of land to Ely abbey. She is, however, present among the witnesses of the third charter, which was given at Headington in Oxfordshire in December 1004. The three charters are catalogued as S 906, 907, and 909 respectively. The last two are the earliest in the charter sequence to adopt a formula in which the senior aetheling Athelstan

---

[29] S 1503 (referencing their grandmother's role).
[30] S 1148.
[31] S 910.

witnesses on behalf of all his brothers. In the charter for Ely (S 907) he attests 'along with my brothers' (*una cum fratribus*). In the charter for St Frideswide's, Oxford (S 909), he again attests 'with my brothers' (*cum fratribus meis*). Given that the formula occludes their names, it might have included Edward. Indeed, the birth of a seventh aetheling – that is, a throneworthy royal son – could account for its introduction as a convenience for including all in the witness list.

Whether the arrival of a seventh son was a point at which a collective formula became preferable, there are other reasons for thinking Edward was born in 1004. Ely, according to later tradition, was visited by Edward's parents to give thanks for his birth.[32] Headington in Oxfordshire, where S 909 was granted on 7 December, places the royal family eleven miles from Islip, Edward's birthplace. In this diploma, moreover, Athelstan has a new title, 'the first-born of the royal sons' (*regalium primogenitus filiorum*). Emma, attesting immediately before him, is described in new terms too, as 'consecrated to the royal bed-chamber' (*thoro consecrata regio*). Juxtaposed in the witness list their titles jostle for attention. Emma's may be making the point that Athelstan's mother was never consecrated. Athelstan's makes the point that he is headed for the throne regardless. An obvious occasion for jostling was the arrival of little Edward and fears about rival claims between the offspring of Æthelred's two marriages. Possibly the king played Athelstan against Emma to keep both dependent upon him, just as he played his viking enemies against each other on at least two occasions.[33]

The *Vita* claims that when Emma was pregnant with Edward, 'all the men of the country took an oath that if a man-child should come forth as the fruit of her labour, they would await in him their lord and king who would rule over the whole race of the English'.[34] Even so, the diplomas display no understanding that Edward was first in line for the throne, and if an oath was sworn its purpose was maybe to affirm her sons were throneworthy. A lesser oath of that sort might still have added to tensions between Emma and Athelstan at Headington – especially if no oaths had been sworn to the sons of Æthelred's first marriage. Whether Athelstan was old enough to appreciate that oaths sworn in one circumstance could take on a different meaning in another, the very arrival of a son by a replacement queen, oath or no oath, was unsettling.

The charter of 1004 in favour of Ely (S 907) reveals something else that occurred about the time of Edward's birth. Though corrupt in its present form, it appears to be based on an authentic document, and the formulae in the witness list place it in the known sequence. It records a royal gift of

---

[32] *LE*, pp. 160–1.

[33] Olaf against Sven in 994; Thorkell against Sven in 1012–13. See Williams, *Æthelred*, pp. 48, 111.

[34] *Vita*, p. 13.

20 hides to the abbey. A story in the *Book of Ely*, compiled by a monk of Ely in the third quarter of the twelfth century, claims that when Edward was a baby, his father and mother brought him to Ely and offered him on the high altar, wrapped in a circular pall decorated with little light-green circles. The pall could still be seen at the monastery.[35] If the story is true, the grant to Ely might have been associated with a royal visit about the time of Edward's birth, in 1004. It is no surprise that Christian parents might express their gratitude for a new boy by offering the first fruits of their union for a blessing, leaving behind the pall as a keepsake. The couple evidently associated their offspring with the outpouring of divine grace, for when Emma gave birth to a daughter, they named her Godgifu, 'God's gift'.

Royal connexions with Ely did not begin with Edward. According to the same writer, King Edgar had given the abbey his purple cloak embroidered with gold, as well as vestments and relics from his chapel. Later, during the reign of Edward the Martyr, Ely's patron – none other than Bishop Æthelwold – took Æthelred to the shrine of its queenly saint, Æthelthryth, where the boy had promised to serve her. As king, he then appointed the abbot of Ely to serve for a third of the year as sacrist to the royal chapel, in rotation with the abbots of Glastonbury and St Augustine's, Canterbury.[36] Even if the writer made this stuff up, Ely's importance in Æthelred's reign is confirmed by contemporary evidence unknown to its later historian. The aetheling Athelstan's gifts to Ely escaped his notice, as did the detail that Abbot Ælfsige of Ely (996 × 999–1012 × 1016) was often at the king's side, where he attested at least 22 of 45 diplomas that can be dated between 999 and 1016.[37] That he was influential with the king is shown by the fact that two monks of Ely in succession were appointed to the East Anglian bishopric about that time.[38]

The *Book of Ely* also claims that – according to the author's predecessors, who used to say they had witnessed it – Edward was brought up with the boys in the cloister, learning the psalms and hymns with them.[39] Though the claim is not implausible, it could be a made-up story that had grown around the presence of the pall. Edward's predecessors were tutored by bishops. King Edgar had studied under Æthelwold, and Edward the Martyr, his son, under Bishop Sidemann of Crediton, while Æthelwold had taken Æthelred under his wing.[40] John of Worcester – a twelfth-century chronicler using a lost version of the Chronicle – identifies Bishop Ælfhun

---

[35] *LE*, p. 160.

[36] Ibid., pp. 117, 146–7.

[37] For Athelstan's alms gift, see S 1503.

[38] Ælfgar and Ælfwine: *LE*, pp. 142, 144.

[39] *LE*, pp. 160–1.

[40] Byrhtferth of Ramsey, *The Lives of St Oswald and St Ecgwine*, ed. and tr. M. Lapidge, OMT (Oxford, 2009), pp. 77–9; E. John, 'The King and the Monks in the Tenth-century Reformation', repr. in idem, *Orbis Britanniae and Other Studies* (Leicester, 1966), 154–80, at pp. 159–60.

of London (1002–14) as the tutor of Edward and his younger brother Alfred; but he may be over-interpreting the Chronicle's remark that Ælfhun was deputed to take care of them in 1013.[41] Still, we might infer that a courtly bishop was considered an appropriate tutor for an aetheling, over a lesser dignitary running a monastic school. Perhaps, however, Edward was sent to Ely to be out of harm's way during viking attacks.

Ely's claim aside, queens bore much of the responsibility for rearing the royal boys, and the evidence of witness lists shows that Emma was Edward's guardian during his early years. As such she had charge of his education. Prior to 1013, Edward only attests charters attested by his mother. Where she is absent, he is too. This is true of S 920 (1008), witnessed by five aethelings, S 921 (1009), S 922 (1009), S 924 (1011), and S 925 (1012), witnessed by three, and S 929 (1012), witnessed by two.[42] That Edward attests every other diploma only in her presence suggests he moved in her orbit and not that of the senior aethelings, who attest five diplomas (cited above) in Emma and Edward's 'absence' – at least as far as their presence or absence in the diplomatic record is concerned. How far she involved herself in his education is unknown. At times he was in the charge of his foster mother. A spurious writ from the last years of Edward's reign names her as Leofrun, the wife of 'Earl' Tostig, but neither she nor Tostig can be identified – and there were no 'earls' in the 1000s, though there were jarls and ealdormen.[43] Like any young bride sent to a foreign country, Emma would soon have been weaned off anything Norman, so it is reasonable to imagine that her children were taught to speak English, whether with her or their foster parents. That Emma moved around with her son more than with his half-brothers was also a token of where her allegiance lay.

Decades before Edward's birth, the witan had conceded that certain lands were to be put aside for royal sons.[44] Edgar had treated them as lands which could be booked and given to the Church – that is, perpetually alienated by royal charter. After his death in 975, the witan judged differently and restored a handful, which Edgar had granted to Abingdon, to Æthelred the aetheling – Edward's father – together with other lands deemed to pertain to aethelings.[45] Æthelred could not have foreseen that he would have eight sons and probably allocated lions' shares to the oldest, redistributing some as more sons arrived. Any divvying up of perquisites would have created tensions. Athelstan occupied the premier

---

[41] JW, ii, p. 475 (calling him their *magister*); cf. ASC E, 1013: he went with them 'se þet he hi bewitan sceolde'.

[42] The exception is S 912, an interpolated diploma with a confused dating clause and a witness list acceptable for early 1006.

[43] S 1137; *Writs*, ed. Harmer, no. 93. His half-brothers, however, had a foster mother (see S 1503).

[44] S 937.

[45] Ibid.

position and came of age, at fourteen or fifteen, about the time of his father's second marriage in 1002. Ten years later, a prince in his twenties, he held land in several counties, some of it purchased or leased from his father, and could boast a collection of prized swords and stallions. His household included a chaplain to say Mass, a steward, a stag-huntsman, a sword-polisher, and armed retainers. He had his own stud farm for breeding horses.[46] Edward, the seventh son, could not have attained the same landed status or pursued the same pastimes with equal capacity. His mother's birthday gift to him of Islip supplemented whatever land remained for his support, but as a minor he could do little to augment it.

Such was the arrangement of family affairs by 1012. On the one hand, the adult princes enjoyed hunting, riding, and sword-play. They travelled with their father and accrued thegnly followers. On the other, Edward, not yet ten, accompanied his mother. This is not to say the experience of his older half-brothers would have been different when they were his age. Their sudden first appearance in a diploma of 993 in conjunction with Ælfthryth's return to court shows that as children they too accompanied a female relation, their grandmother, who brought them up.[47] The important thing to note is the gap between them and Edward. First, we may doubt he spent much time with his half-brothers, participated in their sports, or was made to feel included. Second, we cannot assume he shared their interests and allegiances, though his passions may have been theirs, awaiting their turn to blossom. Nothing is known of his feelings towards his father, mother, and fellow aethelings – not at this date at any rate.

When Edward was born – though it may not have seemed so in hindsight – his dynasty was still riding the crest of its glory. Before Æthelred's day, the unified kingdom he inherited from his ancestors of the West Saxon line had settled into a strong coherence. Ancestral cults now fructified at the tombs of his grandmother Ælfgifu and martyred half-brother Edward at Shaftesbury, and of his half-sister Edith at Wilton nunnery.[48] Wonders reported there proved the sacredness of the bloodline; that its bearers had been chosen by God to join the saints and intercede in the heavenly throne-room. Contemporary writers also praised his father Edgar as a godly ruler who achieved dominion over lesser rulers in Britain.[49] In practical governance, we glimpse the operation of a command structure enabling the king to raise revenue, summon levies, and enforce decisions locally. Ealdormen and high reeves were leading armies against the marauding viking war bands, shire reeves were emerging as agents for justice and fiscal management, and, from the 990s, there are references to

[46] S 1503.
[47] S 876; S 1503.
[48] A. Wilmart, 'La légende de sainte Édithe en prose et vers par le moine Goscelin', *AB* 56 (1938), 5–101, 265–307.
[49] ASC A, 975; Byrhtferth, *Lives*, pp. 75–7.

the king sending his seal to the shire courts, with orders to settle lawsuits.[50] Income flowed to the Crown from improved systems of taxation and regular recoinages, and from gifts made by men raised to officialdom, from monasteries seeking the restoration of lands previously alienated, and from the forfeitures of criminals denounced for conspiracies.

DISASTER

Soon after Edward's birth came the great famine of 1005, so terrible 'that no-one ever remembered one so grim before'.[51] Archbishop Wulfstan of York preached that such evils befell the English because they failed to observe God's laws. 'Heaven strives against us,' he proclaimed, 'when it sternly sends us storms that greatly injure cattle and land. The earth strives against us when it withholds earthly fruits.'[52] Wulfstan was one of Æthelred's close advisors and not the only one aware of the biblical prophecy that Christ and His saints would reign for a thousand years.[53] Others shared his concern that 'a thousand years and more have now passed since Christ was among people in human form, and now Satan's bonds are very loose, and Antichrist's time is well at hand'.[54]

Such foreboding permeated Æthelred's pronouncements and encouraged the belief that penitence was the proper response. A diploma attested by the infant Edward in 1005 opens in this spirit:

> I, Æthelred, in the company of the priests of God and our counsellors, contemplating ... the anger of God raging with ever increasing savagery against us, have decreed that He shall be appeased with the unremitting performance of good works and that there shall be no desisting from His praises. And since in our day we suffer the fires of war and the plundering of our riches, and since, from the cruel depredations of barbarian enemies engaged in ravaging our country and from the manifold sufferings inflicted on us by pagan races threatening us with extermination, we perceive we live in times of great peril ... it is urgent ... we give the utmost care and attention to the wellbeing of our souls.[55]

---

[50] Williams, *Æthelred*, pp. 63–6.

[51] ASC E, 1005.

[52] Wulfstan, *Secundum Lucam*, in *The Homilies of Wulfstan*, ed. D. Bethurum (Oxford, 1957), 123–7, at p. 125. Translation by J. T. Lionarons: http://webpages.ursinus.edu/jlionarons/wulfstan/wulfstan.html (accessed 1 November 2019).

[53] Roach, *Æthelred*, pp. 246–9; J. T. Lionarons, *The Homiletic Writings of Archbishop Wulfstan: A Critical Study* (Woodbridge, 2010), pp. 46–7.

[54] Wulfstan, *Secundum Marcum*, in *Homilies*, ed. Bethurum, 134–41, at pp. 136–7. Translation Lionarons: http://webpages.ursinus.edu/jlionarons/wulfstan/wulfstan.html (accessed 1 November 2019). For the context, see C. Cubitt, 'Apocalyptic and Eschatological Thought in England around the year 1000', *TRHS*, 6th ser. 25 (2015), 27–52.

[55] S 911: translation based on Barlow's, in *Edward*, p. 3.

Wulfstan interpreted the evils of the times through an allegorical reading of the prophecy that the sun would grow dark and the stars fall from the sky because of the people's sins. His preaching fuelled fears that evil men were multiplying and conspiring against God's servants. 'And the stars, it says, will fall from heaven, meaning liars and false Christians will quickly fall from correct belief and eagerly bow down to Antichrist and honour his helpers with all their might.'[56]

As the evils befalling the realm continued unabated, Æthelred began to strike at people around him. In a purge of 1006 he removed three leading thegns and an ealdorman: Wulfgeat was deprived of his territory; Wulfheah and Ufegeat had their eyes put out; and Ælfhelm, their father, the ealdorman in southern Northumbria, was killed the same year.[57] Edward was an infant, but pressure on his father and mother would have affected him in ways parental anxieties do. The breaking of the powerful kindred group in the Danelaw created an opening for Eadric Streona and his allies, a figure whose actions would shape the boy's future. When the raiders returned in 1006 and 1007 they seemed to be everywhere at once. After marking every shire in Wessex with pillaging and burning, they accepted a huge tribute and agreed to depart.[58]

Æthelred wasted no time in the period of peace he had bought. In 1008 he ordered ships to be built all over England. One warship was owed from every 300 hides of land (approximately); and from 8 hides a helmet and mailcoat. In practice it was a tax: the duty of fitting out ships had already been commuted for cash. The revenue was sent to the king to pay his shipwrights and armourers.[59] The fleet that assembled in Sandwich in 1009 was larger than any that was on record.[60] Eadric Streona, now ealdorman of Mercia, had made himself useful. His role in financing the fleet is suggested by the appointment of his brother Beorhtric as one of its two commanders. These were difficult years for the royal family personally. Ecgberht, second of the aethelings, disappears after 1006 (S 912) and must have died about that time. His brother Edgar, the youngest of Edward's half-brothers, died c. 1008. What the Lord had done to Job was beginning to happen to Æthelred, only for Job there was a happy ending.

When the fleet was prepared, Beorhtric scented treachery and denounced the other commander, the Sussex nobleman Wulfnoth. Either his suspicions were justified or Wulfnoth perceived that a tussle with

---

[56] Wulfstan, *Secundum Lucam*, in *Homilies*, ed. Bethurum, 123–7, at p. 125. Translation Lionarons: http://webpages.ursinus.edu/jlionarons/wulfstan/wulfstan.html (accessed 1 November 2019).

[57] S. Keynes, *The Diplomas of King Æthelred 'The Unready', 978–1016: A Study in their Use as Historical Evidence* (Cambridge, 1980), pp. 210–13; Williams, *Æthelred*, pp. 69–70; S. Baxter, *The Earls of Mercia: Lordship and Power in Late Anglo-Saxon England* (Oxford, 2007), pp. 21–2.

[58] ASC E, 1006–7.

[59] Williams, *Æthelred*, pp. 80–1.

[60] ASC E, 1009.

Eadric's brother would go against him, for he promptly detached twenty ships from the fleet and began raiding the south coast. Beorhtric took eighty ships in pursuit, but a mighty wind wrecked his ships and drove them ashore, where Wulfnoth burnt the remainder. This cleared the seaways for an enormous viking fleet led by the Danish jarl Thorkell, comprising Danes, Swedes, and Norwegians. Arriving at Sandwich in August 1009, they brought Canterbury to its knees, taking tribute in east Kent, raiding the coasts of Sussex and Hampshire and inland to Berkshire, attempting attacks on London and blockading the Thames. In 1010 they returned, this time to Ipswich, wreaking a whirlwind in East Anglia.[61]

Busy raising armies to contain the enemy, the king and his witan responded penitently, hoping for a heavenly ceasefire. A new coin was issued in 1009, depicting and invoking the Lamb of God, 'who takes away the sins of the world'.[62] The image of the lamb ready for slaughter was chosen to replace Æthelred's bust, while the bird on the reverse looked like an eagle, though it could pass as a triumphant raven.[63] It was not a long-lived issue. Wulfstan drew up ordinances, more desperate in tone, enjoining the following observances: that on the Monday, Tuesday, and Wednesday preceding the feast of St Michael (29 September) – a saint who combated the devil – every adult Christian should fast on bread and water and raw herbs; and that everyone should go barefoot to church to make confession, and that priests must go barefoot too; and every religious foundation should sing a Mass called 'Against the heathen' daily for the king and all his people, and every priest should celebrate 30 masses for the king and the nation, and every monk should recite all 150 psalms 30 times.[64] Such was the assault upon the enemy.

Edward must have had some memory of the penitential responses. The climate of fear and alarm, the chanting of the barefoot processions, the fervent repetition of psalms, even the little coins with the haloed lamb carrying a cross, lent themselves to vivid impressions for a child of troubled times.[65] His half-brothers were old enough to fight and win glory or be disappointed of a chance to do so. Meanwhile, the remains of a holy martyr were brought to London, out of harm's way. His name was St Edmund, the East Anglian king who had been killed resisting the vikings in 869. In one version of the legend he had offered himself like a lamb – a pacifist laying down his weapons. In another, he had gone down

---

[61] Ibid., 1009–10.

[62] Roach, *Æthelred*, pp. 275–9.

[63] S. Keynes and R. Naismith, 'The *Agnus Dei* Pennies of King Æthelred the Unready', *ASE* 40 (2011), 175–223; D. Woods, 'The *Agnus Dei* Penny of King Æthelred II: A Call to Hope in the Lord (Isaiah XL)?', *ASE* 42 (2013), 299–309. The bird looks like an eagle. It is the eagle of St John the Evangelist, reinforcing the coin's apocalyptic message.

[64] VII Æthelred (*Laws*, pp. 108–12: Latin; pp. 114– 16: Old English); Roach, *Æthelred*, pp. 267–74.

[65] Cf. S 911 ('times of great peril').

fighting.[66] Here was a Christian prince who had withstood the pagans when they shot him full of arrows. He had surrendered this brief life and his earthly kingdom for eternal life and the heavenly one. Archbishop Ælfheah of Canterbury came to pay his respects to the martyr in London, and Edmund's sanctity was proclaimed just as his feast day was entered in the calendars and his name added to the litanies. Here was a model of resistance approved by the Church.[67]

After the regime failed, in 1011, to reach a settlement with Thorkell's army, which continued to raid the southern, eastern, and midland regions, the vikings got into Canterbury and captured the archbishop. Eadric Streona and the witan who assembled in London at Easter 1012 arranged a tribute, but the archbishop refused to be ransomed and paid with his life when the drunken army killed him. Ælfheah's death had a sobering effect, for the next morning a delegation was allowed to collect his body and convey it to St Paul's. Not long afterwards oaths of peace were sworn, and Thorkell took forty-five ships from the raiding army, submitted to the king, and promised to guard the country for payment. The regular tax to pay the crews of hired vessels came to be known later as heregeld, or 'army tax'. Their crewmen were known as lithesmen, 'men of the fleet'. Æthelred was employing the tactic of dividing his enemies, a tactic he used in 994 to set Olaf against Sven. The protection of Thorkell's fleet bought him fifteen months of respite to July 1013.[68]

The anxiety of 1009 now yielded to new perspectives. A diploma of 1012 emphasized the fact that vikings were attacking other nations, dispelling the belief they were a scourge on the English for their sins. 'In almost all nations, contrary to the justice of the eternal Creator, the violence of the tyrannizing pirates is growing worse. They thirst to carry away what is not theirs, as wolves thirst to drink the blood of lambs.'[69] The shift to seeing the bigger picture reflected a new diagnosis. Perhaps penitential responses were failing because God wanted His people to fight? The vikings were not His scourge on the English. They were a plague on everyone. Æthelred now became 'the hammer of the heathens' (*propugnator paganorum*).[70] To Edward, approaching nine, the mood at court may have felt optimistic. After a collective exercise in guilty introspection, the English were recovering their will to fight.

Athelstan, now, was past his mid-twenties, and Edmund, the second aetheling, between twenty and twenty-five. Gaining influence, both may have advocated an aggressive response to the invaders, against the cautious tactics of tailing and containing preferred by their father. That he had not

---

[66] *MSE*, pp. xiii–vii, xxi–ii.
[67] Ibid., pp. xxii–iii; 53.
[68] ASC E, 1011–12.
[69] S 925 (1012).
[70] S 931 (1013).

permitted either to marry suggests he wanted to keep them dependent or was afraid of empowering them lest they become his rivals.[71] He had sat on the throne for thirty-five years, and his sons were champing at the bit. Eadred, in *c.* 1012, was the third to predecease their father. Funerals reminded everyone life was precious and short. In other developments, Eadric Streona was attesting as the leading ealdorman and may have married their sister that year. Æthelred married off a second daughter to Uhtred of Bamburgh, the ealdorman of Northumbria who had served the king by beating back the Scots.[72] Promoted to ealdorman in 1009 or earlier, he had extended his father's command south into the vacancy created by the fall of Ealdorman Ælfhelm. Linking their ambitions to his own by marrying rising stars into his family, Æthelred again shifted its dynamics in ways his sons may not have liked.

Emma, conversely, was a diminishing threat to them, for she witnesses only one of six diplomas datable to 1012, and it is the last of the reign to bear her *signum*.[73] Seven survive from 1013–16, and though not all are irreproachable, none bears her subscription. It may be that in those years Emma became a full-time mother, for her daughter, Godgifu, must have been born at that time if not earlier, and her second son, Alfred, first attests a charter in 1013 and appears in the Chronicle's entry for that year.[74] On that evidence alone, Alfred is likely to have been several years younger than Edward. Godgifu, or Gode as she was known, was possibly the middle sibling. Emma's withdrawal from the political scene, which increasingly centred on London, coincides with a charter of 1012 by which Æthelred granted her an estate at Winchester, including a house and chapel.[75] Though the arrangement may have had to do with her mothering responsibilities, her failure to reappear in the charter record is significant given the fact that her sons – who had attested diplomas previously only in her presence – now began to attest them in her absence. Edward now had a baby brother, but he was too young to grasp the fact that little Alfred was throneworthy too and might be a rival.

The charter witnessed by Alfred in 1013 (S 931) broke the pattern of Emma's sons attesting only in her presence. It is also the only evidence of her sons' presence at court in 1012–13, when she withdrew. If it is a forgery, a case could be made that Emma withdrew with her sons, or Edward at least – for Alfred may not have been born; and the charter is not above suspicion. Among the anomalous features are the strange titles accorded to Æthelred, who is entitled 'king of the Anglo-Saxon and ruler of the Northumbrian monarchy, attacker of the heathens, and emperor of

---

[71] Roach, *Æthelred*, p. 305.
[72] Williams, *Æthelred*, p. 75.
[73] That is, her attestation. S 926 (1012).
[74] S 931 (1013); ASC E 1013.
[75] S 925 (1012).

the Welsh [*Brettonum*] and other provinces'. The witness list is anomalous, since the aetheling Eadwig subscribes after Alfred – the only instance in which the aethelings are not arranged according to age. Yet the mistake is possibly attributable to a copyist having added Eadwig's name after omitting it, for the text of the charter comes from a fourteenth-century cartulary. The list of titles stressing the king's imperial reach would fit with a year in which the Northumbrians plotted with Sven. The claim to sovereignty over the Welsh may relate to an English raid into Wales in 1011–12, noted in a Welsh chronicle.[76] If the charter is authentic it moves Edward and Alfred into the orbit of the king and their older half-brothers. It also reveals Æthelred's grandstanding on the eve of Sven's invasion.

Sven had decided the time was right for a decisive intervention. His arrival at Sandwich in July 1013 broke any new resolve on the part of England's defenders. By the time he had showcased his fleet by sailing around the East Anglian coast into the mouth of the Humber, then up the Trent to Gainsborough, the inhabitants of the Danelaw were ready to yield. First Earl Uhtred and Northumbria, then Lindsey and the Five Boroughs, then the raiders who had settled north of Watling Street, then Oxford, Winchester, and the forces of the south west submitted to the Danish king and gave hostages. London resisted, fighting off the invader, but surrendered once Æthelred had withdrawn with Thorkell's fleet. The nine-year-old Edward saw his father dethroned, as he and his baby brother were bundled into a boat to Normandy in the care of the bishop of London. We do not know whether their sister Gode accompanied them in the same vessel. Emma escaped separately with the abbot of Peterborough – a further clue she now moved separately from her sons. Æthelred wintered with the fleet off the Isle of Wight before joining his wife and her children at the court of her brother, Duke Richard II.[77]

Athelstan, Edmund, and Eadwig, Edward's three surviving half-brothers, are not known to have joined the fugitives in Normandy. Since they hoped to inherit the throne ahead of the duke's nephews, there was a diplomatic argument for leaving them elsewhere. As Æthelred wondered what to do, Sven established his command in England, assisted by his son Cnut, who was a similar age to the aethelings. He had barely held it six months when he died, on 2 February 1014. Never again would any skald sing of a new victory in which Sven reddened bright swords and nourished the raven. After Sven's untimely death, the chief men divided, some favouring Cnut, others Æthelred. Negotiations ensued. The witan sent to Æthelred that no lord was dearer than their natural lord, and they would have him back if he agreed to rule more justly and desist from reprisals. Æthelred replied by sending Edward with messengers and promises he

---

[76] *Brut y Tywysogyon, or The Chronicle of the Princes, Peniarth MS. 20 version*, ed. and tr. T. Jones (Cardiff, 1952), p. 11.
[77] ASC E, 1013.

would be a better king to them in future. That he touted his eldest by
Emma suggests he may have been under pressure to promote Edward's
candidacy for the throne in return for asylum in Normandy. Richard,
after all, had not been averse to cutting deals with Sven. And he had
Æthelred in his power. It is not known when, in that year, Athelstan died,
but the death of the senior aetheling might have been an occasion for
debating whether the throne should pass to Edward over Edmund.[78] For
Norman support was proving pivotal.

Æthelred, of course, was the rightful king in the line of Cerdic, and
Christ's anointed – God's deputy over the English. His other argument
was the force at his disposal under his mercenary allies Thorkell and Olaf
Haraldsson, with the possibility of Norman assistance. Archbishop
Wulfstan used his famed powers of persuasion to remind the English of
their sins. In a sermon reworked in 1014 he chided them for killing one
king (Edward the Martyr) and driving out another, explaining their
calamities as the fruit of their rotten deeds.[79] He referred to the monk
Gildas's account of how the Britons had so angered God He allowed them
to be conquered by the English (i.e. the Angles and Saxons),[80] leaving the
obvious parallel unspoken. Through whatever combination of conscience,
preference, and necessity, Æthelred was restored to the throne. Olaf's
skald, Óttar the Black, boasted it was Olaf who 'assured his realm to
Æthelred'.[81] Thorkell and Richard's flatterers probably made equal asser-
tions on behalf of their patrons. Edward had occasion to feel pride and
success in his own role. It may have been a chance for a moment of closeness between father and son.

Though Æthelred promised no reprisals, he made an exception of
Lindsey, which had harboured Cnut and had little time to prepare for
Æthelred's avenging army. Then, says the chronicler, 'all the inhabitants
that could be got at were raided and burned and killed' – an indication
the victims included women and children.[82] Cnut escaped before the
onslaught, abandoning 'that wretched people', but not before putting

[78] ASC E, 1014; cf. Stafford, *Emma and Edith*, pp. 222–4; S. Keynes, 'Edward the
Ætheling (*c.* 1005–16)', in Mortimer, ed., *Edward*, 41–62, at pp. 51–3. Levi Roach (pers.
comm.) suggests Edward may have been a hostage for the king's future good behaviour – a
possibility that cannot be ruled out.

[79] Wulfstan, *Sermo Lupi ad Anglos*, ed. D. Whitelock (3rd edn, Exeter, 1976).

[80] Gildas, *De excidio et conquestu Britanniae*, in idem, *The Ruin of Britain and Other Works*, ed.
and tr. M. Winterbottom (London, 1978).

[81] Williams, *Æthelred*, p. 126.

[82] ASC C, D, E, 1014: '7 man þa hergode 7 bærnde 7 sloh eal þæt mancynn þæt man
ræcan mihte'. *Mann-cynn* should be translated as 'a race of men, a people' (definition II in
Bosworth and Toller's dictionary). The reasons are that it is preceded by *þæt*, as in other
examples where a 'race' is specified, and it is synonymous with *þæt earme folc* in the following
sentence. It means the people of Lindsey. *An Anglo-Saxon dictionary, based on the manuscript
collections of the late Joseph Bosworth. Supplement, by T. Northcote Toller* (Oxford, 1898), pp. 669,
296.

ashore the hostages taken by his father, minus their noses, hands, and feet. Purges followed in 1015, involving the murder of Morcar and Sigefyrth, leading thegns of the east midland boroughs, lured to their deaths at an assembly in Oxford.[83] Though the chronicler attributed the viciousness to Eadric Streona, Æthelred connived at it, for he confiscated their property and imprisoned Sigefyrth's widow in Malmesbury abbey. The shock collapse and restoration of his regime had reinvigorated his impulse to weed out traitors. Ordinances of 1014, betraying Archbishop Wulfstan's thinking, declared, 'if the land is to be thoroughly purified, inquiry and search must be made for the dwelling place of the wicked'.[84] The regime was inviting denunciations.

Athelstan the aetheling, when he died in 1014, left behind stallions and shining swords. In his will, he made bequests to his surviving brothers Edmund and Eadwig. He left to one beneficiary a mailshirt he had lent to Morcar, and he also bequeathed an estate to Sigefyrth, the thegns to be murdered in 1015. He meanwhile revealed ties to the family of Eadric's late opponent, Wulfnoth, by restoring an estate formerly in his possession to Godwine his son.[85] Nothing went to his new brother-in-law, Eadric himself. The links between the testator and enemies of Eadric's family – Morcar, Sigefyrth, and Wulfnoth – suggest they were in rival camps.[86] It is possible the affection expressed for Æthelred in the will was tactical, since the king might refuse to validate it. Though there were gifts for relatives, friends, and servants, Emma, Edward, and Alfred received nothing. They had no place in Athelstan's circle, and he did not choose to favour them, though he had few blood kin left. His death robbed Morcar and Sigefyrth of a potential protector, smoothing the way to their murder the following year. Edmund, a chief beneficiary of his brother's will, shared his allegiances. After the murder he rebelled, riding to Malmesbury, freeing Sigefyrth's widow, and taking her as a wife, before heading to Cambridgeshire to muster support. Cnut returned at the same time, determined to reconquer. It was September, and Æthelred lay sick at Cosham near Portsmouth harbour.[87] Worn out by tribulation, near to fifty, he may have sensed his approaching death.

Emma's whereabouts in those years is a mystery. Since she attests none of Æthelred's charters after 1012 it is not at all clear whether she returned to England in 1014 or remained in Normandy. A possible cryptic reference to her in the viking poem *Liðsmannaflokkr* might put her in London in 1016; and this would agree with garbled reports that made their way to the

---

[83] ASC C, D, E, 1014–15.
[84] VIII Æthelred 40 (*Laws*, p. 129); on these ordinances, see Roach, *Æthelred*, pp. 297–8.
[85] S 1503.
[86] Williams, *Æthelred*, pp. 115–17.
[87] ASC E, 1015–16.

contemporary German chronicler Thietmar of Merseburg.[88] Wherever his mother ended up, Edward returned to England with his father. A credible diploma of 1015 (S 934) locates him with the king and Edmund. Edward was ten or eleven, a few years from his majority. He was near the age their father had been upon taking the throne in 978. When previous kings had died leaving sons by two marriages, in 924 and 975, the leading men had divided over which son should succeed.[89] Given those precedents, Edmund's decision in 1015 to rebel may have arisen from a fear that his father intended the kingdom to pass to Edward.

Support for the idea that Æthelred alienated Edmund by naming Edward as his heir is found in more than one tradition. The first emanates from the abbey of Saint-Wandrille in Normandy, whose brethren included two of Edward's uncles. A monk writing there in the 1050s claimed that Edward had been anointed and crowned at his father's behest with the approval of his subjects. The date of the alleged episode, shortly before Æthelred's death, suits a context in which the presumed heir was dead and the father was reliant on Norman support.[90] Though associative coronation was a French practice, started by the Capetian monarchs, the claim may reflect a lesser rite of designation. The Norman account chimes with a Scandinavian tradition, that Edmund and Edward succeeded jointly on Æthelred's death.[91] Both reports add noise to the possibility that a party wanted Edward, and indeed, Edward was looking like a contender. By the autumn of 1015, however, and more so after Æthelred's death, the contest was between grown men leading armies. Edmund and Cnut were throneworthy in that crucial respect, where Edward could hardly oppose them.

The wars of succession erupted in Æthelred's lifetime and brought misery to all caught up in them. For both parties the key to victory was command over that area of the Danelaw where loyalties were divided, from the prosperous boroughs of the east midlands, such as Stamford, Lincoln, and Nottingham, northwards into Northumbria. That was the strategic north–south corridor for an invader advancing from the Humber. In Denmark, Sven's elder son Harold had taken the throne at his father's death. Cnut regarded himself as the rightful heir to England. In 1015–16 he and Edmund strengthened their influence in the north–south corridor by marrying into

[88] R. G. Poole, *Viking Poems on War and Peace: A Study in Skaldic Narrative* (Toronto, 1991), pp. 89, 113; Thietmar of Merseburg, *Chronicon*, ed. R. Holtzmann, MGH Scriptores rerum Germanicarum n.s. 9 (Berlin, 1935), pp. 447–8, and see below, p. 43.

[89] S. Foot, *Æthelstan: The First King of England* (New Haven and London, 2011), p. 17; Williams, *Æthelred*, pp. 6–10.

[90] *Inventio et miracula sancti Wulfranni*, ed. J. Laporte, Société de Histoire de Normandie, *Mélanges: Documents publiés et annotés*, 14e série (Rouen and Paris, 1938), 1–87, p. 36. The text is in Le Havre, Bibliothèque Municipale, MS 332, in a hand of s.$^{3/4}$ (my dating: with thanks to Liam Draycott for images).

[91] M. Ashdown, *English and Norse documents relating to the reign of Ethelred the Unready* (Cambridge, 1930), p. 161.

the same dynasty. Edmund, marrying Sigefyrth's widow, became heir to estates Eadric Streona might otherwise have acquired through Sigefyrth's forfeiture. Cnut married Ælfgifu, daughter of the Ealdorman Ælfhelm purged in 1006, whose dynasty Edmund's ally Uhtred had since displaced.[92] Winning approval with his bold and martial strategy, Edmund engaged Cnut's forces in a series of indecisive battles, while both armies sustained themselves by plundering regions associated with their opponents. As the enemy gained strength, Edmund had to coordinate with his father: their differences had to take a back seat in the face of the emergency.

Spring was now returning to the land. It dressed the trees in blossom. As fighting raged around London, the ailing king inside the city gave up his spirit, which flew to the vastness beyond. It was 23 April 1016, and Edward was about eleven: just old enough to understand. On news of Æthelred's death, the witan and garrison chose Edmund to be king, though not unanimously, for some sided with Cnut.[93] Pondering what ensued, from the hindsight of *c.* 1100, a monk put it all in perspective:

> The realm was destabilized, and schisms among the leaders divided the people, who were unsure which way to turn. Factions were forced to war against each other and, by wasting the abundance of their own fruitful land on civil war, turned the blight of devastation back upon themselves. This plague did not end suddenly, even with Æthelred's sudden death, when the dead king's heir Edmund Ironside was elected to the throne. But many of the nobles and the men active in affairs, tiring of the turnaround of kings, went over to Cnut and heartily assisted him so that all men should be subject to him alone.[94]

Æthelred had already alienated many by eliminating lords he suspected of treachery. Yet his same dark vigilance had facilitated his survival through two and a half decades of danger.

Edmund fought on, but holding onto the kingdom was like holding a wolf by the ears. On 18 October at the battle of Assandun, in Essex, his command structure was destroyed. Unlike the Chronicler, who blamed this defeat on the treachery of Eadric Streona, our monk-historian of later years retained his air of detachment: 'One man attacked another, only for another to kill him in the attack. To and fro the fighting continued till nightfall, when the shadows closed in and men started to desert from both sides.'[95]

Nothing is certain in war. Among the dead must have been some Edward admired with that childish assurance which invests adults with

---

[92] T. Bolton, *Cnut the Great* (New Haven and London, 2017), pp. 67–71.
[93] ASC E, 1016.
[94] *MSE*, p. 321 (translation adapted).
[95] *MSE*, p. 159 (translation adapted). The account of the battle in *EER*, p. 27, is similar.

infinite wisdom and strength. We may imagine his bewilderment at the carnage. The slain included Eadnoth, bishop of Dorchester, Wulfsige, abbot of Ramsey, Ealdorman Ælfric of Hampshire, who had survived three decades serving Edward's father, Ealdorman Godwine of Lindsey, the warrior Ulfcytel of East Anglia and, as it seemed, 'all the chief men in the English race'.[96] Edmund obtained a settlement dividing the kingdom, with Cnut as king north of Watling Street and Edmund his tributary in Wessex, but on 30 November 1016 he died too.[97] Cnut inherited the throne of Edward's fathers, and the boy had to be got out of the country lest he join the roll-call of the dead.

> Alas, the gleaming chalice;
> Alas, the armoured warrior;
> Alas, the majesty of the prince!
> Truly, that time has passed away,
> dark under the cover of night,
> as though it had never been![98]

[96] ASC E, 1016.

[97] Williams, *Æthelred*, pp. 146–7. His murder was being rumoured by 1070: *MSE*, pp. 17–19.

[98] *The Wanderer*, in *Anglo-Saxon Poetry*, tr. and ed. S. A. J. Bradley (London, 1982), 322–5, at p. 324 (altered).

Chapter 2

EXILE

heu fuge, nate dea . . .
hostis habet muros
(Alas flee son of a goddess . . .
the enemy holds the walls)

Virgil, *Æneid* II. 289–90

For a prince of eleven or twelve driven into exile by conquest there were precedents to observe and appropriate responses. Virgil provided a fictional model of exile in the *Æneid*, a schoolroom text in England at that time. Stories and songs of Trojan adventure circulated orally among the nobles and formed part of Edward's cultural inheritance. During the 1010s his uncle Richard II was content for the historian Dudo, writing at the ducal court, to trace the ancestry of the Normans to the Trojan exile, Antenor.[1] For Edward the Trojans duly became figures of fabled ancestry. In tales of the Trojan wars, first Antenor then Æneas led followers into exile after the sack of Troy, when the ancient line of kings ended with the deaths of Priam and his many sons, and Greeks storming the citadel. Surviving royals were obliged to wander far in search of new homelands, but the legend ended with redemption when Æneas, favoured by the gods, defeated his enemies in battle and claimed the sceptre of Latium. Not even the embrace of Queen Dido diverted him from his destiny. The Bible supplied patterns of exile from Christian history, much re-told in the world of Edward's childhood and in the preaching which everyone heard. Adam and Eve were the first exiles below the ranks of the angels, driven from Eden for the sin of rebellion. Moses and his people were exiles in their wanderings in search of the land of milk and honey. Then conquerors arrived, the Assyrians and the Babylonians, who expelled the Israelites from the northern and southern kingdoms. Even Christ, Mary, and Joseph had to flee into Egypt to escape the wrath of Herod. In some stories, God had imposed exile as a punishment; in others, He imposed it to test the faith of His people. Yet the Bible, like the *Æneid*, was a saga of redemption, for the Israelites would enter into the Promised Land and would return to rebuild the Temple after their Babylonian

[1] E. Tyler, 'Trojans in Anglo-Saxon England: Precedent without Descent', *Review of English Studies* 64 (2013), 1–20.

captivity; and the Christ-Child would return from Egypt to conquer upon the Cross; and the countless generations of God's people born to original sin would be redeemed from death by His sacrifice and enter their heavenly homeland, a kingdom of beauty and light.

The responses proper to exile barely changed between the ninth century and Edward's day. An exile was expected to feel hardship and affliction and the bitterness of loss. He was to contemplate his state of deprivation, dwelling on comforts he had lost. Accepting that joy yields to sorrow as surely as night follows day, he would transcend earthly cares in wisdom, to seek mercy and comfort from God.[2] This would involve much soul searching, as poems relayed:

> More sorrows and sufferings than anyone else have been my lot.
> I have been driven into banishment from my birthplace.[3]

It also involved profound frustration, helplessness, and a fear of dying in the wilderness like countless Trojans and Israelites.

> A tree flourishes before extending its branches, which is destiny.
> But I cannot pursue mine.[4]

For a prince growing up in an environment where the Danish attacks were regarded more as a divine punishment than a test, there was the added worry that exile was the wages of sin; that God had declared, in the words of Ælfric the preacher:

> For you was the kingdom of heaven ready, and shining structures filled with good things and with eternal light. You have lost all of this through heedlessness and have got for yourselves dark dwellings filled with serpents, and with crackling flames, full of unspeakable torments and horrible stenches, where groaning and howling cease not day or night.[5]

Such were the images evoked for congregations huddled in church for the feast of the exile St John the Evangelist, on 27 December, in that darkness of midwinter, when Christ's birth had just been celebrated but the spring of

---

[2] S. B. Greenfield, 'The Formulaic Expression of the Theme of "Exile" in Anglo-Saxon Poetry', *Speculum* 30 (1955), 200–6; L. H. Frey, 'Exile and Christian Elegy in Anglo-Saxon Epic Poetry', *Journal of English and Germanic Philology* 62 (1963), 293–302.

[3] *Resignation*, in *Anglo-Saxon Poetry*, tr. and ed. Bradley, 387–90, at p. 389, adapted translation, quoted from http://www.hermitary.com/literature/resignation.html (accessed 1 November 2019).

[4] Ibid., p. 390, adapted translation.

[5] *Ælfric, CH: FS*, I. 4, lines 148–53 (pp. 206–16, at p. 211); translation based on B. Thorpe, *The Homilies of the Anglo-Saxon Church: The First Part, containing The Sermones Catholici, or Homilies of Ælfric*, vol. I (London, 1844), p. 69.

His redemption seemed a long way off. In the winter of 1016, Edward and whoever accompanied him imagined a future of storm and wind and frost.

Evidence of Edward's earliest movements in exile comes from a document that combines elements of a diploma and a letter, beginning with an invocation of the Trinity and an address clause. For convenience we will refer to it as a record, since it is neither a writ nor a diploma, nor indeed a letter – but a unique promissory note. Written in the first person, as if by Edward himself, it claims he swore an oath before the altar of the abbey of SS Peter and Paul at Ghent in Flanders, on Christmas Day 1016. The text is preserved on a single sheet of parchment in the hand of a scribe associated with the abbey in the 1030s and 1040s. After the invocation of the Trinity is a salutation to the faithful in the name of Edward, who titles himself 'unworthy of God's mercy, the son of Æthelred'. Edward then explains how he came to swear the oath. Evicted from his father's kingdom, he had gone on a purificatory tour of the shrines of saints, in the hope that God might forgive his sins, through their intervention, take pity on him, and restore him to the throne of his fathers. He had come to the abbey of SS Peter and Paul where several saints were resting, who are named in the record – they included Christ's 'most holy virgin' Amalberga; and there, Abbot Rodbold and the brethren had welcomed him.

After their greeting, the monks asked about the abbey's estates in England at Lewisham, Greenwich, and Woolwich, which – the narrative claims – had been taken from them at some point in the past; and they begged Edward to restore them if one day God restored him to his father's throne. Edward agreed willingly and swore before the high altar that if one day God in His mercy raised him to his father's throne he would restore the abbey's inheritance along with all the appurtenances included in the record and associated with the ports in question. A dating clause follows, using the several forms of dating conventionally used in Cambrai, the diocese in which the abbey lay. Mostly they were taken from the columns of an Easter Table against the year 1016. The year is incorrectly given as 1006, the scribe having missed out the X in the numeral MXVI. After that is the statement: 'And to corroborate the promise I made in my vow, I have ordered it to be written down.' Last is the confirmation: 'I Edward have understood and put it on record.'[6]

The dating clause refers to the occasion on which Edward made the vow, on Christmas day 1016, 'in the time of King Robert' (as noted in the endorsement). The record, however, was made as a promissory note years later. An allusion to the death of Abbot Rodbold (on 23 February 1042),

---

[6] 'Ego Aeduuardus cognoui et notare constitui'. A. Van Lokeren, *Chartes et documents de l'abbaye de Saint Pierre au mont Blandin a Gant* (Ghent, 1868), no. 96 (pp. 72–3). Rijksarchief te Gent, Sint-Pietersabdij, charters, no. 96, reproduced in S. Keynes, 'The Æthelings in Normandy', *ANS* 13 (1991), 173–205, Plate 1 (p. 178) from a facsimile published in 1842 and transcribed in Appendix I of the same article, p. 201.

who is of 'holy memory', and the fact that Edward does not style himself as king, dates it between 23 February and 8 June 1042 (the latter being the day of Harthacnut's death). The dating is corroborated by the date of the scribal hand and by the absence of any notice of a grant made by Edward in the *Liber Traditionum*, an account of gifts to the abbey prior to 30 September 1041, which was compiled by one of its brethren about that time.[7] We may infer that Edward, while at Harthacnut's court, heard of Rodbold's death and wrote to the monks to formalize the vow he had made twenty-five years earlier and to confirm his good intentions. Perhaps a monk arriving from Ghent with news of Rodbold's passing took the opportunity to remind the king-in-waiting of his vow. Domesday Book reveals that the abbot of Ghent held two sulungs at Lewisham with the income of a port in Edward's reign and in William's.[8] Yet there is no mention of the abbey holding estates at Greenwich and Woolwich, which it either never acquired or lost before the Conquest.

As for Edward's movements in late 1016, the record is good evidence for a penitential response to the downfall of his dynasty. It places him in Flanders a month after Edmund's death. Throughout his life, Wulfstan and others in the king's circle had blamed England's afflictions on the sins of the people, demanding penitential countermeasures. Æthelred had internalized the link, finding fault in his own conduct, according to a diploma of 993 (S 876). His son's decision to embark upon a purificatory pilgrimage once God finally disinherited the dynasty looks like the fructification of those thought processes. That the record refers to it in passing suggests the tour was common knowledge. A prince's movements attract interest, not least those of a scion of an ancient House recently overthrown. Edward's penitent wandering pointed to wisdom gained through exile, which lifted the mind heavenwards, and established his reputation as a prince humble before God. Even so, self-abasement was not his objective but a means to an end. Edward had not surrendered to a religious life: he meant to recover his kingdom and was assured enough in his hope to promise bits of it to the monks. He had seen his father regain the throne. Finally, it was a wise move to go in pious guise where he might find supporters. Exile was the art of surviving in the world by persuading others to lend their backing. Ghent was a wealthy, influential abbey patronized by the counts of Flanders. Allies there might mean naval assistance to restore him to the throne.

If Edward's initial response to calamity was to flee to his uncle in Normandy, following his father's precedent, Richard might have conceived the idea of sending or taking him on a tour of saints' shrines to advertise his plight and muster support for him in the principalities confronting

---

[7] *Liber Traditionum sancti Petri Blandiniensis: Livre des donations faites à l'Abbaye de Saint-Pierre de Gand*, ed. A. Fayen, Cartulaire de la ville de Gand (Oorkondenboek der Stad Gent), IIe série, Chartes et Documents, I (Ghent, 1906).

[8] Keynes, 'Æthelings', pp. 177–81.

Cnut on the Frankish side of the Channel. Likely stations on the tour would have included Saint-Bertin at St Omer, Arras, Cambrai, Rheims, Paris, and Rouen. In Æthelred's reign, England and Flanders enjoyed good relations. Trade was flourishing, and ecclesiastical links were strong. Several years before the crisis of 1016, Archbishop Ælfheah of Canterbury had commissioned Adelard, a monk of the abbey Edward visited in Ghent, to prepare a *Life* of St Dunstan, to be read aloud in Canterbury cathedral.[9] Duke Richard also enjoyed good relations with Count Baldwin IV of Flanders (987–1035) and King Robert II of France (996–1031). Emma's whereabouts remain a mystery. She may have gone to Normandy and toured the shrines with Edward, or she may have fallen into Cnut's hands in England. The text does not say whether she or his siblings, Alfred and Godgifu, accompanied Edward to Ghent; but recording who had accompanied him was not part of its purpose.

Cnut meanwhile was securing a hold on the throne. Presiding at a meeting of the witan, he disinherited Edmund's infant sons and the remaining sons of Æthelred, though perhaps not Emma's sons in Normandy.[10] Edmund's two sons escaped execution and ended up in Kiev. We shall hear of them again. Eadwig, the surviving son of Æthelred's first marriage, departed the realm in exile but later returned and was murdered in shadowy circumstances. The confused rumours that reached a chronicler in Saxony, Bishop Thietmar of Merseburg (d. 1018), reported that Emma had remained in London during the siege of 1016 with her 'sons' Athelstan and Edmund, and that Edmund had died in the fighting.[11] Thietmar was a contemporary writer, but at least one of his details was wrong. Wherever Emma ended up, Cnut had to neutralize the threat to his rule posed by a consecrated queen and her offspring. He also had to mend relations with the Norman duke whose nephews he had disinherited. There were differing reports of how he proceeded on both fronts, but the safest comes from the chronicler Rodulf Glaber, a relatively neutral contemporary whose abbot, William, had gone to Normandy at the duke's invitation to reform monastic life at the abbey of Fécamp.

Glaber, a monk who wrote this part of his chronicle in the 1020s at Dijon, claims Cnut 'made a peace with Richard by which he married the duke's sister, Æthelred's widow'. The claim was corroborated in the 1050s by our writer at Saint-Wandrille, who assumed that the marriage between Cnut and Emma took place with Richard's approval.[12] Whether Emma approved

[9] *The Early Lives of St Dunstan*, ed. and tr. M. Winterbottom and M. Lapidge, OMT (Oxford, 2012), pp. cxxv–vi.

[10] *JW*, ii, p. 495; *EER*, p. 33.

[11] Thietmar, *Chronicon*, pp. 447–8.

[12] Rodulfus Glaber, *Historiarum libri quinque*, ed. J. France, in *Rodulfus Glaber Opera*, ed. J. France, N. Bulst, and P. Reynolds, OMT (Oxford, 1989), pp. 54–6. *Inventio*, ed. Laporte, p. 36 ('fratre Richardo consulto fauente').

of it is less clear. The skalds who praised Cnut's victories referred to peace being confirmed by the exchange of women, portraying her as a prize of conquest.[13] The E text of the Chronicle reports that Cnut had Emma 'fetched', an undignified turn of phrase implying either he held her in captivity or she was the object of a marital agreement.[14] As the latter, she might have been 'fetched' from overseas. Emma's own testimony of later years appears in the *Encomium* of 1041–2, which claims that Cnut searched for a bride and found Emma in Normandy.[15] Without mentioning Æthelred, it adds she was a famous queen and a *virgo* – a slippery word meaning both 'young woman' and 'virgin'. Such sleights of hand to eliminate Æthelred's dynasty from the record typify the author's *modus operandi*. He liked to employ deceit without telling outright lies. After Edward's accession, a different narrative emerged, claiming Emma was in London when Æthelred died, and that Cnut kidnapped her, married her, and paid twice her weight in bullion to the army in compensation.[16] This version may, however, be the product of changed political circumstances where Emma needed defending against the charge that she had dispossessed her eldest son.

Cnut's marrying Emma before August 1017 is the most striking of the moves he made to consolidate his position. That he risked alienating Ælfgifu of Northampton's kin by taking a more important second wife exposes him as a skilled player triangulating vested interests. He also had to negotiate a web of diplomacy involving his own ambitions, his brother Harold in Denmark, and the independent war leader Thorkell, who evidently had allies in Normandy, given that he had gone there in 1013 after splitting from the Danish host. The skaldic poem *Liðsmannaflokkr*, composed in 1016–17 to celebrate the recent Danish victories in England, carefully balances its praise for Cnut and Thorkell. It is as if rivalries they set aside during their joint endeavour of conquest threatened to erupt in the aftermath. Nor was Cnut's claim to be a legitimate ruler instantly accepted abroad, for rumour in Paris put about that Cnut was a pagan – meaning at the very least a thinly Christianized barbarian. Cnut tried to impress the bishop who informed him of the rumour, Fulbert of Chartres, by sending him precious gifts. But Fulbert's thank you letter of 1018–19 refers to him only as 'king of the Danes' – a title he acquired after the death of his brother Harold *c.* 1018. That Fulbert does not call him king of the English hints at sympathies with the aethelings.[17]

Richard of Normandy was already a patron to Fulbert, and the existing connexion may account for Fulbert's hesitancy. For Richard was a widely

---

[13] Stafford, *Emma and Edith*, pp. 22, 210.

[14] ASC E, 1017.

[15] *EER*, p. 33.

[16] *GND*, II, p. 21.

[17] *The Letters and Poems of Fulbert of Chartres*, ed. and tr. F. Behrends, OMT (Oxford, 1976), No. 36 (pp. 66–9), cf. p. lxxv.

admired, well-established prince, who was close to the king of France. It is conceivable he and his friends in France held off acknowledging Cnut's title until either Emma bore him a son whom he would recognize as his heir, or he acknowledged the claim of Richard's nephews. Pressure of this kind was not inconsiderable because Cnut obviously cared about his legitimacy and political standing. If he married Emma, he must have cared about his relations with Normandy. The duke merely wanted the hope of having a nephew on the English throne. The boy Edward was a pawn in the power-game, as he would later understand. If he reached the other side of the board, the crown would be his, but rival pawns might emerge to overtake him, and opponents were as ready to swipe at him. Edward could only have learned from Æthelred and his half-brothers that Cnut was a big bad wolf – an impression the twelve-year-old had to reconcile with the manoeuvres of his mother and uncle.

Richard's dealings with Cnut are poorly covered in the scraps of information we have, but those scraps do suggest a picture of amicable relations. For instance, Richard or Emma managed to extract from Cnut a parcel of land and a port at *Rammesleah* in Sussex between modern Rye and Winchelsea, for the Norman ducal abbey of Fécamp. The gift enriched the abbey, facilitated trade, and benefited the dukes, for Fécamp was the site of a ducal palace and their burial place. Richard had shown concern for the brethren by inviting the abbot of Dijon, William of Volpiano, to improve their religious observance. The note by which the gift was conveyed explains that Æthelred had died before fulfilling his promise to give the land – a detail which places the grant early enough in Cnut's reign to be dated to Richard's lifetime. Emma's is the first subscription. If not the petitioner, she appears to have been an intermediary who affirmed her late husband's intentions.[18]

There is also the claim made by Glaber, and possibly derived from his abbot, William of Volpiano, that Richard and Emma persuaded Cnut to settle peace with King Malcolm II of the Scots (1005–34), after warfare that followed the marriage of 1017. It seems to refer to a Scottish victory at Carham in 1018, which asserted Malcolm's dominance over Lothian.[19] Cnut's response to the victory is unknown, but he could have asked his wife's Norman kin to broker a deal, for the Normans were not strangers even to the Scots, being involved in the sea traffic around Britain's western coast, as shown by the discovery of Norman deniers in the Inner

[18] S 949. The note was amplified and presented to Harthacnut in the early 1040s for confirmation (S 982).

[19] A. A. M. Duncan, *The Kingship of the Scots, 842–1292: Succession and Independence* (Edinburgh, 2002), pp. 30–1. Duncan's argument for dating Carham to 1018 (rather than 1016) is stronger than his case for moving Uhtred's death to the former year, which seeks to accommodate Stenton's disbelief that Simeon of Durham could be mistaken about Uhtred's involvement. Simeon was fallible. Cf. Duncan, 'The Battle of Carham, 1018', *SHR* 55 (1976), 20–8.

Hebrides.[20] Richard, moreover, had influence with war leaders involved in Scottish affairs, for only a few years before Carham he had enlisted the help of the Norwegian Olaf Haraldsson and Lagmann Gudrødsson, king in the Hebrides, against the count of Chartres.[21] Glaber did admire Richard, but even if he exaggerates his influence in the conflict between Malcolm and Cnut, it is hard to see why he should link that conflict to Richard and Emma unless the siblings were involved in the peacekeeping.

We also catch glimpses of trouble on the Hampshire coast. At the start of Cnut's reign, Southampton possessed a mint with six moneyers, but it abruptly ceased to issue during his first coin type, the Quatrefoil, in the late 1010s or early 1020s.[22] The sudden closure of a medium-sized mint was exceptional and should be considered with the Chronicle's annal for 1022, which states that Cnut took his ships to the Isle of Wight. Without more information, it is possible only to guess whether Southampton had been attacked. Wight was a haven for raiding fleets, and Hampshire had long been a target, but pirates came into the Channel from as far afield as Denmark and the Irish Sea. There is no suggestion Richard and Cnut had come into conflict. Nor is there evidence that Normandy, though it had harboured Æthelred's enemies in 1000 and 1003, ever accommodated Cnut's; or that Cnut gave refuge to Richard's opponents. Though one of the latter, Count Richard of Avranches, 'fled across the sea' after an attempt on the duke's life, no details are given of his destination or what reception he met there.[23] The aethelings were a special case, for although they were Cnut's opponents it must be assumed there was an agreement not to deploy them. Richard would raise his nephews of course. What is lacking in the sources is any indication that he encouraged them to reclaim their inheritance. Cnut played his part by marrying Emma; raising their son Harthacnut; keeping alive Norman interest in the throne. As Cnut's rule strengthened and his empire expanded, Richard's hold on him would diminish.

Although at the outset Emma was readily regarded as the object of a marriage treaty, her treatment as Cnut's queen was favourable. In 1017, she was herself a vulnerable usurper for having taken the place of Ælfgifu of Northampton, risking the enmity of her faction and the future hostility of her infant sons by Cnut. From another vantage point she was a conse-

---

[20] L. Musset, 'Les relations extérieures de la Normandie du IXe au XIe siècle, d'après quelques trouvailles monétaires récentes', repr. from *Annales de Normandie* 4 (1958), 31–8, in idem, *Nordica et Normannica: Recueil d'études sur la Scandinavie ancienne et médiévale, les expéditions des Vikings et la fondation de la Normandie* (Paris, 1997), 297–306, at p. 303.

[21] *GND*, II, pp. 25–7.

[22] K. Jonsson and G. van der Meer, 'Mints and Moneyers c. 973–1066', in K. Jonsson, ed., *Studies in Late Anglo-Saxon Coinage in Memory of Bror Emil Hildebrand*, Numismatic Essays No. 35 (Stockholm, 1990), 47–136, at p. 100.

[23] *André de Fleury: Vie de Gauzlin, abbé de Fleury*, ed. R.-H. Bautier and G. Labory (Paris 1969), pp. 48–50.

crated queen whose title reinforced Cnut's and enhanced the legitimacy conferred upon him by rites of consecration. In the rites employed for Cnut, references to keys and the sceptre symbolized the delegation of Christ's power to the king via St Peter, a chain of authority already in place in Edgar's reign.[24] If the humble Edward was busily aligning himself with St Peter in Ghent, Cnut could counteract the spectacle by claiming to be the saint's representative. Emma's rites included a set of benedictions for the queen to parallel those for the king. They declared that her role was to be a peaceweaver, to bring tranquillity, to be an English queen, and to be a consort in royal power (*consors imperii* – literally, 'a sharer of rule').[25] According to her encomiast, Emma managed to extract from Cnut a marital oath, that he would never set up a son to succeed him other than one of hers.[26] Such an agreement could have been part of the arrangement brokered with Richard to allow the possibility Edward or Alfred might be king.

With these provisions in place Emma resumed her role at court after an apparent phase of withdrawal in Æthelred's final years. Although few diplomas of Cnut survive in authentic versions, she witnesses regularly, and in S 955 of 1019 employs the formula she had used in 1004, *thoro consecrata regio* – 'consecrated to the royal bed'. The words echo the preface to the queen's consecration rite, suggesting a renewal of status.[27] In 1019 she attested after the archbishops, but by 1022 she had overtaken them to attest after Cnut himself, as we see in S 958 of 1022 and S 984 of 1020 × 1022. In S 970 of 1030 there is a joint attestation in which Cnut subscribes 'with my queen Ælfgifu', elevating Emma, who retained the English name that supplanted her namesake rival, to an unprecedented primacy in the hierarchy of *signa*.

A NEW FAMILY

Edward's movements after 1016 are not well detailed in the records, but a lack of reports of him surfacing elsewhere accords with evidence that he settled at the ducal court. William of Jumièges and our monk of Saint-Wandrille, both writing before 1066, place the aethelings early in Richard's care. The latter remarks that he raised them as if they were his own sons and honourably kept them in Normandy all his life.[28] Whatever Edward

---

[24] C. E. Karkov, *The Ruler Portraits of Anglo-Saxon England* (Woodbridge, 2004), p. 134. On Cnut's coronation, see M. K. Lawson, *Cnut: England's Viking King* (Stroud, 1993; new edn, 2004), p. 82.

[25] Karkov, *Ruler Portraits*, pp. 129, 134; Stafford, *Emma and Edith*, p. 175, and see pp. 177–8 and 188.

[26] *EER*, p. 33.

[27] P. E. Schramm, *Kaiser, Könige und Päpste: Gesammelte Aufsätze zur Geschichte des Mittelalters*, 4 vols (Stuttgart, 1968–71), II, pp. 239–40.

[28] *Inventio*, ed. Laporte, p. 36; *GND*, II, p. 77; *Vita*, p. 13, and *EER*, p. 41.

thought of Richard, the aethelings needed their uncle. Besides, there was more to his duty of care than opportunism, for Richard was a pious man who kept his family close. Such is the case for placing Edward and Alfred in Normandy during Richard's reign, even if they occasionally travelled beyond the duchy on now-forgotten adventures.

At the same time, the princely–paternal model shifted, perhaps in none too subtle ways. For the first twelve years of his life Edward could look to his father, imitating his behaviour as children do. His mother was another profound influence, and that inexorable schedule of characteristics, coded by their genes, nuanced in the womb, and fashioned in the patterns of childhood, would play itself out in Edward as certainly and mysteriously as the scenes of a secret drama. Now his father was dead, a face in his dreams. Richard was filling the vacant outline. Edward had reached an age too when he was able to respond with awareness to the imitable figure before him. He was old enough to admire, resist, emulate, and resent such a figure, all at the same time. Growing to manhood in Richard's court, he could observe how Richard treated friends and enemies, what he valued, and how he comported himself before God. If Edward had a tutor as wise as the one who instructed the German prince Henry, he would have told him to emulate the best in his father and uncle and abhor whatever in their conduct might corrupt his own.[29]

By settling in Normandy, Edward was exchanging memories of constant warfare for a haven of relative peace. In Richard's time, peace above all characterized the duchy's affairs, and it became one of the two great attributes of the duke's legacy, the other being almsgiving. Such was his renown as an almsgiver that the monks of the Sinai desert in Egypt sent one of their brethren to Normandy each year to beg alms of him. They were rewarded with gold and silver.[30] Richard was said to have sent a hundred pounds of gold to the Church of the Holy Sepulchre in Jerusalem and sponsored those who wished to make pilgrimage there. Like his lord, Robert II of France (996–1031), he was remembered as a 'lover of what is good'.[31] If Edward, like his father, associated his tribulations with sin, he might have recognized a link between Richard's piety and the peace in the duchy. The monks who reported on Richard's legacy grasped the link intuitively, and the young exile admired monks and listened to what

---

[29] Wipo, *Gesta Chuonradi II. imperatoris*, in *Die Werke Wipos*, ed. H. Bresslau, MGH Scriptores, 59 (Hanover and Leipzig, 1915), 3–62, at p. 4.

[30] *Inventio*, ed. Laporte, p. 35; T. Heikkilä, *Vita s. Symeonis Treverensis: Ein hochmittelalterlicher Heiligenkult im Kontext* (Helsinki, 2002), pp. 119–21.

[31] Glaber, *Opera*, ed. France et al., pp. 36 and 270, where Richard is described as 'totius boni amator' ('a lover of all that is good'). Cf. Helgaud of Fleury, *Epitoma uitae Rotberti Pii*, ed. R. H. Bautier and G. Labory, *Sources d'histoire médiévale* (Paris 1965), p. 116, where King Robert is described as 'amator bonorum' ('a lover of the good'). Glaber wrote that section at Cluny in the 1030s. Helgaud wrote at Fleury in 1031 × 1041.

they said.[32] Norman monasteries such as Fécamp and Saint-Wandrille remembered Richard as a patron, but the verdict on Æthelred already forming at the time of his death despaired at his ultimate failure. This was never Edward's view – the record from Ghent hints he thought himself 'unworthy' of his father. There were, however, lessons to learn from Richard which extended the logic of his father's perspective on the Danish raids. The contrast with what he had known before Normandy could have persuaded Edward, at an impressionable stage, of the link between a ruler's goodness and the peace and divine favour that accompanied it.

Richard differed from Æthelred in other regards. For one, Æthelred was distrustful and inspired ambivalent loyalty, attributes which re-inforced each other. His distrustfulness bred vigilance, an advantage against conspiracies but a virtue which in excess encouraged him to undermine, and even capriciously strike, established dynasties where his natural support lay. By relying upon royal officials and men dependent on his regime he achieved administrative efficiency but weakened the bonds that united royalty and nobility in respect of their shared interests and ancestries. Too much can be made of those tendencies, but it only took a spate of forfeitures or murders among the king's counsellors to alarm those whose loyalties were transferrable. Richard, in contrast, cultivated an equitable temperament and empowered the people bound to him in established ties of kinship by acknowledging what they would have regarded as their due. He did so by elevating kinsmen to the rank of count and entrusting to them frontier castles, where knights helped keep the peace. Richard's brother, Archbishop Robert of Rouen, was created count of Évreux. His uncle Rodulf, whom he installed at Ivry, consoli-dated Richard's authority on the southern borders of the Évrecin, fulfilling a similar role in the Lieuvin and in Hiémois. His county passed to his son, Hugh, bishop of Bayeux, who was Richard's cousin. Godefrey, another of Richard I's sons, was made count of Eu or Brionne, and Osbern, who may already have been Richard's cousin when he married Rodulf of Ivry's daughter, was solidly implanted albeit without the comital title in Hiémois, Arques, and Breteuil.[33] Richard's objective was a close-knit nobility with a military ethos, kinship affinities, and a shared interest in peacekeeping. Through senior clergy such as Archbishop Robert and Bishop Hugh of Bayeux, the Church in Normandy pulled in the same direction.

Kinship also underpinned relations with neighbouring principalities. Wherever he could, Richard established peaceful links by marriage. His first wife was Judith, sister of Geoffrey, count of Brittany. Their marriage took place early in his reign, near the great abbey of Mont-Saint-Michel, which was situated at the juncture of Brittany, Maine, and Normandy,

[32] On Edward's friendship with monks during his exile, see *Vita*, p. 117.

[33] P. Bauduin, *La première Normandie (Xe–XIe siècle): sur les frontières de la haute Normandie: identité et construction d'une principauté* (Caen, 2004), pp. 194–221, 295.

and influential in all three. Hawisa, one of Richard's sisters, married Count Geoffrey. Matilda, another sister, married Odo II, count of Blois-Chartres. Emma, of course, was married first to Æthelred and then to Cnut, the maintenance of cordial relations with neighbouring powers being of greater import to Richard than the turnaround of princes. Her daughter Godgifu (or Gode for short), who was in exile with Edward and Alfred, was married to Count Drogo of the Vexin, which bordered eastern Normandy. Beneficial exchanges followed. In April 1024, Drogo came to Rouen with a large following and issued charters in favour of the abbey of Saint-Wandrille, granting it estates and exemptions from tolls at ports in the Seine valley.[34]

By establishing ties with England to the north, Brittany to the west, Blois-Chartres to the south-east, and the Vexin to the east, while empowering kinsmen with castles on the southern border of his duchy, Richard built the foundations of a lasting peace. One of his sons and two brothers of his second wife, Papia, entered monasteries, strengthening ducal family influence and procuring intercession. The youngest son of his first marriage, William, was given to the ducal abbey of Fécamp. Papia's two brothers became monks at Saint-Wandrille. While other princes challenged the authority of Robert II of France, Richard remained loyal, assisting his campaigns in Burgundy and Flanders. Loyalty to the king, honouring his familial bonds, and investing in heaven were hallmarks of his piety. They were also survival strategies, for it is doubtful whether Richard possessed the might to face down multiple powerful enemies. In general, princes who could flex their muscle with impunity were more pugnacious, though Richard's commitment to peace may be explained by his unusually religious temperament. Edward could have learned to admire the duke even while realizing Richard would never advance his claim to the throne. His uncle was not one for unsettling the order of things.

What he did not learn from observation Edward could imbibe from stories circulating at court. About the time he arrived in the duchy, Dudo, dean of the collegiate church of Saint-Quentin, was adding the finishing touches to his *History of the Normans*. The learned French cleric enjoyed long-standing ducal favour and had served as Richard's chaplain. With heroic stories told by the likes of Rodulf of Ivry, and with fertile imagining, he fashioned a history of Norman prowess and the feats of ducal ancestors which would do any half-viking people proud. Dudo told of how Normandy's founder Rollo formed a pact of mutual assistance with an English king named Athelstan. When the English rebelled, Rollo came at his summons, crushed the rebels, and secured his throne, receiving in turn

---

[34] E. Van Houts, 'Edward and Normandy', in Mortimer, ed., *Edward*, 63–76, at pp. 65–6.

a gift of half his realm from the grateful king.[35] To query the historical reality is to miss the sense of entitlement underlying the story. In 1014, when Æthelred lost his throne, Richard had received him and assisted his return. Richard's admirers at the ducal court must have thought of him as a new Rollo.

Dudo's tale had a contemporary political resonance which leaves little doubt Æthelred and his sons were supposed to be in Richard's debt. Dudo's work even raised the issue of a grant made to the duke's ancestor for rescuing a shadowy king with a name of the House of Cerdic from his enemies. Whether the tale was intended seriously, a serious point was being made. For as long as Edward was second to Harthacnut in the running for the throne, those narratives of indebtedness could be pressed upon him. And if by some chance he became a player, he could be pressured to repay Norman kindnesses. The longer he spent in Richard's care, the greater his uncle's claim upon him. Still, Edward may have been shrewd enough to detect manipulation and oppose it with grievances. As the heir of an ancient royal line he could nurture his own sense of entitlement; he could argue Richard had done less for him than was his due.

Exile searches the soul, and it teaches patience. Ælfric the Homilist had advice for the depths of winter:

> Many hardships and contumelies anyone would easily endure that he might be accounted the child of some powerful man, and his heir to transitory possessions. Bear now patiently, for the everlasting honour of being accounted children of God and his heirs in heavenly riches, that which the other man would undergo for a frail matter.[36]

And for all the years in which Edward might have considered how to attain both the earthly and the heavenly kingdom, little by little familial joys were restored to him. And God 'Who sets the lonely in a family' and provided a new family for Job, could be credited by anyone mindful of His mercies for blessing Edward with brothers, in the place of those he had lost.

To the brothers he had lost, Edward was substantially their junior and posed a threat as a stepmother's child. In Normandy, his cousins could take their place. Richard and Robert were roughly his age – give or take a few years – and had no reason to feel threatened by him. The three were of an age to find common interests in hunting and martial exploits. If rivalry arose between Richard and Robert, both had an incentive to court

---

[35] Dudo of Saint-Quentin, *De gestis Normannie ducum seu de moribus et actis primorum Normanniae ducum*, ed. J. Lair, *Mémoires de la Société des Antiquaires de Normandie*, vol. xxiii (Caen, 1865), pp. 158–9.

[36] *Ælfric, CH: FS*, I. 3, lines 181–4 (pp. 198–205, at p. 204); translation adapted from Thorpe, *Homilies*, p. 57.

him, and they all had something in common as young men waiting for
their inheritance. Edward had other cousins, potentially friendly figures.
William, his cousin in the cloister, could have been a friend inside the
ducal abbey. Alain III and Eudo I were now joint rulers in Brittany. Sons
of Count Geoffrey by the duke's sister Hawisa, they too were Edward's
cousins. His sister's marriage to Drogo made the count of the Vexin his
brother-in-law. If Edward forged friendships with members of this second
generation, those who favoured him could complicate ducal diplomacy by
promoting his claim to the throne. When the duke died in 1026, Edward
was in his early twenties. Now was his chance to press for recognition.
There was an opportunity to exploit tensions too. Richard had put his
elder son Richard (III) in charge of the duchy, setting Robert over the
county of Hiémois. Within months, Robert rebelled, overturning his
father's arrangement. Richard III besieged him and made him submit,
but in August 1027, the young duke followed his father to the grave.
Adhemar, the contemporary chronicler of Chabannes, reported the
rumour that he had been poisoned. Jumièges reported it too, without
disagreeing.[37] Robert benefited by taking charge of the duchy. He was
champing at the bit.

EDWARD'S STEPFATHER

Eleven years had passed since Edward left England, where other stories
were unfolding. In the cycles of summer and winter, the sun that had
warmed Edward's days had brightened Cnut's, and the faces of Emma's
offspring – Harthacnut and Gunnhilda. Events which at any moment
might have turned one way or another, like streams running down a
mountain, had found their natural course and united severally in their
inexorable motion. Cnut had become the ruler of England and Denmark.
By 1028 he had established his nephew Hákon as a client ruler in
Norway.[38] In England his chief advisors included Godwine, the earl of
Wessex, and Leofric, earl in Mercia. Godwine was the son of the nobleman
Wulfnoth, who had fallen out with Eadric Streona's faction. An ally of
Edmund Ironside's party, his son was a beneficiary of Athelstan's will. By
1023 he was attesting Cnut's charters as the first of the 'earls', this title
having replaced that of ealdorman. Leofric was the son of Leofwine, one
of Æthelred's ealdormen. Their dynasty was the only one of Southumbrian
stature to survive Cnut and his purges, though not without the loss of
kinsmen. Twice its authority in Mercia had suffered erosion from the
installation of other commanders in that region: Eadric in Æthelred's

---

[37] *Ademari Cabannensis Chronicon*, ed. P. Bourgain, assisted by R. Landes and G. Pon,
CCCM 129 (Turnhout, 1999), p. 184; *GND*, II, p. 47.

[38] Bolton, *Cnut*, pp. 154–5.

time, and Danish earls under Cnut.[39] Twice had a parvenu overtaken
Leofwine in the hierarchy: first Eadric then Godwine. Yet knowing not to
overstep was key to the dynasty's survival.

Cnut had also allayed his subjects' fears and exceeded expectations.
Later in the century the monk Herman marvelled at the metamorphosis:

> He that changed Saul,
> the big bad wolf, into Paul,
> transformed this wild man
> into a most Christian king![40]

By marrying Emma and renewing the laws of King Edgar, since reformu-
lated with the help of Archbishop Wulfstan, Cnut showed his willingness
to stand for continuity. When he left England occasionally to see to affairs
in Denmark or in Rome, he would write letters to the English people,
assuring them he was working for their good. At Assandun in Essex, where
many had fallen in battle, he built a minster in atonement and gave it to
his priest Stigand.[41] He also honoured the cults of English saints who had
been martyred by the Danes, arranging for the body of Archbishop
Ælfheah to be translated from St Paul's to Canterbury Cathedral, to the
delight of Archbishop Æthelnoth, and sponsoring the monastic community implanted at Bury St Edmunds, where the martyred St Edmund
rested after his sojourn in London.[42]

In Cnut's time, the church at Bury was rebuilt in stone and dedicated,
by Æthelnoth, in 1032. At New Minster, Winchester, and Thorney in the
Fens, Cnut was commemorated as a benefactor in the Book of Life, which
lay upon the high altar, foretokening the Book which Christ would open
at the Doom.[43] The abbeys of Ramsey and St Benet's at Holme benefited
from his generosity, as did foreign churches such as Chartres. For decades,
the Danish kings and the German emperors had warred against each
other intermittently, but Cnut established peace with his counterpart,
Conrad II. In 1027, he even attended his imperial coronation in Rome.
Returning via Flanders, he stopped to pay his respects at the abbey of
Saint-Bertin in Saint-Omer, weeping before the saint and making rich

---

[39] Baxter, *Earls of Mercia*, pp. 21, 26–7.

[40] *MSE*, p. 43.

[41] ASC F, 1020 (i.e. Ashingdon).

[42] Osbern, *Translatio sancti Ælfegi*, ed. A. R. Rumble, tr. R. Morris and A. R. Rumble, in
Rumble, ed., *The Reign of Cnut, King of England, Denmark and Norway* (London and New York,
1994), 283–315; *MSE*, pp. xxiv– xxvi.

[43] *The 'Liber Vitae' of the New Minster and Hyde Abbey, Winchester, British Library Stowe 944
[etc]*, ed. S. Keynes, Early English Manuscripts in Facsimile 26 (Copenhagen, 1996),
pp. 79–80, 83 (Plate V); *The Thorney 'Liber Vitae': London, British Library, Additional MS 40,000,
fols 1–12r*, ed. L. Rollason (Woodbridge, 2015), p. 102 (Plate 8).

gifts.[44] At a time when the count of Flanders was negotiating with a new duke in Normandy, it served Cnut's interests to remind him he could be generous – and that he had friends in Rome and Germany, Flanders' larger neighbour. He may already have granted privileges to Christ Church, Canterbury, and it did no harm to cultivate loyalty in harbours on both sides of the Channel.[45]

While projecting to the English, and established Christian principalities, the image of a pious ruler, over the northern seas Cnut cast the shadow of a viking warlord. Relaxing at his palace in Winchester where the royal treasury lay, surrounded by Scandinavian nobles – his housecarls – he lavished generosity not on churches but on skalds who sang of his victories over subjugated peoples.[46] Northern affairs often occupied his attention. Denmark, which had passed to Cnut after the death of his brother Harold, was vulnerable to alliances arising between native jarls, who were favourable or indifferent to Cnut's regime, and the rulers of Sweden and Norway, who were ambivalent or hostile. To counteract such threats, he took a lead in the forging of marital bonds between Danish and English nobles. He gave his sister Margaret, also known as Estrith, to the Danish Jarl Ulf. Ulf's sister, Gytha, was married to Earl Godwine, in turn. In the past, England had been a target for viking raids because of its wealth. With Cnut at the helm, the silver went to sustaining a North Sea empire. The taxes were unpopular but perhaps no more than the payments exacted under Æthelred to keep the raiders at bay. Such was the price of peace, with Godwine and other senior figures running the realm in Cnut's absences. Northwards there were setbacks. In 1026 Jarl Ulf, his brother Eilaf, and an army of Swedes and Norwegians ravaged Skåne, the easternmost part of Cnut's domain. Cnut took an army to fight them but secured no clear victory.[47] Worse, the sudden death of his client ruler in Norway forced him to implant a shaky regime under Ælfgifu of Northampton and their elder son, the teenager Swein.

Normandy had posed no threat to Cnut under Richard II and his heir, but now there were signs that the new duke, Robert, might reverse his father's policies. The first indication he was unhappy with his father's disposition of affairs had been his rebellion against Richard III, his father's chosen successor. After obtaining the duchy, he continued in this vein by clashing with his father's stalwarts, Archbishop Robert of Rouen (who was also count of Évreux) and Bishop Hugh of Bayeux (the count of Ivry).[48]

[44] Wipo, *Gesta Chuonradi*, p. 36; *EER*, p. 38.

[45] On his generosity to Christ Church, see Bolton, *Cnut*, pp. 121–2. S 952 and S 959 record purported gifts.

[46] M. Townend, 'Contextualizing the *Knútsdrápur*: Skaldic Praise-poetry at the Court of Cnut', *ASE* 30 (2001), 145–79, at pp. 168–77.

[47] ASC E, 1025 [1026?]; Bolton, *Cnut*, pp. 148–51, argues, however, that Cnut triumphed.

[48] *GND*, II, pp. 49–53; Bauduin, *La première Normandie*, pp. 210–12.

It was probably about this date that Cnut tried to shore up the Norman alliance by negotiating the marriage of his recently widowed sister, Margaret-Estrith, to the duke. But Glaber, writing this part of his history in 1036–41, saw the failure of the marriage as common knowledge, observing how it was well known that Robert 'had married a sister of Cnut whom he had repudiated because she was hateful to him'.[49]

It was also well known, at least in Normandy, that Robert had established brotherly ties with the aethelings Edward and Alfred. William of Jumièges remarks that Robert 'adopted them as brothers', implying that a form of artificial brotherhood was contracted, either blood- or sworn brotherhood, both of which were traditional, artificial, bonds that remained current in the eleventh century.[50] As a potential heir to the dukedom who would swiftly reject his father's posthumous settlement, he had evidently felt that his interests had been overlooked, nurturing a grievance not altogether dissimilar to that of the two aethelings, whom Cnut had robbed of their inheritance and whom Richard II had colluded to keep out of the running for the throne. In any narratives of displaced entitlement cultivated by Robert and the aethelings, Cnut and Richard II were figures whose policies could therefore be linked. Once Robert had rectified his own position, he was bound to assist his artificial brothers with theirs.

KING ACROSS THE WATER

The souring of relations with Cnut after Robert's repudiation of Estrith culminated in a remarkable series of confrontational actions, or gestures, on the part of the duke and one or both aethelings. Before we turn to the sources which allow the following reconstruction, we should consider the most likely outline. In 1033–4, a decision appears to have been made by Robert and his advisors to let Edward call himself 'King' Edward, and to dispatch a mighty fleet with the ostensible task of invading England on the aethelings' behalf and of restoring their inheritance. Those details can be safely accepted as facts. The uncertainty arises about their significance in the power-game that was unfolding and their bearing upon subsequent events.

Jumièges says that towards the end of Robert's reign, the duke took steps to assist the aethelings. He first sent envoys to Cnut, advising him to

---

[49] Glaber, *Opera*, ed. France et al., p. 204: 'quamlibet sororem Anglorum regis Canute manifestum est duxisse uxorem quam odiendo diuortium fecerat'. Glaber is reliable here, *pace* Adam of Bremen, writing forty years later, who muddled the facts (*GHEP*, pp. 114–15): D. C. Douglas, 'Some Problems of Early Norman Chronology', *EHR* 65 (1950), 289–303, at p. 291

[50] E. M. C. Van Houts, 'The Political Relations between Normandy and England before 1066 According to the *Gesta Normannorum ducum*', in R. Foreville, ed., *Les mutations socio-culturelles au tournant des XIe–XIIe siècles* (Paris, 1984), 85–97, at pp. 90–1.

restore to Edward and Alfred their inheritance. When his ambassadors returned empty-handed, the furious duke summoned his chief men and assembled a fleet at Fécamp, enlisting ships from all the ports of Normandy. As it was crossing the Channel a storm blew it to Jersey, where contrary winds detained it, preventing passage to England. 'In despair the duke became more and more distressed', until he accepted the inevitable and directed his ships to Mont-Saint-Michel. There he ordered one part of the fleet to ravage the coast of Brittany while he himself gathered an army of mounted soldiers and prepared to attack the county using the remaining vessels. Alain III of Brittany, who had challenged his authority, was forced to terms. Jumièges claims envoys then arrived from Cnut, declaring he was gravely ill and willing to restore half the kingdom to Æthelred's sons. Contented, Robert delayed his naval expedition and travelled to Jerusalem, but he died on the journey home.[51] Charters lend support to this account in some quite extraordinary ways.

In a charter of Easter 1033 Robert made gifts to the monastery of Saint-Wandrille in the presence of a large company of magnates. They included King Henry of France, the victim of a palace coup. He had been expelled from the royal principality, in preference for Robert, his younger brother, by their mother Queen Constance and Odo II of Blois-Chartres, only to find asylum at Fécamp. In a second charter, issued between 1031 and 1034, Robert restored lands to Fécamp on the advice of counsellors who argued that he had wrongly appropriated them in the first place. Unique formulae common to these charters, and Henry's presence as one of the witnesses in the first, suggest that both were issued at Fécamp, whose scribes did service in lieu of a ducal chancery.[52] The witness list of the second charter is shorter, but it may have been abridged by a copyist. Unlike any charter from Richard's reign, both bear the attestations of Edward and Alfred, whose names appear together in that order without titles.

A third charter is the only one known to have been issued in the name of 'King' Edward before Edward acceded to the English throne. Its text is preserved in two versions, one in the twelfth-century cartulary of Mont-Saint-Michel, the other in a transcript published by the antiquary Sir William Dugdale, from 'the autograph itself at Mont-Saint-Michel'.[53] This is apparently a reference to a lost single-sheet original, transcribed either by Dugdale or by one of the scholars whose transcripts he consulted.[54] Of the 119 charters in the cartulary, 44, including this one,

---

[51] *GND*, II, pp. 77–81, 85.

[52] *RADN*, nos 69, 70; Keynes, 'Æthelings', at pp. 187–9, Appendices 2 and 3.

[53] S 1061. *The Cartulary of the Abbey of Mont-Saint-Michel*, ed. K. S. B. Keats-Rohan (Donington, 2006), no. 10 (pp. 88–9); R. Dodsworth and W. Dugdale, *Monasticon Anglicanum*, 3 vols (London, 1655–73), I, p. 279. A copy of the 'autograph' can be found in the Otterton cartulary. It is not known whether Dugdale saw the original or an apograph.

[54] In 1648, after the death of the French antiquary André Duchesne, Dugdale stayed three months in Calais, consulting his notes and copying his transcriptions of documents

can be checked against originals, pseudo-originals, or copies of originals; and of the 44 only two show signs of tampering having occurred prior to the copying of the charter into the cartulary.[55] Edward's charter is irreproachably authentic. Nor is it the only instance of a would-be king preemptively granting lands not yet come into his possession, for Duke William promised English lands to his followers in anticipation of the invasion of 1066.[56] With no other known precedent, it is likely he had learned the trick from Edward.

In the charter, 'King' Edward grants estates to Mont-Saint-Michel, namely St Michael's Mount in Cornwall, the land of 'Vennesire', and the port called 'Ruminella', neither of which is securely identified, although the former could refer to Winniaton Hundred in Cornwall and the latter to the port of (Old) Romney in Kent. The two extant copies reveal minor variations of orthography and word-order, and moderate variations between the witness lists, which are potentially important. In the 'autograph' copy, the final signatories are Ralph, Vinfred, Nigel, Anschitil Choschet, and Turstin. In the cartulary, they are named as Vinfred, Nigel, Anschitil, Ralph, Choschet, and Turstin, which suggests either that the copyist had a different list or that he copied tabulated names in a different order, while misreading 'Anschitil Choschet' as two witnesses, not one with a byname. A more telling difference is that the copy in the cartulary replicates the *signa* of Duke Robert and an official named Rabel after the *signum* of 'King' Edward and before Archbishop Robert of Rouen, whereas in the 'autograph' copy Robert and Rabel are absent. Their absence from the 'autograph' suggests their *signa* were added later, a practice found in other contemporary Norman charters, in which witness lists were amplified with further names as an afterthought, sometimes by the original scribe.[57] We might infer that the duke was absent when the charter was drawn up but approved it at a later stage.

Rabel attests three charters in the archive of Norman documents, these being Robert's charter for Saint-Wandrille, of Easter 1033, in which he is the fourth signatory after the duke; Edward's charter for Mont-Saint-Michel, as just described; and another charter of Robert for the same monastery.[58] Orderic Vitalis, who amplified William of Jumièges' *Deeds of the Norman Dukes* before 1109, identifies Rabel as the commander of that part of the fleet which ravaged Brittany, while Robert (as Jumièges says)

relating to French monasteries with English possessions: W. Hamper, *The Life, Diary and Correspondence of Sir William Dugdale, Knight, sometime Garter principal King of Arms* ... etc (London, 1827), p. 23.

[55] *Cartulary*, ed. Keats-Rohan, p. 27*ff.*

[56] Bates, *William*, pp. 226, 231–2.

[57] As in the case of *RADN*, no. 85, discussed in Keynes, 'Æthelings', pp. 188–90 and Bates, *William*, pp. 40–1, although his case against Edward's charter for Mont-Saint-Michel, on p. 41, seems unaware of its variants.

[58] *RADN*, no. 65.

gathered an army of mounted soldiers and prepared to attack Brittany using the other part of the fleet.[59] According to Jumièges, Alain of Brittany then sent envoys to Archbishop Robert, an uncle of both Alain and Robert, urging that he come quickly and mediate to avert Robert's attack. The archbishop was soon at Mont-Saint-Michel. These details can be used to explain certain features of Edward's charter, such as the presence of Archbishop Robert and of the bishops of Lisieux and Coutances, who were presumably part of his delegation. The absence of Breton witnesses and any representative of the monastic community of Mont-Saint-Michel suggests they had shut themselves inside the abbey. The initial absence of the duke and his fleet-commander, Rabel, makes good sense if they were away on their respective missions and added their *signa* when they got back to the abbey where negotiations were under way. The English lands given to Mont-Saint-Michel by 'King' Edward cost nothing to a landless king. They could secure its goodwill in the conflict between its rival patrons, Robert and Alain. As cousin to both, Edward would be a mediator, alongside the archbishop, who was everyone's uncle. As 'king', he could enact that role in a manner that set him over the princes as an arbiter.

The charter cannot be dated precisely on internal evidence. Yet it must post-date Easter 1033, when Edward had not yet adopted the royal title. And its association with the Brittany campaign, which Jumièges links to Cnut's final illness and represents as Robert's last action before announcing his intentions to make a pilgrimage to Jerusalem, supplies the outer date limit of January 1035, by which time his intentions were public.[60] Within that time-period, Edward took part in a naval expedition, assumed the title 'king', and granted possessions in England to Mont-Saint-Michel. In the same years his brother Alfred, whose last appearance in charters occurs at Easter 1033 with Edward as co-witness, disappears for a while. He was seemingly not involved in the naval campaign – or at least, his *signum* is not upon Edward's charter. And in two other charters, attested by 'King' Edward, Alfred is no longer with him. Both are charters of Duke Robert which appear to have been confirmed at the beginning of the minority rule of his son, William, by the addition of William's *signum* and the *signa* of members of the minority council, including 'King' Edward himself.[61] One confirms lands granted to Fécamp; the other concerns Mont-Saint-Michel and the Channel Islands – places with which Edward is associated, both in the charter record and in the *Gesta* of William of Jumièges.

---

[59] *GND*, II, p. 78: 'partem quandam classis . . . ad affligendam Britanniam direxit. Ipse uero . . . parabat ab altera parte eam aggredi.' It is highly unlikely that Orderic consulted, and somehow inferred this information from, the charters just mentioned.

[60] *GND*, II, p. 80, n.2.

[61] *RADN*, nos 85, 73 and 111, cf. Keynes, 'Æthelings', pp. 188–90, 196–7, and Bates, *William*, pp. 40–1.

Edward's adoption of the royal title at some point between Easter 1033, when he appears as a witness without it, and January 1035, which is the latest date for the Brittany campaign, reveals that he had ceased to be a pawn and become a player. It involved undermining Cnut and his heirs with claims that could be kept non-specific if necessary, or altered to suit each audience, and which echo in the sources. One such claim was that the English chief men had sworn an oath to recognize his kingship, a claim Edward's character in the fictive *Encomium* is expressly made to deny, in the only direct speech that is attributed to him.[62] The purpose of having his character deny the oath was to defend Emma's recourse to Harthacnut in 1040: a sure indication that Edward was citing an oath which legally bound her to him. That the real Edward was saying the opposite of what his fictional character declares is suggested by the *Vita*'s claim that the people swore an oath to him when he was still in Emma's womb.[63]

A stronger legal claim may lie buried in the Anglo-Saxon Chronicle C/D entry for 1041, which declares that Edward 'had been driven from his country many years before – and yet he was sworn in as king; and he thus stayed at his brother's [i.e. Harthacnut's] court as long as he lived'.[64] The middle clause in this statement is a possible *koinon*, a common element which faces both forward and backward. It thereby creates ambiguity, inviting the reader to infer either that Edward had been sworn in as king before he went into exile, or that he was sworn in at Harthacnut's court in 1041, as co-ruler or heir presumptive. Crafted in the early 1040s, the annal lends weight to the idea that Edward was affirming rumours about an oath sworn before 1016, which others at court were denying, and that the annalist tried to please both camps with a statement designed to admit both possibilities. The reason for thinking it hints at a stronger legal claim is that an oath recognizing an unborn son as king-to-be is less authoritative in the scheme of things than an oath conferring kingship upon an aetheling, as indicated in the phrase 'sworn in as king'. The first oath would not have provided sufficient justification for Edward's adoption of the title 'king'. An oath of the second kind would.

The monk of Saint-Wandrille, writing in the 1050s, pushes the oath story to its absolute limit, claiming that Edward, as a boy, had been anointed and crowned at his father's behest, with the consent of the English people, shortly before Æthelred's death and Cnut's 1016 invasion.[65] If this was a

---

[62] *EER*, p. 49; Williams, *Æthelred*, p. 135, n. 16 (at pp. 222–3). Cf. Stafford, *Emma and Edith*, pp. 221–2.

[63] *Vita*, p. 13.

[64] ASC C, 1041: 'ðe wæs ær for fela gearon of his earde adrifen, 7 ðeh wæs to cinge gesworen, 7 he wunode þa swa on his broðor hirede þa hwile ðe he leofode'; translation from *The Anglo-Saxon Chronicle*, ed. Whitelock et al., p. 106. Æthelred had been driven out in 1013 and sworn in as king again on his return in 1014, but the sentence structure and context favour the view that Edward is the subject.

[65] See above, p. 36 (*Inventio*, ed. Laporte, p. 36).

fiction crafted to further Edward's cause, it was based on Capetian practice, lately rehearsed in 1028 when Henry of France was co-crowned on his father King Robert's orders. Alternatively, the event behind the story may have been a ceremony of *c.* 1015, in which Æthelred demanded oaths recognizing Edward as his successor. If such an event occurred, as posited, the oath-taking was now being presented as a co-coronation, to justify Edward's use of the title 'King'. Saint-Wandrille was an abbey we might expect to promote Edward's claims, given that Edward had two uncles among the monks – Humphrey and Osbern, brothers of Papia – and that his brother-in-law, Drogo of the Vexin, was a benefactor. Taken altogether, the evidence of rumoured oaths suggests that Edward's minimal claim was that an oath had been sworn to him in Emma's womb. A middle claim, which justified his use of the kingly title and was contentious by 1041, was that he had been sworn in as king before 1016. The maximalist story circulating by the 1050s, if only in Normandy, was that Edward had been anointed and crowned before he was driven into exile.

Further evidence of his tactics is found in the *Vita*'s remark that the Franks (meaning the Normans or French at Edward's court) affirmed that a type of miracle performed by Edward during his reign was one he often used to perform in Normandy during his youth. It involved dipping his fingers in water and touching the neck and suppurating face of a woman suffering an infection of the lymph nodes. He also made the sign of the Cross several times.[66] Since this type of miracle was novel in England, Folcard felt obliged to adduce French testimony avowing its precedents. In France, the healing of scrofula by royal touch is first recorded in Helgaud of Fleury's *Life of Robert the Pious*, written shortly after the king's death in the early 1030s. According to the monk Helgaud, King Robert had been granted the grace to heal: 'for by touching with his most pious hands the sores of suffering and signing them with the Holy Cross, he would deliver people from their pains and diseases'.[67] There is no evidence Helgaud's work was read outside the abbey of Fleury-sur-Loire, and Folcard was apparently unaware the royal touch was a type of miracle performed by Capetian kings. Edward had ample opportunity to learn about this miracle or witness its performance either by Robert or by his son Henry, who was with him at Fécamp in 1033. If God granted such a favour to the Capetians, He could grant it to the Cerdicings. By using the royal touch and circulating stories about oaths or co-consecration, Edward could assume the sacrality associated with Capetian monarchs, bolstering the title he already possessed as heir in the line of Cerdic and exposing the Danish usurpation that deprived him of his kingdom.

---

[66] *Vita*, pp. 93–5.
[67] Helgaud, *Epitoma*, p. 128; see also Van Houts, 'Edward and Normandy', pp. 71–5.

How long Edward had spent laying the groundwork for the recognition of his kingship cannot be known, but his rumour-mongering, posturing, and eventual acclamation as 'king' affected Alfred too. For one thing, his assumption of kingly airs reveals Edward's belief in his own precedence. It was based on the gap of seven or eight years between them, and the normative relations between his elder half-brothers, growing up at Æthelred's court, where the eldest – initially Athelstan, then Edmund – had always set himself apart and played the heir presumptive. A similar hierarchy had been plain at the court of Richard II. For all this panoply of precedence, however, the witan acknowledged no model of primogeniture. The eldest son had generally obtained the throne in the past, but in theory at least the chief men were free to elect any candidate to the kingly office, provided he was of the male bloodline. The consecrated king of France, moreover, had been ejected in favour of a younger brother. At Fécamp, in 1033, he had the opportunity to share that story with the aethelings, planting ideas in their heads. It is not known whether he did, but Edward and Alfred surely knew of what had happened to Henry. His presence in Normandy could not otherwise be explained. Edward's assumption of the royal title coincided with Henry's displacement. So perhaps it was partly prompted by fears of Alfred's ambition, fear that Emma preferred Alfred, or an alliance of those fears. Edward may have feared Emma would behave like Henry's mother.

The whereabouts of Alfred during these crucial developments is fundamental, for their decision to attack Cnut forced the Normans into a position where they would have to think hard about which candidate might become king. Prior to the naval campaign the query was irrelevant and potentially divisive. By 1033 it was topical. Alfred's disappearance from the witness lists after Easter that year and Robert's declaration for Edward are chronologically linked, so it is possible the latter was the stimulus for Alfred's withdrawal from affairs. By presenting Robert's plans as an attempt to help both aethelings, and Cnut's offer of half the kingdom as an offer to both, Jumièges covers over the problem that only one could be king. Rivalry between the aethelings, in which the duke sided with Edward, hardly fitted his tale about brotherliness. Whether or not the invasion attempt coincided with a serious illness which afflicted Cnut, it came at the worst possible time for him, for his regime in Norway was on the brink of collapse. Ælfgifu and Swein had to flee about 1034, and war was now brewing for Harthacnut, the teenage regent of Denmark. Perhaps he did write to Robert, to purchase respite, although Jumièges had a motive to inflate any offer which Cnut might have made.

Apart from a similar account by William of Malmesbury, coloured by oral tradition,[68] Jumièges supplies the only record of Robert's naval

---

[68] *GR*, I, § 180 (pp. 319–21).

expedition. We are reliant on a writer who exaggerated ducal achievements, added dramatic flourishes, and telescoped events. It is important
therefore that the charters, particularly Edward's for Mont-Saint-Michel,
fit the report and present some of the missing pieces. There can be little
doubt Robert declared for 'King' Edward and prepared the semblance
of an invasion fleet. Whether it was meant for England or Brittany,
Jumièges made excuses for a failed attempt that left Edward ultimately
disappointed. Robert's deepening distress at the contrary winds, the
encouraging promises from Cnut which allowed him to shelve a risky
expedition, and Jumièges' reflection that it failed 'by the will of God
for the sake of King Edward, whom He meant to reign in future without
bloodshed', are the touches of an apologist.[69] In the final remark, he flattered the reigning king. But his reflection on God's designs neglects to
observe what a blessing it was for Robert that the fleet ended up at
Mont-Saint-Michel, to surprise his Breton enemies. His claim that
Robert's actions forced Cnut to sign over half his kingdom reinvents the
story of Athelstan's gift to Rollo. Robert, as Rollo's heir, now becomes the
donor of half of England to Edward and Alfred, returning to Athelstan's
putative heirs what Athelstan had granted to Rollo. Blame for their failure
to come into their inheritance could be transferred to Cnut or his execu-
tors and away from the duke who had abandoned a promised invasion.
Jumièges was going to some lengths to show Edward was in debt to the
Normans.

Whether Edward felt in their debt depends on the inscrutable particu-
lars of circumstance and character. As the heir of an ancient royal House,
he was vested with his own strong sense of entitlement to counter the idea
he was beholden to another. Besides, God was the only true giver. Those
who hosted Edward could be regarded as merely the executives of a
greater providential design, by which God was restoring what was due to
a wrongfully exiled prince. If Edward did feel indebted to his Norman
hosts there were ways he could repay them to his own satisfaction by
attending the duke, engaging in his diplomacy, and fighting on his
campaigns. When, for example, Baldwin IV of Flanders appealed for
assistance against his rebellious son, Edward might have joined Robert,
who assembled all his warriors, attacked Flanders, and burned down the
stronghold of Choques with everyone inside. He cannot have stood wholly
aloof amid the politics of conflict and conciliation that expedited the
Flanders affair. He may have been involved in celebrating the marriage
of one of Robert's sisters to Baldwin IV about the same time.[70] He was
clearly involved in mediating between Alain of Brittany and Robert at
Mont-Saint-Michel. It is important too that the narrative concerning
Edward's indebtedness to the Normans belongs not to Robert's reign but

---

[69] *GND*, II, p. 79.
[70] Ibid., pp. 53–5

to the reign of his son, William. Robert may not have countenanced the view that his adoptive brother was in his debt. For Robert was a famously generous man.[71]

COMPETING FOR THE THRONE

The year 1035 filled many graves and threw northern affairs into confusion. Edward, for his part, suffered setbacks and loss as death removed friendly princes. Count Baldwin died on 30 May. Then on 2 July Robert died at Nicaea, on his way back from Jerusalem. Drogo of the Vexin died on the same pilgrimage, widowing Edward's sister. The duchy, meanwhile, passed to the guardians of Robert's son William, the seven- or eight-year-old child of Robert's union with Herleva of Falaise. Prior to his departure, Robert had prepared for the eventuality of his death on the pilgrim road by entrusting William to Alain of Brittany, Gilbert of Brionne, and Osbern the Steward.[72] Edward assisted during the regency council, attesting William's early charters, still with the title 'king', but the accession of a child fast began to make the duchy a dangerous place.[73] Edward or Alfred had to involve themselves in finding their sister a new husband if they wished to build their alliances; and amid the creeping uncertainties that beset them, on 12 November Cnut died at Shaftesbury, leaving the witan to dispose his affairs. He also left Harold, a son by Ælfgifu of Northampton, and Harthacnut and Gunnhilda, children by Emma. Swein, his other son by Ælfgifu, would not outlive his father.

Were we to put no flesh on the Chronicle, we might see the ensuing contest as a struggle between factions that emerged when the council of the realm convened at Oxford. There Earl Leofric of Mercia and almost all the thegns from north of the Thames and the men of the fleet in London chose Harold as regent of all England, while Godwine and all the men of Wessex opposed them. It is true that the coinage tells a similar story, with mints north of the Thames striking coins for Harold, southern mints striking for Harthacnut, and a few that were astride the fault-line, including London, striking wisely for both.[74] This, however, is half the story, for Edward and Alfred were in play from the beginning, and since power was maintained in those international circles by intelligence gathering, espionage, and a turnaround of letters, it must be assumed that powerbrokers in England were communicating with both. Hincmar of

---

[71] Ibid., pp. 81–3 and 59–61 for an anecdote, inserted by Orderic, concerning Robert's generosity.

[72] Ibid., p. 81.

[73] Keynes, 'Aethelings', pp. 196–7, Plate 4 and Appendix 6.

[74] Bolton, *Cnut*, p. 198; T. Talvio, 'Harold I and Harthacnut's Jewel Cross Type Reconsidered', in M. Blackburn, ed., *Anglo-Saxon Monetary History: Essays in Memory of Michael Dolley* (Leicester, 1986), pp. 273–90.

Rheims, describing the Carolingian court, explains that anybody who went to the king was expected to bring useful information from friends, strangers, or enemies, and that the king's business was to know every-thing.[75] Where letters survive, as ephemera of diplomacy, they reveal how much the annals occlude. No true 'letter' dictated by Edward survives, yet letters were surely sent by this resourceful man or his agents to lobby persons of influence in 1035.

On the surface, the division was political, with a Mercian faction on one side supporting a midland noble kinship group headed by Harold and his mother Ælfgifu, against a southern Anglo-Danish faction wanting to safeguard its ties to Denmark. At a deeper level, it was an expression of the rivalry between Leofric and Godwine which would become a key factor in the politics of Edward's reign. Leofric was a very religious man from an established noble House. Godwine, who had risen to overtake him in Cnut's reign, was a climber. Both in their different ways may have resented and disdained each other, but they were statesmen enough to put aside their differences in the interests of the realm. The situation that proved to be the exception to that rule arose after Cnut's death, because of the loss of leadership which would normally overrule division, and because of a genuine difference of opinion and interest as to whom to install in his place. Beneath the political and personal differences, at a deeper level still, the tension between Mercian separatism and the expan-sionism of Wessex was straining a kingdom that had been unified by the latter and divided as recently as 1016. It was the first time in many years that the factions represented by Godwine and Leofric had had the chance of an equal contest, and neither meant to lose the advantage by accepting a king who would favour the other.

Emma pre-empted the tense negotiations by establishing herself at Winchester after her husband's burial there, and by assuming command of the king's housecarls and the treasury. E, which tends to favour Godwine, states that he 'was their most loyal man'.[76] The problem for them was that Harthacnut was detained in Denmark, which was under attack by Magnus. The son of Cnut's dead opponent Olaf Haraldsson, he had seized control of Norway after the expulsion of Ælfgifu and Swein. At Winchester, with Godwine's help and in the heart of his earldom, Emma might hold out until Harthacnut returned. But Harold struck early, leading a troop of soldiers to raid the treasury and deprive her of some large part of her late husband's treasure. The compromise hammered out initially conceded that Emma would be regent in Wessex while Harold governed the north. At the same time, her party undermined him, prom-

[75] Hincmar of Rheims, *De ordine palatii*, ed. A. Boretius, MGH Capitularia regum Francorum 2 (Hanover, 1897), 518–30, at p. 529 (trans.: *On the Governance of the Palace*, in D. Herlihy, ed., *The History of Feudalism* (London, 1970), 208–27, at p. 226).
[76] ASC E, 1036 [1035–6].

ulgating rumours that he was not Cnut's son. In the dissimulation of E:
'some said of Harold that he was son of King Cnut and Ælfgifu, daughter
of Ealdorman Ælfhelm, but to many it seemed quite unbelievable'. C is
forthright: 'he said he was the son of Cnut and the other Ælfgifu, although
it was not true'.[77] John of Worcester gives a good idea of what was whis-
pered: that Ælfgifu's sons Swein and Harold were fathered by a priest and
a shoemaker, and that she had duped Cnut into believing that they were
his.[78] Such allegations may have facilitated the archbishop of Canterbury's
announcement that he would neither approve nor consecrate another
man as king while sons of Emma lived.[79]

By adopting this position, Archbishop Æthelnoth adhered to protocol.
His stance was constitutional either because Emma, as the consecrated
queen of two kings, was regarded as the sole bearer of legitimate heirs, or
because oaths had at some time been sworn in favour of one or more of
her three sons, or for both reasons. Politically he may have aligned with
Emma and Godwine. Spiritually he may have been deterred by the bad
odour surrounding Harold. His stance threw open the option that Edward
or Alfred might be crowned. Yet even if this was her secret wish – and
there is no evidence it was – Emma had little choice in her embattled situation but to declare for the son whose claim was preferred by her allies
among the leading men. As king of Denmark moreover, Harthacnut was
well positioned. While there was the prospect of his imminent return – and
we may assume that he was being bombarded with envoys and letters
seeking just that – he was the only safe bet among Emma's offspring.
About this time, if not beforehand, Harold's elder brother Swein died in
exile, and their mother Ælfgifu returned to England. Having lost one
kingdom, Norway, and suffered the loss of a son, she would fight hard for
Harold, knowing that defeat would mean oblivion for them both. If oaths
had been sworn to Emma's children, they would have to be undone. She
would outmanoeuvre Emma.

Across the Channel, one or both aethelings were arranging the
marriage of their sister Gode to Eustace, son of Count Eustace I of
Boulogne. The alliance was auspicious, for the county lay at the narrowest
point of passage from England to France, opposite the Kentish coast, and
enjoyed ties to the exiles' homeland. Normandy to the west remained
supportive. To the east, however, Baldwin V, the new count of Flanders,
had reason to be wary. When strong, the counts of Flanders treated
Boulogne as a subject principality. Eustace I, for his part, adopted a policy
of friendship towards Baldwin V but also built alliances that increased his

---

[77] Ibid., C, 1035.
[78] *JW*, ii, p. 521; cf. *GHEP*, p. 134, remarking that Cnut's sons Harold and Swein were
both illegitimate.
[79] *EER*, p. 41.

independence and weakened the influence of his powerful neighbour.[80] The first such alliance was the marriage forged between Eustace I and the aethelings when his namesake son married Gode. Whether Baldwin V regarded the marriage as a threat is anyone's guess, but it was still only a few years since Edward's adopted brother Robert had marched into Flanders, killed Baldwin's men, and crushed his rebellion against his father. Baldwin may have felt uneasiness, even suspicion towards Edward. Had Edward been on the campaign, Baldwin's feelings might have been darker.

At the same time, he was a new count who needed to tread carefully, aware that in his rebellion he had misjudged the configuration of power. In 1036 relations with England were at stake, and almost anything might happen. The reports coming in to Baldwin via spies and messengers may have been at odds. Officially Emma had declared for Harthacnut. Privately the queen – who had performed a *volte face* before – had other options and might well resort to them if the tide turned for Harold. Edward was gathering ships and would make his assault upon a country that was divided, that lacked a legitimate ruler, and where his mother Emma was acting as regent. Ships from the 1033/4 campaign were perhaps still at his disposal, and support might come through the new alliance with maritime Boulogne. Baldwin also had to factor in relations with the empire, his own superior neighbour. For Cnut had negotiated the betrothal of his and Emma's daughter Gunnhilda to the emperor Conrad's son Henry. The marriage plans for June 1036 were a reminder of Emma's influence with the imperial court.

Emma was well placed to counsel her teenage daughter as she left for a foreign land and a marriage greater than her worries. In 1002 she had taken that path herself to secure peace between England and Normandy, hoping that one day a son of hers would sit on the English throne. Widow of two kings with sons by both, she had not seen that wish fulfilled. But she could at least hope God might ordain a better outcome for her daughter while removing her enemy Harold. Gunnhilda's marriage ratified the alliance Cnut had inaugurated with the emperor Conrad, and at a crucial moment when her brother's inheritance in Denmark and England was under attack. Flanders now had to be mindful of the might of Germany, as did Harold's faction. Like her mother before her, Gunnhilda adopted a native queenly name that was acceptable to the dynasty whose sons she was expected to bear. As Emma had become Ælfgifu, Gunnhilda became Cunegunda. Lonely and disconsolate at the imperial court, she found a comforter in Bishop Azecho of Worms and was saddened when he had to return to usual business.

---

[80] H. J. Tanner, 'The Expansion of the Power and Influence of the Counts of Boulogne under Eustace II', *ANS* 14 (1992), 251–86, at p. 251.

In July or early August 1036, a cleric wrote to Azecho with news.[81] Cunegunda missed him, and envoys had arrived from England to report on the worsening situation. It is helpful for our purposes that the cleric conveys their message with the precision that was vital in diplomatic correspondence. The envoys from Emma had explained that Gunnhilda's 'unjust stepmother' (Ælfgifu of Northampton) was fraudulently lobbying to deprive her brother Harthacnut of the kingdom. She was throwing great banquets 'for all our chief men' and trying to corrupt them, in some cases by entreaty, in others with bribes (*pretio*), tempting them to swear oaths to her and her son. The envoys reported that the chief men refused to concede to her in any of these approaches and had sent messengers to Harthacnut on behalf of them all (*unanimes*), urging his speedy return.[82] The reassurance intended for her gentle daughter belied Emma's fears.

It was at roughly this juncture that another letter was dispatched to Edward and Alfred in Normandy, ostensibly from 'Emma, queen in name only', asking them what they planned to do about the fact that their hereditary kingdom was slipping further from their grasp, and that each day of their procrastination strengthened 'the usurper of your rule' (Harold). Promising that the chief men 'would prefer that one of you should rule over them than that they should be held in the power of him who now commands them', it concluded with a motherly appeal: 'I entreat, therefore, that one of you come to me speedily and privately, to receive from me wholesome counsel, and to know in what manner this matter which I desire must be brought to pass'.[83] In 1041–2, this letter was copied into the *Encomium*, a work – we should recall – that was written for the purpose of indulging and defending Emma's side of the story. Who actually read its involved Latin remains a moot point, but we need not doubt that its version of events reflects the version Emma was putting about at court. By the time the letter, dating from 1036, was copied into the *Encomium*, five years later, it had become an extremely sore memory, partly because its existence was undeniable; largely because its conse-quences were unbearable for Emma. Were we to accept the assertion of Emma's apologist that Harold had it forged in her name and sent deceitful couriers to present it to the aethelings we would surely be deceived ourselves.

Plausible as it may seem that Harold had framed Emma for conspiracy while luring her unwitting offspring into a trap, the letter shares content with the news relayed to Gunnhilda, explaining how Harold (rather than his mother, in this instance) was going around, winning over the chief men

---

[81] *Die ältere Wormser Briefsammlung*, MGH Epistolae. Die Briefe der deutschen Kaiserzeit 3 (Weimar, 1949), no. 5 (pp. 20–2).

[82] Ibid., and W. H. Stevenson, 'An Alleged Son of King Harold Harefoot', *EHR* 28 (1913), 112–17, at p. 115.

[83] *EER*, pp. 41–3.

by gifts (*muneribus*), threats, and entreaty. The narratives are too similar, and *muneribus* too much like *pretio*, for Emma to have composed one letter and Harold the other. We cannot even be sure the news was relayed to Gunnhilda in a letter, but we can be sure Harold was not so artful that he would have intercepted it and styled the narrative and language on that report. He had no reason to do so. Only if he believed that Gunnhilda and the aethelings were comparing notes might he have contemplated such craftiness. But there was no sign they were corresponding, and the flaw in any such plan was the likelihood the aethelings would seek independent confirmation the letter came from their mother. We can hardly believe that Harold was clever enough to borrow Emma's tones and so foolish as to think neither aetheling would check the letter was hers.

There were also reasons for Emma and her encomiast to lie about the letter's authorship. First, at the time the encomiast wrote this part of his work, Harthacnut was king of England. If genuine the letter exposed his mother's support for his rivals, which constituted treason. It may help to imagine a scenario in which Edward had lately made the text available, sending copies where they could sow division between Emma and Harthacnut. An added reason for Emma and her encomiast to dissemble was the unbearableness of the truth. In most actions, we hope for happiness, but sometimes the outcome is so terrible that the only way to solace lies in deceiving ourselves by denying the action that produced it. To say the consequences would not be what Emma wished is a gross understatement of the worst thing a mother can endure. If the letter was Emma's, it made her partly responsible for the death of her beloved child. The letter, moreover, savours too much of a mother's triangulating her sons' rivalries to be someone else's confection, whether Harold's or that of the encomiast using it as a fictive device. Judging by the response, both sons believed that the letter came from Emma. The credence it elicited is the best indicator of its origin.[84]

Emma was now obliged to play that most dangerous of games, reaching out to the sons she had previously sidelined in a desperate attempt to reverse the inexorable rise of Harold. Her letter was carefully worded, eschewing any impression that the chief men had given up on Harthacnut but stating that they would prefer one of the aethelings as king over the man currently lobbying for that office. This was an accurate assessment of Archbishop Æthelnoth's position and no doubt that of a faction comprising senior clergy and secular lords not yet turned by Harold's bribes. It was also a highly provocative letter, crafted to elicit a response. For we may assume when Emma wrote to the aethelings that the nobles would prefer 'one of you', she knew perfectly well Edward had decided he was the rightful king. The corollary is that she saw an opportunity to exploit rivalry between her sons to provoke them both to action. For action was

---

[84] On the letter's authenticity, see also Stafford's argument in *Emma and Edith*, p. 242, n. 136.

what she required, so she added a psychological goad. Alfred's handling in the *Encomium* implies that he was Emma's darling, while Edward's treatment of Emma after he gained the throne punished her for insufficient love.[85] Only a few years earlier, the French queen had driven out her elder son in support of his younger brother, and Emma's letter left open the possibility their mother might declare for Alfred.

Emma's ambivalence landed Godwine in difficulties, as the queen's leading supporter. Harthacnut was his candidate because he owed his lands and status to the king of Denmark's father and could be assured of retaining those benefits under his son, and partly because of the Danish connexion forged through his marriage to Gytha. His nephew Sven, Estrith's son by Ulf, was Harthacnut's ally in Denmark. The aethelings were a less familiar alternative, but given that his father, Wulfnoth, had seized one half of Æthelred's fleet and burned the other while raiding the south coast, and that he, Godwine, had been central to a regime which, for years, had denied their inheritance, he had grounds for trepidation. Harold was less than ideal but would be grateful for his support. There a bargain could be struck if necessary. As the tide began to turn, Godwine could not afford to wait for Danish sails on the horizon. He must have known that Archbishop Æthelnoth's stance gave encouragement to Edward and Alfred, and if he knew of Emma's double-dealing, his continuing association with her threatened to land him in trouble with every claimant, not least Harold, who was gaining strength. By autumn 1036 he had secretly switched allegiance, as his subsequent actions revealed.

ONTO THE ATTACK

The outline I propose for what followed is that the two invasions of 1036, one led by Edward from Normandy, the other by Alfred from Boulogne, were expedited by Emma's letter. Asking whether they were coordinated is like asking the same of the two invasions mounted in 1066, one by Harald Hardrada from Norway, the other by Duke William from Normandy. The answer in both cases is that their preparations coincided, that both leaders surely had intelligence of the other's movements, and that each had distinct and conflicting ambitions. Yet it is also true in both cases that the invasions were launched from separate principalities and relied on troops from those separate principalities. They look as though they were independent, and it is doubtful any of our invaders – if successful – would have handed a crown to another.

Jumièges says that as soon as Edward heard of Cnut's 'long-awaited' death, he sailed with forty ships of soldiers to Southampton, where he met a countless multitude of English ready to join battle with him:

[85] ASC C, 1043; E, 1043.

He started to fight against them the minute he came on land and swiftly sent a considerable part of their number to their death. As a victor, he and his men then returned to their ships. Seeing, however, that he could not possibly obtain the kingdom . . . without a larger army, he turned the fleet about and, richly laden with booty, sailed back to Normandy.[86]

Jumièges' account displays his usual tendencies of dramatization, including the linking of events for narrative effect, compressing time in the process. It is, however, implausible that Edward mustered such a force in the winter of Cnut's death and when the administration in Normandy was securing a child as duke. Jumièges confirms as much by linking Edward's expedition to Alfred's in 1036, stating, 'In the meantime, Alfred went with a considerable force to the port of Wissant and crossed from there to Dover.'[87] His earlier statement that Edward sailed as soon as he heard of Cnut's death was intended for narrational effect.

William of Poitiers, by and large rewriting Jumièges in the 1070s, found enough leeway in his source to claim that Alfred crossed 'a little while after Edward'. A stricter reading of Jumièges belies that interpretation. Either Poitiers wanted to reconcile Jumièges' statement that Edward's crossing occurred very soon after Cnut's death with knowledge that Alfred's expedition occurred in 1036, or he simply inferred the chronology from the order in which Jumièges placed them. Jumièges regarded them as simultaneous, as did John of Worcester.[88] Their testimony also fits the idea the brothers were responding to Emma's letter. If Jumièges' figure of forty ships is accurate, Edward probably took a remnant of the ship-army of 1033/4. It was not quite an invasion fleet, but the letter gave Edward reason to believe he would meet with support. His plan was to land at Southampton, probably to rendezvous with his mother at Winchester. On arriving in Godwine's earldom he hoped for a friendly reception, but the troops he brought could fight his way out of a corner. In the event, the army ready to greet him attacked as he put ashore. Edward beat them off but wasted no more time on a broken strategy.

Alfred meanwhile embarked from Wissant with soldiers from Boulogne, supplied surely by his brother-in-law Eustace. Although the encomiast, stressing Alfred's innocence, avoids suggesting it was an invasion, Jumièges envisaged a considerable band of warriors ('militibus non parui numeri assumptis'), and Poitiers says that 'he was better prepared than his brother before him for armed opposition'.[89] No writer ventures the number of ships. The encomiast claims Alfred declined troops offered by the count

[86] *GND*, II, pp. 105–7.
[87] Ibid., p. 107.
[88] *GG*, pp. 3–5; *JW*, ii, p. 523.
[89] *GND*, II, p. 107; *GG*, p. 5.

of Flanders. But this detail is unreliable, for Baldwin may later have pretended he had offered Alfred assistance, to gain Emma's favour. Interpreting Alfred's expedition as a bid for power where Edward had failed, Poitiers inferred that 'he too sought his father's sceptre'.[90] Sulcard, writing independently at Westminster abbey in 1076 × 1085, shared his opinion that Alfred was after the throne.[91] Rivalries aside, Edward and Alfred would have been unwise not to coordinate on such a venture. It is possible they did so as competitors united in the cause of restoring their bloodline. Still there are firmer grounds for thinking Alfred was colluding with agents in England, who were to meet him in Kent. While Edward aimed at Winchester, Alfred set sail to liaise with representatives of Godwine or the archbishop of Canterbury. In 1028, Cnut had taken fifty ships and expelled Olaf of Norway with the help of local forces.[92] Edward and Alfred's armies were strong enough for each of them to achieve a similar coup independently, provided their English allies materialized.

Somewhere not far from the White Cliffs Alfred's forces put ashore and advanced inland until they met the earl of Wessex. The exact details of what happened next are blurred by the plangent responses of writers overwhelmed by the enormity of events. The C text, describing the aetheling as blameless, states that he wished to see his mother in Winchester but Godwine and other powerful men would not allow him to do so 'because the murmur was very much in Harold's favour, although it was unjust'. At this point, the source annal, which surely derives from Emma and Harthacnut's regime (1040–2), broke into a poetic lament of a sort reserved for the deaths of princes, explaining that Godwine stopped him and set him in captivity, and sold some of his companions into slavery, and killed others, and put some in chains, and blinded others, or maimed them, or scalped them.

No more horrible deed was done in this country
Since the Danes came and made peace here.[93]

The D text repeats the detail but removes Godwine's name, allowing the reader to infer that Harold perpetrated the deed. The E text, friendly to Godwine, omits the source annal entirely.

Jumièges, dramatizing as usual, casts Godwine as the traitor Judas, alleging he gave Alfred the kiss of peace and had a meal with him – details he was including to enhance the allegory. Then in the middle of the night,

---

[90] *GG*, p. 5.

[91] B. W. Scholz, ed., 'Sulcard of Westminster: *Prologus de Constructione Westmonasterii*', *Traditio* 20 (1964), 59–91, at p. 90.

[92] ASC E, 1028; Bolton, *Cnut*, pp. 152–5.

[93] ASC C, 1036. Cf. ASC E, 978 [979]. A parallel is being drawn with the murder of Edward the Martyr.

he continues, Godwine had him bound with his hands behind his back and sent him with some of his following to King Harold in London. The account of what happened to his followers is like the poem's but with less detail.[94] In the encomiast's version, the allegory is slightly different. Alfred is mocked and put on trial like Christ – a saintly parallel created for Emma's comfort. In a reversal of the legend of the Theban legion, for whom decimation meant killing one in ten, the encomiast alleges that Alfred's captors spared one in ten and killed nine. This too was embellishment, emphasizing their wickedness. In his version, Godwine welcomes Alfred, guides his forces to Guildford, and gives them food and lodging. There Harold's soldiers capture them during the night.[95] Since Godwine was gaining strength at the time of writing, the artful encomiast introduced just enough doubt to lead anyone foolish enough to do so to infer that Harold's action was unexpected. Eventually Alfred was taken to Ely where they sliced out his eyes. He lingered there at the abbey before dying of injuries on 5 February, probably in 1037.[96]

Truths that speak too much of our humanity we hide in the glass of make-believe. Once upon a time there was a mother who loved her sons, gave them birthday gifts, offered them up for God's blessing, accompanied them in their childhood, pressed for their right to inherit: but these things had happened long ago. Whether Emma should have acted differently in the intervening years was a question that would trouble her relationship with Edward.[97] Yet her marriage to Cnut had preserved the peace between England and Normandy and kept alive the hope she should bear a future king. In the darkening diplomacy of the 1010s it was a greater good than the lost cause of championing the House of Cerdic. After Cnut's death, declaring for Harthacnut had been her best strategy. Emma was still mindful of Edward, but Harthacnut and Alfred were her favourite sons. Still, in 1036 she had little choice but to play all three. Godwine too had little choice but to prove himself loyal to the emerging victor by performing a nasty deed. If Godwine also reckoned upon serving the kingdom's interests, posterity would have nothing to say to vindicate him. Scalpings and mutilations left an acrid aftertaste. Perhaps at the time, however, the earl saw no better way to avoid civil war. In the raging winter as her son languished at Ely, Emma was forced into exile. She fled to Flanders, where Baldwin gave her a house in Bruges.

Edward's reaction to Alfred's death cannot be inferred from the Chronicle, since the C source annals of 1035–9 appear to belong to Emma and Harthacnut's regime of 1040–2. Their blackening of Harold, lament

---

[94] *GND*, II, p. 107.

[95] *EER*, pp. 43–7.

[96] B. Dickins, 'The Day of Byrhtnoth's Death and Other Obits from a Twelfth-century Ely Kalendar', *Leeds Studies in English and Kindred Languages* 6 (1937), 14–24, at p. 19.

[97] ASC C, D, E, 1043.

for Alfred, and sympathy for Emma are not reliable indicators of Edward's sentiments. On seizing the opportunity implied by his mother's pleading letter, he had run into a trap that had nearly cost him dearly. His feelings towards Alfred may have cast him simultaneously as his beloved brother, Emma's favourite, a rival for his throne, a traitor, and a fool who played with fire. Whether he entertained those thoughts is anybody's guess, but thoughts habitually come, invited or uninvited. The brutal part of the reality that may have come into Edward's thoughts was that Godwine had done him a favour. It is not inconceivable that Godwine had factored such a consideration into his political gamble.

Emma soon summoned her eldest, who mounted his horse and came forthwith; but the encomiast's account of their meeting is crafted to give the impression that he cultivated no design upon the throne. Edward's character in the narrative sympathizes with his mother's plight but acknowledges his inability to help, stating that the English nobles had sworn no oath to him; and this, the encomiast adds, was an indication that she should ask the help of Harthacnut instead.[98] Whatever really transpired at the meeting when mother and son saw each other's faces, possibly for the first time in twenty years, the encomiast had to excuse Emma for not doing more to help Edward. He even reverses their roles, making Emma the plaintiff and Edward the defendant. In truth, Edward was doing everything to advance his title, and unless Alfred's death dispirited him, we may suppose he went to Flanders to seek Emma's support and left disappointed. One possible reason for this is that Emma was now receiving encouraging signals from Harthacnut, a claimant Godwine might still have been willing to welcome. Baldwin of Flanders likewise may have preferred to back Harthacnut.

The emperor and his son were part of the configuration but were off campaigning through Italy. Returning from that faraway land in 1038, Gunnhilda fell prey to a rampant sickness and joined the ranks of the dead.[99] Emma's sorrow left no more mark in the record than Bishop Azecho's mourning, but the encomiast anticipated the pain she would feel when he wrote about Alfred. A Flemish cleric, it was during her exile in Bruges that he entered her service. In Normandy peace was deteriorating as castellans fought private battles and Henry of France made incursions to stabilize unruly borders. Several of Duke William's tutors and guardians were murdered. England scarcely rested easy under Harold, with the Welsh in the ascendant and the Danish problem unsolved. In Denmark, Harthacnut reached a peace with Magnus, appointed Sven Estrithsson his deputy, and sailed for Bruges. The fiction of happy families forged by the encomiast claims that he burned to avenge the harm done to his (half) brother Alfred. But the claim is one of several casting Harthacnut as

[98] *EER*, pp. 47–9.
[99] Wipo, *Gesta Chuonradi*, p. 57.

Emma's truest son and Alfred's elder brother, as if both were sons of Cnut. It was early in 1040. Civil war loomed, with Harthacnut and Emma poised across the sea. Ælfgifu and Harold would have counted upon the support of Godwine and Leofric, but the king fell sick and died on 17 March.[100]

ENDGAME

For Leofric, Harold's attraction had lain partly in the northern ties of his mother's line and partly in the prospect of extricating England from Danish affairs. Godwine had opposed Harold until the stance became dangerous, then burned his bridges with Emma by betraying her and destroying her darling. Now both earls were in the deeply uncomfortable position of having to choose between declaring for Harthacnut, who had already been offered the throne and who lay at Bruges with an invasion force upwards of sixty ships, and Edward, who may or may not have commanded a fleet at that time. Recent events had taught them the folly of backing the claimant who could not enforce his claim, but the inevitable alternative was the installation of a regime that would bide its time until it secured their downfall. Godwine, at least, was no stranger to impossible choices, and it was probably obvious to all that inviting Harthacnut to take the throne was a safer way to delay retribution than resisting his growing fleet. Envoys were sent to Bruges to make the offer, and in summer 1040, Harthacnut came with sixty-two ships and immediately extended the heregeld to pay for them all. This was a tax imposed since Æthelred's time to pay the oarsmen of sixteen hired ships at 8 marks per rowlock.[101] By extending it to pay for hiring sixty-two ships of lithesmen, Harthacnut nearly quadrupled the tax.

Then many who had sent for him, and 'supposed they did well', regretted their decision, 'and all who had hankered for him before were then disloyal to him'.[102] The heregeld was so severe that it occasioned a rise in the price of wheat – the first recorded instance of inflation – and in 1041 'raider-money' was collected to buy respite from an unidentified naval threat. E claims that the latter amounted to £21,099, and that £11,048 was paid to thirty-two ships. It was a reduction in the size of the fleet being supported, but an increase in the tax overall. In Worcester, rebellion broke out, and two of the king's housecarls, sent to collect the tax, were killed. Leofric, whose earldom this was, had never wanted Harthacnut in the first place. The king responded, sending his earls – including the unhappy Leofric – with an army to ravage Worcestershire. A Northumbrian revolt led by Earl Eadwulf of Bamburgh was also stamped upon when Harthacnut had the earl murdered under his

---

[100] ASC E, 1039 [1040].
[101] Ibid.
[102] ASC C, 1040.

safe-conduct, a crime which earned him the odious reputation of a pledge-breaker.

Emma was probably biding her time until power shifted far enough for her to punish the men who had supported Harold and tortured her son. John of Worcester – writing in the early decades of the twelfth century but using a lost version of the Chronicle – hints at a poisonous atmosphere where those interested in their downfall denounced Harold's supporters. He cites the case of Bishop Lyfing of Crediton and Worcester, who had been installed in the second of his conjointly held bishoprics by Harold in 1038. After Harold's death, Archbishop Ælfric of York denounced Lyfing to Harthacnut for his alleged part in Alfred's betrayal. The king duly confiscated his second bishopric, Worcester, which may have been interpreted as the reward for his complicity, bestowing it on Ælfric. The latter thereby succeeded in re-establishing the status quo of Æthelred's reign, when archbishops had usually occupied York and Worcester in plurality. Conveniently for Lyfing, however, Ælfric was barely settled in the see when the two housecarls were murdered in a tower of Worcester cathedral. Harthacnut then relented and reinstated Lyfing.[103] Such unpredictable behaviour unsettled friends and enemies alike.

Godwine was wondering how long all of it would last. Though he survived, he was forced to swear he had played no part in Harold's decision to blind Alfred. He might have bought Harthacnut's favour by giving him a richly equipped ship and war gear, though in that detail John of Worcester is likely to err, mistaking the recipient of the ship Godwine presented to Edward two years later.[104] Harthacnut insulted Harold's erstwhile supporters by having his corpse dug up and flung into the marshes near Westminster abbey, where the king had been buried. John identifies Godwine as one of those tasked with this fine duty. So it was that the turnaround of kings churned up festering rancour and dumped it on the heads of both camps. A king is like a stronghold. When he is cast down, the enemy storms in and ruins those who relied on his protection. Neither of Cnut's sons, in hindsight, had much to recommend them, and on top of the lack of benefit to be had from either, their rapid rotation dragged first one faction then the other into the mire.

Edward's appeal as a candidate who might decouple England from Denmark proceeded from his legitimacy. For he was the heir of the ancient ruling dynasty, usurped with violence within living memory. From the era of Alfred the Great the mystical quality of kingship was held to reside in the male bloodline of the House of Wessex, a lineage extending back in time for centuries to the semi-mythical founder Cerdic and forward in time even up to the present day. Edward had the single attribute on which all could agree, and to which those with noble ties to

---

[103] *JW*, ii, pp. 529–33.
[104] Ibid., pp. 530–3; Keynes and Love, 'Earl Godwine's Ship', pp. 202–3.

his kindred were disposed by inclination. Whatever claims he had made
to bolster it in France, concerning an oath, his own associative coronation,
even his grace of healing by the royal touch, his blood-claim was the absolute foundation of his hopes. It alone opened doors and purses. True
English kingship could not be usurped, nor could it be passed or promised
away to someone not of the blood. In 1040 Harthacnut had a strong argument in the form of sixty ships at Bruges and invitations from the witan,
but by 1041 the mood was changing.

It is safe to suppose that Edward and his foreign and English allies were
in contact with influential agents in England, pressing his case, offering
incentives, seducing the disgruntled. To disregard the possibility that he
also posed a military threat is to overlook the evidence of 1033 and 1036.
Edward had already been a leader in two documented naval expeditions
and had attacked successfully with forty ships. Even if Poitiers had reason
to magnify the threat Edward's Norman supporters presented to the
English, an attack by the claimant would have been in character.[105] In the
initial year of his reign Harthacnut paid off half his crews from the invasion fleet he had gathered, retaining thirty-two ships in 1041.[106] This was
still double the number Harold and Cnut had retained, on top of the
excessive raider-money. Why both were needed is unclear, for there is no
indication the raider-money was for paying off half the original sixty-two
crews. Tribute was for buying off threats. One possibility is that England
faced an attack from vikings aligned with Magnus or acting independently. The other is that it had to pay off a fleet that accompanied Edward
from Normandy. Either way, amid discontent and domestic rebellion,
there were strong arguments for involving Edward in the government.

Negotiations proceeded in 1041. The *Quadripartitus*, a work compiled at
Winchester *c.* 1108, provides local detail. From this, it emerges that an
assembly met Edward on the Hurst spit, at the mouth of the Solent, opposite the Isle of Wight. The author, interested in the legal dimensions,
claimed Edward was made to swear he would uphold Cnut's laws in
return for the allegiance of the chief men.[107] By Cnut's laws he meant the
corpus of laws revised over the centuries and issued most recently by Cnut
with the approval of the witan. There, on the head of a shingle spit, a
delegation offered to receive Edward as king once he had sworn the oath.
Yet the author names no negotiator but Godwine and Bishop Ælfwine of
Winchester, and the question remains whether the delegation was acting
unilaterally. If the leading men had decided Harthacnut had abrogated
the laws and forfeited their allegiance, as C, D, and E rather imply, the

---

[105] *GG*, p. 19.

[106] ASC E, 1040 [1041].

[107] *Die Gesetze der Angelsachsen*, ed. F. Liebermann, 3 vols (Halle, 1903–16), I, 529–46, at p.
533; J. R. Maddicott, 'Edward's the Confessor's Return to England in 1041', *EHR* 119
(2004), 650–66.

invitation to Edward was the first stage of a coup. C is damning, declaring that everyone who had sent for Harthacnut was regretting the decision. Its cryptic statement that they were 'disloyal to him' is significant, for the alternative was Edward.[108] Though in other respects a poor parallel, Ælfgifu and Swein's regime in Norway shows that on the last occasion a wife and son of Cnut had been left in charge of a conquered kingdom, they were expelled in a putsch by the native nobility.[109] If the disloyalty noted by the chronicler meant the refusal by Harthacnut's earls to carry out orders, the king was no longer in control.

The location of the assembly on the Hurst spit hints at the presence of Edward's fleet off the Isle of Wight, a favourite base for raiding armies, not far from where Edward had landed and fought a battle five years earlier. A Lotharingian cleric named Herman was one of those who was with Edward in 1041, so it is worth noting the remarks of Goscelin, his protégé in later years. 'Edward,' he wrote, 'sailed out of Normandy with a mighty army of household and hired troops alike; and though scarred by his brother's fate and naturally fearing similar, he had not given up on reclaiming his paternal inheritance.'[110] He then states that those who had sent for him received him with the utmost joy. Goscelin reported these things in c. 1100, long after Herman's death, while rewriting a work tackling the cult of St Edmund. They are not in the earlier work or any other text, and while the details concerning the mixture of the troops and Edward's state of mind could well be imaginative touches, it is just as likely they derive from memories passed on by Edward's companion, Herman. If Edward was meeting with a unilateral assembly critical of the regime, it is reasonable to infer that the chief men invited him to sail from Normandy to force events. Still, Goscelin appears to imply that the expedition occurred after Harthacnut's death: a mistake not at all surprising in a writer who remembered stories but neglected chronology. The near-contemporary annal copied in C/D leaves all possibilities open, stating that Edward came from beyond the sea, was sworn in as king, and dwelt at his brother's court. To preserve fictions of harmony, it could be masking some episode like this: Edward was invited over, against the wishes of his half-brother and mother, and was confirmed as the rightful heir before rebellious lords and a host of foreign soldiers who had to be paid off.[111]

Goscelin provides our only detailed account of the company Edward brought with him. Poitiers remarks that the duke lent Norman support, but his idea that the English were cowed by rumours of the duke's prowess in war is fanciful, given that the duke was about thirteen at the time. He

[108] ASC C, 1040.
[109] Bolton, *Cnut*, pp. 186–9.
[110] *MSE*, p. 193.
[111] ASC C, D, 1041.

also suggests that Edward took a small escort of Norman soldiers.[112] Goscelin, however, refers to household troops and mercenaries, indicating that Edward assembled his army out of camp followers and hired men. There is no mention of ducal support, and it may be that Edward had won enough friends to launch his bids for the throne in 1036 and 1041 quite independently. As a boy struggling to control his duchy, the duke was in no position either to help him or stop him. Edward could take advantage of his existing alliances, weak ducal authority, and his influence with members of the minority council to pull together an army. His letter to the monks of Ghent, written while he was at Harthacnut's court, is further proof of his lobbying. It reflects his earlier grant of lands in England to Mont-Saint-Michel and looks like evidence of a broader, long-term strategy to incentivize potential supporters. What is more interesting is that after becoming king he would lavish favour not on foreign allies but on Godwine and Bishop Ælfwine, the men who negotiated his return. This could imply it was English silver, sent by Harthacnut's opponents, which paid for his mercenary fleet and forced Emma and Harthacnut to involve him in the government.[113]

The encomiast, writing in 1041–2, paints a picture of harmony, in which Harthacnut is moved by brotherly love to offer Edward a share in ruling the kingdom. Having welcomed him on board, Harthacnut and Emma create a trinity of familial affection at the helm of the ship of state. The encomiast lauds their mutual trust and inviolable bonds of love, asserting that they had 'no quarrel between them'.[114] Poitiers adds that Harthacnut was a sickly man, more concerned with the life to come.[115] His aim, however, was to emphasize the brotherly affection between the two half-Norman kings, fleshing out the tale of harmony. None of the contemporary sources suggests that Harthacnut was dying, and the annals for 1041 nowhere state that Edward was summoned. The *Encomium*'s claim that Emma and Harthacnut asked him to share power is a pretence that they had the choice. The annals for Harthacnut's reign are one of the most damning indictments of a ruler. And they derive from Edward's regime. As soon as Edward took power, moreover, the encomiast had to totally redesign his ending. The conclusion we must draw is that Edward was angry that Harthacnut had been given the throne, deemed his reign a disaster, and felt like pursuing a standing quarrel with his mother and half-brother. That all strengthened Godwine's position as he had intended it would. His readiness to go over to Edward in 1041 reveals he had come to regard him as a lesser threat, possibly because Edward did not share

[112] *GG*, p. 18.
[113] The *Vita*, p. 15, and ASC E, 1041 [1042] indicate that Edward was welcomed. His rewards to Godwine and Ælfwine are described below, pp. 100, 101–2.
[114] *EER*, p. 53
[115] *GG*, p. 7.

Emma's desire to avenge Alfred's death. Aware that power was shifting, the encomiast scribbled his fiction, hoping that the pole star of familial affection would guide them through the night.

Harthacnut was at a wedding feast in Lambeth in June 1042, when, as C describes it, he 'died as he stood at his drink, and he suddenly fell to the earth with an awful convulsion; and those close by took hold of him, and he spoke no word afterwards'.[116] Even if the author of the annal, who regarded Harthacnut as a pledge-breaker and tyrant 'who never accomplished anything kingly so long as he ruled', dramatized his fate and inability to confess as code for the destruction of his soul, it was not the death of a languishing man. While nobody claimed foul play, death could not have struck at a more opportune moment. In Æthelred's time, the Homilist had written that once the people have chosen a king and he has been hallowed, 'he has power over the people, and they may not shake his yoke from their necks'.[117] This, like many preachers' analogies, was a bit of hyperbole – a parable contending that a person who chose the devil could never break his power. In truth, on coming to the realization that they had bound themselves to the devil Harthacnut, the chief men brought over Edward, and the devil vanished like smoke. As Goscelin wrote many years later, God 'the champion planter, Who knows how to root out bad apples . . . grafted on a branch from His olive' – which was Æthelred's shoot.[118] Mourners did their duty over the coffin of Emma's youngest son. The annalists prepared to defame him to posterity, 'and all the people then received Edward as king, as was his natural right'.[119]

---

[116] ASC C, 1041.
[117] Ælfric, CH: FS, I. 14, lines 111–15 (pp. 290–8, at p. 294); translation from Thorpe, The Homilies, p. 213.
[118] MSE, pp. 191–3.
[119] ASC C, 1042.

Chapter 3

KINGSHIP

A gentle breeze arises from the west – and a warming sun comes
forth;
now the earth bares her bosom – and flows out with her sweetness.
Spring has come forth, crimson, – and donned her finery;
she scatters the earth with flowers, – the trees of the wood with
leaves.[1]

CONSTRUCTING A NARRATIVE

Writing shortly before Harthacnut's sudden death, the encomiast had
explained how his work revolved around the praise due to his patron
Emma. Like a circle, which is drawn from one point in a continuous arc
until it joins itself in completion, praise for the queen, the writer insists, 'is
evident at the beginning, thrives in the middle, is present at the end, and
embraces absolutely all of what the book amounts to'.[2] Mapping the
circular outline onto the content, he suggests that Sven is the beginning,
Cnut the middle, and Harthacnut the end, and that the attentive reader
will notice how the achievements of all three redound to Emma's praises.
In the Virgilian framework, which he is also at pains to use, Emma takes
the place of Virgil's patron Octavian, for the *Encomium*, like the *Æneid*,
praises its patron by praising its patron's dynasty. In this scheme, Emma
is Octavian, Sven Anchises, Cnut Æneas, and Harthacnut his son
Ascanius/ Julus, ancestor to Julius Caesar. Grandfather, father, and son
thus complete the laudatory circle drawn around the queen and anticipate
the foundations of a glorious empire.

Unfortunately, the mysterious agency turning the wheel of history had
other ideas. After Harthacnut's death, in 1042, the encomiast rewrote the
ending of his work to account for the cycle of dynasties:

Now, o watchful reader, let your careful attention show itself and recall
what I said in my preface about the circle. I indeed recollect that I said

---

[1] From a Latin poem of the early/mid eleventh century, known in England in
Edward's reign: *The Cambridge Songs (Carmina Cantabrigiensia)*, ed. and tr. J. M. Ziolkowski
(New York and London, 1994), p. 117.
[2] *EER*, p. 7.

that in making a circle there must be a returning to one and the same point so that the circle may attain the orbit of its round form.[3]

He then explains that this is what was brought about in the English realm, accordingly. First there was Æthelred, who died when his son Edward was too young to reign. Providence then made provision for his posterity and after a space of years restored the monarchy 'to the one to whom it was due'. Clearly this was not the circle the author had envisaged in the preface, but a separate one and greater, drawn around its outside and sealing within itself the expired vision of a Norman-Danish Troy. His revised ending buried Cnut's dynasty as effectively as the original work had buried Æthelred's, acknowledging that each turn of events displayed God's glory. He now perceived the glory of God (and Emma) as a wheel within a wheel.

The encomiast was like the Roman cheerleader trying to augur the outcome of the battle of Actium.[4] He had trained one raven to croak 'Hail Caesar' and another one to croak 'Hail Antony', the difference being that the encomiast had to deploy each voice in turn. His revised ending reveals how the narrative changed on Edward's accession in 1042. Courtiers who had said one thing were now stridently asserting another. Those who wrote to please the powerful parroted their new sentiments. The original *Encomium* suppressed Æthelred's name probably because Emma did not countenance its utterance. The Edwardian recension of the *Encomium*, in contrast, not only names him but magnifies him as 'the most outstanding of all of those of his time', which could be taken to include Sven, Cnut, and Emma herself. It also declares that the whole land, evidently during the circle of years joining Æthelred's death to Edward's accession, 'had longed with a thousand times a thousand prayers for the day of his lordship, since it saw shining out in him the mark of his father's goodness'.[5] Suddenly the tide was turning on the encomiast and on Emma, who were now desperately paddling back to shore.

No doubt many in England had been praying for Edward's restoration during the reigns of Harold and Harthacnut, but an equally important development in the narrative is the myth of Æthelred's virtue which accompanied it, a myth the encomiast could hardly have authored, for events had overtaken him. He was not shaping the narrative as much as being swept along by it. A surge of enthusiasm for Edward is perceptible in C's declaration that he was chosen as king 'as was his natural right'. Borne on the same current, the *Encomium*'s revised ending makes the point three times: that Edward had been due to succeed 'by hereditary right';

[3] Keynes and Love, 'Earl Godwine's Ship', p. 196.

[4] Macrobius, *Saturnalia*, II. 4. 29, tr. R. A. Kaster, 3 vols, Loeb Classical Library 510–12 (Cambridge, MA, 2011), I, p. 359.

[5] Keynes and Love, 'Earl Godwine's Ship', p. 196.

that God had restored the monarchy 'to the one to whom it was due', and that Edward was 'the legitimate heir'.[6] There was also praise for him in the revised ending but none for Emma, who is not mentioned. Whether this was enough to placate the king and secure the author's commission is doubtful because he vanishes from view. He had shown he could change his tune, but what is written cannot be undone.

Time and tide, time and tide, they wait for no one: except that the future now waited on Edward, while a tide of nostalgia threatened to submerge the legacy of Cnut. The medieval conception of time, while determining that time was linear, undermined itself with cyclical reckonings – one of the many unresolved dialectics which made contemporary thinking so fertile. By the calculation of chroniclers, Edward and his contemporaries lived in the sixth age of the world, which corresponded to the sixth age of man: extreme senescence. As the world grew weary, so the passage of years mirrored and measured its decline, relentless as the lapping of waves upon the shore; the dripping in a cave. Yet the linear view of time seemed incongruous in a world where so much was cyclical. Annals and chronology were for the literate; and even literate people were immersed by common habituation in the seasonal cycles of growth and decay, planting and reaping, and in the annual cycle of feast days; the cycles of the moon; the all-encompassing cycle of life and death. Beyond time, in heaven, were God and the saints. Events on earth below were merely a reflection of eternal truths. David, Solomon, Edgar – those rulers were types of the holy king, who happened to have been incarnate in time and to have won renown somewhere along a timeline known to chronographers, but a David, a Solomon, an Edgar could reappear. In time, scholars hoped they would. The Trojan exiles were heroes who, unless deemed to be mythical as they were by some, had attained their promised land and founded the greatest empire in the fourth age of the world, the age of David and Solomon, when the world was in the prime of manhood. They too were an eternal type that might reappear. Scholars who kept watch for the mysteries of providence unfolding in history awaited the recurrence of such types, trying to match them to known persons. Edward heading into exile was like the exiled Æneas, but there the parallel ended. Cnut's conquering dynasty resembled the Trojans in Latium, but there the parallel ended. Disappointment often befell those who peered into the dimness of events for patterns foretelling the future. Until the future became the now, however, the belief that a pattern was recurring served to calm the anxieties of uncertainty and to offer hope of renewal in a world spiralling out of control. Not only was a positive narrative instantly built around Edward, it had to be. The alternative was to admit God's displeasure.

---

[6] ASC C, 1042; Keynes and Love, 'Earl Godwine's Ship', pp. 195–6.

No less to his advantage, in this providential rationale, was the extraordinary trajectory by which the exiled claimant had been rid of every obstacle. For twenty-five years, Edward had said his prayers in Normandy as Cnut, Harold, and Harthacnut – the last two only young men in their twenties – were swept away. Prior to that, six older brothers had predeceased him. Edward was rarer than the Israelite destined to complete the journey from Egypt to the land of milk and honey. Not everyone at that time attributed events to the hand of God, but the tendency was common and among the pious instinctive. The encomiast for example had already written that God took back to Himself, in 1016, the prince who had been defending London (i.e. Æthelred), 'in order to spare those in the fight'; and that God had determined that Edmund Ironside should die, to open the way for Cnut.[7] Though the point is not made explicit in his Edwardian recension, it could by extension of this logic be argued that Cnut, Harold, and Harthacnut were removed in time for Edward. The circle drawn around their dynasty implies as much, and such an idea is apparent at the end of the reign, in the *Vita*.

The *Vita*, we may recall, was begun shortly before Edward's death and finished in 1067 or thereabouts. It likens God to a father who restores to his children the gifts he has removed to punish their misbehaviour. Having removed Edward and brought the English to repentance under the scourge of barbarian rule, God led them to seek the flower He had been preserving from the ancient root of kings, and finally answered their prayers by returning the gift, ending their sorrows, and ushering in an age of mercy. Folcard explains that God cut down Cnut and his whole stock because He had preserved among His seed the one whom He had destined to rule the English kingdom. The phase of Danish rule is described as a barbarian yoke, evoking images of Egyptian and Babylonian captivity. Edward's accession, in contrast, is cast as the jubilee of redemption for the English, a biblical reference which implied their liberation from slavery under the Danes.[8] There should be no doubt that these ideas grew up in 1042 since the seeds of them and the requisite framework are evident in the encomiast's revised ending.

C, which was compiled or copied *c.* 1045 (and continued annually or in stints thereafter), registers a change of tone as clearly as the *Encomium*. To start with, its annals for 1035–9 were written by a supporter of Emma.[9] They signal their allegiance to her by reporting sympathetically how Harold plundered her treasures, and how 'she was driven out without

---

[7] *EER*, pp. 23, 31.

[8] *Vita*, pp. 11–15.

[9] Cf. D. N. Dumville, 'Some Aspects of Annalistic Writing at Canterbury in the Eleventh and Twelfth Centuries', *Peritia: Journal of the Medieval Academy of Ireland* 2 (1983), 23–57, at p. 25. If the source annals for 1035–44 were written by a 'royalist ecclesiastic', as Dumville proposes (p. 25), he suddenly changes tune at this point.

mercy to face the raging winter' (C 1035, 1037). They also impugn Harold's legitimacy by suggesting he was the son of an affair. The annalist, more-over, includes a poem blaming Godwine for the atrocities that led to Alfred's death and paved the way for his martyr cult (C 1036). He expresses his admiration for 'the good' Archbishop Æthelnoth – the prelate who had refused to crown anyone but a son of Emma.[10] From 1040, however, a change of tone occurs. Not only is the annal for 1040 the first to reveal it was written retrospectively – its remark that Harthacnut did nothing worthy of a king as long as he reigned must date it to Edward's reign – the damning of Harthacnut's memory in the annals for 1040–2 is at odds with the pro-Emma annals for 1035–9. Even Æthelred got a better write-up than C 1040–2's damning verdict on Emma's son by Cnut. The *Encomium/*C show that a narrative kind to Emma's regime suddenly u-turned in 1042. It is proof that the new 'official line' was that Harthacnut had been a disaster. The claim that those who had summoned him had regretted it looks like an indictment of their election of him instead of Edward. Twenty-four years of hurt and indignation were erupting, blasting the narrative into reverse.

The E text for 1042 says that all the people chose Edward as king in London, remarking 'may he hold it as long as God grants him!' It then describes a year of famine and disease:

> And all that year was a very heavy time in many and various ways: both in bad weather and crops of the earth; and during the year more cattle died than anyone remembered before, both through various diseases and through bad weather.[11]

This juxtaposition of kingmaking and famine was politically charged. Not only was it normal to interpret bad weather as a sign of divine displeasure, it was also thought that an unjust king would bring disasters on the realm, such as storms and infertile soil, though the people's sins could have the same effect.[12] Conversely, a good king brought blessings upon his people – an idea found in the *Life of Robert the Pious*.[13] If the land did not rejoice at Edward's coming in 1042, it might be taken as evidence of God's disapproval. To counter that claim, the narrative Edward was propa-gating could be deployed to blame the barrenness of the land on the sins of Harthacnut and the sins of the people who had chosen him.

---

[10] ASC C, 1039; *EER*, p. 41.

[11] ASC E, 1041.

[12] M. Clayton, 'De Duodecim Abusiuis, Lordship and Kingship in Anglo-Saxon England', in S. McWilliams, ed., *Saints and Scholars: New Perspectives on Anglo-Saxon Literature and Culture in Honour of Hugh Magennis* (Woodbridge, 2012), 141–63, at pp. 146–7, 153–6; T. Lambert, *Law and Order in Anglo-Saxon England* (Oxford, 2017), pp. 216–19; Roach, *Æthelred*, pp. 113–14.

[13] Helgaud, *Epitoma*, p. 58.

The coronation ceremony was an important opportunity to develop the 'official story'. It was customarily delayed, to allow for preparations.[14] Waiting until the famine and sickness had abated, Edward was crowned the following spring. He was even so bold as to fix the date for Easter Day, 1043. No previous king is known to have linked himself to Christ in this way, superimposing the drama of kingmaking on the mystery of the Resurrection. Easter falls upon the Sunday during the week of the full moon that follows the vernal equinox. From that point the days become longer than the nights, and at the spring full moon the world is continuously illuminated for twenty-four hours. The festival was celebrated at this special lunar moment to mark the triumph of Christ, the Light, over the darkness of death; and because the shift in the phases of the moon taught the contemplative mind to exchange earthly things for heavenly glory.[15] In the mapping of the occasion onto its symbolism, Edward signified Christ in his role as the Lord's anointed. Exile was the darkness of death overcome by the resurrection of his dynasty, and spring brought renewal to a stricken land. The themes of spring and Christ's rebirth were becoming popular in continental poetry:

> When new buds are brought forth in spring from the earth,
> and on all sides in the groves boughs burst into leaf,
> how sweet an odour wafts fragrantly amid the flowering herbs!

A second poem, about Easter Day, links the two themes:

> For everywhere the wood with foliage and the grass with flowers show
> favour to Christ triumphant after the gloomy underworld.[16]

Easter, in 1043, fell on 3 April, providing ten months for diplomatic exchanges and the readying of embassies to attend the coronation. Winchester was the stage where the drama would be acted out.[17] Up to the late ninth century the Old Minster had been the ceremonial centre and mausoleum for kings of Wessex. Early in the tenth, the New Minster had taken over that role, becoming the resting place of King Alfred (after his body was moved from the Old Minster) and of his heirs as far as King Eadwig (d. 959). Breaking the pattern, Edgar had chosen Glastonbury as his burial place, Æthelred St Paul's in London, and Edmund Ironside Glastonbury. Cnut's dynasty had returned to the Old Minster, forging a

---

[14] G. Garnett, 'Coronation and Propaganda: Some Implications of the Norman Claim to the Throne of England in 1066', *TRHS*, 5th ser. 36 (1986), 91–116, at p. 92.

[15] Bede, *De temporibus* 15 (*Bedae Opera de Temporibus*, ed. C. W. Jones (Cambridge, MA, 1943)); tr. C. B. Kendall and F. Wallis, in *Bede, On the Nature of Things* and *On Times* (Liverpool, 2010), 106–31, at p. 117).

[16] *Cambridge Songs*, ed. Ziolkowski, pp. 45, 87, and cf. 117.

[17] *Vita*, p. 15, n. 32.

link with the ancient kings of Wessex. Cnut was buried there in 1035, Harthacnut in 1042. It is not known which minster was chosen for Edward's ceremony, though Old Minster, the cathedral, seems more likely. The choice might have made a statement about whose heir he thought himself to be. Winchester's complex identity as a seat of Edward's dynasty and likewise Cnut's enabled those who were enacting the drama to play with multiple meanings.

As well as the two great minsters, there was the royal palace – probably a considerable arrangement of stone buildings – and a soaring tower which Æthelred had added to the New Minster. It stood as a reminder of the piety of Edward's father. Six storeys high, the exterior was embellished at every level with sculpture depicting the saints. The towering westworks of the Old Minster included a balcony where the king could appear to his people. Somewhere amid this complex was the treasury; and the Old Minster, palace, and treasury were in close proximity.[18] Hereabouts dignitaries could be accommodated. Feasting and ceremony could go hand in hand. Guests interested in the law might have recalled that the ordinances now known as I and II Cnut had been promulgated at Winchester a little over twenty years earlier. Regarded as a digest of all that was useful in past decrees, they were fundamental to Edward's kingship, since the witan received him upon the condition that he uphold 'the laws of Cnut'.[19]

What we refer to as the coronation ceremony was an ancient transformational ritual that changed a man chosen by the people into their king. After the ritual was Christianized, the creation of a liturgy made it into a rite of the Church, in which the transformative moment was the suffusion of God's grace which accompanied the man's anointing with holy oil (chrism). It was at that moment – not the point when the crown was put on his head – that the king-elect was made into a king. The transformation involved his exchanging the mere name of king, which was conferred at the time of his 'election', for the office of kingship with its sacral associations. For that reason, some writers preferred to date a king's reign from his coronation, though in practice the title was effective from the point of accession – a convention that had arisen out of the Frankish-Germanic tradition of choosing the king in an assembly. Pagan traditions aside, the models invoked in the rites – Abraham, Moses, Joshua, David, and Solomon – were all individuals chosen by God. There were no auspicious precedents for kings chosen by the people. Saul was the example from the Bible, but since God chose David rather than Saul, his name is absent from the liturgy. He was a reminder of the tension between elective and divine kingship which the ceremony tried to resolve.

[18] F. Barlow, M. Biddle, O. von Feilitzen, and D. J. Keene, with various contributors, *Winchester in the Early Middle Ages: An Edition and Discussion of the Winton Domesday*, ed. M. Biddle et al., Winchester Studies 1 (Oxford, 1976), pp. 291, 313–21; Stafford, *Unification and Conquest*, p. 105.

[19] *Die Gesetze*, ed. Liebermann, I, p. 533.

The service used at Edward's coronation would have been a version of the 'Second Ordo', which appeared in the tenth century.[20] It stressed at almost every point in the rituals the role of the officiating clergy as mediators of transformative grace. Like the sacrament of ordination by which a man became a priest, the mystery of consecration set the king apart as a sacred conduit through whom God might act for His people. Abraham had fathered God's people Israel. Moses had led them out of captivity. Joshua had brought them to the Promised Land and victory over their enemies. David had established the divine basis of kingship, and Solomon had adorned it with wisdom and gold. Christians saw themselves as the Israelites' successors, the gentiles who had supplanted the Jews according to the new covenant of grace. Though the liturgy sought to fortify Edward with the faithfulness of Abraham, the obedience of Moses, the courage of Joshua, David's humility, and the wisdom of Solomon, he must be first and foremost the servant of Christ, placed over the Church and all Christian people.

Since Christ was the ultimate model for any Christian monarch, Edward decided to be made into a king on the day of His resurrection. From the time of his grandfather Edgar, the image of Christ the King had been appearing in art emanating from Winchester and its alumni. Enthroned, He wears on His head a golden diadem.[21] The diplomas issued by Edward's father and grandfather had stressed the importance of humility, labouring the point that God reserves His grace for those who approach Him in a humble and penitent spirit. Edward's diplomas would continue this theme.[22] Similar ideals of kingship prevailed in France while Edward was growing up there. Helgaud's *Life of Robert the Pious* (d. 1031) stated that 'to serve God is to reign', meaning that kings who lacked humility were no kings at all. It presents King Robert as the 'blessed man' of the Psalms, who walks in the ways of the Lord.[23] Humility was performative, expected in the king's demeanour. Arrogance betrayed itself in the eyes, the window of the soul. First on the list of things God abhorred, according to the Book of Proverbs, were haughty eyes. Edward, conversely, walked around 'with the eyes of humility', graciously affable to one and all.[24]

---

[20] For the details below, Schramm, *Kaiser, Könige und Päpste*, II, pp. 233–41, and Barlow, *Edward*, pp. 61–5.

[21] B. C. Raw, *Anglo-Saxon Crucifixion Iconography and the Art of the Monastic Revival* (Cambridge, 1990), pp. 139–41.

[22] C. Insley, 'Charters, Ritual and Late Tenth-century Kingship', in J. L. Nelson et al., ed., *Gender and Historiography*, 75–89, at p. 85.

[23] Helgaud, *Epitoma*, p. 100.

[24] Prov. 6:17 ('oculos sublimes'); *Vita*, p. 18, which I amend to *humilitatis . . . uisibus*, treating *humiliatis* as a misreading of *humilitatis*, as attested in Richard of Cirencester (ibid., note ᵃ). Cf. Hincmar quoting King David (Ps. 130:1): 'Quique in eius humilitatis augmento subiunxit: *neque elati sunt oculi mei*, atque addidit: *Neque ambulaui in magnis*': Hincmar, *De regis persona*, cols 836–7, on David's humility as an example for kings.

Prior to the ceremony of consecration, Edward and his nobles would have attended Mass and heard the liturgy for Easter Day. Veiled during Lent, the altar cross would now again be visible. God and penitents were reconciled in the risen Christ. It was usual for spring flowers to be strewn on the floor, exuding a delicate fragrance. Afterwards, two bishops led the king into the church where the ceremony was to take place. There he prostrated himself before the altar – a penitent gesture – while the *Te Deum* was sung. Then he made the triple promise in the name of Christ: to maintain peace on behalf of the Church and Christian people; to forbid plundering and all forms of wickedness to men of every rank, and to uphold equity and mercy in every legal judgment. His ability to keep that oath was the test of his kingship, whatever else he might have promised in prior negotiations. Prayers followed, then the consecration and the anthem: *They anointed Solomon* (1 Chron. 29:22). Afterwards Edward was invested with the regalia, the symbols of his office as Christ's ruler in earthly affairs. These were five, the ring, sword, crown, sceptre, and rod, in that order. Each had its special meaning. The ring was 'the seal of the holy faith' on which the realm was founded and whence its power would increase. By faith the king would overcome his enemies, destroy heresies, and bind together his subjects in the Catholic religion. The sword stood for the might of God's army by which to defeat his foes. The crown looked to the glory obtained through justice. The sceptre stood for righteousness and the strength of the realm. Like the other regalia it was entrusted along with a prayer that the king might be granted blessings, including children. Last came the rod of virtue and equity by which the proud would be scattered and the meek raised on high.

Each of the regalia denoted a resource only God could dispense or adduce in response to prayer. After Edward received them, the officiating bishops invoked Christ, the key of David and sceptre of the House of Israel, calling upon Him as the door to salvation and as the helper Who leads sin's captives from their prison and from the shadow of death, that the king might be worthy to follow Him in all things. Then there was the benediction and the anthem – *May the king live forever! Vivat rex! Vivat rex! Vivat rex in aeternum!* For the true path of humble kingship led to eternal life. Finally, the king was put in command of his estate, and a separate Mass may have been said, a Mass for a consecrated monarch.[25] Easter meant the end of days of fasting and exile from grace. Everyone now could proceed to the banqueting hall:

The Lord from the dead is arisen!
He has conquered the power of the grave!

---

[25] As above, see Schramm, *Kaiser, Könige und Päpste*, II, pp. 233–41.

He has broken the gates of the prison!
He is arisen in glory to save!²⁶

Just as the innovation of scheduling his coronation for Easter Day proclaimed a bold message about Edward's vision of kingship, so too did the word put out to his people on the first coin issue in his name. For in a second innovative move without obvious precedent, he introduced the word 'PEACE' around Christ's cross on the reverse (i.e. the tails side) of his first coinage. The two statements combined in a narrative that was difficult to misinterpret. Edward was the resurrected Christ, ushering in the reign of peace. In Normandy he had put about stories of an oath sworn to him, even a coronation, justifying his use of the title 'king'. Now on the throne, he drove home the message that he was England's saviour by damning the memory of Harthacnut, trumpeting Æthelred's paternal virtues, and casting himself as Christ, who would bring God's kingdom to earth. If monarchy is the art of cultivating awe that turns sceptics into subjects, Edward had a flair for it from the start.

POWER RELATIONSHIPS

Of course, no invented narrative is as persuasive as one promulgated with conviction. Yet amid all the talk of destiny, his accession would have been an anxious time. Indeed, who but the impervious attains the pinnacle of their hopes after so many years of struggle without a fear of plummeting into the abyss? If Edward's brain was normal it would have been churning at the events, full of dreams and nightmares. His father's demons had been legion – the fear of having incurred a curse; the fear of God's displeasure; haunting fears of treachery or viking invasion. Edward had inherited some of those demons or their effluvial vestiges. He also inherited power over people whose desserts had been a topic of mental debate. Previously he had been free to dismiss them from his mind or parade them as crude caricatures. Now he had to handle them deftly; look them in the eye; decide what to exhume and what to bury. Years abroad had taught him patience and resourcefulness. Exile taught him resilience, and dealings with many princes had honed his diplomacy. Æthelred's watchfulness, Richard's dedication to peace, and Robert's magnanimity were models for his conduct too. The encomiast was resigned to flattery, but as an observer he exercised choice in praising the ruler's virtues. Edward, he observed, was notable for his faculties, displaying strength of mind and judgement, and a quick intellect. He possessed Æthelred's 'goodness and wisdom', a remark which could be taken two ways.²⁷ Such attributes were

---

²⁶ An adaptation of the lyrics of the Easter Hymn from *Cavalleria rusticana* captures the right note.

²⁷ Depending on whether he dissembled: Keynes and Love, 'Earl Godwine's Ship', p. 196.

standard in courtly praise, as were others, including piety, generosity, vigour, manliness, and greatness. The encomiast's praise was proportionate. Edward might still achieve great things.

Diplomatic exchanges were frequent early in a reign. Neighbouring princes had to know how they stood with a new ruler, and Edward would have dispatched envoys of his own. The *Vita* casts Edward as the peaceable Solomon, who received legations from all the princes of the earth. It mentions three monarchs who sought his friendship with ambassadors and gifts. Henry, king of the Germans and the future emperor of the Romans, had married Harthacnut's sister, the late Gunnhilda. He had no argument with Edward, his brother-in-law. The French king Henry responded positively too. Like Edward, but briefly in 1033, he had been an exile in Normandy sidelined by maternal politicking. He and Edward had witnessed charters there together. Possibly, he had offered him insights into Capetian kingship. Even if Folcard was mistaken in thinking the two were close kinsmen, they had much in common and were both Francophones. A third ruler, the king of the Danes, was evidently Sven Estrithsson. Folcard says he sent ambassadors and submitted as a vassal to Edward, swearing an oath of fidelity and confirming it with hostages.[28]

We can compare the *Vita*'s account of their interaction with Adam of Bremen's story, which Adam, writing in the 1070s, claimed to have heard from Sven himself. In Adam's version, Sven had been sent on an expedition against Magnus of Norway while serving as Harthacnut's deputy in Denmark. Upon his return he found Harthacnut dead and Edward elected king in his place. Edward feared his claim to the English throne and made a treaty appointing Sven his immediate successor, ahead of any children he might have. Satisfied, Sven resumed his war with Magnus.[29] The context in which the two conflicting accounts surface encourages us to see them as mirror-opposites. Adam was telling a story invented around 1066 to strengthen Sven's claim to England. Folcard tells a story that reverses the power relationship by having Sven submit to Edward instead of Edward cowering before Sven. Their stories cancel each other. The truth is that in 1042 Sven was struggling rather desperately to fend off Magnus of Norway and probably came to England as a petitioner. Emma was his aunt, Godwine his uncle, Edward a cousin. Sven lacked the strength to be bullish with his relations and may have been obeisant, as Folcard implies.

Folcard mentions other ambassadors arriving on behalf of unnamed Frankish princes, dukes and rulers, some from 'the outlying islands'.[30] To the south, the counts of Brittany, Normandy, and Boulogne were Edward's kin by blood or marriage. All had an incentive to affirm their friendship

[28] *Vita*, p. 17.
[29] *GHEP*, pp. 135–6.
[30] *Vita*, p. 18 ('angularibus insulis'). My translation.

on Edward's accession. Baldwin of Flanders was less enamoured of Edward. In 1040 he had assisted Harthacnut. Earlier he may have associated Edward with Robert and his part in suppressing his rebellion against his father Baldwin IV. The marital link between his smaller neighbour Boulogne and mighty England would not have pleased him. Still, the monks of Ghent in Flanders made friendly approaches to the king, and other petitioners doubtless did the same. The king of Dublin at that time was Ímar mac Availt. In 1038 he had driven out Echmarcach, his Hiberno-Norse predecessor, who remained at large as a rival ruler in the Hebrides.[31] In Leinster, Diarmait mac Máel na mBó was gaining in strength and would soon achieve supremacy in Ireland. By Ímar and Diarmait's campaigns, Norwegian influence in the Irish Sea was gradually being weakened. But there were many pirates around its coasts who would ally with Scandinavian adventurers, or warmongering paymasters from Ireland, Wales or the Scottish or Cumbrian seaboard. Conflict within that zone was persistent and inward looking until the late 1040s, strengthening Edward's hand.

Any of those princes may have sent ambassadors to Edward to seek support against their rivals. We know client rulers weighed their options in this way because King Alfred's Welsh biographer tells us that Welsh princes submitted to his overlordship to gain protection from other more aggressive princes. One even abandoned his alliance with the Northumbrians to do so, since it had brought him no benefit, only a good deal of misfortune.[32] Trade, in the Irish Sea, was a stimulus for good relations between Ireland and Chester and, increasingly, Bristol, via the Severn estuary. Dublin exported slaves, skins, grain, timber, and fish among its commodities and imported pottery, jewellery, and woollens. Godwine had dealings with Ireland, for his wife Gytha was involved in the slave trade, and his daughter Edith learned Irish.[33] The men of Alfred's following who were sold as slaves in 1036 may have passed through the human markets of Dublin or Waterford.

To the north, the Scottish king Macbeth (Mac bethad mac Findláech) had incentives to show respect to Edward, not only to keep the earl of Northumbria south of their disputable border, but also to strengthen his hand against the earls of the Orkneys, who wanted to increase their influence in Caithness and the Moray Firth, as did the nearby Norwegians. An alliance with Edward could be a counterbalance to Orcadian-Norwegian

---

[31] B. T. Hudson, 'Cnut and the Scottish Kings', *EHR* 107 (1992), 350–60, at pp. 355–6, and R. A. McDonald, *The Kingdom of the Isles: Scotland's Western Seaboard, c. 1100–c. 1336* (East Linton, 1997), p. 33.

[32] *Asser's Life of King Alfred, Together with the Annals of St Neots, Erroneously Ascribed to Asser*, ed. W. H. Stevenson, new impression with an article by D. Whitelock (Oxford, 1959), ch. 80 (pp. 66–7).

[33] E. Mason, *The House of Godwine: The History of a Dynasty* (London and New York, 2004), pp. 34–5; *Vita*, p. 23.

incursion and a way to curb Northumbrian expansion. When Cnut marched into Scotland after returning from Rome in 1031, Macbeth and two other kings had submitted to him, because Cnut's hegemony at that time, over England and Norway, threatened the Scots from both directions.[34] Edward, in contrast, posed no immediate threat, but it was sensible for Macbeth to approach him. Wales was in a stormy phase of internal conflict that sometimes relied on border raids to fund itself. Borders there were murky. Territory and tribute were disputed, and a strong Welsh king was a menace. Gruffudd ap Llywelyn, king of Gwynedd, was the dominant figure in North Wales. In 1039, he had defeated the English in battle at Rhyd-y-Groes on the upper Severn, forcing back his neighbour Earl Leofric of Mercia, whose brother had been killed in the fighting. By the early 1040s, Gruffudd's ambitions were focused on southern Wales, which remained their object for over a decade. Like the infighting in Ireland, this was to England's advantage.

Between Wales and Scotland was the kingdom of the Cumbrians and the kingdom of the Isles. We do not know who ruled the former in 1042, but Edward came to regard it as a client territory by 1055. Echmarcach, king of Man and the Hebrides, was the ruler of the Isles. He had submitted to Cnut with other Scottish rulers in 1031, and his weakened position since his expulsion from Dublin in 1038 was grounds for considering an alliance with Edward.[35] Not to have allied with Edward in some way could have left him exposed to Irish and Norwegian princes competing to dominate the Irish Sea. It would also have left him exposed to the ruler of the Cumbrians, whoever that was. For their rulers liked to dominate Galloway, the buffer zone between the Cumbrian kingdom and the Isles.

Unlike other rulers who might have made overtures, Scottish and Welsh princes were answerable to claims that English kings were their overlords and they their tributaries. For over a hundred years, Edward's predecessors had been styling themselves kings of the whole island of Britain (referring to the territory) or as rulers of all Albion. 'Albion' was an archaic name for Britain and the name of a virtual polity, the conception of which strengthened their territorial claims. Sometimes their overlordship was made explicit in diplomas that described them as kings of the English 'and of all the peoples settled round about' or that upgraded the title of 'king' (rex) to 'basileus' – a title with imperial connotations, employed by the Greek emperor.[36] Officially – and correctly by international protocol – the English king was never granted the title 'emperor'

---

[34] Hudson, 'Cnut', identifies Macbeth as one of the three.

[35] On Echmarcach, see A. Woolf, *From Pictland to Alba, 789–1070* (Edinburgh, 2007), pp. 244–6.

[36] Foot, *Æthelstan*, pp. 212–13; J. Crick, 'Edgar, Albion and Insular Dominion', in D. Scragg, ed., *Edgar, King of the English, 959–975* (Woodbridge, 2008), 158–70, at pp. 162–3.

(*imperator*), which belonged solely to the emperor of the Greeks and to the German emperor (i.e. the emperor of the Romans). Still, it appeared in historical works, such as the *Life of St Oswald*, written in Æthelred's reign, which describes Edward's grandfather King Edgar as 'emperor of the whole of Albion' (*totius Albionis imperator*).[37]

Whether imperial aspirations were pursued actively depended on the king in question. Their originator, King Athelstan (d. 939), had been strong enough, on occasion, to compel Welsh and Scottish rulers to subscribe his diplomas, and Edgar had assembled several kings of the neighbouring peoples of Britain for his quasi-imperial coronation of 973. But none of their successors is known to have extracted tribute from client rulers, even though clientage, for all we know, may have been the normal state of affairs.[38] Adopting the title Harthacnut had assumed, Edward's earliest extant diploma, of 1042, styles him as 'king of the whole of Britain'.[39] Rulers subject to the overlordship that was implied by that title had an interest in discovering what it meant in practice. That peace prevailed for more than a decade thereafter between Edward and Macbeth and Gruffudd ap Llywelyn suggests their opening exchanges established good relations. The only rulers who fell out with Edward early in the reign were Gruffudd ap Rhydderch – a ruler of southern Wales after 1044 – and Baldwin of Flanders.

Another title, first applied to King Athelstan in a diploma of 938, provides an insight into how such titulature was inherited and how it was adapted to develop new claims to dominion. In the dispositive clause of the diploma, Athelstan is described as 'industrious king (*basileus*) of the English and of all the peoples settled round about'.[40] Preserved in the archives of Old Minster, Winchester, the diploma became a model for another, drawn up in 1046 in the name of King Edward, which incorporated the same title, word for word.[41] By this means Edward became the titular ruler of the Welsh, Scots, Britons and potentially other peoples, whether or not they regarded him as such. An earlier diploma for Old Minster, drawn up in 1045, looked to the same model or a similar one now lost but adapted the wording, describing Edward not as king of adjacent peoples but as 'industrious king (*rex*) of the English and of all the islands set

---

[37] Crick, 'Edgar, Albion and Insular Dominion', p. 163; Byrhtferth, *Lives*, p. 136; cf. the use of *imperator* by a contemporary referring to the Irish king Brian Boru ('emperor of the Gaels'): Woolf, *Pictland to Alba*, p. 225.

[38] A poem of Athelstan's time reports that Welsh princes paid him tribute: Foot, *Æthelstan*, p. 163.

[39] S 994, S 998.

[40] S 441 (938, Old Minster, Winchester): 'basileus industrius Anglorum cunctarumque gentium in circuitu persistentium'; Foot, *Æthelstan*, p. 213 (and ibid., note 8).

[41] S 1013 (1046, Old Minster, Winchester): 'basileus industrius Anglorum cunctarumque gentium in circuitu persistentium'.

round about'.[42] It is possible his titles were modified on either occasion to acknowledge the submission of new clients. Winchester at any rate was the centre of royal operations. If a draftsman thought fit to adapt an older title, to show that his rule extended to surrounding islands, it was a way of expanding his claim to dominion over Britain. It associated the king with his ancestors' achievements too.

It was customary for the chief men to offer gifts to a new monarch, as well as swearing allegiance. Acceptance of the gifts signalled the establishment of trust between the king and the men who would enter his service. In Godwine's case we know that the gift was a warship, because Folcard describes it. Typically, a warship had a crew of sixty-something. The largest one surviving from the viking age is Skuldelev 2. Built in Ireland *c.* 1042, it was raised from Roskilde Fjord and held a number nearer eighty. Folcard claims that Godwine's dragon-prowed vessel was splendidly adorned, laden with treasure, and provided with equipment for 120 warriors. The aim may have been to arm a crew and a reserve crew, each of sixty men, to serve in rotation. For each man there was a helmet, hauberk, spear, a sword, a Gallic shield, and a Danish axe. The ship had a seat for the king to command them.[43] For there was nothing subtle about the earl's gift. Edward was a naval commander. He valued ships. He had three expeditions to his name, in 1033/4, 1036, and 1041. Such a gift would flatter his vanity, or it would appeal to his practicality. In the past he had needed men and ships, and his father's reign had been bedevilled by sea-borne raiders. The message was that Godwine would help defend the coast. He also demonstrated the quality of the war gear he could source.

Earl Leofric had got on the wrong side of Harthacnut at the outset by supporting Harold in 1035. Harthacnut had his revenge by making him ravage his own earldom, and the earl of Mercia could not have been too aggrieved at news of his sudden death. His father had served Æthelred. Leofric would serve his son. Earl Siward's position inclined him to be cooperative too. Installed by Cnut in strongly Danish York, he had married into the House of Bamburgh, traditionally the ruling dynasty of Bernicia, the northern part of Northumbria. To bolster his legitimacy as an incomer he had married a daughter of Earl Ealdred of the Bernician House. Eadwulf's half-brother and successor Eadwulf had been killed on Harthacnut's orders for partaking in a northern rebellion. Siward, who was probably involved in the murder, then annexed his earldom of northern Northumbria, as the husband of Ealdred's sister. He thereby

---

[42] S 1012 (1045, Old Minster, Winchester): 'industrius rex Anglorum omniumque insularum in circuitu persistentium'.

[43] Keynes and Love, 'Earl Godwine's Ship', pp. 188, 219–20, 186; R. P. Abels, *Lordship and Military Obligation in Anglo-Saxon England* (Berkeley and Los Angeles, CA, and London, 1988), pp. 109–10.

dominated what are now the northern counties, but it is doubtful he was much loved by the native lords for his part in the murder of the last ancestral earl, and his usurpation of the earldom. To put it simply, he needed to retain Edward's support. He regularly attended his court in the south.

Edward was fortunate to inherit these earls, all competent and experienced. Nothing in their conduct indicates that their desire to advance their interests was habitually misaligned with the interests of the realm, although a case or two could be made. All were, in modern parlance, professional officers. So too was Edward, who knew enough of diplomacy not to bear a grudge against deputies who for their own reasons had served Cnut. Nor was he one for reprisals, purges, or humiliating his opponents. No corpses of rival monarchs would be dragged from the grave and dumped in a ditch, though the verdict on Harthacnut achieved just that in a figurative sense. No cohort of nobles would be killed on the king's orders, as happened in 1017. No wavering earl wrong-footed by intrigue would be made to prove his loyalty by entrapping a foe. Difficult as it must have been, Edward decided to let go of the past. For the most part he managed to do so, but in one case there was too much hurt to let wrongs go unpunished.

Emma, indeed, should have realized that the narrative lambasting Harthacnut was also aimed at her. Yet it could be said that Edward had been learning from his mother. Not only had she spread rumours of Harold's illegitimacy; she had manipulated their shared memory concerning her first marriage in ways that gaslighted Edward. Æthelred his father had been written out of the story. Edward seems to have been cast, preposterously, as another son by Cnut, with a lesser claim to the throne than Harthacnut. She had also written to suggest that Alfred's claim was equal to his. The frontispiece to the *Encomium* depicted Emma, and her alone, sitting on the throne. Her two sons stand to one side, emerging from an archway that forms the border of the drawing.[44] The image is one of supreme queenly dominance. In the charters of Harthacnut, Edward attests as 'the king's brother', as though his regality inhered in that relationship rather than his filial one to Æthelred.[45] This was the illusion Emma was maintaining in the *Encomium* and one Edward quickly dispelled when he became king. It is possible Emma had come to see things in that way. Surrounded by flatterers, she could have been delusional. Still, we must remember that forging a narrative is a campaign of violence. The narrative forged by Emma had been slicing Edward apart.

Emma was in her fifties when her eldest child was crowned. Hers was the misfortune of having seen the cycle of life convey most of her children from the womb to the earth. Yet the continuum in Emma's case

---

[44] Karkov, *Ruler Portraits*, pp. 152–5, and Fig. 21.

[45] S 997; S 993 (which I treat as a product of the see of Ramsbury: Brihtwold, the diocesan, concludes the senior group of witnesses); in S 994 Edward is absent.

determined the fates of kingdoms. In Winchester she had a grand house.[46] There she could watch Archbishop Eadsige admonish and instruct her son before all the people. Whatever her feelings at Edward's coronation, she would play the part of a queen, mindful of Harold's precedent of raiding the royal treasury. Being resident in Winchester she was well placed to assert her role as the custodian of that treasure or at least to move some of it around, lest all of it fall into the hands of the king. In times of uncertainty, treasure secured one's position and bought allies. Edward needed riches too. Coronations were costly, as was entertaining a slew of foreign envoys arriving to pay the respects of friendly potentates. And Edward had to reward the agents who had helped him to power.

Harthacnut, faced with a deficit on coming to the throne, had alienated his subjects by quadrupling the heregeld and collecting 'raider-money'. Edward had no intention of repeating that mistake, and in a year of famine. (One wonders whether the suffering of the people was overstated to dissuade him from such measures.) The witan, however, may have pressed him about the money Harthacnut had accumulated, suspicious that some of it may have come into Emma's hands. There were political reasons for recovering whatever could be recovered, not least to appease ratepayers and finance government operations.[47] Years of mistreatment were also a goad to the king to strike out at his mother. On 15 or 16 November, Edward rode from Gloucester to Winchester with Godwine, Leofric, and Siward and deprived his mother of her treasures and lands. The official reason as given in C and E was that Emma had withheld her riches from him. D explains that earlier she had been very hard on him by doing less for him than he wanted, both before and after he became king.[48] Politically speaking, Edward also had to dispel any lingering notion that his mother was the power behind the throne.

The breaking of Emma's power involved action in East Anglia, where her reeve, Ælfric son of Wihtgar, collected revenue from a private liberty comprising eight and a half hundreds in West Suffolk. When in 1043 the bishop of East Anglia had died or retired, Emma's priest Stigand had been manoeuvred into the bishopric. His was a logical appointment, for Stigand was a senior priest of the royal chapel and may have been next in line for promotion. Edward was still reliant on advisors and approved the nomination in good faith. Besides, Stigand had roots in East Anglia, so everything seemed in order. Stigand, however, proceeded to offend.

---

[46] S 925; *Winchester*, ed. Biddle et al., p. 340; Stafford, *Emma and Edith*, pp. 111–12.

[47] Compare the situation when Henry IV took over from Richard II: C. Given-Wilson, *Henry IV* (New Haven and London, 2017), p. 176.

[48] ASC C, 1043; E, 1042 [1043]; D, 1043. Freeman invites us to consider whether Emma might have opposed Edward's election to royal office: *NC*, II, p. 64.

He may have demoted the abbot of Bury St Edmunds and taken charge of the monastery to enrich himself and secure Emma's grasp on her liberty.[49]

It was common enough for a monarch – especially a new one – to find that he had been played. Having confirmed Stigand's appointment in good faith, he found the prelate bent on mischief. Stigand nevertheless misjudged the situation, for Edward was determined to break Emma and any of her minions who stood in his way. Since the king is known to have visited St Edmund's abbey and put it in possession of the liberty in the time of Abbot Ufi (c. 1039–44), he may have ridden there from Winchester to complete his strike against Emma.[50] Arriving in Winchester on 15 or 16 November, he would have reached Bury in the week following St Edmund's feast day on 20 November – a symbolic time for repairing any harm that had been done. At Bury, if he had not already done so, he relieved Stigand of office. C reports he was put out of his bishopric soon after Edward struck against Emma, noting the king confiscated his assets – possibly including the liberty. The reason C gives for this sudden reversal is that he was Emma's closest advisor and that she did what he advised, but if that were so Edward must have discovered it after appointing him.[51] After confiscating Stigand's assets, Edward ordered another bishop to administer the bishopric. Then he put Ufi in charge of the liberty and granted the monks the royal vill of Mildenhall.[52]

Suffolk lay outside the normal royal itinerary. Visiting St Edmund gave Edward a chance to build relations in the Danelaw. He began by dismounting a mile outside Bury to complete the journey on foot as a pilgrim, prompting his companions to do the same. His devotion was probably genuine, but the gesture was also performative, expressing maximum respect for the saint. Evidently it succeeded, for it was remembered thirty years later, as was the grant of the liberty and of Mildenhall which proved the sincerity of the gesture.[53] As a monarch who had once lost his inheritance to Danish invaders, Edward had reasons to admire the king who had made a stand against them. His early visit to Edmund sent multiple messages – that he would resist foreign invaders as the martyr had done; that he too would be a humble and godly king. Bury, rather like Winchester, was meaningful to Danes and English, for whereas the English regarded Edmund as a champion against invaders, the Christianized Danes had adopted him, and Cnut had sponsored the abbey. By visiting Edmund's shrine and enriching the saint with the gift of the liberty, the foreign-reared

---

[49] T. Licence, 'Herbert Losinga's Trip to Rome and the Bishopric of Bury St Edmunds', *ANS* 34 (2012), 151–68, at p. 166.

[50] *MSE*, pp. 45–7.

[51] ASC C, 1043. ASC E, which is Stigand's, conceals his deposition.

[52] S 1069.

[53] *MSE*, pp. 45–7.

king could display support for England's interests as well as the piety he had promised at his coronation.

Stigand had hitherto enjoyed a smooth career. Loyal and dependable, he had built his reputation as a royal servant. The business of 1043 discomfited him, and he soon learned his lesson. Three years later in 1046 he was reinstated in his bishopric, and, in 1047, promoted, upon the death of Bishop Ælfwine, to Winchester. Emma was provided with a pension and ordered to live quietly in that same town.[54] She had to accept the transition from queen to dowager.[55] Even her relic collection was pillaged. On news of her disgrace, her goldsmith nabbed the head of St Ouen and sold it to Malmesbury abbey.[56] As queen, she had been a benefactress to the Church, finding Cnut a kindred donor. For Ely she had woven precious textiles.[57] To Abingdon she and her second husband had given a gold and silver shrine. At Winchester she had competed with Ælfwine to adorn the Old Minster, and she had given to Canterbury and Sherborne cathedrals and recipients overseas. Bury and St Augustine's, Canterbury, would remember the queen fondly.[58] Yet for all her generosity, she had mistreated her firstborn son. Better for her he should seize her treasure and seem to do her wrong. For it would counter the accusation that she had wronged him all those years.

REWARDING THE FAITHFUL

Though Edward must have arrived in England with a household, there is no record of who accompanied him. Folcard seems to say that Abbot Robert of Jumièges was one such companion, but this may be short-hand for saying he joined Edward early in the reign. His presence in England before 1045 cannot be confirmed. A twelfth-century writer at Ramsey abbey believed that Edward's nephew Ralph (Gode's son) came to England with him. But there is no argument for placing Ralph here before c. 1050.[59] About the time of Edward's arrival in 1041, two priests make their first appearance in charter witness lists at the end of the group of royal chaplains. Herman, who was probably from Lotharingia, and Leofric, a Cornishman or Breton who trained there, may have arrived in England with Edward as his chaplains, but it is equally possible

---

[54] On Stigand's reinstatement, see Appendix 1, p. 256; *JW*, ii, p. 535.

[55] Stafford, *Emma and Edith*, p. 115.

[56] William of Malmesbury, *Gesta Pontificum Anglorum*, ed. and tr. M. Winterbottom, with the assistance of R. M. Thomson, OMT, 2 vols (Oxford, 2007), I, pp. 627–9.

[57] *LE*, pp. 292, 294.

[58] Stafford, *Emma and Edith*, pp. 143–4; *MSE*, p. 110.

[59] *Vita*, p. 29; *Chronicon Abbatiae Rameseiensis*, ed. W. D. Macray, RS 83 (London, 1886), p. 171.

they came with Harthacnut and Emma from Bruges.[60] In the mid-eleventh century the cathedral schools of Lorraine were the premier gymnasium for urbane court clerics. The fact both men were promoted to bishoprics early in Edward's reign is not proof they were his creatures, because most of the chaplains on the list were promoted in order of seniority. No Norman is known to have arrived with Edward, but foreign friends and kin would start trickling into the realm, reaching a critical mass by 1050.

For the years 1042–8, we have little information from the *Vita*, more from the Chronicle, two diplomas of Harthacnut and sixteen of Edward which are likely to be authentic.[61] There is also a scattering of writs. On examining the circle that basked in royal favour, we find that in every grouping – namely bishops, abbots, earls, and thegns – Edward retained Harthacnut's men. The leading thegns, for example, who carry over in the witness lists are Ordgar, Osgod, Brihtric, Odda, Ælfstan, and Ælfgar. They attest in no strict order, though Osgod often heads the list. He was a staller, a title given to officers below the rank of earl who served the royal household. A source from Bury refers to him as a 'major-domo', a term for a palace official with charge of its affairs and personnel.[62] Osgod was Cnut's man. Ordgar, in 1044, received land from the king in Cornwall, as his 'faithful servant' (the Latin word 'minister' equating to the Old English 'thegn').[63] He and Ælfgar were brothers, West-country thegns, and Edward's kin.[64] Odda attests diplomas from 1013 onwards, had served Edward's father, and was likewise his kinsman. His family seat was in Gloucestershire. The last three thegns – if not Osgod – were the sort of men who might have pushed for Edward's restoration in 1041.

Osgod alone among the stallers is known to have cultivated a Danish identity, but other thegns who regularly attest diplomas had Scandinavian names. They included Karl, Urk and Thored (Thorth). A few received lands from Edward in return for military service. Urk, who was given land at Abbott's Wootton in Dorset, was a housecarl inherited from Cnut and his sons – a member of the king's troop and bodyguard. Thorth may have been a housecarl, and likewise Tofig, to whom Edward granted land probably at Burghill in Herefordshire in 1048. The diploma describes him as

---

[60] Cf. F. Barlow, 'Leofric and his Times', in idem, K. M. Dexter, A. M. Erskine, and L. J. Lloyd, *Leofric of Exeter: Essays in Commemoration of the Foundation of Exeter Cathedral Library in A.D. 1072* (Exeter, 1972), 1–16, at p. 3.

[61] S 993 (the text of which is suspect but the witness list acceptable) and S 994 of Harthacnut, and S 998, S 999, S 1001, S 1003, S 1004, S 1005, S 1006, S 1007, S 1008, S 1010, S 1012, S 1013, S 1014, S 1015, S 1017, and S 1044 of Edward.

[62] *MSE*, p. 56.

[63] S 1005.

[64] Barlow, *Edward*, p. 75.

Edward's *comes* – a military companion.[65] Ælfstan, another royal thegn, who may be the prominent witness of that name, received land reckoned at 10 hides in Wiltshire in 1043, in the heart of the royal domain.[66]

Some of these men were surely among those who had been 'disloyal' to Harthacnut. In other cases, we can be sure Edward was rewarding agents who had helped him to the throne. In 1041, Bishop Ælfwine of Winchester and Earl Godwine had led the embassy that brought him into the government, and both duly received more than any other beneficiary. Grants by the king to Bishop Ælfwine and his cathedral, the Old Minster, Winchester, express gratitude not only in their phraseology but also in the magnitude of the gifts. In 1044 Edward gave 30 hides at Witney in Oxfordshire to 'his dear bishop' Ælfwine – possibly the draftsman of the diploma – 'as a reward for faithful service'.[67] The same year he gave the Old Minster itself 15 hides in Somerset. A series of land grants in Hampshire followed in 1045: one to the Old Minster of 8 hides; two to Bishop Ælfwine of 7 and 8 hides.[68] Ælfwine received another 6 hides in Hampshire in 1046.[69] His closeness to the king indicates he was a trusted advisor, for he witnessed twelve diplomas between 1042 and his death on 29 August 1047.

During these years the king began repaying his foreign debts. One of his earliest actions, two days after becoming king, may have been to issue a writ putting the monks of Christ, St Peter and St Ouen of Rouen in possession of an estate at West Mersea in Essex. The gift was formalized with the drawing up of a diploma in 1046.[70] Mersea could boast oyster beds and saltpans, and it was easy enough for traders crossing from Normandy to sail up the Wantsum Channel into the Thames estuary and follow the coast around to Mersea. Whoever controlled Mersea, additionally, dominated the seaward approach to Colchester and Maldon. The monks were therefore well rewarded. Merchants travelled to Rouen from the North Sea, the Atlantic, the Baltic, and the Mediterranean. This sort of grant fostering trade could be treated as a debt repaid to Edward's Norman supporters. It is striking, nevertheless, how little the king gave to foreign recipients in comparison with the favours he lavished on power brokers in England who had assisted him to the throne. Poitiers would

---

[65] For Urk, see S 1004, S 1063, and Harmer, *Writs*, p. 576. For Thorth and Tofig see S 1010, S 1017, Lawson, *Cnut*, p. 152, and S. Keynes, 'Cnut's Earls', in Rumble, ed., *The Reign of Cnut*, 43–88, at p. 80. On S 1017 and Burghill, see below, p. 111, n. 118.

[66] S 999.

[67] S 1001.

[68] S 1006 (1044); S 1012, S 1008, S 1007 (1045).

[69] S 1013.

[70] S 1015. This is how I interpret the diploma's reference to the estate being in Edward's possession for two days after he became king. See C. Hart, 'The Mersea Charter of Edward the Confessor', *Essex Archaeology and History* 12 (1980), 94–102; repr. in idem, *The Danelaw* (London and Rio Grande, 1992), pp. 495–508.

credit his accession to the Normans, but Edward's actions imply he felt little debt to the Normans on that score. They reinforce the impression that William had not been very much help.

Clergy were promoted in order of precedence. A diploma of Harthacnut of 1042 and one of Edward's of 1043 include among the witnesses several royal chaplains.[71] The first charter lists Eadwold, Stigand, Ælfwine, Spirites, Herman, and Leofric.[72] The second lists Eadwold, Herman, and Leofric. In the interim, it would appear that Harthacnut had installed Spirites as the head cleric of St Guthlac's, a royal minster in Hereford, and Edward promoted Stigand to the bishopric of East Anglia.[73] Herman received the bishopric of Ramsbury in Wiltshire on the death of Edward's supporter Bishop Brihtwold in 1045, and Leofric received Crediton on the death of Bishop Lyfing: an appointment foretokened by Leofric's installation in an estate of 7 hides at Dawlish in Devon in 1044.[74] It may have been a prebend, signifying Leofric's admission to the cathedral chapter. These four royal chaplains were promoted in roughly the order they attest the two diplomas, so there was an understanding that royal chaplains had to wait their turn. This could be one reason friends from Edward's exile were not all rewarded immediately but trickled into place over the course of the 1040s. In 1045 or 1046, when the non-monastic see of London became vacant, Edward installed Abbot Robert of Jumièges, a Norman monk.[75] The Chronicle's strange silence over his appointment hints at controversy. Perhaps the powerful body of clergy at St Paul's demanded one of their own or disliked the imposition of a monk-bishop incomer. Edward was nevertheless determined to empower his friend. If a plum was needed to tempt him from Normandy, it was the diocese of London.

The chief harvester of plums was the redoubtable earl of Wessex. Early in the reign, the king heaped favours on Godwine in acknowledgement of his support and because Godwine pushed harder for favour while Leofric acquiesced. That was how the two earls had retained their respective positions. Godwine was not short of land, but one of Edward's early actions was to extend his earldom to include Kent, transferring the third penny from the archbishop to Godwine in recognition of the transferral of

---

[71] S 993, S 999.

[72] Duduc, Eadwold, and Stigand attest in that order in a diploma of 1033 (S 969), the year in which Duduc was appointed to Wells. S. Keynes, 'Giso, Bishop of Wells (1061–88)', *ANS* 19 (1997), 203–71, at p. 208 and ibid., n. 30, is right to challenge the view that Herman and Leofric arrived with Edward (but note that S 982 is corrupt).

[73] *Hemingi chartularium ecclesiae Wigornensis*, ed. T. Hearne, 2 vols (Oxford, 1723), I, p. 254 on Spirites and Harthacnut. He does not attest again, so his promotion from the chapel to the deanship may be dated *c.* 1042.

[74] S 1003.

[75] He first attests a diploma in 1046 (S 1015).

comital duties.[76] The context for the transfer was the illness of Archbishop Eadsige in 1044, which obliged him to give up his duties both as diocesan and earl. C reveals how closely Edward and Godwine were collaborating at this stage, remarking that they agreed in private to install the abbot of Abingdon as the suffragan bishop in Canterbury. Abingdon had links with Godwine; and the abbot, Siward, was surely his client. Eadsige was in on the plan because he feared another candidate might ask for the post if more people knew. Siward's promotion was therefore presented to the witan as a *fait accompli*.[77]

Godwine had children, nephews, and protégés who shared his ambition. He wanted the king to advance them, and Edward obliged. In 1043, Godwine's eldest son Swegn received an earldom in the south-west midlands, covering part of the region encompassing Somerset, Herefordshire, Gloucestershire, Oxfordshire, and Berkshire.[78] Then, in 1045, the Danish king's brother, Beorn Estrithsson, was made earl in the east midlands.[79] Godwine was his uncle, but his promotion may have had more to do with building peace with Denmark than with Godwine's demands. In 1045 Godwine's second son Harold was given the earldom of East Anglia.[80] Prior to those appointments, officials of lesser rank had overseen the south west and the East Anglian earldom, which lacked an earl for many years. The creation of earls in those regions elevated their administration and tied it more to central government. Whether the king's aim was to strengthen the state or create roles for Godwine's sons, the two objectives were compatible.

While Edward's ecclesiastical promotions followed an orderly logic, broken only by his appointment of Robert of Jumièges to St Paul's, his secular ones reveal whom he wished to reward or please. Experienced servants of the state such as Odda and Osgod, who may have been well qualified, were passed over in favour of men in their twenties who were members of the most powerful noble House. It was practicable for the king to ally with the Godwines and feed their ambitions, thereby securing the loyalty of the House most able to uphold his regime. Edward understood the power-equation from the outset, and for most of the reign it worked. Each of his promotions had something to recommend it. In Swegn's case, Leofric might have valued his assistance in the Welsh marches, even if Swegn's command chafed at his own. Admittedly Swegn

[76] A third of the revenue of each shire (the 'third penny') went to supporting the earl. On Godwine's tenure of Kent, see S. Baxter, 'MS C of the Anglo-Saxon Chronicle and the Politics of Mid-eleventh-century England', *EHR* 122 (2007), 1189–1227, at p. 1191, n. 114.

[77] ASC C, 1044.

[78] He first attests in 1043 (S 999); on his earldom, see Barlow, *Edward*, p. 91; S. Baxter, 'Edward the Confessor and the Succession Question', in Mortimer, ed., *Edward*, pp. 76–118, Map 1.

[79] His earliest attestations are in S 1008 and S 1010 (both datable to 1045).

[80] He attests as earl in S 1008 (of 1045) but as a thegn in other charters of 1045.

was unruly. He claimed that Cnut rather than Godwine was his father, a boast that annoyed his mother Gytha.[81] His earldom had once been controlled by Leofric's father, and soon after his appointment Swegn seized land in Shropshire formerly held by Leofric's dead brother.[82] Still, there were advantages in having a bullish man and self-identified Dane implanted in the region. Cnut had pursued a policy of installing military men in the marches, minor Danish earls – Hrani in Herefordshire, Eilífr in Gloucestershire, and Hákon in Worcestershire.[83] Swegn's appointment was a revival of that policy after an interval in which the Welsh had scored a victory in 1039 at Rhyd-y-Groes. His claim to be Cnut's son was bluster that would impress the war-hardened Danes settled there by Cnut.

The east midlands earldom, which bordered Swegn's, had a longer history of Danish settlement and a mixed population. It comprised London, Hertfordshire, Buckinghamshire, and Bedfordshire, possibly reaching north into Huntingdonshire and Northamptonshire, and had outlets via the Thames and perhaps the riverine system of the Wash. Earl Thuri, Beorn's predecessor, fades from view early in the reign. He attests a diploma of Harthacnut but no extant charter of Edward, though he remained active in his earldom and received the king's writ.[84] Beorn was living in Wessex with his brother Osbeorn. His appointment maintained the tradition of having a Danish earl north of London. Edward could use it to build relations with the Danish king Sven Estrithsson, Beorn's brother. Godwine could claim credit for it if he wanted to foster influence in Denmark. Beorn's was a lucrative and comfortable earldom, different to his cousin's in the west, where resources thinned towards the marches and peace was a lull in fighting. He probably commanded the lithesmen – the hired crews of the fleet.

East Anglia was largely unreconstructed, with pockets of royal influence among vast tracts dominated by an Anglo-Danish elite. The Crown held little land here, and it lay outside the king's normal itinerary. The earldom, comprising Norfolk, Suffolk, Cambridgeshire, and Essex, straddled territory that had fallen to Danish invaders in the ninth century. It embraced many inhabitants who looked to Denmark as a second homeland. Trade in furs and skins, in antler and amber, brought Scandinavian merchants across the North Sea to emporia such as Norwich and Ipswich, where they mingled with traders from the Rhineland, selling wine and buying cloth. As an administrative unit it was a perpetual experiment. In Æthelred's day there was no ealdorman after the death of Æthelwine in 992, but Ulfcytel acted like one, at least as a military commander. Their lordship never extended to Essex. Cnut had assigned the region to the warrior Jarl

---

[81] *Hemingi chartularium*, ed. Hearne, I, pp. 275–6.
[82] Baxter, 'MS C', p. 1195.
[83] Lawson, *Cnut*, pp. 152–3; Keynes, 'Cnut's Earls', pp. 58–62.
[84] S 994, S 1106, S 1228.

Thorkell, an appointment which ended in his exile. No earl took his place. By the 1030s royal officials such as Osgod and Tofi the Proud were prominent in the eastern counties. Like Swegn, Harold was in his early twenties when he came into his command.

It was not uncommon for an heir to put off marrying until established in his inheritance. Edward and his brother Alfred exemplify this trend insofar as neither is known to have taken a wife in exile. Godwine's glittering achievement in these years was the coronation of his daughter Edith, whom Edward wed on 23 January 1045.[85] Her age is unknown. Though Folcard hails her as the first of Godwine's 'offspring', he meant first in virtue rather than first-born.[86] Had she been older than her eldest brothers, Swegn and Harold, well into her twenties, she would have been old indeed for an unmarried noblewoman; but if she was born *c.* 1030, and still in her teens, she would have been a good age. Edith was a suitable match for the forty-year-old bachelor, for kings of his line had often chosen wives from among the nobility. His English might have been old-fashioned, overlain by French. Edith would have been able to help him in that regard. The *Vita* remarks that Edward contracted the marriage 'because he knew that with the advice and help of Godwine he would have a firmer hold on his hereditary rights in England'.[87] This is not far from the mark. The monarch also wanted a son to continue the line of Cerdic. He had not campaigned to recover his inheritance only to be the last of his House. Nor had Godwine given him Edith so she could practise abstinence. There was an assumption that marriage involved cohabitation, coitus, and a prior intention to procreate.[88] Their marriage negotiations probably followed the Easter coronation of 1043, pursuing the themes of new life, fertility, and the resurrection of the dynasty.

By offering Godwine the chance to be grandfather to a king, Edward finally harnessed the ambition of his mightiest subject. The marriage set the seal upon a network of alliances which in its intricacy, extent, and weaving of peaceful ties proclaimed Edward to be a man like his uncle, Duke Richard II. Maintaining the peace and perpetuating the bloodline were priorities from the outset. In 1045 Edward and Godwine were looking forward to defending the realm and securing its future. Edith would be the Lady of the English and the keeper of the royal household. She too was crowned, and her arrival in the witness lists as queen and consort coincides with Emma's departure thence and the conclusion of her queenly career.

---

[85] ASC C, 1044 [1044–5].

[86] *Vita*, p. 27. The implication of 'prior' in line 3 of the poem (p. 26) is uncertain.

[87] Ibid.

[88] P. L. Reynolds, *Marriage in the Western Church: The Christianization of Marriage during the Patristic and Early Medieval Periods* (new edn, Boston; Leiden, 2001), p. 338.

BUILDING PEACE

The Anglo-Saxon age is often presented as an age of warrior kings. To an extent it was, for in the first few centuries before the emergence of the Anglo-Saxon state, kings acquired followers by being successful military leaders, and they paid for their growing followings by frequent warfare and tribute taking. Warrior culture manifested in the bling that was worn on the battlefield and in tales of epic heroism. By the time of Edward's grandfather, Edgar (957–75), such were the trappings of a bygone age. The balance of attributes that made up a king's authority had tipped away from military prowess towards blood lineage, sacral status, moral worth, wisdom, and skills of government. Fleets and armies were expensive and better used as deterrents. Fighting was only contemplated when the odds were securely in one's favour, or in apocalyptic situations when invaders were in the land. Scrutinizing Edward's reign, we see an additional stimulus to peace in the idea that the king, like Solomon, did not engage in bloodshed.[89] It was for having kept his hands clean that God had allowed him – and not his warring father David – to build the First Temple. When the parallel began to gain traction is hard to say, but we may wonder whether Edward had an idealistic vision in mind from 1042. To serve God and earn the Solomonic blessings of peace, prosperity, and wisdom he needed to be pure. Reports of his bloody battle in 1036 find no notice in the Chronicle; and William of Jumièges discusses it, paradoxically, in relation to Edward's bloodless route to power.[90]

The ideal of kingship that had come to prevail by Edward's time held that the earthly kingdom should minister to the heavenly one. Informed by political theory drawing on the ideas of St Augustine, the ministerial conception of kingship envisioned a polity ruled by Wisdom, impregnated by the Spiritual, preparing the City of God for transmigration into eternity.[91] Some attributes still thought desirable in a ruler were left over from Antiquity. Several are evident in the eighth-century portrayal of the Merovingian monarch Dagobert I, whose bravery, severe justice, reputation among many tribes, and ability to strike fear into neighbouring kings would have impressed Suetonius. Yet his generosity to churches was a Christian attribute, and his maintenance of peace, for which he was called *pacificus*, made him another Solomon.[92] Nor would a classical biographer such as Suetonius have looked askance at Hincmar's critique of Alexander the Great, who, for all his conquests, failed to subdue his passions. It was, after all, a classical critique. But Hincmar added the Christian advice that

---

[89] *Vita*, p. 7; *GND*, II, p. 79.

[90] *GND*, II, p. 79.

[91] R. Folz, *The Concept of Empire in Western Europe from the Fifth to the Fourteenth Century*, tr. S. A. Ogilvie (Frome and London, 1969), p. 10.

[92] *Liber historiae Francorum*, ed. B. Krusch, MGH Scriptores rerum Merovingicarum 2 (Hanover, 1888), 215–328, at pp. 314–15.

kings should appoint ministers of religion whose conduct would neither offend God nor be a stumbling block to others. He should, moreover, appoint officials who hated greed and loved justice.[93] Given that Edward's ideal of kingship was moulded to a large degree in France, Hincmar and later Frankish theorists may have influenced his thinking.

The eleventh-century ideal to which Edward aspired had been refined in England by Wulfstan II of York (d. 1023) and in France by Abbo of Fleury (d. 1005), whose ideals of kingship were encapsulated in his account of the martyrdom of St Edmund, written in the 980s. Wulfstan believed that a king's chief duties were to promote Christianity, encourage and protect the Church, work to bring about peace with the aid of just laws, support those who sought justice, and restrain evildoers. The seven things appropriate to a righteous king were a very great fear of God; a constant love of righteousness; humility before the virtuous; steadfastness against evil; comforting and feeding God's poor; promoting and protecting God's Church; and judging justly without regard for persons.[94] Abbo's ideal king hardly differed, being generous towards the needy, gentle to orphans and widows, humble before God despite his exalted office, kind to his subjects, and severe in dealing with criminals.[95] Abbo also observed that his duties according to the laws of the Church included oppressing nobody unlawfully; judging without regard for persons; defending strangers, orphans, and widows; defending churches; cleansing the wicked from the earth; nourishing the poor with alms; putting just men in charge of affairs; restraining his wrath; defending the fatherland against enemies strongly and justly; retaining a humble spirit, and attending prayer at the allotted hours, as well as punishing theft, adultery, and the like.[96]

Helgaud of Fleury, continuing the tradition, found several of those duties upheld in the conduct of Robert of France, whose biography he wrote in the 1030s. His protagonist was a just king who lived without guile and prayed daily. He loved goodness, cultivated humility, and believed that ruling was about serving God, subscribing to the ministerial conception of kingship. He gave alms copiously and supported many monasteries.[97] Unlike the skalds who praised Scandinavian rulers for their victories in battle, theorists such as Wulfstan, Abbo, and Helgaud regarded warfare as a last resort and nothing to glory in. Wulfstan wrote that a king should subdue rebels 'by force if he cannot do otherwise'.[98] War was the lamentable breach of the king's God-given peace. Many men admired belligerent

---

[93] Hincmar, *De ordine*, p. 521 (*Governance*, tr. Herlihy, at pp. 213–14).

[94] *The Political Writings of Archbishop Wulfstan of York*, ed. and tr. A. Rabin (Manchester, 2015), pp. 103–5, and Clayton, 'De Duodecim Abusiuis', pp. 146–7.

[95] M. Mostert, *The Political Theology of Abbo of Fleury: A Study of the Ideas about Society and Law of the Tenth-century Monastic Reform Movement* (Hilversum, 1987), pp. 162–79.

[96] Abbo of Fleury, *Collectio canonum*, PL 139, cols 473–508, at col. 477.

[97] Helgaud, *Epitoma*, pp. 58–60, 66, 78, 100, 102, 128.

[98] *Political Writings*, tr. Rabin, p. 105.

rulers, but wisdom taught that a king should aspire to maintain God's peace without bloodshed. Kings, however, could only keep the peace by showing their readiness to resort to considerable force when necessary.[99]

Edward was regarded, later, as a king who had kept the peace and abided by the precepts espoused by theorists of Christian kingship. His biographer, who was one of them, described how he went about fulfilling his duties:

> Entrusting the affairs of God to his bishops, and the affairs of His ministry to men of the law, Edward instructed them to act in accordance with God's will. Entrusting the world's affairs to his earls, sheriffs, and palace lawyers, he ordered them to judge equitably, that righteousness should have royal support, and evil, wherever it appeared, the condemnation it deserved.[100]

The premise here is that kingship was an onerous business – that God delegated to the king vicarious responsibility both for the pastoral business of the Church and for the ministry of justice. The king in turn delegated both because he had enough work to do in governing the realm. Strong, active kingship was regarded with suspicion, as savouring of a tyrant's taste for power. Kings who stood back and let others run the realm were better kings, though the act of delegation still left them vicariously responsible for the conduct of their ministers.[101]

Abbo had explained the importance of delegation not long before Edward's birth:

> Since the king's ministry is to scrutinize the affairs of the entire kingdom with an eye to hidden injustice, how else can he cope but with the co-operation of bishops and the chief men of the realm. . . . For he alone cannot accomplish everything that is profitable for the realm.[102]

His English contemporary Ælfric made a similar point in his tract *Wyrdwriteras*, explaining that kings should delegate tasks such as leading

---

[99] L. Roach, *Kingship and Consent in Anglo-Saxon England, 871–978: Assemblies and the State in the Early Middle Ages* (Cambridge, 2013), p. 106.

[100] *Vita*, pp. 18–20. The word Barlow transcribed as 'misterii' appears, in the manuscript, to have a superscript 'i' after the 'm', signifying the omission of 'n' (and must, anyway, be 'ministerii'). Barlow proposed '? ministerii' in the critical apparatus of his first edition, but decided against this reading in his second edition, removing the suggestion. See *The Life of King Edward who rests at Westminster*, ed. and tr. F. Barlow (London, 1962), p. 12, critical apparatus, ᵃ. In my modified translation, I retain 'iuris', which Barlow discards: 'Causam dei episcopis suis, et eius ministerii iuris uiris imponens, monebat ut secundum deum agerent, *etc*'.

[101] P. Stafford, 'The Laws of Cnut and the History of the Anglo-Saxon Royal Promise', *ASE* 10 (1982), 173–90, at p. 189; M. Clayton, 'The Old English *Promissio Regis*', *ASE* 37 (2008), 91–150, at pp. 148–9 ('and rihtwise mæn him to wicnerum sette . . .').

[102] Abbo, *Canones*, col. 478A: 'Cum regis ministerium sit totius regni *etc*'.

armies, to focus on more important things.[103] Perhaps Edward's biographer had this advice of delegation in mind. Certainly, the theme of delegation is key to his conception of Edward's way of ruling, to the extent that Harold and Tostig appear as twin pillars holding up the sky in the cosmos of his rule. There is no doubt that in the coming decades the king would rely heavily on agents of the Crown. His reliance on earls and bishops would have been taken as evidence of wisdom and good governance.

Edward now ruled a polity that was headed by an elite of maybe no more than 150 great landowners and officials. Among them were complex ties of kinship, lordship, friendship and business affiliations. Some were Edward's relations. Many had ties to elites in neighbouring kingdoms and principalities. A holder of public office such as a monarch, earl, or bishop was expected to use his position to reward his kin and followers. Not to do so would have been a violation of social obligations. Clientelism was nevertheless at odds with the ideals of courtly advice literature, which urged rulers to promote godly men, 'who valued nothing more than the king and the realm'. Ideal ministers would be swayed by 'neither friends nor enemies, nor relatives, nor those who offered gifts, nor flatterers, nor those who made threats'.[104] After a year or so, an intelligent king would have formed opinions of his leading counsellors, noting their traits. He would have learned which were cautious or bold; which had interests to press; who was forthright and who subtle, and where tensions were. The beginning of a reign was a time when a king was vulnerable to manipulation. He might misjudge a few appointments.

In a strongly hierarchical polity, the ruler's favour was the key to influence and power. While the few who enjoyed it could shape his decisions, everyone else either had to buy his favour with gifts or hope for generosity. Just as God showered blessings on those He loved, the king lavished benefits on his favourites, with visible results. For those near the king sat near him, rode near him, dined near him, hunted near him, and enjoyed his private audience. Envy and jealousy arose when lords felt entitled to a greater share of the king's favour. The more he shared it out, the less it concentrated on those who already had it. The best thing a king could do, while bearing in mind the theory of good kingship, was to learn that it was a balancing act and learn such from experience. When delegating the spiritual, executive, and judicial functions of governance, he had to choose who should minister to the realm. When choosing, he had to balance ideals and expectations, lordship and kinship, loyalty and talent. Edward had to disburse offices and favours without so empowering one faction that he lost the consent of the witan, which legitimized his governance. From the theorist's perspective kingship was about ministering to the King

---

[103] 'Wyrdwriteras: An Unpublished Ælfrician Text in Manuscript Hatton 115', ed. W. Brackman, *Revue belge de philologie et d'histoire* 44 (1966), 959–70.

[104] Hincmar, *De ordine*, p. 527 (*Governance*, tr. Herlihy, p. 223).

of heaven. From a practical perspective, it was concerned with commanding loyalty by even-handedness and consensual decision making.

Though Edward got off to a good start, building foreign alliances, keeping Cnut's earls, and working with the officials he had inherited, a few notable figures found no place in the peace he planned to build. What seems at first glance to define them as a group is that they were relics of Cnut's regime who failed to adapt to the new one. Edward was content to be served by adaptable ministers who would do his bidding, but those who resisted him or his narrative, or who held out for alternative candidates, were sent elsewhere. One of them was an earl named Harald, son of Thorkell, Cnut's earl of East Anglia. In 1042, he left England for Denmark, where Magnus of Norway had him killed.[105] In 1044, for unspecified reasons, Edward banished his widow and her sons. The lady, Gunnhild, was a person of importance, the daughter of Cnut's sister and the king of the Wends. Wary of seeking help in Denmark, she took her sons to Flanders and 'stayed at Bruges for a long time'.[106]

At home the staller Osgod was increasingly a misfit. His nickname meant 'coarse', and coarseness may have stood against him. A diploma of 1044 inserts a category of 'nobles' in the witness list between the earls and the thegns. In this charter alone, thegns who normally witness with, and after, Osgod appear ahead of him in the hierarchy, in that category. They include Odda, Ælfgar, and Ordulf, at least two of whom were Edward's kinsmen. Heading the coterie of 'nobles' are Godwine's sons Harold, Tostig, and Leofwine.[107] The draftsman did not consider Osgod a noble and placed him among the thegns. The variation in protocol shows that a distinction was being drawn, at least in some contexts, between noble and non-noble – a distinction privileging the old aristocracy, with the restored House of Cerdic at its head. If Osgod wanted an earldom, it did not augur well – and, indeed, one of those 'nobles', Harold, his junior, leapfrogged him into the earldom of East Anglia, where Osgod resided.

At some point between 1044 and 1046, Osgod joined the king on a second visit to Bury. Dressing in his finest animal skins, with armlets on both arms, he slung a gilt-inlaid axe over his shoulder. The gear was unapologetically Danish, and gold armlets denoted noble status.[108] Perhaps Osgod was making a point. Edward was visiting Bury to enter confraternity with the monks. As Edward and the brethren busied themselves in the chapter house, the stallers were having a meal. Osgod kept at the drink. Suddenly he arose and staggered towards the church, his colleagues calling after him. He was not supposed to take an axe inside, but he

---

[105] For Harald, see *EER*, pp. 84–5; Keynes, 'Cnut's Earls', p. 66.

[106] ASC D, 1045 [1044]; *JW*, ii, p. 541.

[107] S 1003. Cf. S 1019, another charter from the combined south-western see, with a category of *nobiles*.

[108] *MSE*, p. 57, and p. 37 for the idea that gold armlets marked out the Danish nobility.

seemed to be bent on confronting the saint who meant so much to
Edward. Entering the church, he tried to remove his axe but suffered a
stroke. Edward was first on the scene and ordered the monks to tend him,
and he recovered, but for paralysis in his hands. Before midwinter 1046,
he was outlawed.[109] Given his record of service and the fact he was the
closest man East Anglia had to an earl, his offence may have been to
oppose Harold's advance to the earldom that year.

ALLIANCES AND DEFENCE

Never one to miss an opportunity to send a strong message, in 1044 the
king went out to Sandwich with a fleet of thirty-five ships. The action
demonstrated his resolve to guard in person the coasts often attacked in
his childhood. It also suggests raids were anticipated around the south-
east. The following summer in 1045, Edward was back in Sandwich with
a fleet so large 'that no one had ever seen a greater raiding ship-army in
this land'.[110] Perhaps the statement itself was a piece of Edwardian propaganda, but it does reinforce the impression that Edward made it a priority
to put in place a naval deterrent from the start. Nor can it have escaped
him from experiencing the process in Normandy that raising fleets was
hugely expensive; maintaining them maybe more so. The felling of trees,
opening of shipyards, employment of shipwrights, and provisioning of
crews created burdens which rulers transferred to their subjects, usually by
the imposition of taxes or military obligations. Seldom do the latter show
up in the scanty records, but an intention of financing grand operations
may be discernible in the large-scale recruitment of moneyers, in the mid-
1040s, to strike coin in London – a royal command centre and rear opera-
tional base of the fleet, which had its forward base at Sandwich.[111]

The policy of establishing a naval deterrent, though burdensome to
Edward's subjects, was well judged, since ships were power itself in that
increasingly maritime political arena. At that time, the North Sea and its
approach to the Channel was the principal zone of threat. Sven Estrithsson
and Magnus of Norway were warring for control of Denmark, and
Magnus might raid England to pay his troops.[112] Baldwin of Flanders was
another menace. A friend more to Emma and Harthacnut in the past, he
opened his harbours to Edward's enemies by helping first Gunnhild then
Osgod after Edward drove them out. Yet it is doubtful whether Baldwin's

---

[109] ASC C, 1046.

[110] Ibid., 1045.

[111] H. Pagan, 'The *PACX* Type of Edward the Confessor', *British Numismatic Journal* 81
(2011), 9–106, at p. 38. The number of known moneyers at the London mint increased from
twenty-eight in the time of Edward's first issue, to forty-four, in the time of his second, *RSC*
(Radiate Small Cross), conventionally dated to the mid-1040s.

[112] Cf. ASC D, 1046 [1045].

motive for harbouring exiles had more to do with weakening Edward than with enlisting allies to protect his prosperous ports, since Flanders was not a land renowned for building warships, so its counts had reason to find allies who possessed them.[113] Flanders, moreover, could not be too overtly hostile to England, an important trading partner.[114]

Meanwhile, conflict in Wales forced Edward to clarify his Welsh policies. In 1044, the northern king Gruffudd ap Llewelyn had killed the southern king Hywel ap Edwin in battle. Hywel's other enemies, Gruffudd and Rhys, the sons of Rhydderch, assumed his command, but they had fallen out with Gruffudd ap Llewelyn. At different points in the past the English had clashed with both Houses. In 1035 they had killed Caradog, the brother of Gruffudd and Rhys. In 1039 they had fought against Gruffudd ap Llewelyn.[115] Edward now had to decide whom to back in the conflict. In 1046 he sent Earl Swegn to join ap Llewelyn in a raid upon southern Wales. The action was a success. Hostages were taken, and a strategy was initiated of containing the southern rulers in the pincers that were Gruffudd ap Llewelyn and Swegn.

All was going to plan until Swegn decided to reward himself by abducting the abbess of Leominster. Even if she took to his bed willingly – and the chroniclers suggest otherwise – it was a scandal, and a sin, and an embarrassment to all. Chief among the abbey's patrons were Earl Leofric and his wife Godgifu, who were already liable to taking exception to Swegn for having occupied the land of Leofric's dead brother and allying with the Welsh king who had killed him. Pressure of some sort was brought to bear on the renegade, and in 1047 he sailed for Bruges and spent the winter there. He might have found a drinking companion in Osgod, who had also gone over to Baldwin.[116] The abbess was freed, and Edward shared the bulk of Swegn's perquisites between Beorn and Harold.[117] By making Beorn the beneficiary of this re-shuffle, he nullified the potency of any appeal Swegn might make to the king of Denmark, Beorn's brother. The marches were still without two earls, and in 1048 to shore up defences, Edward planted his housecarl Tofig in the fort at Burghill, north of Hereford, a vital outpost overlooking Offa's Dyke.[118] The earl of Mercia may have regained estates formerly held by his kinsman, now forfeited by

---

[113] R. W. Unger, *The Ship in the Medieval Economy 600–1600* (London, 1980), pp. 77–8.

[114] M. Gardiner, 'Shipping and Trade between England and the Continent during the Eleventh Century', *ANS* 21 (2000), 71–93, at pp. 92–3.

[115] ASC C, 1039; and generally K. Maund, *Ireland, Wales, and England in the Eleventh Century* (Woodbridge, 1991), pp. 22–5, 64–5, 115, 122.

[116] Osgod was certainly in Flanders in 1049 (ASC C, 1049).

[117] ASC C, 1049.

[118] S 1017. The case for it being a Herefordshire diploma is explained in Appendix 2, and this makes *Berghe* the earliest form of the place-name Burghill. I translate *comes* as housecarl. He was, perhaps, Tofi the Proud: see A. Williams, *The World before Domesday: The English Aristocracy, 900–1066* (London, 2008), p. 28; Fleming, *Kings and Lords*, pp. 99–100.

Swegn. And he – Earl Leofric, Tofig, and Bishop Ealdred of Worcester were left to watch the Welsh.

Meanwhile across the North Sea Magnus of Norway was gaining strength. Edward had to decide whether to intervene there too. In 1047 Sven Estrithsson sent for help, requesting fifty ships to assist him against the Norwegian aggressor, but the witan opposed fighting someone else's battles, not least because of the magnitude of Magnus's fleet. Shamed by the actions of his son, Godwine found himself on the wrong side of the argument, advocating intervention on behalf of his Danish nephew. John of Worcester, who alone comments on how the witan divided, identifies Earl Leofric as Godwine's opponent in the debate. It is also clear Leofric commanded the majority and that Edward sided with him.[119] In this, the latest political duel between the earls, the choice was between policies of neutrality and intervention. As in the debate over who should succeed Cnut, Godwine struggled against a tide of isolationism to involve England in Danish affairs. Leofric moved with the tide, and Edward let the earl of Mercia win the argument for him. The ships were duly withheld.

Magnus then fought against Sven, expelled him with immense slaughter, and obtained Denmark for himself. The Danes paid him tribute and received him as king, but he died that October. In 1048, Sven returned to Denmark and again sent to England for fifty ships, in this instance to subdue the kingdom. There was a swell of opposition, and Edward declined. An additional factor in the debate this time around was the accession of Harald Hardrada as the sole king of Norway, who sent to England, seeking terms of peace.[120] The threat of English naval assistance to Sven was a stimulus to his peace negotiations. Delivering ships to Sven under the new circumstances would jeopardize a worthwhile deal with Norway. Once more Sven was sent away, disabused of any idea that his uncle Godwine could pull strings on his behalf. As in 1045, Edward kept peace with a deterrent. Amassing ships while Sven and the Norwegian kings weakened each other, he was able to broker durable treaties with both.

Begging for English help was new to the Danes, as was its refusal. In the past they had taken what they wanted, and a couple of Danish chieftains resolved to do so again. In 1048 Lothen and Yrling sailed west to Flanders. Crossing to Sandwich with twenty-five ships, they raided the port, enslaving people and taking gold and silver. Intelligence might have reached them that Edward was elsewhere. When they raided the Isle of Wight they ran into fighting, for the Chronicle mentions casualties. Then the king and his earls went after them in their ships. The vikings turned back and attempted to raid Thanet, but the local people had been warned and 'kept them both from landing and from water'. E's remarks hint at the

---

[119] ASC D, 1048 [1047]; *JW*, ii, p. 545.
[120] ASC D, 1049 [1048].

blocking of harbours or naval action against them. Put to flight from there, the Danes raided up the Essex coast for slaves and booty before sailing east to Flanders – 'to Baldwin's land' – where they sold their loot.[121] Though Baldwin was turning into a problem, the raiders had not had an easy strike.

BUILDING PEACE WITH GOD

In those watchful years when the king guarded the coast, the earls were frequently with him. It is in this context we glimpse the peace they were busily building with God. Leofric was prayerful, undertaking long vigils. Sometimes he witnessed spiritual phenomena, which he recounted to his confessor, who wrote them down. His report preserves the untidiness of genuine narration. There is no theological gloss; no attempt at coherence; no imperative to explain. Mysteries are respected for their integrity. We find that Leofric was summoned to St Clement's church in Sandwich where the king was attending Mass. Normally Leofric would attend two masses or more each day, and all his services together in the morning, before he went out. Entering the sanctuary, he stood at the north side. Edward stood at the south. At the altar cross the priest was celebrating Mass. The church was filled with people. A cross stood on the ground in the north-east corner of the sanctuary, largely hidden by a tapestry hanging on the eastern wall. As the priest celebrated Mass, Leofric saw a hand raised in blessing over the hidden cross. Peering at it, he saw the whole cross as if nothing was in front of it, and the blessing hand was moving and turning upwards. Then he became afraid and doubted himself, but on looking again he saw the hand clearly. 'Its fair fingers were slender and long, and the nails distinct, and the thick flesh beneath the thumb was all visible, as was the part from the little finger towards the arm and some of the sleeve.'[122] He did not dare look any longer and hung his head. Leofric told his vision to his confessor but otherwise never spoke of it. The hand of God was with the king as he watched the coast.

Edward was credited with visions, but his piety was reflected in his almsgiving, which favoured monks and the poor. From early on he showed concern for human wellbeing. By granting estates at Chartham and Mildenhall, for example, to Christ Church and Bury, for food rents for the monks, Edward was putting their needs above showier forms of giving.[123] On his second visit to Bury, he became a lay member of the community 'for the benefit of past and future generations'. An account

---

[121] ASC E, 1046 [1048].

[122] P. A. Stokes, 'The Vision of Leofric: Manuscript, Text and Context', *Review of English Studies* 63 (2012), 529–50, at p. 550.

[123] S 1047; *MSE*, p. 45, and cf. S 1101, on the granting of sake and soke to support a religious community.

written at the abbey presents him as a keen and conscientious patron.[124] A writ for the abbey about the time of his visit (1044 × 1047), in which he calls St Edmund 'my kinsman', suggests that his putative ancestors were in his thoughts and that he identified with the saintly king who died for his people.[125] Herman, a monk writing at Bury c. 1070, recalls the connexion Edward felt towards St Edmund, 'on account of their kinship', and the oath he swore to protect the saint's community.[126] The king's special regard for this saint is reflected in his granting of a mint to the abbot of St Edmund's, a privilege enjoyed by no other abbot in the realm.[127]

Ely remembered Edward as the most generous of all its royal benefactors, explaining his generosity as a fructification of his gratitude for the schooling he received there. Though the diploma in Ely's archive is a later forgery in Edward's name, confirming the abbey in all its privileges and possessions, we need not doubt its claim that he was the donor of Lakenheath in Suffolk. Abbot Wulfric, whom the king installed in 1044/5, was Edward's kinsman and a likely recipient of his munificence.[128] Among elements that may be original in the diploma, Edward is reported as saying that he donated Lakenheath 'so that, in a way, I may join their community', and to gain the intercession of saints who rested there.[129] This can be taken to mean Edward entered confraternity (consortio) with the brethren, probably at the behest of his kinsman Abbot Wulfric on the occasion of his gift of Lakenheath. If he did it soon after Wulfric's accession, it was about the time (1044–6) he entered confraternity with the monks of Bury, soon after the accession of Abbot Leofstan. By then, he may already have entered the confraternity of Mont-Saint-Michel, having promised English lands to the abbey in the 1030s.[130]

Evesham's monastic archive contains few documents that survive in authentic form, but its list of benefactors and a doctored diploma in Edward's name agree he was the donor of Upper Swell in Gloucestershire. Whoever was abbot at the time – a point on which versions of the diploma disagree – apparently made a gift to the king of 6 marks of gold. A layman had forfeited the estate, and the gift was to ensure it passed into the

[124] *MSE*, pp. 57–9.

[125] S 1074.

[126] *MSE*, p. 61.

[127] R. J. Eaglen, *The Abbey and Mint of Bury St Edmunds to 1279* (London, 2006), pp. 25–30. The earliest coins recorded from the mint are type 4, Small Flan, provisionally dated c. 1048–50.

[128] S 1051; S 1100; *LE*, pp. 160–1, 164.

[129] *LE*, p. 161: 'quo illorum aliquo modo iungar consortio'.

[130] He appears in the abbey's martyrology-necrology, which was reserved for those who had entered into some form of confraternity with the brethren: K. S. B. Keats-Rohan, 'Testimonies of the Living Dead: The Martyrology-Necrology and the Necrology in the Chapter Book of Mont-Saint-Michel (Avranches, Bibliothèque municipale, MS 214)', in D. Rollason, A. J. Piper and M. Harvey, ed., *The Durham Liber Vitae and its Context* (Woodbridge, 2004), 165–90, at p. 178.

possession of the abbey. The stipulation that the revenue from the estate should provide a food rent for the monks is likely to be authentic because it is paralleled in the terms of Edward's gifts to Christ Church and Bury. So is the king's comment that the gift was made 'for the good of my soul and [the souls] of my successors' – a remark which echoes the observation that Edward forged links with Bury 'for the benefit of past and future generations'.[131] That was about the time of his marriage to Edith. Requests for prayers for his successors imply he was hoping for an heir.

Ramsey abbey maintained that Edward made friends with two of its monks who lived as hermits on a nearby island. Withman, a German, was a retired abbot. Oswald, his companion, was a nephew of the saintly Archbishop Oswald of York (d. 992). Being ascetics, both monks were the sort Edward admired, and both were literary men whose hagiographical writing and poetry might have commended them to Edith – a refined patron of the arts who was skilled in prose and poetry. Still, the twelfth-century story of how Edward granted estates in Norfolk to Ramsey in response to their petitions is nowhere corroborated in the abbey's muniments. The only estate certainly granted by Edward to Ramsey was Broughton in Huntingdonshire, and that was probably a gift to Abbot Ælfwine for serving as Edward's ambassador in 1049.[132]

Other monasteries received nothing from the king, including several of the greatest in the land. Glastonbury was an ancient and immensely wealthy abbey where Edward's grandfather Edgar and half-brother Edmund Ironside lay buried. It could list Æthelred and Cnut among its benefactors, but not Edward – a hint he disapproved of his dead half-brother. New Minster, a royal abbey in Winchester, received gifts from Æthelred and Cnut, but nothing from Edward until near the end of the reign, when his kinsman became abbot. As with Ely, this appears to have prompted him to enter confraternity.[133] Peterborough, another wealthy monastery, had to content itself with purchasing confirmations of its estates. No gifts associated with Edward were commemorated at the abbeys of Malmesbury, St Albans, Bath, Eynsham, St Benet's at Holme, Burton, Crowland, Thorney, Athelney, and Muchelney. Emma shared and may have inspired his enthusiasm for Old Minster, Winchester, Bury, and Ely.[134] In all these cases the king showed no concern for his material legacy. He was not yet – like his mother and father – a builder of towers

---

[131] S 1026; Thomas of Marlborough, *History of the Abbey of Evesham*, ed. and tr. J. Sayers and L. Watkiss, OMT (Oxford, 2003), p. 135; cf. above, n. 124.

[132] *Chronicon*, ed. Macray, pp. 159–60; S 1107.

[133] *LE*, p. 161; T. Licence, 'Edward the Confessor and the Succession Question: A Fresh Look at the Sources', *ANS* 39 (2017), 113–27, at pp. 121–3. Even so, no gifts are recorded in connexion with the ceremony.

[134] Stafford, *Emma and Edith*, pp. 143–4; L. Jones, 'Emma's Greek *Scrine*', in S. Baxter, C. Karkov, J. L. Nelson, and D. Pelteret, eds, *Early Medieval Studies in Memory of Patrick Wormald* (Farnham, 2009), pp. 499–507.

and sponsor of opulent works, but a provider for the brethren, a seeker of prayers, and an associate in confraternity. Intercession seems to have mattered more to him, in these years, than material legacy.

Almsgiving benefited not only the recipients, for it washed clean a giver's soul. Folcard nevertheless exaggerates when he says that Edward lived in the squalor of the world like an angel.[135] Had he sought no worldly entanglements and never stained his record it would be a miracle indeed. The point was that Edward was a spiritual man. He was in the world, not of it – a citizen of heaven abiding in the slums. Angels were beings created to glorify and honour God's majesty.[136] Whenever Edward did likewise he became as one of them. His generosity involved hospitality and maintenance of the poor. For many poor and infirm, he made daily provision at his court and at many places in the kingdom. They included people who claimed to have been cured of illness by his royal touch. Abiding at court, some were living proof of the power he channelled: the human equivalents of crutches and walking sticks left behind at a shrine.[137] Whether they knew it, they were props to a narrative he was constructing around the holiness of his bloodline. Edward also gained a reputation for entertaining foreign monks, whose discipline he knew to be stricter. Savouring their company and showering them with gifts, he held them up as role models to the monks of England.[138]

Edward's strategies for building peace with God speak of influences that shaped him. The monasteries he honoured – Bury, Ely, Christ Church, Old Minster – were, ironically, Emma's favourites too. His penchant for foreign ascetics recalls the predilection of Dukes Richard II and Robert. Robert had promoted John of Ravenna to the abbacy of Fécamp in 1028, and his fellow Italian Suppo to the abbacy of Mont-Saint-Michel in 1033.[139] By that date Edward was hanging around in both locations in their company, and he may later have acquired a taste for Lotharingians. Though the channels his devotion took had been carved out early on, the attention to practical necessities appears to have been his own, and it is worth noting that his desire to make material provision for God's servants paralleled his practical concern to create systems of coastal and marcher defence. For all the theory and numinous spin of kingship, we see here his care and duty.

The style of Edward's court in those early years reflected the grandeur of the heavenly imperium. A diploma of 1043 exalts the king with the title 'monarch of the English by the imperial command of the Ruler enthroned

---

[135] *Vita*, p. 63.

[136] *Ælfric, CH: FS*, 36. 2, 486–96, at pp. 489–90.

[137] *Vita*, pp. 65, 93–5.

[138] Ibid., p. 63.

[139] V. Gazeau, *Normannia Monastica (Xe–XIIe siècle): Princes normands et abbés bénédictins; Prosopographie des abbés bénédictins*, 2 vols (Caen, 2007), II, pp. 105–10, 203.

on high'.[140] In the coronation year, this indicated that God had intervened to restore the old dynasty. The draftsman used the Greek loan word *basileus* to denote the monarchic office, a noun with imperial connotations. Additional Greek loan words familiar from Anglo-Saxon and Capetian diplomas created an aura of gravity and majesty. Greek, the language of the Gospels, was used to describe the sign of the cross with which Edward marked his diplomas. They were *agie Crucis taumate* ('marked with the sign of the Holy Cross').[141] His use of the formula in his earliest diploma, of 1042, issued before the coronation, recalls the sign of the cross he made in Normandy to cure people of scrofula. The proems of his diplomas are lofty and grave, addressing themes such as the Fall of Man and the spiritual rewards of giving.[142] Never does Edward seem vulnerable or undignified. Never is there a narrative glitch amid the grandeur.

Edith, like her husband, tried to be 'dignified and reserved'. More open with her views, she actively practised discretion. Her generosity matched her husband's, and she encouraged him in his. Literary and artistic, she excelled in painting, needlework, prose, and poetry, and she spoke fluent French as well as Danish – her mother was Danish – and Irish.[143] She was, moreover, the stage manager of Edward's kingship and a collaborator in designing the royal narrative:

> From the very beginning of her marriage, she dressed him in garments either embroidered by herself or of her choice, and of such a kind that it could not be thought that even Solomon in all his glory was ever thus arrayed. In the ornamentation of these no count was made of the cost of the precious stones, rare gems and shining pearls that were used. As regards mantles, tunics, boots and shoes, the amount of gold [thread] which flowed in the various complicated floral designs was not weighed. The throne, adorned with coverings embroidered with gold, gleamed in every part; the floors were strewn with precious [Andalusi?] carpets from Spain. Edward's staff, for everyday use when walking, was encrusted in gold and gems. His saddle and horse-trappings were hung with little beasts and birds made from gold by smiths under her direction.[144]

Seldom are we told how kings of that age presented themselves, but it does appear that the decoration of Edward was exceptional. To outshine

---

[140] S 999 (1043): 'Ego Eadwardus annuente altithroni moderatoris imperio Anglorum basileus'.

[141] S 998 (1042).

[142] E.g. the Gospel formula, 'Date et dabitur' (S 1006, S 1015, S 1022), and for the Fall as a theme, see S 1004 and S 1015.

[143] *Vita*, p. 23 (from Richard of Cirencester).

[144] Ibid. (from Richard of Cirencester) – translation modified.

Solomon was quite a feat. We have seen that the king was casting himself in the guise of the resurrected Christ; and what we are seeing in this description of his attire is his modelling as a quasi-divine figure, a saviour come down to earth. Edith was like the priestess of his cult, dressing him as a saint and sitting at his feet. The few permitted to draw near to him may have claimed to speak for the oracle. Perhaps the idea was to transform his outer man into a vision of the soul within. Edward was as beautiful as Solomon; as radiant as Christ the King. His finery united heaven and earth in the panoply of Holy Wisdom.[145] His serenity proclaimed perpetual peace.

[145] Cf. *Psy.* 823–88.

Chapter 4

CONFLICT

publica sed requies privatis rure foroque
constat amicitiis
(But the nation's peace depends on goodwill
between its citizens in field and town)

Prudentius, *Psychomachia* 755–6

The years 1049–53 delineated a period of political struggle which reconfigured Edward's alliances. During these years he had to contend with the developing threats from Flanders to the east and Gruffudd ap Rhydderch to the west. He would also fill both archbishoprics and install his own candidates in several important offices, colliding with other powerful agents who sought to install theirs. Looking abroad, he had to raise his political game to become a European player. At home, he had to integrate newcomers into a small and jealous circle of lords without somehow upsetting the balance. Finally, he would negotiate the first rebellion of his reign. Like the later one of 1065 it resulted largely from a perception that he shielded his favourites from justice when they committed breaches of the peace. Both threatened the unity of the family Edward had built up around him. Both threatened his ancient royal line.

For most of the 1040s Edward's opponent Flanders had enjoyed good relations with Edward's ally, the German emperor Henry. Baldwin had even done Henry the occasional favour, such as attacking the West Frisians in 1045 when their count lent support to Duke Godfrey II of Upper Lorraine, who was in rebellion against Henry.[1] In 1047 Godfrey initiated a second rebellion against the emperor, this time persuading Baldwin to join him. Eustace of Boulogne was now drawn into the rebel alliance through the influence of those two mighty neighbours of his. As part of this manoeuvre, if he had not already done so, he repudiated his wife, Edward's sister Gode, and married Godfrey's daughter, Ida of Lorraine. Gode made her way to England, where her brother endowed her with estates.[2] Ralph, the son of her previous marriage to Drogo of the Vexin, may have joined his uncle Edward prior to that point. But the

---

[1] *Les Annales de Saint-Pierre de Gand et de Saint-Amand*, ed. P. Grierson (Brussels, 1937), p. 91.
[2] See below, p. 166.

absence of his name from Edward's charters before 1050 makes it more likely that he arrived with Gode.[3] By repudiating Edward's sister and joining an alliance that included his opponent Flanders, Eustace showed his willingness to sacrifice relations with England to fulfil his ambitions. One of those ambitions was to remain a player in the power struggle fast developing on his side of the Channel. Another was to procure the heir lacking from his union with Gode.

Such was the political theatre in which our actors were increasingly performing, yet it engaged the attention of the chroniclers far less than a flashpoint of domestic politics which occurred in 1051. In that year Edward fell out with Earl Godwine. The struggle that ensued brought England to the brink of civil war. Different voices can be heard in the accounts of these events, as can strong opinions, but they show little interest in the storm of objectives, impulses, and emotions that resolves in political decision making. Unlike the king and his earls, the chroniclers who devoted much attention to those years of conflict were not well appraised of the shifting equipoise of northern European politics. The row in 1051 between the earl of Wessex and the visiting count of Boulogne – the incident that sparked conflict between Edward and Godwine – threatened the equilibrium the king was trying to maintain. The chroniclers saw only the storm in front of them, not the ripples. Edward had to worry about distant waves crashing elsewhere. In 1053 he would emerge from the conflict, rid of divisive underlings. He would strengthen his ties with the emperor and aspire to be his peer.

TROUBLE BEGINS TO BREW

By 1049 the emperor could no longer ignore Baldwin's part in Duke Godfrey's second rebellion, so he raised a mighty army to march into Flanders. With him was his kinsman the pope, Leo IX, formerly the imperial bishop Bruno of Toul, who owed his position, influence, and allegiance to the emperor. Henry now sent to Edward and to Sven of Denmark for naval assistance to blockade Baldwin in case he attempted to escape from Bruges.[4] Edward, who had refused naval support to Denmark in 1047 and 1048, was more inclined to offer it to the emperor and punish Flanders at the same time, though he would send no troops abroad, and such may not

---

[3] Ann Williams suggests that Eustace's marriage to Gode was dissolved at the Council of Rheims later that year, but Leo was striking down marital alliances between the emperor's opponents. It is, accordingly, more likely that Eustace repudiated Gode to marry Ida. Her return to England may also have prompted Edward to intervene against the allies: A. Williams, 'Regional Communities and Royal Authority in the Late Old English Kingdom: The Crisis of 1051–1052 Revisited', *History* 98 (2013), 23–40, at pp. 27–8. Tanner, *Families, Friends and Allies*, p. 87, notes: 'The papal action was designed to weaken the bonds between the allies and disrupt their authority within their territories.'

[4] ASC C, 1049; Tanner, 'Counts of Boulogne', pp. 264–5.

have been asked of him. Baldwin, moreover, still had the support of Henry of France his brother-in-law, who in other regards was Edward's ally.

Edward answered the emperor's request by assembling a 'great raiding ship-army' off the coast at Sandwich. It included forty-two ships led by Godwine and Earl Beorn, who may have commanded fourteen ships of lithesmen that made up the standing fleet. There were also Mercian vessels, possibly under Leofric, who was at the king's side at Sandwich on other occasions, plus the king's own contingent. A spike in coin production at the Sandwich mint, involving multiple dies under the aegis of one moneyer, evidences a factory-style initiative to finance the operation.[5] Once the men of the fleet had been deployed, the king had to meet the cost of their daily pay. With conflict brewing, on 20 April the bishop of Noyon visited St Peter's, Ghent, where he elevated the relics of St Florbert to supplicate the heavens.[6] As Henry III marched on Bruges, Edward's fleet menaced its count, conducting naval exercises. Edward cultivated his reputation as a naval commander, guarding against raids that might come as a by-product of Flanders' discomfiture. Henry of France played a similar game, marching an army through northern France in a show of support for Baldwin. Through messengers the kings of England and France could have agreed their responses in advance.

While Edward and his commanders lay at Sandwich, Godwine's son Swegn returned with eight ships, landing at his family's Sussex estate at Bosham harbour.[7] After fleeing into exile in 1047, he had wintered with Baldwin in Bruges before setting out for Denmark in summer 1048, where he had 'ruined himself with the Danes'.[8] Now the prodigal son came overland to Sandwich to seek Edward's pardon. The chronicles reflect differently the greeting he received. E maintains that, while the king was willing to make peace with him and restore all he formerly possessed, Harold and Beorn insisted he should not be entitled to the things the king had granted to them out of his forfeited earldom. D appears not to comment on the first round of discussions. C notes Harold and Beorn's opposition to Swegn and claims the king refused him everything. E adds that he was granted four days' safe-conduct to return to his ships. It may be that C jumps straight to the conclusion of the affair whereas E offers a glimpse of how it unfolded. For Edward there were political benefits in restoring Swegn to his earldom. Not least, there was a hole to plug in the defence of the Welsh marches, where Swegn's alliance with Gruffudd ap Llywelyn, the king in North Wales, was needed to keep the sons of Rhydderch in check. His restoration would place Godwine in Edward's debt and create fruitful rivalries among the earl's protégés. Ultimately,

---

[5] Pagan, 'The *PACX* Type', p. 12, and pers. comm.
[6] *Les Annales*, ed. Grierson, p. 26.
[7] ASC D, 1050 [1049]; *JW*, ii, p. 549.
[8] ASC D, 1050 [1049]. Perhaps he squandered resources in attempts to buy support.

however, the king had to rule consensually. He sent Swegn back to his ships, perhaps with the advice that he should work on winning over Harold and Beorn.

As Swegn was returning to Bosham, word came to the king that hostile ships lay to the west and were raiding.[9] This was in July or August, when a fleet of Hiberno-Scandinavian vikings – thirty-six ships were counted – sailed out of the Irish Sea and around the southern Welsh coast. At first, they ravaged Deheubarth, the southern Welsh kingdom, but its ruler Gruffudd ap Rhydderch, who was strong in Glamorgan, persuaded them to join with him in attacking the English instead. They may have found an opening for attack in the absence of a fleet at Bristol, if it is assumed that the ship-service of the shires around the Severn was then being deployed at Sandwich. Raiding up the Wye into Gloucestershire, they burned down Tidenham, a valuable manor belonging to Bath abbey. No earl was available, so it fell to Ealdred, bishop of Worcester, to raise the levies of Herefordshire and Gloucestershire, whose fluid loyalties ensured that his plans were betrayed to Gruffudd. Ealdred's troops were caught by surprise and defeated; the bishop was forced to flee. D, which supports Ealdred, complains that they had 'too little help'. Perhaps Tofig was killed, for the fort at Burghill came into Godwinson hands about this time.[10] Reports of the attack came to Edward, who dispatched the Wessex squadron under Godwine and Tostig, reinforced by two royal ships under Beorn, to meet the enemy. He also released the Mercian fleet, which must have been anxious to return home.

Although D muddles the sequence of events, claiming that Edward waited until Baldwin had made a pact with the emperor before dispersing the fleet, E was abreast of events in the south-east and reveals that Edward responded immediately to the threat in the Severn estuary. Realizing he had to choose between deploying a large part of his fleet there and detaining it for another month until the Flanders affair concluded, he sent squadrons from Wessex and Mercia to deal with the new danger and remained at Sandwich with a few ships in case the diminishing threat from Flanders happened to flare up in the endgame – and to honour his promise to the emperor. The pact mentioned by D must be the treaty Baldwin was forced to sign at Aachen in mid-September, by which point Duke Godfrey's capitulation had put an end to the rebellion. Edward might have learned the affair was moving to a conclusion, but there was still some tense manoeuvring to be done before the treaty would be agreed.

No sooner had Edward dismissed the Mercians than he heard that Osgod Clapa, in exile since 1046, was at Wulpe, an island north of Bruges, with twenty-nine ships.[11] Either the king of the Danes, who was now in

---

[9] For the account that follows, ASC E, 1046 [1049]; D, 1050 [1049]; *JW*, ii, pp. 549–53.

[10] *GDB* 186a; Williams, *World before Domesday*, p. 23.

[11] ASC C, 1049; *JW*, ii, p. 551, also reports twenty-nine ships; ASC D, 1050 [1049] has thirty-nine ships, probably a copying error.

command of his realm, had been taking advantage of his resurgence to expel interlopers, or Osgod was exploiting the chaos of war. Edward quickly recalled such ships as he could. Many had got no farther than the north mouth of the Wantsum.[12] Sensing danger, Osgod set his wife in Bruges and waited with six ships at Wulpe, sending the rest to attack the Naze in Essex. There they did harm until a storm overtook them and destroyed all but a remnant, which ended up overseas, where their crews were captured and killed. Maybe they fell into the hands of Edward's allies in Denmark or Normandy. The combination of an effective intelligence network, rapid responses, and the luck of the winds and the waves had enabled England to weather multiple threats.

Meanwhile the Wessex squadron lay weather-bound at Pevensey, hindered by storms allied to those that were pounding Osgod's ships. Swegn was at Bosham pondering his next moves. Had he known of the raids in Gloucestershire he might well have turned them to his advantage as an argument for restoring him to his earldom. Without Swegn there, the sons of Rhydderch were encroaching, inciting treachery in Edward's subjects, and enticing vikings from the Irish Sea into the prosperous Severn valley. Still, nothing could be achieved while Beorn and Harold stood in the way. Swegn journeyed to Pevensey and spoke with his father Godwine and cousin Beorn, appealing to the latter for help with the king. Possibly because Harold was not there to steady him, or because Godwine pressured him, Beorn acquiesced. Swegn offered oaths of loyalty, but Beorn trusted his kinsman and rode with him to Bosham, taking only three attendants. There he was overpowered, bound, and carried aboard. Swegn's ships sailed west past Wight and Portland; and at Dartmouth Beorn was murdered 'and buried deep'.[13] No one seems to have suspected Godwine's involvement, though he and Swegn had conversed before Swegn lured Beorn to his death, and similar plans had been sprung to entrap Alfred in 1036. Only Adam of Bremen nurtured a conspiracy theory, perceiving a Godwinist plot to destroy Sven Estrithsson's chances of succeeding to the English throne by killing his supporters in England, Beorn among them.[14] But Adam's theory was a later fantasy.

One way to interpret these events is to characterize Swegn as a reckless man whose rash actions twice ruined his prospects – once when he absconded with the abbess of Leominster, and again when, instead of attempting a second round of negotiations, he murdered the cousin who had offered to assist. This interpretation has in its favour the undoubted folly of the first action, the risks associated with the second, and the possibility that Beorn's murder was the result of a quarrel that arose after

[12] ASC C, 1049.
[13] Ibid.
[14] *GHEP*, pp. 154–5.

Swegn got him aboard. Had it not been, Swegn might as easily have killed him at Bosham. A different reading of 1049 is that Swegn's actions were premeditated and bold. That he had gambled foolishly in the past is no evidence that he did so again. While Beorn and Harold were both in office, Swegn had no prospects in England, and it is doubtful he had any in Denmark or Flanders. Killing Beorn could create a vacancy with a hope that friends in England might plead on his behalf. C and D agree in stating that Swegn went to Pevensey 'with guile'. Whatever transpired, he may have calculated that Godwine would support him; and Ealdred, bishop of Worcester, needed him in the marches. Beorn was playing a double game, trying to please both camps while looking after himself. Swegn could turn that fact to his advantage by claiming Beorn had gone against Harold – a claim his father and brother might believe. As in 1036, the victim was led to a remote place before the fatal attack. Maybe Swegn had no wish to cause trouble for his father by killing Beorn at Bosham, a family estate.

When the crime was discovered, the king and the raiding army at Sandwich declared Swegn *nithing* – a man in disgrace. Two of his ships were captured by the men of Hastings, who killed the crews and took the ships to Edward. Others abandoned the former earl. With two remaining vessels, Swegn sailed for Flanders and was granted asylum at Bruges for the second time by Baldwin. Harold arranged for his cousin's body to be honourably re-interred with his uncle King Cnut at the Old Minster, Winchester, where Beorn's friends and men of the fleet gathered for his funeral.[15] It was a high-class murder, a scandal of the first degree. With messages buzzing to and fro among those caught up in the ongoing conflict, fingers of blame would soon have been pointing in several directions.

GETTING ON BOARD WITH THE POPE

As Edward was concluding his campaign with the emperor, news came that the latter's friendly pope planned to convene a synod at Rheims. Seldom had his predecessors ventured north of the Alps, but Leo IX wanted to enlist rulers and bishops of northern principalities in a campaign to tackle abuses. Dates were fixed for the first week of October. Clerical and lay dignitaries began preparations for the journey. Edward dispatched the German bishop Duduc of Wells, Wulfric, the abbot of St Augustine's, and Ælfwine, abbot of Ramsey, ordering that they should report to him what was decided there for Christendom.[16] For Ælfwine the timing could not have been worse. On 18 or 19 September the bishopric of Dorchester

---

[15] ASC C, 1049; D 1050 [1049].

[16] ASC E, 1046 [1049]. Duduc was either German or Lotharingian; A. Bihrer, *Begegnungen zwischen dem ostfränkisch-deutschen Reich und England (850–1100). Kontakte – Konstellationen – Funktionalisierungen – Wirkungen* (Ostfildern, 2012), pp. 182–3, argues for Lotharingian.

fell vacant at the death of Bishop Eadnoth II. Since 1006 it had gone to monks of Ramsey abbey who had lavished the benefits upon Ramsey. Either Ælfwine had already left by this point or he was sent off to Rheims by higher powers who did not care for his lobbying. Edward bestowed the bishopric on his Norman priest Ulf. Being the king's man, he could be trusted to employ the see's resources to the advantage of the Crown and not some other interest. Besides, he may have been the next chaplain in line for a bishopric. The appointment met with opposition. C and D, under C's influence, signal that Ulf was a terrible choice. D and E agree that he was unable to fulfil the duties of episcopal office, though the papal privilege Ælfwine went on to obtain at Rheims could have had something to do with that, if, for example, it excluded Ulf from officiating at Ramsey, which lay within his diocese.[17]

Leo's ecclesiastical business had secular ramifications. With the rebellious duke Godfrey safely incarcerated and Baldwin bound by the September treaty, Leo used his synod to finish the emperor's work by quashing marital alliances forged during the rebellion. At Rheims the marriage of William of Normandy to Baldwin's daughter Matilda of Flanders was prohibited on grounds of incest. Eustace of Boulogne, on a similar pretext, was excommunicated for his marriage to Ida, Godfrey's daughter; and Enguerrand of Ponthieu incurred the same fate for his recent strategic marriage.[18] The verdicts passed at Rheims reveal the importance to the rebels of allying with the maritime powers, and the emperor's desire, conversely, to isolate Lorraine and Flanders. Edward too may have been gratified by Leo's treatment of Eustace. Possibly his embassy upheld it. There were, besides, added grounds for excommunication if the count had put aside Gode unlawfully. Even so, from England's perspective the marriage between Normandy and Flanders was a greater concern, for even if it served the young duke William merely to flatter his ambitions, Edward could not allow a hostile alliance to develop between the major maritime players that were once forward bases for Scandinavian raiders. Leo's prohibition of the marriage between William and Matilda would buy Edward time, but Baldwin and William, as well as Godfrey and Eustace, would look to turn the pope around.

Rheims marked the beginning of warm relations between England and the new papacy, which assisted Edward in his efforts to court the emperor's friendship and establish himself as a negotiator on the European stage. They also reflected his concern to put the business of the Church in order.

[17] *Chronicon*, ed. Macray, p. 171; B. Savill, 'Papal Privileges in Early Medieval England, c. 680–1073', D.Phil. dissertation (Oxford, 2017), p. 234: the privilege gave him *protectio* for the *iura* of his abbey.

[18] *Anselme de Saint-Rémy, Histoire de la dédicace de Saint-Rémy*, ed. and tr. J. Hourlier, in *La Champagne bénédictine: contribution à l'année saint Benoît*, Travaux de l'Academie nationale de Reims, vol. clx (Rheims, 1981), 181–297, at p. 252; Tanner, 'Counts of Boulogne', p. 263.

As the monarch chosen by God to govern its affairs, Edward signalled that his actions were open to scrutiny; that Leo might offer guidance. Clergy discontent with their situation exploited the tentative dialogue. After Rheims, Leo wrote that it had come to his attention that Leofric, bishop of Crediton, and other bishops presided in obscure villages, though Church law decreed that sees be situated in the administrative centres of the dioceses. He wrote to Edward 'to command and request' that Leofric's bishopric be moved to Exeter, telling him he was sending a legate to England to inquire into other matters.[19] No pope in living memory had intervened to this extent, but Edward showed willingness to comply. In 1050 he sent two bishops, Herman of Ramsbury and Ealdred of Worcester, to Leo's Easter synod in Rome, where Herman delivered an adulatory speech. The English, he proclaimed, were hospitable to all peoples – he was, like the pope, a Lotharingian. England was full of churches, daily adding new ones to the old; in those churches were innumerable ornaments and bells, and the king and chief men were generous benefactors to Christ.[20] No doubt his audience appreciated the irony, given that Herman had left the cathedral cities of Lorraine and ended up in rural Wiltshire. A few years later he would follow Leofric's precedent by petitioning to relocate his see to the prosperous abbey of Malmesbury.[21]

Sensing the significance of Leo's religious mission, Edward proved responsive. He had instructed the clerics setting off for Rheims that whatever was done or spoken there should be written in English and a copy of the report kept in the king's treasury under the care of Hugolin the chamberlain.[22] After discussions with Leo or his legate it was decided that the combined dioceses of Devon and Cornwall should be governed from a single see, which would be established in St Peter's minster, within the walls of Exeter. The transference of Leofric's operations to the administrative centre of the south west redressed the irregularities of a bishop holding two dioceses and residing in obscure places. Mindful of defence as ever, Edward now abolished the old cathedrals of Crediton and St German's, which had suffered the onslaughts of pirates, in favour of a fortified location (which in 1068 would withstand the Conqueror for eighteen days with the loss of much of his attack force). The strategic enhancement of Exeter involved the concentration of regional minting there as well.[23] In the summer of 1050 a charter was drawn up, confirming St Peter's in its new

[19] *The Leofric Missal*, ed. F. E. Warren (Oxford, 1883), p. 2. This version of the letter is unlikely to be original.

[20] ASC E, 1047 [1050]; F. Barlow, *The English Church 1000–1066* (London and New York, 2nd edn, 1979), p. 94.

[21] Malmesbury, *Gesta Pontificum*, I, pp. 287–9, 629.

[22] *Chronicon*, ed. Macray, p. 170.

[23] ASC D, 1067 [1067–8]. The siege succeeded through treachery. A. Freeman, *The Moneyer and the Mint in the Reign of Edward the Confessor 1042–1066*, BAR British Series 145 (1985), p. 62.

possessions. Edward attended the ceremony, laying the charter upon the altar. Leading Leofric by the right hand and Edith by the left, he installed the bishop in his new cathedral before a great assembly. It was agreed that Leofric should govern the canons of St Peter's by the precepts of the revised Rule of St Chrodegang of Metz, a quasi-monastic template of living.[24] Favoured by cathedral churches in the empire, it was the constitution Leo had observed as a canon of St Stephen's in Toul.

Pleasing the pope by enacting useful reforms cost Edward little. It demonstrated respect for the conciliar legislation Leo was renewing and commitment to improving the life of the clergy in accordance with an approved template. Leo in turn expressed his delight on hearing that Edward was 'diligent and devoted in his concern for churches and churchmen'.[25] Still, there were limits to what could be expected from the king. It is doubtful, for example, that virtue and merit weighed more in his appointments to the royal chapel than the influence of relatives and friends who wanted him to create careers for their protégés, or whose protégés became his own through the affection he bore them. One such was Élinand, the protégé of Edward's nephew Count Walter of the Vexin, the son of Gode by her first husband. Another was Osbern fitz Osbern, a son of Osbern the Steward, whom Edward had known as an officer in the court of Duke Robert. Osbern the Steward had been killed while protecting the young duke William. When his son later failed to inherit a share of family estates, Edward found a place for him in his chapel.[26]

Edward nominated many bishops from among the ranks of his chaplains, participating in the Franco-Germanic trend of preferring courtly prelates. Ulf of Dorchester, however, found rivals ready to denounce him. Summoned to the Council of Vercelli (1 September 1050), he was threatened with deposition: 'they nearly had to break his staff – and would have done so, if he had not given more treasure – because he could not perform his duties as he ought'.[27] Ulf was then made to accompany the pope to Toul, where a council was scheduled for late October. Leo IX in fact was one of the more moderate reforming voices. Cardinal Humbert advocated deposing not only prelates who had purchased office, a stance Leo shared, but the clergy ordained by them as well. Peter Damian, an ascetic, wished to defrock all clerics who indulged in masturbation.[28] Edward, for his

---

[24] S 1021 ('una aecclesiastica regula').

[25] *The Leofric Missal*, ed. Warren, p. 2: 'audiuimus te circa dei ecclesias et ecclesiasticos uiros studiosum et religiosum esse, inde multum gaudemus'.

[26] S. Martinet, 'Élinand, évêque de Laon méconnu (1052–1098)', *Mémoires de la Fédération des sociétés d'histoire et d'archéologie de l'Aisne* 36 (1991), 58–78, at p. 58; Bauduin, *La première Normandie*, pp. 223–7.

[27] ASC E, 1047 [1050].

[28] W. D. McCready, *'Odiosa sanctitas': St Peter Damian, Simony, and Reform* (Toronto, 2011), pp. 52–3, 70–9; G. W. Olsen, *Of Sodomites, Effeminates, Hermaphrodites, and Androgynes: Sodomy in the Age of Peter Damian* (Toronto, 2011), p. 206.

part, had a kingdom to run. His prelates had to possess the requisite secular qualities to serve as agents of the Crown. Like the pope, he was answerable to God, but for different duties. Ulf's humiliation proved that the two would not always agree.

TENSIONS DEVELOP

Edward's thoughts were not entirely occupied with Leo. At home, there were pressing matters of state. Swegn's earldom was vacant and vulnerable; Beorn's, in the east midlands, was rudderless, and Edward was beginning to doubt the policy of appeasing factions among the native nobility by empowering only their protégés. In the years 1050–2 incomers from the French principalities multiply in the records. They are too numerous to be identified as camp followers from Edward's exile all suddenly promoted within a few years. Rather, they signal a political strategy concerned with strengthening Edward's command on the frontiers and in the shires, and with renewing links with cross-Channel powers in response to the shifting of alliances in Europe's northerly sea-zone. Employing a stratagem that had served Richard II and later dukes in Normandy, Edward installed castellans in the Herefordshire marches, in Swegn's vacant earldom, where Bishop Ealdred had failed to rout the Welsh. Castles arose, probably of the ring-work type, with ditch and palisade. One in the northern march, labelled Richard's castle, was named after Richard Scrob. Another, at Hereford, became Pentecost's castle, after the castellan Osbern Pentecost. By 1052 a castellan called Hugh was operating nearby.[29] Their advantage to Edward was that they lacked the ambivalence associated with border loyalties, which made local levies unreliable.

Beorn's earldom went to Edward's nephew Ralph of the Vexin, a son of his sister Gode. He first attests, as earl, in two diplomas of 1050, ahead of Tostig, who may or may not have been his junior.[30] A second Ralph, the Anglo-Breton Ralph the Staller, received a command in the king's household in or before 1050. Edward then established him in East Anglia, which had been Osgod's stamping ground. Osgod too had been a royal officer. Ralph now replaced him. Born in Norfolk about the beginning of the century, he had migrated to Brittany, served in the entourage of Edward's cousin Count Alain III in the 1030s, and was the sort of person who could have made Edward's acquaintance overseas.[31] Edward's French kinsman Robert fitz Wimarc also appears as a staller, one of the elite royal officers. At Clavering in Essex, he built a castle of his own.

---

[29] Barlow, *Edward*, p. 94; Williams, 'Regional Communities', p. 38.

[30] He appears in this position in S 1020 and S 1021, both dated to 1050.

[31] K. S. B. Keats-Rohan, 'Raoul *Anglicus* et Raoul de Gaël: un réexamen des données anglaises et bretonnes', *MSHAB* 94 (2016), 63–93, at pp. 72–4, 89, 90.

Within a short time, the king had created a French earl, two foreign stallers, and two or three Norman castellans. Meanwhile, foreign priests were multiplying in the royal chapel, among them Élinand, Robert, Regenbald, and William.[32]

By 1050 the advancement of foreign courtiers was also impacting the shires. When Ælfwine of Ramsey returned from Rheims to find the Norman chaplain Ulf installed as his bishop, it was not his only difficulty. A noble benefactor of Ramsey had lately died, leaving property to the abbey, but the dead man's kinsman, Ælfric son of Wihtgar, opposed the will in his absence and claimed right of inheritance. The abbot was fearful of confronting such a powerful man in public, for Ælfric was the royal reeve responsible for the eight and a half hundreds centred on the abbey of Bury St Edmunds. So he approached the king privately and paid him 20 gold pieces (mancuses), and 5 to Edith, to sway the verdict. At a hearing before the chief men the king ruled in his favour, but the abbot was obliged to lease one of the estates to the incomer Earl Ralph for his life-time. Even if Ralph had helped him win his case and agreed to leave the estate to Ramsey in his will, it is doubtful Ælfwine was in any position to dictate the terms.[33] Edward probably encouraged him to lease the estate to his nephew while pocketing the gold. Ælfwine, for his part, would have observed that the earl and bishop now presiding at the shire court conversed in a foreign tongue.

It was only diplomatic for Edward to temper his promotion of foreign men with gestures that would appease his senior earl. The clearest instance was his restoration of Swegn, whom Ealdred led back from Flanders and reconciled to the king upon his return from Leo's Easter synod in Rome in 1050.[34] Swegn may have bargained on this: he was a better marcher lord than Ealdred. He would not have bargained on returning to discover a nest of Frenchmen in his earldom, but Edward was taking no chances with defence. Before Leo's synod, Baldwin had reneged on his treaty with the emperor. This led to a second invasion in which Henry took an army through Cambrai to Bruges, burning settlements and killing their inhabitants. Baldwin surrendered and swore fealty. Then the emperor went home, though he confiscated the march of Anvers (Antwerp).[35] All of this gave Godwine and Harold cause for concern at the prospect of renewed embargoes, because the flow of Flemish commerce enriched their earldoms in the south and the east. Their service in Edward's fleet conflicted with their economic interests. It is likely to have been in the autumn of 1050 that Baldwin approached Godwine about a marital alliance that

[32] S 1020; S 1022.

[33] *Chronicon*, ed. Macray, pp. 169–70, 171–2. For a similar case, see *Hemingi chartularium*, ed. Hearne, II, pp. 396–8.

[34] ASC C, 1050.

[35] *Les Annales*, ed. Grierson, pp. 91, 156.

would see Tostig marry Baldwin's half-sister Judith in September 1051. At
that social level Edward's consent was prerequisite for Godwine if he
wished to marry off his son while retaining the king's favour, and Baldwin
would court trouble if he failed to consult the emperor. Edward had a
further stake in the union, arising from the fact that Judith was his second
cousin, the daughter of his cousin Eleanor. The betrothal represented an
effort by all parties to weave a meaningful peace.[36]

Just as the raids in the Welsh marches exposed a weakness that
prompted Edward to install foreign castellans, the fleet's deployment
re-energized debates about its cost and the efficient use of resources.
Harthacnut had made himself very unpopular by demanding 8 marks to
the rowlock for a fleet of sixty ships. Edward had reduced the heregeld to
the point of retaining only fourteen hired crews. His frequent presence at
Sandwich during the 1040s allowed him to negotiate a system of defence
based around the towns which later became the head harbours of the
Cinque Ports, namely Hastings, Romney, Hythe, Dover, and Sandwich.
As sea-borne trade increased there, merchant ships were multiplying. The
king was contracting agreements with prosperous ports. By extending
their privileges to include toll exemptions and rights to profits of justice
from their courts, Edward secured a commitment from Dover and
Sandwich and probably also Romney, Hythe, and Hastings to supply
ships and seamen for naval defence. Lightening other customary dues, he
increased their defensive duties.[37] This is when we find the earliest references to butsecarls – boatmen of the maritime towns. The fact that the
men of Hastings captured two of Swegn's ships and took them to the king
shows they were providing a service in 1049. Their duties may be found
fossilized in Domesday Book, which states that Dover owed its service of
fifteen ships each with twenty-one men, for fifteen days when summoned
to guard the coast.[38] For service above fifteen days, the king had to pay.

Arrangements of this sort now enabled Edward to phase out the mercenary crews – the lithesmen – who had been instituted in Æthelred's final
years as auxiliaries from Denmark. No source suggests they had given
unsatisfactory service, but the tax which paid for them – the heregeld –
was expensive and unpopular. The mercenaries were a supplementary
force, augmenting the maritime powers which kings otherwise had at their
disposal when calling out the ship-fyrd. It could have been Edward's
intention for some time to substitute a new ancillary force, furnishable

---

[36] *Vita*, p. 39. I am grateful to Liesbeth van Houts (pers. comm.) for her advice on the
marriage.

[37] C. W. Hollister, *Anglo-Saxon Military Institutions on the Eve of the Norman Conquest*
(Oxford, 1962), pp. 117–21.

[38] N. Hooper, 'Some Observations on the Navy in late Anglo-Saxon England', in
C. Harper-Bill, C. J. Holdsworth, and J. L. Nelson, eds, *Studies in Medieval History presented
to R. Allen Brown* (Woodbridge, 1989), pp. 203–13.

from the south-eastern ports, hence the arrangements he made. The service those ports were providing at any rate made the retention of a mercenary fleet look more like an extravagance. At a Lenten council in 1050, the king paid off nine of the mercenary crews, retaining five and promising them twelve months' pay. Then, at another Lenten council, in London the following year, he dismissed the remainder and pleased his ratepayers by abolishing the heregeld.[39]

About that time, in another act aimed at the monied elite, whose favour had to be curried, the regime increased the standard of the silver penny. Before the early 1050s, that standard was fairly stable at about 1.08g, though with variance among different mints. With the recoinage that brought in the 'Expanding Cross' issue, it rose to approximately 1.66g. Two versions of this type were issued, a light one at the previous standard weight, and the heavy version just mentioned. Although it is not clear which came first, the heavy version signalled an attempt to reform the weight of the coinage which was carried through into later issues, albeit to a lesser degree, by the maintenance of the penny at approximately 1.30g.[40] An increase in the weight of the penny might not only have aided the king by increasing the bullion value of the fixed farms paid to him by royal officials; it might also have appealed to landholders generally whose income was based on fixed rents. With the abolition of the heregeld about that time, the king may have been responding to pressure from his nobles to alleviate fiscal burdens. Whether such burdens related to the costs of defence, they were exacerbating tensions in the polity.

Edward's decision in 1050 to phase out the mercenary crews marked a downgrading of the threat level attached to Denmark and Flanders. It sent the important message that England could trust to the defences Edward had put in place, and it placated those, whoever they were, who felt the burdens of Edward's regime. Prior to the autumn of 1050 Edward's actions have a placatory quality, as though he acted for political reasons to please others. While this is not true of the promotion of foreigners, which suited his own ends, it is discernible in his phased scheme for abolishing the heregeld; in Swegn's restoration after Easter; and in the betrothal of Tostig and Judith of Flanders about that time. Then on 29 October 1050, the archbishop of Canterbury died, and the placatory actions came to an end. In fact, the king had stood to gain from them, but he could not install his own candidate in Archbishop Eadsige's shoes without trampling on powerful interests.

After Eadsige's death the monks of Canterbury elected one of their own to replace him. This was Godwine's kinsman Æthelric, and the earl became

---

[39] ASC D, 1052 [1051]; cf. Lambert, *Law and Order*, pp. 307–8.

[40] S. Lyon, 'The "Expanding Cross" Type of Edward the Confessor and the Appledore (1997) Hoard', *Numismatic Circular* 106 (1998), 426–8, at p. 426; and Rory Naismith, pers. comm.

his advocate. Edward favoured a rival candidate, Robert of Jumièges, bishop of London. Lobbying and manoeuvring by both camps ran into 1051, when York fell vacant too, on 22 January, with the death of Archbishop Ælfric.[41] About this time, Edward's kinsman Rudolph appeared at court. Formerly bishop of Nidaros in Norway, he was looking for a comfortable retirement. Ælfric was replaced with Cynesige, who was either a royal chaplain or a monk of Peterborough.[42] Then at the same mid-Lent council, when Edward abolished the heregeld, Robert was appointed to Canterbury. The *Vita* reports that his appointment caused much anger, while E alludes to the overruling of Æthelric's election in its statement that Robert was installed 'against God's will'.[43] London went to Spearhafoc, who may well have been Stigand's protégé, since Stigand's chronicle, E, takes an interest in him.[44] He was also Edward's man, having become the king's goldsmith. Abingdon, which he vacated on his elevation to London, was given to the rootless Rudolph, depriving more monks of an elective voice. In all those appointments, Edward had his way.

REBELLION

Fifteen years later, when writing the *Vita*, Folcard identified Robert's appointment to Canterbury as the catalyst in the conflict that would occur later that year. In his opinion the appointment was the moment when the king abandoned the counsel of the nobles and clergy and sided with a cabal of Frenchmen who had followed him from Normandy, Robert being their spokesman and the king's closest advisor. Through the favour he enjoyed with Edward he received first London then Canterbury and involved himself more than was proper in the running of the realm. Edward began to offend his courtiers by preferring Robert's advice to theirs, and the realm grew troubled as factions vied for Edward's favour.[45] Folcard goes on to recount how the new archbishop was bent on attacking Godwine with assorted schemes, including a lawsuit claiming the earl had invaded the lands of his archbishopric. Adding to his madness, he managed to convince the king the earl was plotting to harm him 'as he had

[41] *Vita*, p. 31.

[42] Cf. J. Cooper, 'Cynesige [St Cynesige, Kynsige] (d. 1060), archbishop of York', *ODNB*. John of Worcester and Simeon of Durham, surely not independently, describe him as a royal clerk at the time of his appointment. A 'Cynesige presbiter' appears among the royal chaplains in S 1020 (for Abingdon, 1050) and in the fabricated witness lists of S 1023 and S 1025 which depend on it, but that may be a mistake for 'Cynesige minister' who appears in a similar position in S 1022. None of the witness lists is above suspicion.

[43] *Vita*, p. 31; ASC E, 1052.

[44] He was formerly a monk of Bury St Edmunds, whence he had gone from St Benet's at Holme: T. Licence, 'The Origins of the Monastic Communities of St Benedict at Holme and Bury St Edmunds', *Revue bénédictine* 116 (2006), 42–61, at pp. 57–8.

[45] *Vita*, pp. 28–30.

harmed his brother Alfred' – so Robert is meant to have said. Worried by the allegation, the king assembled the witan and, in his absence, charged 'the guiltless earl' with treason.[46]

Folcard, it should be noted, did not witness these events, nor was he critical of the story he received. The account he put together involves two main elements: a one-sided narrative created by the earl's supporters to exculpate Godwine, and the motif of the evil advisor who leads the king astray. Examples of that topos were to be found in the Bible, so it is possible Folcard inserted it into the narrative himself.[47] The flaws of his account from our historical perspective include its assumptions, simplifications, and omissions. First, the author assumes that the French had followed Edward from Normandy, an easy way to explain their presence. Second, he assumes Edward appointed Robert simply because he was the king's favourite, forgetting that the king was giving Robert a job to do. Third, Folcard was unaware of the conflict that arose almost immediately between Robert and Edward. Their relationship was stormier than he portrays. Fourth, he omits an incident involving Eustace of Boulogne that sparked open conflict between Godwine and Edward. Fifth, he neglects to mention that the earl was in open rebellion when he was charged in his absence with treason at Gloucester.

There were good strategic reasons for appointing Robert to Canterbury, given Edward's concerns in 1050–1. One of them was the alliance between Normandy and Flanders, which was coming to fruition thanks to a campaign lobbying Pope Leo to overturn his prohibition on the marriage of William to Matilda. At this juncture, a Norman archbishop of Canterbury could strengthen relations with Normandy and help to maintain diplomatic equilibrium. A second concern was finance. Edward regarded Robert as capable and dependable. In posting him to Canterbury he would have contemplated the utility of the Kentish archbishopric as a source of revenue to the treasury. Archbishop Eadsige and his predecessor had exercised the earl's authority in the shire. This involved the office-holder sending two thirds of the profits of his jurisdiction to the king and keeping a third for his own use, known as the earl's 'third penny'. In 1044, however, a suffragan bishop had been nominated to assist Eadsige, whom illness incapacitated. Godwine had manoeuvred his own candidate Siward into this role and assumed the earl's authority in the shire, taking the third penny for himself.[48] It is unlikely he did so without encroaching on Canterbury's estates in a manner which resulted in loss of income to both the archbishopric and the Crown, although the evidence is open to debate.[49] Godwine, as a rule, did not meddle in ecclesiastical appointments, but he did in

[46] Ibid., p. 34
[47] E.g. Haman (Esther 3:1–6); Achitophel (2 Sam. (2 Kgs) 17:7).
[48] Williams, 'Regional Communities', p. 26.
[49] A. Williams, 'The Piety of Earl Godwine', *ANS* 34 (2012), 237–56, at p. 242.

the case of Canterbury, which lay upon his doorstep. In 1050, as in 1044, he recommended a candidate who would bend to his interests, but on this occasion Edward decided that the archbishopric should not be Godwine's private fiefdom and sent in Robert of Jumièges to sort things out.

Whether he knew what conflict awaited him, Robert left for Rome in the spring to ask the pope for a pallium – the woollen vestment signifying that he was authorized in his office. There the matter of Spearhafoc's nomination to London arose. His opponents found a way to sway Leo, and Leo forbade Robert to bless him. It is possible that a delegate of the canons of St Paul's had gone to Rome, complaining that the king had imposed his candidate without an election, or that Spearhafoc purchased office. Word of Leo's veto might well have reached Edward before Robert's return, for the king chose not to attend the archbishop's installation at Canterbury on 29 June 1051, although he had attended Leofric's at Exeter one year earlier. Only when he had taken the precaution of securing himself in office did the archbishop make his way to the king, but before he reached him Spearhafoc rode out to meet him, bearing the king's writ and seal. If it was not clear already, it should have been clear then what Edward expected of Robert. Spearhafoc asked to be consecrated. Robert declined. Spearhafoc begged to be consecrated bishop of London. Robert refused, stating the pope had forbidden it. Then Spearhafoc returned to London, and all that summer and autumn he occupied the bishopric with Edward's full consent.[50]

Leo was beginning to suspect Edward's choice of bishops, though not in Robert's case. Robert shared his scruples, but scruples have a habit of aligning with politics. Leo had been flexible enough to change his mind about William and Matilda's betrothal, and Edward saw Robert's inability to sway his verdict on Spearhafoc as a failure, or worse. By allowing him entry into his bishopric – Robert's old see – Edward publicly undermined his archbishop, as Robert's recalcitrance undermined him. Gossip might say that Robert was playing the pope against the king to oust the king's candidate and replace him with one of Robert's choosing. Edward now had to choose whom to back between an archbishop who was loyal but defied him in this one matter and an earl whose influence in Kent he wished to check. To the latter, the archbishop showed himself a malign genius, bent on disarming him. Here too his ideals aligned with his politics. Robert not only headed a faction which was inimical to Godwine's interests, he was fighting him in court over estates he claimed for Canterbury, manoeuvring in a way that wrong-footed him.[51] Though Robert weakened his cause by antagonizing the king, his opponents' inability to find fault in his conduct made him a dangerous adversary.

[50] ASC E, 1048 [1051].
[51] *Vita*, p. 33.

Godwine, whose discomposure echoes in the *Vita*, did not know how to handle him.

The king was scarcely more in charge of the situation and was already jeopardizing relations with the papacy and Normandy by opposing his Norman primate. Having forced his own candidates on several influential religious communities, including Canterbury, London, Ramsey, and Abingdon, he found he had pushed through Robert's controversial appointment only for his protégé to slap him in the face. Perhaps Robert felt too much in Edward's power and wanted to regain a bit of control. Like Thomas Becket a century later, he could counter any charges of cronyism that might have been levelled against him by opposing the king on a matter of principle. Whatever Robert's motives were, there is truth in Folcard's claim that he was trying to turn Edward against Godwine, and he may have been sowing division by asking about the royal marriage, which was still without issue after six years. King Robert of France had put aside more than one wife who did not give him an heir. Edward's 'evil advisor' would be advising him to do the same.[52]

That summer, after Robert returned from Rome, Eustace of Boulogne came to visit the king with a band of companions. Since 1049 he had been distancing himself from Baldwin, but Normandy and Flanders were negotiating around him, threatening to engulf his interests in their maritime alliance.[53] Tostig's imminent marriage to Judith, meanwhile, betokened a rapprochement between Flanders and England which might prove prejudicial to Boulogne's trade in the Channel. In such circumstances, Eustace was obliged to repair his relations with Edward. Whatever the two men discussed, Eustace could hardly have forgotten Godwine's outrage against the men of Boulogne and his brother-in-law, Alfred. That matter must have come up in the conflict that followed, otherwise Folcard would not have touched on it in the *Vita*. For Eustace the topic would have helped reaffirm his bond with Edward by reminding him of a grievance they shared and drawing his attention away from the more divisive matter of his treatment of Edward's sister. Godwine, already caught up in conflict with Robert and conscious of being undermined, now had to fear the politicking of a new antagonist.

Homeward-bound, Eustace and his men stopped for a meal in Canterbury, which was Robert's domain. A rendezvous there would have provided an opportunity for Robert and Eustace to talk about such matters as where Eustace and his men should lodge for the night, before their return crossing. The hill-top burh at Dover, where St Mary's minster stood, was an obvious destination; but with current tensions and the potentially inflammatory lobbying of Eustace it could well turn into a hornets' nest. Dover was an ancient royal vill. Robert, as archbishop, had jurisdiction over the

---

[52] Robert certainly turned his attention to it later in the year: see below, p. 141.

[53] Tanner, 'Counts of Boulogne', p. 264.

minster, its dependent churches, and any ecclesiastical tenements that might offer hospitality. Godwine, as earl, had long enjoyed comital authority and secular patronage there, although Robert's appointment threatened that. What reception awaited Eustace and his men riding from Canterbury thus depended on the state of relations between Robert, Godwine, and the king, and the allegiances of the burgesses whose houses they wished to lodge in. Proceeding to the burh, they put on mail coats. Eustace was either anticipating trouble or intending to start a fight. D remarks that they 'looked for lodgings foolishly', alluding to provocation.[54] Violence broke out, causing the death of a score of burgesses and a similar number of Eustace's men.[55] Then Eustace galloped to the king at Gloucester and roused his anger by telling him his version of events. It was always a good idea to get to a king first. Whatever Edward's view of the affair, the blow to his diplomacy and harm to visitors, who were legally under royal protection, demanded a robust response.

E, which preserves the other side of the story, blames Eustace for the trouble at Dover, claiming he had forced his way into a house and killed the householder, after the man had killed one of Eustace's men in self-defence. By accusing the count of attacking the man in his home, the chronicler charged him with *hamsocn*, a crime so serious it was reserved for the king's judgment. But there is no indication Edward waited to hear the case for the defence. Nor does D imply that Godwine was eager to hear Eustace's story. Edward sent for the earl and ordered him to ravage the burh. Action of this kind was a standard method of punishing offending communities. King Eadred had dealt in such a manner with the men of Thetford, where an abbot had been murdered. Edgar had ordered a harrying of Thanet because traders from York had been killed there, and Harthacnut had ordered his earls to sack Worcester after its inhabitants killed two of his housecarls.[56] Edward too had to uphold royal authority. He could not be seen to tolerate a breach of his peace in a royal vill. Maybe the whisperings of Robert and Eustace had tempted him to put the earl to the test, but we should remember that Robert was not entirely in the king's favour, while Eustace had come as a petitioner seeking to rebuild relations. Between Edward and Godwine would soon be evidence of that gradual erosion of trust where two parties are unsure whether to embrace or attack each other. In that non-dialogue, friendship and menace elide, and neither party knows whether the tide is turning.

---

[54] ASC D, 1052 [1051].

[55] ASC E is better informed than D, which seems to associate the incident with Eustace's arrival in England, though the chronicler may have abridged events: ASC E, 1048 [1051].

[56] F. M. Stenton, *Anglo-Saxon England* (Oxford, 3rd edn, 1971), p. 554; S. Baxter, 'The Earls of Mercia and Their Commended Men in the Mid Eleventh Century', *ANS* 23 (2001), 23–46, at p. 34, n. 75.

No source implies that Edward had been expecting an incident at Dover, and from the king's perspective it was better to punish a few burgesses than to seem weak and erode the fragile friendship with Boulogne. Godwine on the other hand cared little for Boulogne and realized that an enemy had manoeuvred him into a storm. It was not only the latest in what the earl perceived as a series of wrongs, but the worst. The king had seemingly accepted the version he had from Eustace without regard for justice, and this was all too much for a man long accustomed to getting his way. The fracas, followed by the king's response, drove him to uncharacteristic opposition. Protesting Edward's order, he began to assemble an army at Beverstone in Gloucestershire near where the king was staying, gathering men from all over his earldom. Swegn and Harold joined him, swelling his forces with theirs. E, which stands up for the earl, claims they gathered their troops to seek the king's advice on how to avenge the insult the foreigners had done to Edward and the realm. But D unmasks the threat that was posed by 'a great and countless army all ready for war against the king unless Eustace and his men were given into their hands, likewise the French who were in the castle'.[57]

John of Worcester later guessed that 'the castle' referred to the burh at Dover, but since Eustace and his men had been driven from there, E is surely correct in referring to the castle in Herefordshire where – the rebels alleged – foreigners had 'inflicted every injury and insult they could upon the king's men'.[58] As a partisan account, E is useful because it shows that Swegn resented the Norman presence in his earldom and cited it as a grievance in support of his father's argument that foreigners were harming the realm. The crucial point is that when Godwine and his sons took up arms they had to decide which enemies they might overcome and devise a narrative that would allow the king to capitulate with dignity. The enemies they targeted were parvenus whose ambitions conflicted with their own. Their narrative asserted that foreigners were harming the realm. Edward could demonstrate resolve (i.e. back down) by punishing the foreigners in question.

The rebels put their demands to Edward on 1 September.[59] He could only temporize, having failed to perceive the magnitude of Godwine's grievance and the inflammatory effect of his order to punish Dover. Alleging a need for deliberation, he sent orders to his earls that they should come to the royal palace of Gloucester on the feast of the Nativity on 8 September. Leofric and Siward arrived with moderate support, 'but

[57] ASC E, 1048 [1051]; D 1052 [1051].

[58] ASC E, 1048 [1051] and *JW*, ii, p. 561. It is unlikely Frenchmen lingered in the burh at Dover after Godwine summoned the forces of his earldom against them.

[59] ASC D, 1052 [1051]; *JW*, ii, p. 561, claims they did so after the feast of St Mary on 8 September, probably because he misread a reference to 'the later feast of St Mary' (cf. ASC D) as 'later' (i.e. after the feast).

after they knew how it was there in the south, they sent north all over their earldoms – and Earl Ralph also over his – and had a great army called out for the support of their lord'.[60] Their response reveals that in this case there was no doubt that the line between lawful remonstrance and rebellion had been crossed. At Gloucester, Edward complained of Godwine's treason, and the earl was formally charged in his absence.[61] The royal army mustering there was ready to attack the rebels, but the king was apprised of the evils of civil war and devised a safer plan to overcome his opponents by the stealth of his prerogative. Granting his peace to both sides, he deferred judgment until a meeting of the witan, to be held at Southwark on 24 September. It was the autumn equinox, when day and night were equal, and justice would hang in the balance. A summons was sent out across the land. Edward then called out the fyrd north and south of the Thames, forcing men of the levies who had rallied to the rebel earls to choose between serving the king and disobeying his mandate. As Edward's forces swelled and the rebel host dwindled, Godwine and his sons received a summons of their own: they were to attend the council at Southwark to answer charges against them.

Fifteen years later, Folcard claimed that Robert of Jumièges had convinced Edward that Godwine was plotting to harm him, as he had supposedly plotted against Alfred in 1036. He complained that the accusation was unfounded, blaming Robert's malice. What Folcard does not mention is the rebel army Edward could see for himself. If his advisors sensed a threat and reminded him of 1036 their advice was apposite. Edward, in any case, did not need to be told that he had put Godwine to the test and found him rebellious. As king, he was within his rights to be angry that earls, caught up in their grievances, failed to see the bigger picture of kingly obligations, which required him to respond to the incident in Dover. At Gloucester, Godwine was charged with plotting against the king. The charges were laid in his absence, because the rebel earls were refused access to the king, for fear they might harm him.[62] In the breakdown of dialogue which was fast occurring, Edward had committed the affront of siding first with Eustace, then indicting Godwine in his absence. E, like the *Vita*, blames the foreigners for turning Edward's mind, arguing that the earl found it abhorrent that he had to make a stand against his lord. E, nevertheless, retains the awkward facts omitted from the *Vita*: that Godwine had disobeyed the king's order and raised an army against him.[63]

When Godwine arrived in Southwark prior to the meeting, his suspicions were growing. Though the fact he was being readmitted to the king's

---

[60] ASC D, 1052 [1051].

[61] *Vita*, p. 35.

[62] Ibid.; ASC E, 1048 [1051].

[63] ASC E, 1048 [1051].

presence suggested the king wanted to reopen dialogue, Godwine feared that his opponents had manipulated the king and would block the path to reconciliation. Worse, he could not be sure Edward had had no hand in a plot to undermine him. Remembering talk at Gloucester, that hostages should be exchanged, his first move was to demand safe-conduct and hostages, that he might come and go without treachery.[64] But the balance of power had shifted in favour of the king, whose response was to demand the service of the thegns who were accompanying the rebels, either as levies or as commended men. E's claim that all the thegns were dutifully surrendered serves to present the rebels as compliant, but D indicates that only Harold's thegns were handed over to the king. For Godwine and Swegn to have delivered all theirs as well would be tantamount to capitulation. Edward responded by outlawing Swegn, who was still on probation after his restoration that summer. His failure to obey royal orders was a violation of the terms.

Edward was exploiting a division exposed by Harold and Swegn's differing responses to his mandate. It is likely that by this stage he wanted rid of Swegn, but his intention regarding Godwine and Harold was to bring them to heel. As a token of that intention he ordered them now to present themselves at the assembly in a company of twelve men. According to Cnut's laws, which Edward had sworn to uphold, a person who stood accused of plotting against the king could clear himself by undergoing a triple ordeal. He would start by choosing five men as oath-helpers and be himself a sixth.[65] By commanding Godwine and Harold to attend in a company of twelve Edward was initiating that process. He was within his rights to refuse hostages to the defendants, because they had no right to them under the law. The ordeal was a way of assessing the validity of the oath by direct appeal to God as supreme witness.[66] The triple ordeal involved carrying a red-hot piece of iron, weighing three pounds, nine feet or plunging the arm elbow-deep in boiling water to lift out a stone. A burn that was clean after three days was proof of innocence, but a festering wound determined guilt. In the case of a man accused of plotting against the king, guilt meant death and the forfeiture of all possessions, though a judge might decree exile.[67] Godwine, understandably, feared a plot against him. Again, he demanded safe-conduct and hostages, as a precondition to the chance to clear his name. Then Edward sent Stigand to Godwine's house in Southwark to deliver an ultimatum.

[64] ASC D, 1052 [1051] implies that it was decided at Gloucester that hostages should be exchanged at some point in the future, but we are not told that they were.

[65] ASC E 1048 [1051]; II Cnut 57; and 30, § 3a (Laws, pp. 204, 190); on oath-helpers, see J. Hudson, The Oxford History of the Laws of England, vol. 2: 871–1216 (Oxford, 2012), pp. 81–2; and Lambert, Law and Order, p. 255.

[66] J. D. Niles, 'Trial by Ordeal in Anglo-Saxon England: What's the Problem with Barley?', in Baxter et al., eds, Early Medieval Studies, 369–82, at pp. 371–2.

[67] II Cnut 17 (Laws, p. 204).

Stigand was an acceptable mediator. As events would show, he was no friend to Robert, who despised his protégé Spearhafoc. Yet he was also a man broken by the king for a lesser offence than the one Godwine was committing, who had learned his lesson, served the king loyally, and been restored to favour. Godwine, he declared, could hope for the king's peace only when he gave him back his brother alive, along with all his men and their possessions which had been taken from them.[68] The impossible demand proved the point. Godwine, as everyone knew, could not return Alfred because the earl had acted upon worse royal orders than an order to punish Dover. Either he was a willing executive who could have no qualms about ravaging the burh, or he chose which orders to follow and was therefore culpable for Alfred's capture and, by the same reasoning, for rebellion in the Dover affair. Edward had exposed Godwine's hypocrisy and was one move away from checkmate. It was time for the earl and his son to back down and accept a way out. Godwine, however, was incapable of yielding. Overturning the table even as Stigand pleaded for sense, he rode for Bosham that night. His sons escaped too. Since the defendants had failed to make a formal denial at the proof stage, their guilt was effectively established, and it was up to the assembly to decide their punishment.[69] In the morning, the king and the witan outlawed them.

There can be no doubt that this was a saddening turn of events. True, Godwine might have resolved the affair by undergoing the ordeal, just as Edward might have rescued it by guaranteeing his father-in-law an escape route. Yet it is enough to observe the shadow of Alfred over the conflict to perceive the pain and confusion clouding the judgement of both sides. Justice for the dead weighed heavily in that society: in Alfred's case, it was doubtful whether the debt had been paid. From one perspective, the Godwines were an overweening faction that dominated the king. From another they were the adopted family of an exile who had lost two families in succession. For nine years Godwine and his sons had served Edward loyally. Even Swegn's offences were not directed against the king. Nor is there any evidence that Edward himself had been planning to be rid of them. D says that to everyone in England their fall could scarcely have been imaginable 'when formerly Godwine stood so high in Edward's favour, and his sons were earls and the king's favourites, and his daughter married to the king'.[70] It was a way of saying that the proper order had been upset.

On hearing of Godwine's flight, Robert sent a large force of soldiers from the royal palace to pursue him, while another troop under Bishop Ealdred went to intercept Harold and his younger brother Leofwine, who were sailing west for Bristol. But Ealdred, unlike Robert, shared the king's

---

[68] *Vita*, p. 37.
[69] On the process in such cases, see Lambert, *Law and Order*, p. 254; *Vita*, p. 37.
[70] ASC D, 1052 [1051].

restraint, and he 'could not or would not' apprehend them.[71] Exile had its own lessons to teach, as Edward knew well. For a time, bad weather detained Harold's party in the mouth of the Avon. As soon as it cleared, they sailed for Ireland. Godwine, Gytha his wife, Swegn, the newly-wed Tostig, and Gyrth, a younger brother, had meanwhile gathered their treasures and set sail for Bruges, where Baldwin would offer comfort and assistance.

The routing of the rebels reveals the adroitness of Edward's manoeuvring. Stalling, he increased his strength while weakening his opponents by exploiting his prerogative. Harold he had coaxed into giving up his thegns; Swegn he confounded by withdrawing his pardon; Godwine he isolated and finally trapped in a knotty point of law. If Robert was the king's advisor, it is easy to see why he valued his advice even against his better judgement. Forced to confront a rebellion arising from an order he could not withdraw, he had little choice but to connive at the machinations that brought about the incident at Dover, out of which the whole unwonted conflict erupted. As king, he had no option but to uphold his office, lest rebellion be seen to go unpunished. At the same time, he intimated his willingness to offer a way out by providing for the earls to clear themselves. Godwine's unanticipated flight reinvented the crisis. Had the earl been sensitive to subtleties, Stigand's plea might have offered a clue that the king – who had twice reinstated Swegn – sought reconciliation. It would necessarily have involved Godwine's grovelling submission and readmission into the king's favour. Possibly that would have been enough for his enemies. Instead Godwine had upped the brinkmanship. Edward was not so naïve to imagine he would go quietly. At the same time, the banishment of the rebels offered temporary relief from the tensions that had been brewing in the polity.

Edward could now give serious thought to a problem that had exacerbated those tensions. Soon after the earls' banishment, he seized Edith's assets and placed her in the custody of his sister, the abbess of Wherwell nunnery in Hampshire.[72] E, implying formal separation, states he 'put her aside'. The *Vita*, which is less blunt, depicts Robert as the schemer who instigated divorce plans, which the king 'did not reject'.[73] He deemed that point admissible because the king he admired was acting under a malign influence. Neither source provides an insight into Edward's motives, but the timing is revealing, for it suggests that discussions about a divorce may have fuelled the row between Edward and his in-laws. The king most probably wanted a bride who could provide him with an heir and was thinking of divorcing Edith for that reason, though other sources of

---

[71] Ibid. The annal hints at discretion.
[72] ASC E, 1048 [1051]; Folcard, who closely associates Edith with Wilton, gives Wilton instead of Wherwell. The sister was a half sister, we assume.
[73] ASC E, 1048 [1051]; *Vita*, p. 37.

tension, such as possible charges of adultery, cannot be ruled out.[74] Certainly, Edward was under pressure and in a mood to believe evil accusations in 1051.

Notions of the indissolubility of marriage had not hardened into stricture, but they were moving in that direction, and there was the additional difficulty that Edith was a consecrated queen. Both obstacles could be got around with the help of a concession in ecclesiastical law, which permitted remarriage to a divorcee if his spouse entered a monastery.[75] There was no precedent in Anglo-Saxon England for divorcing a woman on the presupposition that she was barren, though a king less scrupulous than Edward, encouraged by a scheming advisor, might have done as he pleased. Still, if Edith could be induced to become a nun, Edward might remarry without censure. At Wherwell, she would be poised to take the veil; by taking it she would renounce her queenship and estate, while freeing her husband to marry a woman who might provide an heir. Yet there is no evidence she did take the veil. And Edward veiled his intentions. As the *Vita* relays, he entertained Robert's designs only to a point.

Edward's deliberation was religious as well as political. There was much to be said for trusting in God. Childless couples in the Bible had done so and been blessed, and only a year before, in 1050, the six-year-old marriage of the emperor Henry III and Agnes of Poitou had yielded a son.[76] Edward had been married six years in 1051, and Folcard describes him as *caelebs*, meaning faithful to his wife.[77] Elsewhere in the *Vita*, Folcard refers to Tostig as *caelebs* too.[78] If this provides an insight into Edward's attitudes to marriage, divorce might have offended his sensibilities. The heightened respect for wedlock which is implied accords with his heightened devotion to the saints, revealed by his pilgrimage on foot to St Edmund. Edward retained not only childhood experiences of a climate of penitential fervour, but also his father's anxiety about incurring divine displeasure. Exile and restoration had taught him patience; that God blesses those who wait on Him. Yet it was his energetic instinct that had urged him on to secure the throne. Without an heir, his bloodline would die; and he was fast nearing the age his father was when he died. Yet whatever might be decided by him or God, his immediate problem was familial conflict, which divorce could only inflame. By placing Edith where she could neither harm nor conspire, he kept his options open.

---

[74] Stafford, *Emma and Edith*, p. 265.

[75] *Das altenglische Bussbuch: (sog. Confessionale pseudo-Egberti) ein Beitrag zu den kirchlichen Gesetzen der Angelsachsen*, ed. R. Spindler (Leipzig, 1934), pp. 180–1.

[76] Stafford, *Emma and Edith*, p. 264. At the age of thirty-two, however, the emperor was a much younger man.

[77] Cf. Baxter, 'Succession Question', pp. 84–5.

[78] *Vita*, p. 50. The noun 'caelebs' is the subject of the sentence. It is a metonym for Tostig, meaning 'the chaste man'. Barlow's translation on p. 51 obscures the metonymy by inserting 'and' before 'chastely'; but Freeman read the passage correctly: *NC*, II, pp. 539–40.

The flight of the rebel earls left vacancies for Edward's supporters. Swegn's former command in the south-west midlands was divided between Leofric of Mercia, who took charge of Oxfordshire and Worcestershire – unless Ealdred commanded the latter – and Osbern Pentecost in Herefordshire, who was left to defend the march, receiving comital manors and the earl's third penny to sustain his administration. Ealdred, who had pursued Harold to Bristol, appears once again to have been performing an earl's military duties in Gloucestershire, where he fought Gruffudd ap Rhydderch and his pirates in 1049.[79] The south-western shires of Dorset, Somerset, Devon, and Cornwall were assigned to Edward's kinsman Odda, a responsible elder statesman who had served Edward's father as well as Cnut's dynasty.[80] The eastern half of Wessex remained vacant under the king's officials. This was a region that included large parts of Godwine's patrimony and where his support was strongest. The *Vita* says that some across the land openly declared for the exiled earl.[81] If that is true, Edward had cause to make his presence felt there, though Robert may have briefly assumed a comital role in Kent. Siward possibly received Huntingdonshire, but the bulk of Harold's East Anglian earldom went to Ælfgar, son of Earl Leofric.[82] Meanwhile, Edward yielded in his stand-off with the archbishop and, by extension, the pope, neither of whom he could offend any longer, by expelling Spearhafoc from London. Stuffing money-bags with gold and gems acquired from the king for making a crown, the artful goldsmith departed the realm, never to return.[83] His place was taken by one of Edward's chaplains, William, another Norman. It certainly seemed Robert was now implanted at the helm.

THE VISIT OF DUKE WILLIAM

The ship of state sailed onwards into darkness, now dissipating, now gathering over an ever-changing horizon. Edward had expelled a powerful and dangerous kinship group with allies in Denmark, Flanders, and Ireland. Advisors told him Godwine wanted him dead, and few kings

[79] Williams, *World before Domesday*, pp. 23, 143; and Baxter, 'Succession Question', notes to Map 5. Ealdred had commanded the levies in Swegn's absence, when Gruffudd and his allies were raiding in Gloucestershire, and pursued Harold through Gloucestershire in 1051.

[80] A. Williams, *Land, Power and Politics: the Family and Career of Odda of Deerhurst* (Deerhurst: The Deerhurst Lecture, 1997).

[81] *Vita*, p. 41.

[82] I speculate about Robert, in view of the gap left by Godwine's absence, and in view of the archbishop's comital role before 1044. For the other reassignments, see Baxter, 'Succession Question', Map 5; cf. S 1107, for Siward's authority in Huntingdonshire.

[83] *Historia Ecclesie Abbendonensis: The History of the Church of Abingdon*, ed. and tr. J. Hudson, OMT, 2 vols (Oxford, 2002–7), I, p. 196.

could have been more aware of the throne's precariousness. His uncle, Edward the Martyr, had been murdered. His father had been overthrown. There was a danger something bad would happen to him. Across the Channel, the young duke William had passed through storms. In 1047, with the aid of the French king, he had overcome his opponents at the battle of Val-ès-Dunes, strengthening his hold on the duchy. By 1051 he had appeased the pope and sealed his marriage with Flanders. Meanwhile, Henry of France was helpfully distracting the energies of his aggressive neighbour, Count Geoffrey of Anjou. Conflict with both lay in the future but could not be foreseen. Nor could William have known that his uncle, William of Arques, would also turn against him. In 1051 he still attended the ducal entourage.[84] Like Eustace before him, William had a moment to turn his attention to England, where Edward wished to entertain him. That autumn, he crossed to visit his kinsman with a large troop of companions and enjoyed the king's hospitality.[85] He would ascertain the drift of Edward's thinking now Godwine and his sons were driven out and Edward had rid himself of Edith.

The timing of William's visit suggests that Edward's motive in inviting him was to counter the threat of the exiles, and their allies at home and abroad, by securing the duke's undertaking to assist in any emergency. William's grandfather Richard II had assisted in 1013–14 when Æthelred lost his throne, and he had done so again c. 1016 when Edward fled to Normandy. Both Edward and William had spent long enough at the Norman court to have heard Dudo's story about Rollo rescuing an English king from the rebels who threatened his realm. Now there was a need for a similar understanding, in case rebels returned to England with ships full of allies. A bit of political balancing was required. Edward could not expect William (nor the latter consent) to brandish arms against Baldwin, his father-in-law. What he could ask was that William be ready to assist him if Godwine and his sons sought out Norman harbours or came into Edward's realm with violence. William's arrival in England with a large troop of Normans was a warning to everybody that the king was prepared to summon help, even to lay the realm open to foreign attack in the event of civil war. It was another example of the strong messages Edward liked to send.

Princes put in place such arrangements to preserve peace when conflict threatened to erupt. Obtaining William's support was a way of neutralizing the threat posed by Baldwin. Privately Baldwin and William might resolve not to escalate the conflict, in much the same way as Edward and Henry of France mustered their forces in 1049, on opposing sides in the conflict between the emperor and Baldwin, without offering their allies military assistance. Neither Baldwin nor William is known to have sent

---

[84] Bauduin, *La première Normandie*, p. 309
[85] ASC D, 1052 [1051]; *JW*, ii, p. 563.

troops into England in 1052, when the rebel earls would return, though the fear of attacks from such quarters registers in the C/D entry for that year, which refers to the concerns that many seem to have had, that civil war would lay the country more open to foreign attack.[86] For William it was an opportunity to visit his relations, including the famous Emma, whom he may not have met. Nearing death, she had lived to see the banishment of the earl she blamed for Alfred's murder, and it may have been her wish too that her great-nephew should visit. She was, after all, a letter writer with a track record of inviting over relatives in Normandy. With the departure of Edward's Godwinson in-laws, it was time for his Norman family to pull together. If moved to rethink his relationships, the king could remind William how close he had been to his father. They could feast together. Just as Edward's father in a phase of anxiety learned to appreciate his departed mentor Bishop Æthelwold, Edward now had the opportunity of the crisis to draw closer to Robert's son.[87] If William resembled Robert, there was a visual cue. Whether in such a scenario Edward might have come to regard William as a potential heir is a crucial question, though not one any writer considered at the time.

Could we be a fly on the wall, it would certainly be at that meeting, for what transpired between Edward and William has overshadowed the reign. In later years various kinsmen of Edward, including Harold, William, and Sven Estrithsson, claimed he had promised them the throne, but no source written before 1066 implies he offered it to any of them. All the sources written after his death by supporters of the rival claimants are suspect because they cannot be corroborated, contradict each other (and sometimes themselves), and are manifestly engaging in legitimization. Men who seize power invent justifications for their actions. The basic story circulated by William's supporters was that Edward promised him the throne because he was Edward's deserving kinsman. There were embellishments on the theme and minor variations. Putting that aside for a moment, a better way of thinking about the problem is to approach it by inductive reasoning. The question we need to address is whether Edward ever considered who might succeed him in the absence of an heir of Cerdic's blood. Since this was a natural and pressing interest for a king in his position, the question should rather be, when might he have thought about it? The answer is when he feared he might die in that situation, or when he realized he might not have children. In 1051, he was in danger and sent away his wife. It was a moment when his thoughts could well have turned to the question we are addressing.

Our next step is to examine evidence from the sources. The record of William's visit in 1051 sheds no light on Edward's intentions for the succession because it can be explained by his need to forge alliances to combat an

[86] ASC C/D, 1052.
[87] Above, p. 18.

urgent danger. It does, however, place William with the king when worries about the succession were probably weighing on his mind. Jumièges, a supporter of William writing in defence of the Conquest c. 1069, was seemingly unaware of the visit, yet he provides circumstantial detail that reinforces the impression that Edward and William had a conversation about the throne c. 1051. The detail he provides is that Edward, allegedly, sent Archbishop Robert of Canterbury to name the duke as his heir; and given that Robert only commanded authority in England as an archbishop in the years 1051–2, it seems to point us to negotiations occurring at that time.[88] In the mid-1070s, Poitiers reworked and embellished Jumièges' account of William's career, adding that Robert conveyed hostages to the duke as pledges of Edward's commitment.[89] Jumièges does not mention the hostages, so Poitiers must have linked them to the arrangements about the succession independently. We know from other sources that the hostages were Godwine's son Wulfnoth and Swegn's son Hakon, Godwine's grandson.[90] They were delivered to William in the same window of time, in 1051–2, as we shall see below. By bringing in the hostages, Poitiers, like Jumièges, seems to provide independent detail pointing to an arrangement made in 1051 about the succession. He too makes no mention – so seems to be unaware – of William's visit to England that year.

Taken together, it looks as if it may add up to something. We have Edward at the moment he would have been thinking about the succession, with circumstantial detail from Jumièges and separate detail from Poitiers pointing to the same year. All of this nevertheless begins to fall apart when we pick away at Poitiers. First, it is important to note that Poitiers' account is responding to Jumièges' defence of the Conquest and to the slightly earlier account (1067–8) by Bishop Guy of Amiens. A vital detail from Guy which he altered was the story about the pledges, for whereas Guy makes William's character say that the pledges Edward had given him were a ring and a sword, conveyed by Harold, Poitiers replaces the ring and sword with hostages brought by Robert.[91] While the ring and sword, along with the crown and sceptre, were certainly royal insignia for investing a king, the first two could also be used to invest a follower with land or office, or merely be gifts. Poitiers realized the hostages seemed like a more impressive pledge, and since he knew Robert had conveyed them to William, he took the detail about pledges, linked it to Robert's conveyance of a promise to the duke (a detail found in Jumièges), and landed on the idea that the hostages were a pledge for the throne.

Poitiers' separate detail pointing to 1051 is therefore incidental, insofar as Jumièges put him on the scent. His idea that the hostages were a pledge

[88] *GND*, II, p. 158
[89] *GG*, pp. 19, 121.
[90] See below, p. 154.
[91] *Carmen*, p. 20. Cf. *GG*, pp. 19, 121.

was either pure surmise or a lie to improve Guy's pledge story, which must reflect a story told by William's supporters shortly after the Conquest. (Jumièges does not mention pledges.) This still leaves the likelihood that Edward was worrying about the succession when William visited, and Jumièges' claim that Robert conveyed a promise to William, presumably in 1051–2. The problem with making an argument out of it is the *Vita's* assertion that Robert was masterminding a royal divorce, for Edward would only have contemplated divorcing Godwine's daughter – a move that would destroy foundational alliances and endanger his position – if the higher priority of procuring an heir obliged him to remarry. By mentioning Robert's scheme and Edward's interest in it, Folcard risked destroying the picture he was painting of marital harmony between the king and queen, so we should trust his testimony. It means, of course, that the very figure whose involvement seems to confirm the making of the promise in 1051 was pursuing a policy that was incompatible with that promise. Robert either wanted Edward to remarry, or he wanted William to be his heir. Edward's thoughts about the succession, in other words, were not on William but on how to procure a blood-heir, and Robert was investigating divorce as one of the options. Jumièges, seventeen years later, recalled that Robert came to Normandy in 1052 and assumed he must have been the person who conveyed the promise of the throne, which had been rumoured since 1066.[92]

It always bears repeating that if Edward promised William the throne, Norman worthies such as the monk of Saint-Wandrille, writing in the mid-1050s, and Jumièges, compiling the first part of his work up to *c.* 1063, would have shouted it from the rooftops. A telling change Poitiers made when rewriting Jumièges was his insertion of a notice of the promise in the pre-Conquest section.[93] Jumièges never included such a notice where it should have come in the timeline later espoused by William's apologists, because, at the time he wrote (prior to 1063), the story of the promise had not been invented. In fact, the first portion of his work conveys the impression that the Normans had done a good deal for Edward, without the favour being repaid. He then attempts a transition to the second section, in which William, all of a sudden, is in Edward's debt for having been promised the throne. We can try to rescue the Norman sources by proposing a compromise scenario in which Edward wanted William to succeed him if no heir of the blood came forth. Norman writers might have been reluctant to record such an arrangement, since doing so could work to the duke's disadvantage if a blood-heir emerged. The danger of twisting the facts and alleging an unconditional promise was that it might anger the king, who could withdraw it. If Edward made a conditional arrangement of this variety the silence of pre-Conquest sources can

---

[92] *MSE*, p. 63.
[93] *GG*, pp. 21, 69.

be squared with their insistence that an agreement of some kind was reached.

There is, however, a problem even here. English kings could not simply promise away the throne. The authority to confer it lay with the witan, as demonstrated in the deliberations of 1035–6, 1040, and 1041, when Godwine's faction spoke for the witan on Edward's behalf. Edward could nevertheless do as he wished in signalling who should succeed him, and there were no conventions around who that should be in the absence of an heir of the blood. Those were uncharted waters. What was clear was that heirs of the blood took precedence over other aspiring claimants. The proofs of this convention lay in the fact that nobody besides the royal sons of Wessex had been called 'aetheling' (throneworthy), and in the fact that in all the time Cerdic's ancestors had been the reigning dynasty in Wessex and over all England, no one but them – barring usurpers and their whelps – had risen to obtain the throne. In 1014, the witan recalled Æthelred because 'no lord was dearer to them than their natural lord'.[94] In 1041 the leaders recalled Edward after twenty-four years because of his blood-title, the uniqueness of which had sustained him in exile and secured him the throne. Given his contacts in Germany and Norway, he should have been aware that Edmund Ironside's sons were in Hungary, and that if he died childless the witan would offer the throne to them. Though we may be certain Edward made gifts to William in 1051, he could hardly have treated him as his first or even second choice as successor.

SHIPS ON THE HORIZON

Like a sequel to the struggles of 1049, the cold conflict between England and Flanders was renewing itself. On the one hand, the count harboured and energized Edward's enemies. On the other, the king deployed a minatory William, and retained Eustace, who had become detached from Baldwin, as potential back-up. Baldwin responded by persuading his brother-in-law Henry of France to dispatch ambassadors to Edward's court, appealing for Godwine's restoration. Baldwin too sent ambassadors to Edward in the winter of 1051–2, when the earl was in Bruges.[95] In matters of diplomacy he calculated that Edward's cordial relations with the French king were a better route to securing the outcome he wanted, but on this occasion Henry's entreaties fell on deaf ears, and the latter was left to contemplate the possibility that William enjoyed more traction with Edward than *he* did. Emma, whose view of these events is not recorded, died on 6 March 1052. In later years the epigrammist Godfrey of Winchester would represent her as a gemstone whose virtues shone more

---

[94] ASC E, 1014.
[95] *Vita*, p. 41.

brightly than her splendours.[96] Her funeral in Winchester, where she was buried beside Cnut, evoked complex relationships. Whatever Edward felt about his mother, waves of sadness follow such losses and must have swelled those already washing over him after the unexpected exiling of his third family.

When the campaigning season arrived that year, Gruffudd ap Rhydderch led a war band up the Wye valley near the eastern tip of his kingdom and raided in Herefordshire, almost as far as Leominster.[97] On his previous raid in 1049 he had surprised the levies led by Bishop Ealdred, whose chronicler, D, complained of traitors in the ranks and a lack of support. This time he encountered not only the levies but also a troop of French (possibly Normans) 'from the castle'. As in the account of the events of September 1051, only one castle is mentioned – probably the castle at Hereford held by Osbern Pentecost, who was deputizing as earl in Swegn's absence. The impact of the encounter, in which numerous English and French were killed fighting side by side, may have reminded the king to reinforce the march. It may well explain the decision, at roughly that date, to build a second castle – Richard's castle – north of the one at Hereford. At least on this occasion there was no mention of treachery. The French garrison was loyal to Edward, a fact which vindicated his decision to plant it there in the first place, in the porous Wye valley, where loyalties were fluid.

Gruffudd, as in 1049, chose a moment when the king was distracted, for Edward and the witan had taken the decision to deploy forty longships at Sandwich under the command of Earl Ralph and Earl Odda. Though the strategy limited their military capabilities in the west, it countered the developing threat from Flanders. Godwine readied his forces in the River Yser. On 22 June, he sailed to Dungeness on the tip of the Kentish coast. It is hard to judge what he intended to do because we do not know how many ships he commanded.[98] From this point the chronicles diverge. C and D, which are substantially the same here, having a common source, claim the earl won over many to his cause and swelled his ranks with supporters. E is better informed about the events unfolding in the southeast, and though the author favoured the earl, he is also clear that his chief device was coercion. The *Vita* provides an account not unlike that in E, but it exaggerates the extent of the earl's support, claiming that all available Englishmen in the south and east came flocking to him like children

[96] Godfrey of Winchester, *Epigrammata Historica*, II, in *The Anglo-Latin Satirical Poets and Epigrammatists of the Twelfth Century*, ed. T. Wright, RS 59, 2 vols (London, 1872), II, p. 148

[97] It is often supposed that the king involved was Gruffudd ap Llewelyn (not least because the raid occurred on the anniversary of the latter's battle with Eadwine in the Shropshire marches in 1039), but a stronger case can be made for his namesake: T. M. Charles-Edwards, *Wales and the Britons 350–1064* (Oxford, 2013), p. 564. The assumption may derive from an erroneous inference made by John of Worcester: *JW*, ii, p. 567.

[98] *JW*, ii, p. 569: 'a few ships'; *Vita*, p. 41, perhaps exaggerating, 'a large fleet'.

to their long-awaited father.[99] Its rosy picture of a triumphal return was created to please Edith *c.* 1066. Even the chroniclers wrote from hindsight after what was judged to be a happy outcome, so they too were inclined to smooth over – if not always to deny – unsettling elements of the campaign.

According to E, when the earls at Sandwich learned of Godwine's arrival they sailed around the coast in pursuit, and a land-army was ordered out against him. Though it could not have taken long for a message from Edward's watchmen to reach the fleet, the C/D version claims that Godwine was able to entice to him all the Kentish and the boatmen from Hastings and all the coastal area around, and all Essex and Surrey and other support in addition.[100] He did all of this supposedly before the earls learned of his arrival and set out after him. In conjuring up images of his secret campaign, the C/D version provides a glimpse of rumours that were circulating, including a belief – or fear – that Godwine commanded support in the south-east. Its reference to secret negotiations smacks of retrospective surmise that served to account for the large following Godwine later brought to London, although the idea that he had come to rendezvous with supporters should not be dismissed. E, a Kentish account, is more credible on what he accomplished. It says that when Godwine was warned about the earls' seaward approach he sailed to Pevensey, away from his pursuers. His plan therefore was not to fight them. Bad weather descended. The earls lost sight of their quarry and were obliged to return to Sandwich, and Godwine to Bruges. His reconnaissance mission had been curtailed.

In France that summer King Henry was manoeuvring to tilt the balance of powers in his favour. It would involve an overhaul, even a reversal, of alliances, but Henry perceived that the game had changed. Since the 1040s he had allied with William against the overly mighty count of Anjou, Geoffrey Martel. (His name meant 'The Hammer'.) He now abandoned that strategy and made peace with Count Geoffrey on 15 August 1052. William, who must have heard of this *volte face*, was in for an uncomfortable summer. He is last recorded in Henry's company near Orléans on 20 September 1052. Afterwards, relations between the two would deteriorate into war.[101] Henry's motives are a mystery, but the following factors are salient. First, William was looking more dangerous after triumphs over Geoffrey in their proxy war in Maine during the winter of 1051–2. At that point, Geoffrey would have urged Henry that William had gone too far. Second, William had manoeuvred into a position in which both Flanders and England were bidding for his support.

[99] *Vita*, pp. 41–3.

[100] ASC C/D, 1052.

[101] O. Guillot, *Le comte d'Anjou et son entourage au XIe siècle*, 2 vols (Paris, 1972), I, p. 79; Bates, *William*, pp. 125–6.

This could only have aroused suspicion in Henry and in his northern followers, such as the counts of Boulogne and Ponthieu. Henry had empowered a young duke who was beginning to outshine his master. Third, of course, if there was any talk of William becoming Edward's client, Henry had cause for concern.

Power was also shifting in Ireland, around Harold and Leofwine, who had sailed there from Bristol the previous autumn. The *Vita* names their host as Diarmait mac Máel na mBó, who was king of Dublin at the time it was written. He evidently had been Harold's ally, for he sheltered Harold's sons after the Conquest.[102] In 1051, however, the king of Dublin was the Hiberno-Scandinavian ruler Echmarcach, who also dominated the kingdom of the Isles, which included the Isle of Man and Galloway.[103] Diarmait at that time was king in Leinster. Harold and Leofwine found themselves in his company just as he was preparing to expand his realm. In 1052, Diarmait finally expelled Echmarcach and took command of Dublin. If Echmarcach was Edward's client and Diarmait was not, the turnaround in Dublin played to the rebels' advantage; and it roughly co-incided with the departure of Harold and Leofwine that summer to raid the south west of England.

The nine ships Harold and Leofwine took with them were manned either by their own men or hirelings, active possibly because of the current tumult. They set out for the Bristol Channel and landed at Porlock in Somerset, near the Devon border. There they seized cattle, 'people', and property.[104] Slave raids were ugly affairs, typically involving the slaughter of men and the seizure of women and children for an overseas market. Normally they targeted foreign peoples deemed to be barbarous and infe-rior, but on this occasion the brothers were shaming Edward by enslaving his English subjects.[105] Heading inland, they ran into a force from the two shires, which drove them back to their ships but with the loss of more than thirty thegns and many ordinary soldiers. The raiding party then sailed round Land's End and into the English Channel. They too must have suffered losses, and they resolved at this point to seek out Godwine and his other sons and join forces.

In the meantime, Edward recalled his ships to London to exchange the commanders and oarsmen for fresh ones. This allowed for the deployment of Earl Ralph in Herefordshire and Earl Odda in Somerset where raids had occurred that summer. Yet in a repeat of the sorts of difficulties that had dogged his father, the business of exchanging the crews was delayed so long that the ship-campaign was abandoned, and they all made their

[102] *Vita*, p. 41; and p. 40, note 94.

[103] Hudson, 'Cnut', pp. 355–6; McDonald, *The Kingdom of the Isles*, p. 33.

[104] ASC E, 1052.

[105] D. A. E. Pelteret, *Slavery in Early Medieval England from the Reign of Alfred until the Twelfth Century* (Woodbridge, 1995), p. 72.

way home. Perhaps the king was struggling to find fresh crews in the coastal regions where Godwine's support lay; and it was not a time to annoy his subjects with the burden of continued deployment. When his spies relayed the news, Godwine and his fleet sailed straight to the Isle of Wight, where they raided until the inhabitants paid what they wanted. Then they set out westwards to the isle of Portland, a royal estate, and attacked that. Thereabouts, after Godwine's fleet joined Harold's, they all turned east again to the Isle of Wight to collect plunder they had stashed. Safety in numbers would counter the danger that heavily laden ships might be intercepted.

The rebel campaign now gained momentum. Advancing to Pevensey, the leaders of the flotilla commandeered all the ships that were fit for service. When they came to Dungeness, they seized ships from Romney, Hythe, and Folkestone before heading around to Dover and Sandwich, taking ships, hostages, and supplies. The C/D version remarks that the rebel earls 'enticed to them all the local people along the sea-coast and up inland'. If Godwine did find supporters, it was either because he had commended men in those areas, or because the cost of maintaining the royal fleet that year had fallen heavily on the ports he targeted. Edward's abolition of the heregeld had pleased ratepayers, and ports had received assorted privileges, but now that they were feeling the burden of the king's demands, murmurings of discontent were inevitable. It is telling that Edward, uncharacteristically, sent home the ships before the danger passed. E, nevertheless, maintains that the men of the ports had little choice but to do Godwine's bidding. Contrary to what the *Vita* claims, they did not flock to him as to a long-awaited father. No father figure needs to take hostages.[106]

When Edward learned that the rebels were at Sandwich with a great flotilla, he sent for more help, but it came too slowly to check Godwine's advance. Godwine then sailed up the Wantsum Channel and into the Thames estuary, while some of the ships went via Sheppey, where the raiders burned down the royal town of Milton Regis in another act of aggression towards the king. At Southwark, Godwine waited for the tide to turn and carry him through London Bridge. The C/D version claims that he settled terms with the city's inhabitants 'so that they wanted almost all that he wanted'. It also refers to the presence of the earl's land-army, which came down and arrayed itself along the shore.[107] With this array the guards at the bridge were in no position to argue. Edward was inside London with his earls, about fifty ships, and a great land-army, with reinforcements arriving all the time. The *Vita* reports that his temper was inflamed, and he was in a militant mood; but few wished to proceed to

---

[106] ASC C/D, 1052; E, 1052.
[107] ASC C/D, 1052.

civil war.[108] The rebels wanted their offices and lands back and to be rid of their enemies. Lords loyal to Edward were unwilling to lose what they had gained from the rebels' dispossession. The king, militant or not, required a peaceful solution that would preserve key tenets of his diplomacy, even if by this stage he realized he would have to make painful compromises.

HOSTAGES TO FORTUNE

During that pivotal year, after the banishment of their enemies, the French faction that had strained the loyalties of the native ruling elite had attained an even greater influence in guiding the king's counsel. Leofric and the other English leaders now had a chance to decide whether they preferred the new situation to the previous one in which Godwine and his sons, though a dominant party, had been kept in check. Not infrequently since 1047, Godwine had lost his arguments, initially with the king's refusal to send a fleet to Denmark to assist Sven Estrithsson; later, over the Canterbury appointment; then with the fight at Dover and, finally, in what was the last straw, the dispute over hostages and whether the earl should stand trial. Robert of Jumièges had impressed Edward with his righteous and absolute opposition to the earl. Leofric had gone along with it to an extent. Yet his disapproval of Godwine was less zealous, and he had generally been opposed to strengthening foreign links.[109]

The earls opened negotiations with their maximum demand: that all their entitlements be restored to them. Swegn was not directly included in the bid, for instead of joining the raiding party he had gone on pilgrimage to Jerusalem to complete the penance due for murdering his cousin Beorn. Edward delayed, buying time and retorting with objections. Whatever his own views were, he had to work around Leofric and his son Earl Ælfgar, neither of whom would have been keen on the idea of Ælfgar returning his earldom to Harold without compensation. Nor would Robert and the Norman faction countenance Godwine's restoration. While he was procrastinating, a rumour began that some in Godwine's camp, losing patience with the king, wanted to attack him, and that the earl was struggling to restrain them.[110] Then Stigand went to Godwine, with other acceptable mediators, and advised that both sides exchange hostages. This time Edward agreed, renewing his offer that they might clear themselves of the charges previously brought against them. The terms of their restoration would be decided afterwards in assembly, where Leofric or anyone who opposed them could take it up with the petitioners. Edward's thoughts were racing, as Æthelred's had been in 993. The *Vita* remarks

[108] *Vita*, pp. 43–5.
[109] On C as a possible reflection of Leofric's views, see Baxter, 'MS C', pp. 1204–5.
[110] ASC E, 1052.

that it took a while for him to calm the tumult of his mind.[111] By offering his pardon graciously Edward disguised the fact that he was the one now backed into a corner. A way out had been offered and, to preserve peace and unity, he had to be capable of yielding.

Hostages were meant to safeguard parties in treaties and negotiations. By handing over loved ones into the temporary custody of the other side, one or both parties agreed to render themselves vulnerable, so that if the hostage givers betrayed their side of the agreement, the hostages might be killed or mutilated in retaliation. We know that Godwine's son Wulfnoth and Swegn's son Hakon were handed over as hostages in 1051 or 1052, but our two sources disagree over the occasion.[112] E refers to hostages being readied in the negotiations of 1052, whereas John of Worcester, who used a lost chronicle, mentions an exchange of hostages at Gloucester a year earlier, in September 1051.[113] Yet his account is at odds with E's claim that Godwine twice demanded hostages from the king at Southwark and received none (for those demands would not have been necessary if hostages had been exchanged at Gloucester). We could try to accommodate John by hypothesizing that Godwine had sent hostages to Edward and received none in return, but John does not say that and seems to indicate the opposite by implying both parties were happy with the exchange. The hypothesis also creates difficulties around the account provided by E, for if Edward had given no hostages in 1051, it is hard to believe that the earl agreed to hand over additional hostages as part of an exchange in 1052, when he was in the stronger position.

Since E is clear that both sides arranged for hostages in 1052, John's problematic claim that hostages were exchanged in 1051 is best explained as the attempt of a writer who knew about their importance in hindsight to fit them into the story. It is safer to trust E's indication that Wulfnoth and Hakon were to be handed over to Edward about 14 September 1052. How they fell into William's hands is the key to many mysteries. The central issue is that William should not have had the hostages at all, for he was not one of the parties directly involved in the negotiations of September 1051 or September 1052, and if the hostages were transferred into his care by Edward for safekeeping, they should have been returned once the Godwines had proved their good behaviour. The only writers

[111] *Vita*, p. 44: 'paulatim deferuente animi motu sedatus'. Note, however, that Folcard was playing with the theme of disturbance in the microcosm and macrocosm.

[112] For a handing over of hostages in 1051, see Barlow, *Edward*, pp. 112–13, and 301–6, and K. E. Cutler, 'The Godwinist Hostages: The Case for 1051', *Annuale Mediaevale* 12 (1972), 70–7.

[113] Barlow, *Edward*, p. 304 observes that E 'does not state explicitly that hostages were actually exchanged': '7 ge ræddon the man tremede gislas on ægðer healfe. 7 man swa dyde' ('and they decided that hostages should be arranged for on both sides. And so it was done').

who shed light on this matter are Poitiers and Eadmer, a monk at Canterbury writing before 1109. Both were well positioned. Poitiers was an adult at the ducal court while the hostages were in William's custody. Eadmer was in his thirties and active at court when Wulfnoth died in the 1090s.[114] He was, moreover, a boy-monk at Christ Church in the years E was being compiled in Canterbury.[115] Poitiers' story is that Edward sent the hostages to William in the company of Robert of Jumièges, although he does not tell us when. Eadmer says Edward sent them to Normandy, before settling peace in 1052, since he suspected treachery on Godwine's part.[116]

Both accounts have corroborating evidence to recommend them. E reports that Robert's response to the hostage exchange was to mount his horse and flee the realm with a troop of companions. He would have arrived in Normandy about the time Eadmer places the arrival of the hostages in the duchy – a fact which would account for Poitiers' belief he was part of the legation that brought them over. Eadmer's claim that Edward sent them to Normandy because he suspected treachery from Godwine resonates with Folcard's revelation that an opportunity to kill the king presented itself to the earl. It also chimes with his disingenuous assertion that the earl would not have dreamt of doing such a thing.[117] There is no indication Eadmer drew his information from the *Vita*. The crucial point, on which Poitiers and Eadmer agree, is that the hostages arrived in Normandy at the same time as Robert of Jumièges. This fits with E's evidence of hostages being readied immediately before Robert's flight. As might be expected of two writers bearing separate witness to events, Poitiers lacks the date and context for the hostages' transfer to William, while Eadmer supplies both but fails to refer to Robert's role.

Taken together, the evidence strongly suggests that Robert took the hostages with him when he fled. E can be used to support this idea because after reporting the hostage exchange it tells us that Robert and his faction fled as soon as they found out about it. Seizing their horses, they made for strongholds, some heading west to Pentecost's castle at Hereford, others riding north to Robert fitz Wimarc's at Clavering in Essex. The archbishop himself with Bishop Ulf and their men rode for the east gate of London. There, fighting broke out, and lives were lost, but they managed to escape through Essex and take a ship from the Naze which carried them across the sea. E links Robert's flight to the hostage exchange, stating that the latter was the event that prompted it, but stops short of saying Robert took the hostages with him, perhaps because their

[114] Barlow, *Edward*, p. 305, n. 1, and idem, *William Rufus* (New Haven and London, 2nd edn, 2000), p. 65.

[115] On E's Christ Church origins, see Appendix 1.

[116] *GG*, p. 21; *HN*, pp. 5–6.

[117] *Vita*, pp. 45–7.

transfer to William was so controversial that it was best left off the record.[118]

As far as we know, the bishops' party was the only one of the three to run into fighting on trying to flee London. That, coupled with the fact that the other parties fled 'north' and 'west', probably via Bishopsgate and Newgate, may evince a plan to smuggle out something important by East Gate (i.e. Aldgate).[119] E, which is critical of Robert and his faction, says they killed and injured many young men in making their escape. It may, however, conceal injuries done to them. Bishop Ulf was dead by 1053, and there is no suggestion he reached Normandy. Indeed, the E chronicler, taking Stigand's side, had an incentive to conceal any injury to Robert's party, since it justified the charge that he had used force to expel Robert from his see.[120] If Edward did send the hostages with one of the escaping parties, using two as decoys, the bishops' party might have been thought the least likely to come under attack. There is the possibility he did so without handing over hostages of his own – a daring move by a king dodging checkmate. The king could always blame Robert, but it was surely done with his knowledge. Poitiers later presented the move as a pledge of the crown to William, but Edward was thinking about nothing so much as keeping the crown on his own head.

Prior to this manoeuvre, if he had hoped for assistance from Normandy, none would be forthcoming. It was 14 September. William was on his way to Orléans, possibly in Henry's company, seeking assurances of his royal goodwill. The C/D version's account of the stand-off of 1052 mentions the fear that civil war would lay the country even more open to foreign men. It may refer to the Welsh but could also refer to the Normans or others whose alliances might cause them to become involved. The following day, after Robert's party had departed, a great meeting was declared in London where Godwine and Harold cleared themselves and were restored to the king's friendship. The chroniclers agree that the pardoned earls received back their estates, although they may be glossing over complexities. Edith was led from her confinement, reinstated, and restored to the king's side. If Edward wanted rid of her it would be harder for him now. Several of the foreigners who had offended the rebels were outlawed, and the story spun in 1051 was allowed to prevail: that foreign men 'had promoted illegality and passed unjust judgements and counselled bad advice'.[121] No one begged to disagree.

---

[118] I. W. Walker, *Harold, the Last Anglo-Saxon King* (Stroud, 1997), p. 47, and Mason, *House of Godwine*, pp. 77–8, also conclude that Robert fled with the hostages but disagree over Edward's possible complicity.

[119] On gates and roads out of London, see A. Vince, *Saxon London: An Archaeological Investigation* (London, 1990), pp. 77, 118–29.

[120] The charge was laid at his door at the council of Winchester in 1070: Barlow, *The English Church*, pp. 302–3.

[121] ASC C, 1052.

Osbern Pentecost and Hugh surrendered their castles. With Leofric's permission, they passed through Mercia on their way to Scotland, where they offered their military services to Macbeth.[122] His decision to receive them is hard to read in diplomatic terms, for it may have been friendly to Edward – supposing he was hoping for their return – or it may have been an attempt to undermine him. Macbeth possibly saw its potential on both counts. Robert, we are proposing, delivered the two hostages to William. He then went off in search of the pope to complain of his eviction. Having fled without trial, he was within his rights to argue he had been driven from his estates and office without legal proceedings, in contravention of canon rulings.[123] Leo, however, was in Germany until February 1053, so Robert's attempt to find him had to be sure of its bearings. Stigand took on the administration of Canterbury, and to counter the claim that Robert had been driven from his office, the report was put about that the incumbent had wilfully abandoned his pallium.[124] Both sides were trading half-truths, for Robert had departed voluntarily but intended to return with his archiepiscopal office intact.

Swegn's earthly ambitions ended at Constantinople where he died on his way home from Jerusalem, a fortnight after Godwine's restoration. About the same time, his father was taken ill. He recovered, but in the opinion of C, he 'made all too little reparation for God's property which he had from many holy places'. Normally the annalist's disapproval of Godwine and his sons was less explicit. Here he knew the sequel. It was Easter 1053, the tenth anniversary of Edward's coronation. Edward was in Winchester dining with Godwine, Harold, and Tostig when Godwine suddenly sank down at his footstall, deprived of strength and speech. He was carried into the king's chamber but remained in this state and died a couple of days later. Few deaths are described in the chronicles. When they are, there is usually a moral. C's treatments of Harthacnut and Godwine follow the same formula by censuring those men, then revealing that death caught them by surprise and deprived them of speech (along with the opportunity for making confession). The formula was a coded way of saying that suffering awaited them in the afterlife. It was not quite the heavenward ending for Godwine implied in the *Vita*.

C, with its concern for propriety, is also candid about the unsatisfactory disposition of church affairs in that year, complaining that there was 'no archbishop in the land'.[125] Stigand had occupied Robert's seat in Canterbury, and Cynesige in York was still without a pallium. The two bishops appointed in 1053, Leofwine of Lichfield and Wulfwig of

---

[122] *JW*, ii, p. 573.

[123] T. Licence, 'Robert of Jumièges, Archbishop in Exile (1052–5)', *ASE* 42 (2013), 313–29, at p. 328.

[124] ASC E, 1052 (adopting Stigand's line).

[125] ASC C, 1053.

Dorchester (replacing Ulf who had not survived his flight), had to go across the sea to find an archbishop to ordain them.[126] As suffragans of Canterbury, they presumably headed to Robert, who was poised to return, having outlived his enemies Godwine and Swegn and obtained papal letters confirming him in office. None but Leo the pope, or his legates, was authorized to depose an archbishop. In June 1053, Robert attended an exhibition of the relics of St Denis at the royal abbey outside Paris. There he was received as the archbishop of Canterbury and could lobby other dignitaries to petition Edward. The gathering included Edward's nephew, Count Walter of the Vexin; his former chaplain Élinand, who had recently been made the bishop of Laon; Odo, brother to Henry of France, and Edward's old acquaintance, Abbot John of Fécamp.[127] The last of these had had plenty of occasions to cross paths with Edward in Normandy.

By restoring Robert, Edward would be able to mend relations with the papacy and the Normans, whose interests had suffered in the settlement of 1052, and to end the international embarrassment of having lost his only functioning archbishop. The king must have given the matter a great deal of thought and considered all possible outcomes, but it is doubtful that the witan would have tolerated Robert's return, and in hindsight it was clear that Robert was too willing to destroy the family Edward had created, including his wife and father-in-law.[128]

CARVING UP THE CAKE

The return of the rebel earls and Godwine's death were opportunities for Edward to resume the task of balancing competing interests and defusing noble rivalries, a task he had previously complicated by introducing foreigners into the equation. Managing the great of the realm was the foundation of consensual government. Still, Edward needed to accommodate the expectations of his kin, and of established dynasties who were coming to regard earldoms as heritable. In the re-shuffle of 1052, Swegn's death enabled Odda, who had to give up the south-western shires, to assume a command in Gloucestershire. Ralph retained his earldom. The loser was Ælfgar, who had to return East Anglia to Harold. Ælfgar could not have been pleased with the outcome, for he had done no apparent wrong, was about Harold's age, and would have expected to come into an earldom. Having got one (several years after Harold), he was promptly shoved out of it, so that his competitor, who had lately rebelled against the king, could have it back. Even if Ælfgar was used to seeing his father settle

---

[126] Licence, 'Robert', p. 327; Ulf was dead. ASC C 1053 refers to Wulfwig taking over the bishopric which Ulf 'had had while Ulf was still alive and expelled'.

[127] Licence, 'Robert', p. 315.

[128] He had also destroyed Edward's London appointment, Spearhafoc.

for second place, he had to decide for himself how long he would tolerate the privileging of Edward's in-laws.

Fortunately for Ælfgar, in 1053 Godwine's death occasioned a second re-shuffle. It was an opportunity for the king to restore Ælfgar to the East Anglian earldom, but the shine was taken off his restoration by Harold's simultaneous promotion to Wessex. As Harold stepped into his father's shoes, it must have seemed that he could do no wrong; certainly, he had been one of Edward's favourites from the start. Wessex was vast. Edward's golden boy lay spread across the south like a great lounging mastiff. There were, however, dividends for Leofric's kin in the midlands. Prior to the early 1050s, we are unsure who commanded Lincolnshire and Nottinghamshire, though Leofric and Siward are contenders. Then from 1052, Leofric's dynasty exercised at least ecclesiastical influence there. In that year, it was agreed the abbot of Peterborough should stand down in favour of Leofric's nephew, also called Leofric, who received rights of presentation to four other abbeys in Mercia and the midlands. Earl Leofric, his wife Godgifu, and Ælfgar, about the same time, assumed the patronage of other religious houses in the midland corridor.[129] By allowing them new influence in those counties, Edward balanced the vastness of Harold's earldom by entrusting the Leofwinesons with a swathe of territory from the Welsh march to the Norfolk coast. Unlike Wessex, where the king's perambulation sat heavily with the earl, their territory was freer from his surveillance.

Osgod, always a minor player, might have regained lands. D reports that in 1054 he died in his bed, an odd detail to include had he ended his days in exile. Osgod's reappearance reminds us that Ælfgar might not have been the first to lose power in East Anglia to Harold: for it is a fair guess that Osgod had coveted the earldom in 1045 and been outlawed for daring to oppose Harold's appointment. Ælfgar had bitten his lip in 1052 and been rewarded for his patience the following year, when the earldom was restored to him. The obstacle now to his further ambitions was Tostig's desire for an earldom. Tostig's marriage to Judith of Flanders gave him an advantage, because it was a prop to the precarious peace lately established with Baldwin, which Tostig's promotion to the rank of earl might well solidify. Edward therefore had a greater incentive to advance Tostig in the next re-shuffle; and Tostig's empire would most likely be carved from the midlands or the north, where he would compete with Ælfgar's kin. It always suited the king to placate the ministers he relied on to maintain his government; but the cubs were getting bigger; they were bulkier and fiercer. One day they would have to fight it out.

---

[129] Baxter, *Earls of Mercia*, pp. 68, 190.

Chapter 5

DOMINION

And He will speak peace to the nations;
And His dominion will be from sea to sea.

(Zech. 9:10)

LEGACY PREPARATIONS

Let us pause Time. For we have the ability to do so. For Time is the illusion of motion in the continuum of Being. Working Edward's life into a story, we replicate that illusion. Events pass before our mind's eye, as clouds scudding across the sky. There – it is the morning of 14 September. Edward is lost in the Mass, caught up in eternity.[1] Light falls dappled through a leafy place, somewhere outside. Farther away a skylark hangs motionless, dissolving Time in its song. The sun shines on London, Rome, and Jerusalem. Its dominion ebbs into shadows at the farthest reaches of the earth. It illuminates the Feast of the Exaltation of the Holy Cross. It illuminates the day – perhaps a few years ago – when Godwine returned to confront our king; when peace, and his dominion, and the future of his ancient line, hung in suspense.[2] Where now is Godwine? Where is Emma? Where is Alfred? Where are Æthelred and Edmund, Cnut and Harold and Harthacnut, Gunnhilda and Azecho, Richard II and Robert? Edward is mostly flown through life's journey, and so many souls are flown before. Outside, the sun spreads its warmth; the morning is barely in motion. Edward is lost in Time. Maybe he is thinking of his legacy. Maybe he is contemplating Westminster, rising through the mists of the Thames.

Since the days of Edward's father, London had recovered its Roman pre-eminence as the principal city of the realm. For Æthelred, his son Edmund, and Cnut, its defence had been the key to controlling both halves of England, the English territory and the Danish territory, lying either side of a line from London to Chester, along the Roman road known as Watling Street. Winchester remained the capital of Wessex, the site of the royal treasury and palace, where Cnut's courtiers had their residences and Edward was crowned. But the strategic importance of

---

[1] Cf. *Vita*, p. 63.
[2] *JW*, ii, p. 569; *Vita*, pp. 43–7.

London and its international reputation as a port for luxury trade raised it to another level. In the past, Winchester had been a base for Cerdic's heirs as they extended their dominion from Wessex across what would become England, but eleventh-century kings with imperial aspirations looked beyond the Channel and the North Sea. London became their inevitable seat of government. They were players on a European stage.

There were signs already in the reign of Harold I that power was shifting to London. In 1039–40, trees were felled to provide timber for the construction of the first Anglo-Saxon waterfront at Billingsgate, east of the old London Bridge. The creation of the wharf implies interest on the part of the monarch and citizens in furnishing a landing stage where custom could be gathered. Merchants' houses were being equipped with storage cellars, which attest a healthy surplus. Among luxury imports were casks of wine, fine woollens, and silks, while the only industry of note was the working of non-ferrous metals. These were characteristics London had in common with early royal centres such as Rendlesham in Suffolk, where high-status exchange and non-ferrous metalworking were definitive activities. Still, London was getting crowded, with the infilling of the eastern half of the city. The smaller size of some of the wards there reveals that the densest settlement fronted the Billingsgate to London Bridge route and major streets leading off it. The area to the west of the St Paul's minster complex was also infilling.[3] Two miles upriver, in the pleasant environs of Westminster, Harold I may already have had a hall, for a palace was there in Edward's reign, and Harold chose the adjacent abbey as his burial place. When he died in 1040 his body was brought down-river from Oxford to Westminster abbey. Doubtless there was a royal residence within the walled city of London, but royalty tends to flee bustling places in favour of amenable spots nearby. The fact that Osgod, one of Harthacnut's stallers, had a house already at Lambeth, just over the river from Westminster, indicates that courtiers were congregating in that area.[4]

Folcard, whose interest in Westminster was chiefly in the monastery, explains that Edward chose to re-found Westminster abbey because it occupied a delightful spot near the rich and famous city and lay near the main channel of the river, 'which bore abundant merchandise of wares of

[3] A. Vince, ed., *Aspects of Saxo-Norman London, 2: Finds and Environmental Evidence*, London and Middlesex Archaeological Society, Special Paper 12 (Over Wallop, Hants, 1991), pp. 21, 427–34; J. Ayre and R. Wroe-Brown, 'The Post-Roman Foreshore and the Origins of the Late Anglo-Saxon Waterfront and Dock of Æthelred's Hithe: Excavations at Bull Wharf, City of London', *Archaeological Journal* 172 (2015), 121–94, at pp. 129, 139, 181. For Rendlesham, see C. Scull, F. Minter, and J. Plouviez, 'Social and Economic Complexity in Early Medieval England: A Central Place Complex of the East Anglian Kingdom at Rendlesham, Suffolk', *Antiquity* 90 (2016), 1594–612.

[4] *JW*, ii, pp. 533–5.

every kind for sale from the whole world to the city on its banks'.[5] Such considerations applied equally to any hall that already stood there, and given that the palace was finished before the abbey,[6] it is likely the king began work at Westminster by improving his secular residence, a possibility his biographer would have had reason to pass over as distracting from the spiritual edifice which manifested Edward's piety. There is no reason to suppose the choice of location was Edward's rather than that of a more obscure predecessor (such as Harold), or that it had more to do with religion than with amenity and consumption. The king was the top consumer, or at least the court. Westminster's location enabled the provision of the finest consumables, away from the bother of London. It was also well situated for the reception of foreign embassies. Distinguished visitors could be rowed through London Bridge past the walled city with its bustling wharves and around the river-bend to the oasis of Thorney Island, with its palace, and with the new abbey of Westminster, displaying in rising synthesis the finest elements of European Romanesque. There Edward could proclaim his status as a European monarch not inferior to the German emperor, commanding a global network that brought him Asian silks, Andalusi carpets, and spices from the Arabian Sea.[7]

Another point of reference, though Edward may not have seen it, was St Peter's basilica, the Vatican, in Rome. Like many Anglo-Saxon churches, Westminster bore a dedication to St Peter, and this detail fuelled speculation about the king's personal devotion to the Prince of the Apostles, a fondness for St Peter which was implicit in his early visit to St Peter's, Ghent. The charter Edward approved for the monks there reveals that, even in the 1040s, there were rumours of a vow made to St Peter, to be honoured once the apostle had restored him to the throne. At Ghent, the vow was said to involve the restoration of English lands to St Peter's abbey. At Westminster in the 1070s or 1080s, Sulcard told a different tale, of how Edward, on gaining the throne, had planned a pilgrimage to Rome, with the intention of thanking St Peter for the glory and peace that had been granted him by the apostle's agency. The witan, however, fearing disturbance in his absence, persuaded him to spend the funds put aside for his pilgrimage on re-founding a monastery in Peter's honour.[8] Neither story is reliable, for the monks of Ghent wished to acquire estates by placing Edward in a debt-relationship to their saint, and Sulcard wished to credit the success of Edward's reign to St Peter. He had read of the glory and peace of Edward's reign in his biography, but the latter mentions his devotion to Peter without reference to a pilgrimage, which is Sulcard's embellishment. Nor can we believe Edward was so ready to

---

[5] *Vita*, pp. 67–9.

[6] Edward died at the palace before the abbey was finished: *Vita*, p. 113 (from Osbert).

[7] On the spices, see below, p. 170.

[8] Sulcard, *Prologus*, pp. 90–1.

leave behind the throne he had longed to win. The *Vita* does reveal that Edward paid for the re-foundation of the abbey out of the tithes of the royal estate, channelling what was due to God into a project of Solomonic ambitions. If it betokened a departure from humble gifts of food rents to monks, it also hints at Edward's assuredness of his kingly dignity which was beginning to adorn his humility with grandeur.

We do not know when work began on the palace or abbey. The business of dating either depends on an assessment of relevant documents, architectural influences, and the speed and likely extent of the progress that had been made by 1066. Even judging the latter is by no means straightforward, for Folcard gives us two accounts of the building, one suggesting it was largely incomplete, the other stating that it was complete apart from the porch.[9] The second account comes in the second part of his work, which depicts Edward as a saint, and may therefore exaggerate the completeness of the building to make Edward's death appear timelier. Saints were supposed to anticipate their demise, not die leaving their burial place unfinished. The Bayeux Tapestry makes the point perfectly, by showing the hand of God blessing the abbey and a worker topping it with a weathercock just as Edward's cortège is about to enter.[10] Although such accounts bear witness to the growing legend that the king had died at just the right moment, they are not reliable evidence for the building's state of completion. Nor can it be objected that contemporaries would have rejected accounts that were patently untrue, for we know eleventh-century writers made up all sorts of untruths, foisting them on contemporaries.

Documents that may help us date the inception of the building work include a series of writs which, at first glance, seem to date it to the 1040s. In one writ, addressed to Ælfweard, bishop of London, Edward confirms to St Peter's, Westminster, a gift of land at Kelvedon in Essex, given by Æthelric the chamberlain and his wife Gode.[11] The address seems to imply that courtiers were sponsoring his foundation before 1044, the year of Ælfweard's death. Domesday Book reveals, however, that the gift was made in 1066, late in Harold II's reign or shortly after his death, when a forged writ would have helped secure Westminster's claim to an estate which was potentially forfeit to the Conqueror, since all acts of Harold's reign were vulnerable to annulment in William's. The forger would have pushed the invented transaction as far back in time as possible, to the start of Edward's reign, hoping that anyone who could have contradicted it would by now be dead.[12] Other writs

---

[9] See below, pp. 164–5.

[10] *BT*, 29.

[11] S 1118.

[12] Harmer, *Writs*, no. 74, and pp. 297–306 for discussion. Cf. R. D. H. Gem, 'The Romanesque Rebuilding of Westminster Abbey (with a reconstruction by W. T. Ball)', *ANS* 3 (1981), 33–60, at p. 34, who cites spurious writs (Harmer, *Writs*, nos 73, 75) to posit an endowment under way by 1050.

in the series are demonstrable forgeries, as are the Latin diplomas for the abbey, though they may draw on lost originals.

If the documents do not reveal whether the abbey was begun in the 1040s or 1050s, neither do remains that have been discovered. Westminster had design features in common with the church of Jumièges, which is thought to have been built in the 1050s or thereabouts, but it is not known whether Jumièges or Westminster was laid out first, and one of those features, the base mouldings, was the sort of detail the master-builder would have left to one of his craftsmen. It tells us nothing about the patron's inspiration. Doubt also surrounds the termination of the eastern arm and whether it was aisled. If Westminster had an apse-and-ambulatory plan, a model might have been Rouen cathedral, but there is no archaeological evidence for aisles or ambulatory, and the Tapestry, which may or may not depict the structure accurately, indicates neither, while illustrating an aisled nave. If the eastern arm was aisleless, the obvious models would have been German imperial buildings such as Speyer and Hersfeld. Speyer was begun by the emperor Conrad in 1030 but collapsed in 1052, had to be rebuilt, and was consecrated in 1061. Unlike Jumièges, it shared with Westminster the distinction of being a dynastic burial church. And in scale as well as pretensions, it offered a fitting model for a ruler conscious of his image on a European stage. In short, Westminster's remains do not establish the date the abbey was begun, while the structure is best thought of as a point of synthesis in a European setting – a moment of architectural creation.[13]

Though the archive and remains reveal little about the chronology of construction, the description in the first part of the *Vita* captures the progress of building work at a fixed point in time. The author mentions the presbytery – always the first part to be built – and remarks that the crossing was in place and roofed. The central tower, however, which the crossing was to support, is not described at this juncture, where the use of the conditional tense may imply it had not been built.[14] The chapels, with their altars, had not yet been consecrated, and no part of the nave is described. The author mentions that enough space had been left between

[13] Gem, 'Romanesque Rebuilding', p. 54; E. Fernie, 'Edward the Confessor's Westminster Abbey', in Mortimer, ed., *Edward*, 139–50, at p. 141 for Jumièges and p. 150 for Speyer; and F. Woodman, 'Edward the Confessor's Church at Westminster: An Alternative View', in W. Rodwell and T. Tatton-Brown, eds, *Westminster: The Art, Architecture and Archaeology of the Royal Abbey and Palace*, BAA Conference Transactions 39, 2 Pts (Leeds, 2015), I (Royal Abbey), 61–8; and T. A. Heslop, pers. comm.

[14] This was Francis Bond's reading. He remarks, 'what was finished [by January 1066] consisted probably of the eastern limb, the south wall of the south aisle of the nave, and as much of the transepts and nave as was needed to prop up the lower stage of a central tower': F. Bond, *Westminster Abbey* (Oxford, 1909), p. 8. Cf. *Vita*, pp. 68/9–70/1. The continuous sentence starting 'Porro crux templi' refers to the crossing, which is its subject throughout. It appears not to describe the tower.

the work in progress and the east end of the old church to accommodate what he calls 'some part of the *vestibulum*', a word that may refer either to a western porch or the nave. If a porch is meant, like the one at Jumièges, the author would be passing in silence over the nave, as he passes over the tower. Alternatively, he may be describing a yawning western entrance, still unfinished.

The second part of the *Vita* contained details of the buildings as they stood in December 1065. Although the Latin text is lost, a translation made in the sixteenth century reports that the monastery was 'for the moste parte finyshed' and 'there remayned nothynge unbuylded but the Entry or porche'.[15] One of the nouns probably translates *vestibulum*, and since it is glossed as 'porch', we may prefer that reading. This also supports the idea that the account given earlier in the work neglects to describe bits of the church that had already been built, including the tower and the nave. Perhaps it is not an eyewitness account, or perhaps those parts were covered in scaffolding. Normally, a church of such size could be built in 15–20 years. This was a royal project with no expense spared.[16] Quarries for supplying the stone had been opened not far away at Reigate in Surrey, 30 kilometres to the south west.[17] Work should have advanced rapidly, and in the absence of known setbacks such as the collapse at Speyer and the fire that burnt down Edith's half-finished church at Wilton, it is a reasonable guess that rebuilding of the abbey began in the years around 1050.[18]

The palace was either completed before work began on the abbey or arose at the same time. Spearhafoc's appointment to the see of London in 1050 may offer a clue: for the king's decision to install his goldsmith, who might oversee the working of precious metals in the capital, and to commission from him a new crown, is possibly indicative of a stage when the palace was nearing completion and when the work of adorning it and providing new regalia was paramount. Still, it is possible that he installed him in London to oversee the cutting of coin dies, which had all been cut there since Cnut's reign, or simply because an opportunity to have him there presented itself. If the palace was in place by 1050, the rebuilding of the abbey might have followed, but all we can say for certain is that works were under way at Westminster by the second decade of the reign.

[15] Summerson, 'Tudor Antiquaries', p. 177.

[16] *Vita*, p. 69.

[17] R. Gem, 'Craftsmen and Administrators in the Building of the Confessor's Abbey', in Mortimer, ed., *Edward*, 168–72, at p. 171.

[18] This calculation fits with twelfth-century Westminster tradition associating the re-foundation with Leo's pontificate. S 1039, Edward's 'Telligraphus' for Westminster (forged by Osbert of Clare) contains a fake letter purporting to be from Leo IX, granting Edward permission to rebuild the abbey.

EDWARD AND EDITH

The settlement of courtiers across the river at Lambeth continued in Edward's reign, although in his time Lambeth became the residence of the king's closest relatives. In 1066, according to Domesday Book, the lords of Lambeth were Edward's sister Gode and his brother-in-law Harold. This was evidently Gode's principal abode, for she kept her treasure there.[19] Amicable relations between Harold and Gode's family are implied not only by the fact that Ralph, her son, was one of the Frenchmen whose presence the Godwinsons had not thought objectionable, but also by his decision to name his son Harold, apparently after the child's great uncle. As earl of the south-east midlands, which included London, Ralph was close at hand. Gode likewise may have attended court, for although she never appears as a witness to Edward's diplomas, she had no official business in that capacity. Edith was now back at her husband's side; indeed the storm of 1052, and Godwine's death more so, had cleared the air between them and alleviated parental pressure. Folcard would later sow the seed of an idea that the couple practised sexual abstinence, but this is best taken as another narrative designed to gild the king and queen, in this case by defending against the ancient notion that a lack of heirs (and fertility) was a mark of divine disfavour. At the time of her father's death, Edith was still a young woman, perhaps in her early twenties; and she may have returned to her husband's bed and further attempts to conceive a child. The sources, naturally, are silent. For all we know, there may have been moments of intense pain. The queen may have miscarried, once or several times, or borne a child or children who died. There may, alternatively, have been no glimmer of light, as their hopes gradually faded.

An anecdote relayed by a foreign visitor shows how Edward and Edith interacted. One time, Abbot Gervin of Saint-Riquier crossed to England from Ponthieu. He was a man well known for his holiness,[20] and Edith was eager to greet him. She probably thought he would be flattered when she offered him the kiss of peace, for the gesture signified that they were equals, though in worldly terms she outranked him. Gervin, however, shrank back in horror. Not a woman to be scorned, she vented her fury by confiscating the gifts she had given him, before Edward intervened and advised her not to take offence, because the abbot was bound by a vow to avoid contact with women.[21] Mollified, she went back to Gervin with greater respect, giving him an amice adorned with gold and gems. Converted to his way of thinking, she began rebuking native bishops and abbots for their readiness to be greeted by women. Prelates like Stigand's

---

[19] S. Baxter, 'Gode 2: Gode, Sister of King Edward, fl. 1066', *PASE Domesday*, www.domesday.pase.ac.uk (accessed 3 June 2018).

[20] *MSE*, p. 87.

[21] *Chronique*, ed. Lot, pp. 237–8.

married brother Æthelmær (whom Stigand had manoeuvred into the bishopric of East Anglia after installing himself in Canterbury) probably wished Gervin had never left Ponthieu. Still, the anecdote conveys Edith's goodwill, reasonableness, and impressionableness, alongside Edward's desire to nurture harmony and to avert diplomatic incident by getting people to see others' points of view. It may show she had a temper like her husband but was less inclined to check it.[22] She seems to have learned to mask her anger with time, but Folcard notes that, for the most part, she wore her heart on her sleeve.[23]

KINGLY ASPIRATIONS

Like all kings, Edward communicated his aspirations through multiple media, of which the royal court was the theatre, and official perambulation and visitation the parade. We saw how Edith presided over the set and props, selecting and embroidering the king's garments, the coverings of his throne, and the carpets under his feet. Everything glistened with gold and gems, not least the staff Edward used when walking. When he rode, his saddle and harness glinted with miniature beasts and birds wrought by goldsmiths under Edith's direction.[24] A desired effect on those who glimpsed the king in his hall, palace, or tent, or on an expedition, was the inculcation of awe akin to the awe induced by jewelled and gilded effigies of saints. Those who never saw the king in his ship upon the Thames could nevertheless marvel at the works at Westminster, but for most people only the coinage provided a ready image. Kings were Christ's regents whose coins displayed His cross on one side (the 'reverse') and their bust on the other (the 'obverse'). Only one unit of currency, the silver penny, was minted in England, and the busts communicated messages about the monarch. Like much medieval art, they tended to be stylized, not lifelike. Frequent recoinages in a reign were opportunities to project new aspirations or alter the message presented to the populace. A king might write to his subjects as Cnut did, or promulgate a decree, or he could change his image on the coins.

Before the early 1050s, Edward's messages were conservative. Except for the 'PACX' coinage at the reign's outset, which proclaimed a timely peace after much infighting, all the types issued during his first decade on the throne recalled the coinages of his predecessors. These types, Radiate/ Small Cross, Trefoil Quadrilateral, Small Flan and Expanding Cross

---

[22] Ibid.: Gervin's snub made Edith *ferox* ('wild') and *irata* ('enraged'). Cf. *Vita*, p. 19.

[23] *Vita*, p. 23 (from Richard of Cirencester): 'When offended, she curbed or hid her anger by holding her tongue'; cf. 'When faced with some distressful or squalid scene, she could barely pause for a moment but immediately made a suitable comment on it to the company.'

[24] Ibid., p. 25 (from Richard of Cirencester).

(named and ordered in their chronological sequence by modern experts), display crowned, helmeted, or diademed left-facing busts, all features which are anticipated in the issues of Æthelred and his successors. The last two coinages in the sequence, Small Flan and Expanding Cross, reveal experimentation with the size and weight of the penny, the former issue comprising smaller, lighter coins of greater thickness, the latter comprising, uniquely, two different series within a single issue: a lighter series and a heavier one. It is difficult to determine why in the late 1040s or early 1050s experiments were undertaken, but whatever the reasons for changes in size and weight, the conservatism of the designs was maintained.

The next issue, Pointed Helmet, in two respects marked a turning point. First, the experiments with the size and weight of the coinage yielded, in this issue, to a relatively consistent standard, which was retained thereafter. Second, the imagery moved sharply away from previous designs and became more imperial, assuming features of the coins of Byzantine emperors and of German emperors of the Ottonian and reigning Salian dynasty. Pointed Helmet coins portrayed a bearded and helmeted monarch, with a right-facing bust, holding a fleur-de-lis. The beard, which was a German feature, remained in subsequent portraits. In the next coinage, Sovereign/ Eagles, which is datable to the mid-1050s, a full-length repre-sentation of the king enthroned in majesty, holding a staff and orb, replaced the bust on the obverse, and birds appeared on the reverse in the quarters of the cross – another innovation. The departures again show Edward constructing a narrative of his kingship.

Images of rulers enthroned in majesty can be traced back through Ottonian and Salian seals to sixth-century Byzantine coins and to represen-tations of Christ in several different media.[25] Even so, the closest parallel geographically and in date is the majesty portrait of Edward on the earliest extant royal seal, which shows the monarch crowned, with beard and moustache, seated in frontal pose on a stool or backless throne. On one side of this double-sided seal he holds an orb in one hand and a sceptre in the other; on the other side, he holds a sceptre and a sword. Three impressions from Edward's genuine seal matrix are attested, and the earliest sealed a writ issued between 1053 and 1057, a space of time in which Sovereign/ Eagles is likely to have been designed. Whether the coinage imitated the seal or vice versa, models for the latter lay in the range of representations and insignia found on the seals of German emperors.[26] Their seals were

---

[25] R. Naismith, *Medieval European Coinage, with a catalogue of the coins in the Fitzwilliam Museum, Cambridge: 8 Britain and Ireland c. 400–1066* (Cambridge, 2017), p. 274. See also T. Talvio, 'The Design of Edward the Confessor's Coins', in Jonsson, ed., *Studies in Late Anglo-Saxon Coinage*, 487–99, at p. 490.

[26] *Writs*, ed. Harmer, pp. 95–105; T. A. M. Bishop and P. Chaplais, *Facsimiles of English Royal Writs to A.D. 1100, Presented to Vivian Hunter Galbraith* (Oxford, 1957), pp. xi–xiii, xxii–xxiv, and No. 3 (Plate III), No. 20 (Plate XVIII), and No. 25 (Plate XXIII (b) and (c)).

one-sided, but there were precedents for two-sided seals in the lead seals (papal bulls) that were attached to papal documents. In general terms, the iconography of Edward's seals and coins in the 1050s suggests that the regime had come to think of itself as more imperial, and it is worth observing that this shift accompanied an increase in its dealings with foreign powers and in its interventions in client kingdoms.

Novel designs aside, we may wonder whether a king who left his wardrobe to Edith's care would have gone to the trouble of poring over antique coins, to plan each numismatic makeover. By saying Edward cared little for his appearance, Folcard may nevertheless be engaged in apologetics, just as Eusebius excused Constantine for wearing too much bling.[27] Henry III of Germany, to whose eminence Edward aspired, was criticized for conspicuous consumption.[28] By crediting his wardrobe to Edith, Edward could dodge accusations of ostentation while dressing up as the king he had always longed to be. Yet we should bear in mind that designs were tasked to goldsmiths. Spearhafoc fled in 1051, a casualty of politics. If his replacement was the German Theodoric, who would later be regarded as the greatest goldsmith in London, the change in office-holder might account for the stylistic turning point.[29] Spearhafoc was an English monk whose career can be traced from St Benet's abbey in Norfolk via Bury St Edmunds and Abingdon. Moulded in a native tradition of monastic goldsmiths, he would have favoured conservative designs, unlike Theodoric, who may have favoured German ones. The same argument can be posited for the seal, for although Cnut appears to have had a seal, its design is unknown, and there is no evidence beyond the prior trait of conservatism that it was the model for Edward's seal of the mid-1050s.[30] For both seal and coinage, novel designs of the 1050s can be explained as the innovations of a new designer. Edward must, however, have approved the changes, and their implementation in tandem with the construction of Westminster accompanied the outward-facing turn in his kingship, signposted in 1049 by his dealings with the German emperor and the papacy.

As Edward approached fifty, the projections of Solomonic and imperial majesty were accompanied by an acknowledgement of human frailty. For it was about this point that the king's physician began to appear at court. Baldwin was a Frenchman, a native of Chartres, and an expert practitioner of medicine. That the king gave him property in Deerhurst hints

[27] Eusebius, *Oration in Praise of Constantine*, 5. 6–7: in *Eusebius: Church History, Life of Constantine the Great and Oration in Praise of Constantine*, tr. A. C. McGiffert and E. C. Richardson, A select library of Nicene and Post-Nicene Fathers of the Christian Church, ed. H. Wace and P. Schaff, 2nd ser., 14 vols (Oxford; London, and [later] New York, 1890–1900), I, p. 586.

[28] S. Weinfurter, *The Salian Century: Main Currents in an Age of Transition*, tr. B. M. Bowlus (Philadelphia, PA, 1999), p. 102.

[29] Cf. Naismith, *Medieval European Coinage*, pp. 274–5.

[30] Harmer, *Writs*, pp. 17–18; *pace* pp. 98–101.

that his patient was often in Gloucestershire – visiting his palace in Gloucester, hunting, or surveilling the Welsh march.[31] A show of royal power was needed there on and off to cow Welsh enemies, as it had been needed in Sandwich in the 1040s to defend the Kentish coast. Baldwin imported a more learned medicine than that known in England, which was gaining advocates on the Continent. Its language was Latin, which crossed the same borders as its educated proponents, and it integrated medical theory, such as humoral theory, and practice. There is no evidence medicine of the new kind had been known in England before, though Edward may have come across it in exile.[32]

In a book of medical recipes Baldwin brought to England are several written in a hand which may be identified as his own.[33] As well as requiring native plants such as costmary, they also demand exotica such as pepper, ginger, myrrh, cardamom, saffron, cinnamon, and frankincense. Most of the spices were transported to Europe via the Red Sea and traded, with silks and other goods, in the bazaars of Constantinople, but not before passing between the ships or caravans of merchants along the way.[34] Pepper came mainly from Malabar (modern Kerala), leaving India from ports on the Arabian Sea. Frankincense originated in the Dhofari region of Oman, while myrrh too could be found on the Arabian Peninsula in Yemen, or in the African countries of Ethiopia, Eritrea, and Somalia.[35] What made this medicine fit for a king was its insistence on ingredients only the rich could afford. Edward the consumer tapped a confluence of global supply-routes, and by those same routes vivifying spices arrived at his halls and palaces in the hands of a French physician, who had to be careful not to spill them on his Andalusi carpets and Byzantine patterned silks. One of the recipes Baldwin wrote out, called 'Imperial remedy', produced 'a nice-smelling mouth and a good stomach' and rid the body of phlegm. (Too much phlegm made a king meek and indulgent towards his favourites.) A second remedy claimed to cure dysentery and diarrhoea. Two others were for fevers.[36]

[31] Bates, *Regesta*, no. 254.

[32] D. Banham, 'A Millennium in Medicine: New Medical Texts and Ideas in England in the Eleventh Century', in S. Keynes and A. P. Smyth, eds, *Anglo-Saxons: Studies Presented to Cyril Roy Hart* (Dublin, 2006), pp. 230–42.

[33] D. Banham, 'Medicine at Bury in the Time of Abbot Baldwin', in T. Licence, ed., *Bury St Edmunds and the Norman Conquest* (Woodbridge, 2014), 226–46, at pp. 237–8, and see below, pp. 270–1.

[34] M. Van der Veen and J. Morales, 'The Roman and Islamic Spice Trade: New Archaeological Evidence', *Journal of Ethnopharmacology* 167 (2015), 54–63, at pp. 55–6. Saffron was grown in England in the later Middle Ages.

[35] V. Turner, 'To what extent was Sloane 1621 a useful medical document for Abbot Baldwin and the monks of Bury St Edmunds in the late eleventh century?', unpublished MA essay, University of East Anglia, 2015.

[36] Banham, 'Medicine at Bury', p. 237.

Hints of human frailty remind us that the images of command were aspirational. For all that buildings, regalia, and coins may reveal is how a regime that was sometimes vulnerable wished to appear to onlookers. However outward-facing they seem, they were also a mirror that appealed to its inward gaze. Other mirrors could be less flattering. Edward, beneath his glittering robes, was a childless king whose recent brawl with his in-laws had achieved little and played into the hands of foreign powers. The subsequent expulsion of the archbishop of Canterbury was a reversal more humiliating than his refusal to consecrate Spearhafoc, not to mention Spearhafoc's absconding with the gold Edward had given him for making a crown, an incident which made a mockery of an attempt to project kingly authority. At the end of the affair he had no functioning archbishop, and two of his kinsmen were in William's keeping. Peace had been restored but at a cost to easy relations with the pope and Normandy, and his lack of an heir and Robert of Jumièges were headaches no physician could dispel.

ARCHBISHOP ACROSS THE WATER

Robert, we will recall, had fled in 1052 and arrived in Normandy at the same time as the hostages. He then sought the pope to complain of his eviction, but he could not have had his audience before February 1053 when Leo returned from Germany.[37] Afterwards he appears in the company of John of Fécamp, an abbot Edward would have got to know in Normandy. John invited Robert to his abbey to perform spiritual offices that had once been the preserve of the archbishops of Rouen before Duke Robert exempted the abbey from their authority. In 1053 or 1054, Robert of Jumièges dedicated two of Fécamp's churches and ordained several of its clergy.[38] He and John were among the prelates whose attendance was recorded at the exhibition of the relics of St Denis at Paris in June 1053. Given they were the only Norman clergy present, it is likely they went there together. It is also likely that the bishops-elect of Lichfield and Dorchester took advantage of Robert's proximity to cross the Channel and be ordained by him.[39] None of this reflected well on Edward's management of the Church.

Robert's activity at Fécamp, just across the water, was embarrassing for two reasons. First, it was reminiscent of Edward's posturing there as an exile backed by Normandy two decades earlier. The parallel would not have been lost on any of the men involved. Second, the Normans were aligning with the papacy against Edward by acknowledging an archbishop

---

[37] For Leo's itinerary, see JL, I, pp. 529–49.
[38] L. Musset, 'Notules fécampoises', *Bulletin de la Société des Antiquaires de Normandie* 54 (1957–8), 584–98, at p. 596.
[39] Licence, 'Robert', pp. 315 and 327.

whom the witan had repudiated. In 1051, when the count of Anjou had invaded the adjacent county of Maine, William had provided refuge for Gervase, bishop of Le Mans.[40] Now, in 1053, the duke could again pose as the protector of a prelate wrongfully driven from his see, and at a time when the aggression of Norman settlers in southern Italy generated a constant background strain upon Normandy's relations with the pope. William, who could not have been overjoyed about the expulsion of Normans from England, was pressuring Edward to reinstate Robert. At the same time, he was content to retain his two hostage in-laws.

Just when Robert seemed poised to return, events conspired against him. In June 1053, when he was in Paris touting his credentials as the exiled archbishop, Leo his advocate was defeated and captured in Italy at the battle of Civitate, having led a troop of mercenaries in a desperate campaign against Norman invaders in the south. He remained their prisoner until March 1054 and died a month later. Protracted negotiations postponed the installation of his successor Victor II until March 1055, all of which deprived the Church of a viable pontiff for almost two years. William, meanwhile, was being drawn ever deeper into a conflict sparked by the rebellion of his uncle, Count William of Arques. It was a dangerous affair because it encouraged a hostile alliance headed by the French king and the count of Anjou to intervene in Normandy.[41] The duke eventually routed their armies, but the fallout occupied him well into 1054, and with the papacy inactive and William busy, Robert had no help from either.

Notes copied in the seventeenth century from a manuscript now lost may provide an insight into the diplomacy of those years, for they record a visit to England by Abbot John of Fécamp in early December 1054. The date and nature of the original source are unknown, but its author was interested in the abbey's estates in England and interpreted John's visit as an attempt to set their affairs in order and petition Edward for additional gifts. The vagueness of his account suggests he neither knew nor cared to include details of other business the abbot might have been pursuing. But Robert's situation and the hostages were pressing matters.

The notes begin by mentioning a 'little charter' in Fécamp's possession, in which Edward ordered that Steyning in Sussex should pass to Fécamp upon the death of Bishop Ælfwine (of Winchester). Given that Ælfwine died in 1047, the 'little charter' would have had to have been issued before that date. The notes then describe John's visit to England, to inspect the abbey's English estates, but they mention neither *Rammesleah*, which the abbey acquired from Cnut, nor Steyning, which should have come into its possession by the terms of the 'little charter'.[42] Instead, they claim John obtained from Edward a gift or confirmation of estates clustering in

[40] Bates, *William*, pp. 98–9.
[41] Ibid., pp. 129–33.
[42] See above, p. 45; *Neustria Pia*, ed. A. du Monstier (Rouen, 1633), p. 233.

Eastbourne (Sussex), but the absence of even the ghost of a charter from Edward confirming such lands to the abbey raises the suspicion that the story was invented after 1066, with a view to claiming possessions the abbey never acquired but had a chance of acquiring when the lands of the vanquished English became available. Conquest is a cynical enterprise. It was not for nothing that Fécamp sent ships in 1066. Even before the duke sailed, the monks made him promise to 'restore' to them Steyning, which Harold held.[43] William had no qualms about promising his enemy's land to a ducal monastery. Edward had set the precedent in the 1030s, when he promised land in England to Mont-Saint-Michel.

As for the 'little charter', there is no reason to think that it differed from the vernacular record, preserved in a thirteenth-century copy, in which Edward declares that Steyning is to pass to Fécamp on the death of Bishop Ælfwine (S 1054). This record arouses suspicion by literally stating that it is a writ – something drafters of genuine writs never had cause to do – and by its lack of an address clause, which by the 1040s was a standard element.[44] William the Conqueror was evidently content with the 'sealed letters' of Edward, shown to him in the 1070s by the monks of Fécamp, for they are mentioned in his charter confirming Steyning to the abbey.[45] Still, it is doubtful that he would have rejected a forged writ, if written over the erased text of an authentic writ, on a slip of parchment with Edward's seal still attached.[46] To do so would have required the critical study of writ formulas current in the 1040s; and besides, William was willing to grant Steyning to Fécamp anyway. The description of the 'little charter' (i.e. writ) – probably S 1054 – and the reference to 'sealed letters' of Edward point to the forging of a writ in the years around the Conquest by fécampois brethren who desired the lucrative port of Steyning. Later they tried their luck again by claiming Edward had given them estates in Eastbourne.

It is possible of course that John visited England for no reason besides attending to his abbey's English possessions. Earlier that year he resigned the abbacy of Dijon, which he had held conjointly with Fécamp since 1052, and having thus disburdened himself, he could turn to his English

---

[43] Bates, *William*, p. 226.

[44] S 1054 begins: 'Eadweard cyngc cyð on ðysan gewrite ðæt ic habbe geunnen ðæs lands æt Stæningan into ðan halgan mynstre æt Feskamp . . .' ('King Edward declares in this writ that I have given the estate at Steyning to the holy minster at Fécamp . . .').

[45] See *Regesta*, nos 141, 141a and 144.

[46] Erasing the text of a writ, to which a genuine seal was attached, then writing over the erasure was a trick employed after the Conquest by the monks of Christ Church, Canterbury, apparently to good effect. S 1088, a writ with Edward's seal attached, was overwritten by two scribes, possibly on different occasions. A. Hudson, 'Anglo-Saxon Seal Impressions at the British Library', unpublished paper given for the British Academy–Royal Historical Society Joint Committee on Anglo-Saxon Charters', 22nd Annual Symposium, at the British Academy, 11 September 2017.

interests. He had, however, earlier served as an ambassador for Leo's
regime, and might have acted on this occasion in Leo's name, though
Leo was in captivity. Leo had written before of dispatching a legate to
England in his letter to Edward of *c.* 1050. In 1070, when Bishop Wulfstan
of Worcester made his profession to the new Norman archbishop of
Canterbury, he said that Leo and four subsequent popes had summoned
Stigand to answer a charge that he had expelled Robert from his see and
worn his pallium. Wulfstan also stated that the popes excommunicated
and condemned him, presumably on his failure to respond.[47] Though the
regime which forced him to demolish his beloved cathedral could doubtless get Wulfstan to declare whatever it liked, there may be some truth to
the claim that admonitory letters from the pope were delivered to
Stigand.[48] Robert acquired letters from Leo, before joining John of
Fécamp, in 1053, in Paris and Normandy; and John is found in England
the following year. News of Leo's captivity, however, would have blunted
a papal reprimand. If John was pleading for Robert, it would not have
been the first time he failed in an embassy. As Leo's ambassador to the
Normans of southern Italy in 1050, he had suffered insults and influenced
no one.[49] Edward was known for his generosity to foreign ascetics, but he
had reasons not to restore Robert. There were besides more pressing
matters. England was still without an heir.

NEXT IN LINE

As work advanced on the abbey, his mausoleum, the king resolved on a
course of action to address the problem of the succession. As early as 1051
he had revealed his determination by considering divorce; but the triumphal return of Edith's father and Edward's ambivalence had postponed
any resolution. Whether Edward and Edith were still trying to have a
child, an alternative plan was needed; and since the king had given up on
the idea of remarriage out of moral duty, devotion, or political necessity,
customs of royal succession dictated an approach to the senior eligible
claimant of the bloodline. In a faraway land, that line was thriving in the
son of Edmund Ironside, who had been exiled in infancy long ago, in 1016.
His name too was Edward, and it is no surprise that his namesake uncle,
who had passed his exile in Normandy abiding in the absolute conviction
of his own right to inherit the throne, turned to him as the back-up candidate once it became clear, or increasingly clear, he would beget no son.

[47] *Canterbury Professions*, ed. M. Richter, Canterbury and York Society, 67 (Torquay,
1973), no. 31 (p. 26).
[48] William of Malmesbury, *Life of Wulfstan*, in idem, *Saints' Lives*, ed. and tr. M.
Winterbottom and R. M. Thomson, OMT (Oxford, 2002), p. 123.
[49] J. Leclercq and J.-P. Bonnes, *Un maître de la vie spirituelle au XIe siècle* (Paris, 1946),
p. 18.

1. Emma with her children Edward and Alfred (exiting right), as depicted in an illustrated Anglo-Norman verse *Life* of St Edward the Confessor.

2. Emma (entering left) presenting her children to Duke Richard II of Normandy, as depicted in an illustrated verse *Life* of St Edward the Confessor.

3. *Encomium Emma Reginae*, prefatory image. Emma, enthroned, receiving the work from its author, while her sons, Harthacnut and Edward, look on.

4. Wisdom enthroned in her temple, from a Canterbury manuscript of *Psychomachia* by Prudentius. Inspired by Prudentius, Folcard presents Edward (as Faith) and Edith (Concord) ushering in the reign of Holy Wisdom.

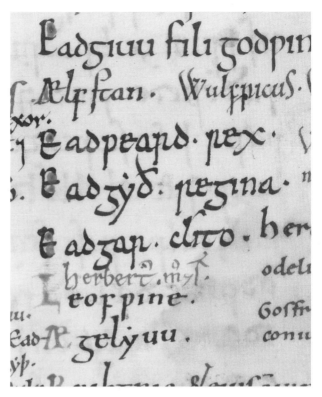

5. Detail of a page from the Book of Life of New Minster abbey, Winchester, showing the names of King Edward, Queen Edith and Edgar Ætheling, entered in a block of three as a single entry.

6. The king in his court (England, *c.* 1000).

7. The first issue of the reign, Edward's new coinage proclaims the message, 'PEACE', around the cross on the reverse. *Pacx, c.* 1042–4.

8. The king sits enthroned, facing, holding orb and sceptre. *Sovereign Eagles, c.* 1056–9.

9. Edward is bearded and crowned, facing. *Facing Bust, c.* 1062–5.

10. Edward is bearded and crowned, facing right. He holds a sceptre. *Pyramids*, *c*. 1065–6.

11. Harold, crowned and bearded, faces left and holds a sceptre. His first and only issue, imitating Edward's first issue (reverse) and last issue (obverse), proclaims the message, 'PEACE'. *Pax*, 1066.

12. 341 Edward *Pacx* pennies, from a hoard of about 2,300 coins, buried in an earthenware wine bottle (a 'costrel') at Leziate in Norfolk, *c*. 1043. The hoard was reported in 2019.

13. Writ of Edward the Confessor with seal. Portions of the text have been erased and rewritten by forgers. The seal is authentic.

14. Byzantine gold and enamel reliquary cross, c. 950–c. 1050, from Constantinople (Istanbul). Edward was buried with a similar reliquary cross, likewise depicting saints identified by Greek inscriptions.

15. Edward in conversation with Harold and another man; the opening scene of the Bayeux Tapestry.

16. William and Harold discuss a man whom Harold is leading by the hand; above, peacocks confronted, one displaying its tail.

17. Edward reprimands Harold upon his return from Normandy.

18. Edward's body is borne to the newly completed church at Westminster. The hand of God blesses the place of burial. Bell-ringers attend the cortège.

19. Edward addresses close companions on his deathbed; below, his corpse is wrapped in a shroud.

20. Harold is offered the symbols of royal power and is proclaimed king by the assent of the people (on the left) and by Stigand (right); Harold and Stigand look directly at the viewer.

21. The reconstructed head of King Sven Estrithsson of Denmark (modelled on his skull in Roskilde cathedral). The head is on display in the National Museum in Copenhagen.

22. The Sea Stallion from Glendalough, built 2000–4: a reconstruction of the great longship Skuldelev 2. Thirty metres long, it can be rowed by a crew of sixty. Skuldelev 2 was built in 1042, probably in Dublin.

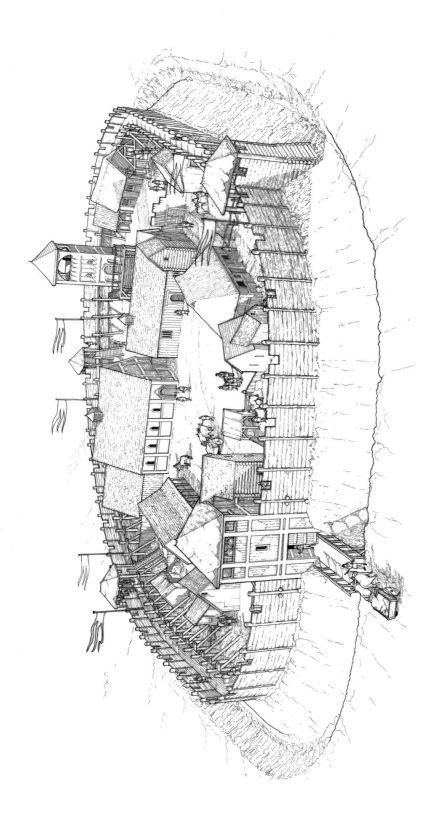

23. Impression of a hypothetical castle, England, c. 1050.

24. Detail from a Byzantine silk shroud, buried with Bishop Gunther of Bamberg in 1065. Edward was buried in a Byzantine silk shroud the following year.

25. Fragments of eleventh-century Byzantine silk from the funerary clothes of Edward the Confessor, removed from his tomb in 1686. The pattern shows birds confronted.

Duty-bound to his bloodline and the provision of an heir, the king imple-mented a plan to bring the aetheling to England. The fact that he would be the second foreignly reared aetheling – after Edward in 1041 – to be invited to return as the heir apparent attests the shared understanding among the political elite, both at home and abroad, that the throne should properly pass to a son of Cerdic's line, even if he was a virtual foreigner, who had not set foot in England and may have spoken no English.

Trusting to Bishop Ealdred, an experienced ambassador who had been on a mission to Rome, Edward ordered him to make ready, which Ealdred evidently did, for he deputed the spiritual offices of his episcopacy to a neighbour, Bishop Leofwine of Lichfield; assigned the temporalities of Worcester diocese to the monk Æthelwig of Evesham, a good adminis-trator who could be trusted to take care of military operations in the Welsh marches (as he would demonstrate in 1074); and installed an abbot at Winchcombe, which he had held in plurality since the death of its last incumbent the previous year.[50] Organizational proficiency of this sort was no small consideration in Edward's choice of servants, but such prepara-tory efforts do imply the expectation of a prolonged absence. Negotiating the return of an aetheling was no straightforward matter. Edward may have instructed Ealdred to take the time he needed.

After Edmund Ironside's death in 1016, his infant sons, Edward and Edgar, had been conveyed overseas, but instead of arriving in Normandy like their uncles Edward and Alfred, they had ended up in Russia at the court of the grand prince of Kiev. Iaroslav I (1019–54) controlled the passage of sea-borne trade from Scandinavia to Byzantium, making him a power-broker in the Baltic region.[51] Politically a speculative investor, he harboured exiled princes and made a policy of marrying them to his daughters, whose Greek names (like all things Greek to rudimentary civi-lizations in the West) were cultural signifiers, denoting elegance, piety, and taste. Anastasia and Elisabeth were wed to future kings when they were still aspiring exiles at Iaroslav's court. The Hungarian duke Andrew, Anastasia's husband, became Andrew I of Hungary (1046–60). Elisabeth's husband, Harald Sigurdsson, became Harald Hardrada of Norway (1046–66), and about the time Duke Robert of Normandy was encour-aging Edward's bid for the throne, Iaroslav was supporting Edward the Exile, son of Edmund Ironside, by marrying him to his daughter Agatha.[52] Although the twenty-year-old prince was not a contender in the

---

[50] Freeman, *NC*, II, pp. 379–80. On Æthelwig's later military role, see *JW*, iii, p. 25.

[51] E. Melnikova, 'The Baltic Policy of Jaroslav the Wise', in U. Fransson, M. Svedin, S. Bergerbrant, and F. Androshchuk, eds, *Cultural Interaction between East and West: Archaeology, Artefacts and Human Contacts in Northern Europe* (Stockholm, 2007), pp. 73–7.

[52] R. Jetté, 'Is the Mystery of the Origins of Agatha, Wife of Edward the Exile, Finally Solved?', *New England Historical and Genealogical Register* 150 (1996), 417–32; N. Ingham, 'Has a Missing Daughter of Iaroslav Mudyri been Found?', *Russian History* 25 (1999), 231–70. Alternative pedigrees rely on injudicious appraisals of the evidence or the multiplication of

succession dispute of 1036, Iaroslav's policy reached far enough to influence its course, for another young prince living in exile with Edward at the
Kievan court left in that year to claim his father's kingdom of Norway. He
was Magnus, whom we encountered earlier, son of Olaf Haraldsson; and
it was his belligerence that kept Harthacnut in Denmark and threatened
Edward in the early 1040s. Without the support he had received from
Iaroslav, events of 1036 might have taken a different turn. And while
Magnus was threatening first Harthacnut then Edward, Iaroslav was
nurturing the son of Edmund Ironside.

In 1051, when Edward was pondering what to do about the succession,
Kievan dynastic politics became topical again with the wedding of
Iaroslav's fourth daughter, Anna, to Henry of France. Anointed and
crowned in Rheims cathedral, she soon bore the son Henry lacked from
his first marriage and gave him the Greek name Philip.[53] Edward maintained contact with the French court through his chaplain-ambassador
Élinand. Anna, sister to Agatha, was an obvious possible source of news
about Edward the Exile and might have been an avenue of communica-
tion in the discussions around his potential return. By 1054, Edward,
Agatha, and their children, Margaret, Christina, and Edgar, were living
in Hungary. On the death of Edgar's eponymous uncle, Edward and his
son had become the sole conveyors of Cerdic's bloodline. Moreover,
Iaroslav's habit of marrying his daughters to ambitious exiled princes, and
the decision to invest in a mission to bring him back to England, suggest
that the Exile had not abandoned his birthright. So it was decided that
Ealdred should go to the German court and approach the emperor about
how to proceed, for the emperor was England's ally and Hungary's overlord. The difficulty was that the emperor refused to acknowledge King
Andrew of Hungary, who had come to power after a rebellion against the
emperor's client-king Peter. Whether the English king was aware of the
obstacle to negotiations, bypassing Henry III would have been an affront,
so Ealdred's party made its dutiful way to Cologne.

The D author, who certainly moved in Ealdred's orbit, describes
Agatha vaguely as the emperor's kinswoman, hinting at another reason
for Edward's ambassador to have turned to Henry III. To the chronicler,
who took an interest in the emperor, Henry was Agatha's most powerful
relation and the only one worth naming.[54] Possibly he knew no additional

suppositions with a view to reconciling irreconcilable sources. For the settled view, see now
C. Raffensperger and D. J. Birnbaum, *Rusian Genealogy*: http://genealogy.obdurodon.org/
findPerson.php?person=agafia (accessed 30 October 2017).

[53] T. Zajac, 'Gloriosa Regina or "Alien Queen"? Some Reconsiderations on Anna
Yaroslavna's Queenship (r. 1050–1075)', *Royal Studies Journal* 3 (2016), 23–70, at pp. 31,
34, 35.

[54] ASC D, 1057; John of Worcester, trying to make sense of the relationship, identifies
her as the daughter of a brother of the emperor: *JW*, ii, pp. 503–5. Her name alone makes
this theory highly unlikely.

details, but his claim was not incorrect. Henry of France had taken Anna as his second wife after first marrying the daughter of Henry III's uterine brother Liudolf of Frisia. His first marriage had made him the emperor's nephew-in-law. His second made Agatha the emperor's kinswoman. What the chronicler's emphasis on her imperial kinship obscures is the extent of her and her husband's connectedness to various royal courts. Not only would the marriage of 1051 have made the Kievan dynasty the talk of the courts of Europe – and it should be noted that King Edward communicated with Anna's husband until at least 1052 through the embassies of his French chaplain Élinand – it also made Edward the Exile the brother-in-law of three kings, namely Henry of France, Harald of Norway, and Andrew of Hungary.[55] Ealdred's mission to bring back the blood-heir had international dimensions. Several mighty rulers had an interest in the Exile's return.

SCOTLAND AND WALES

As Edward refashioned his image and planned to entertain an heir, his military priorities were shifting. In the 1040s, sea-borne attacks from the Danish-Flemish piracy zone had been his main concern, but with the abatement of conflict in the North Sea and the stabilization of the Norwegian and Danish regimes, the threat there had subsided. In the 1040s, the king had been frequently at Sandwich. In the 1050s, no visits to Sandwich are recorded, as if Edward the naval commander no longer needed to watch the coast. Flanders was now an ally, albeit perhaps, like Normandy, a sulky and an ambitious one. The other military zone of the 1040s was the Welsh march, where Edward had pursued an aggressive policy in alliance with the northern Gruffudd against his southern Welsh namesake. After the southern king's raid into Herefordshire in 1052, the policy had culminated in the political assassination of his brother Rhys in retaliation for injuries. Edward had demanded his head, as a warning to the southern king, and it was delivered to him at Gloucester upon Twelfth Night (5 January 1053).[56] His dealings with both Gruffudds – sending Earl Swegn to campaign with one and beheading the brother of the other – delivered a stern message. They also displayed the airs of an overlord towards his underlings.

After 1053, events not of Edward's choosing but partly of his making drew him deeper into Welsh and Scottish affairs and further towards the insular dominion credited to his most celebrated forebears, notably Athelstan and Edgar. He was spurred along this path by what the *Vita* describes as the near-simultaneous rebellions of the Welsh and Scottish

---

[55] Adam of Bremen mentions only daughters of Iaroslav who were married to kings: *GHEP*, p. 153.

[56] ASC C, 1052 [1052–3]; D, 1053.

kings. The author gives the impression of two uprisings. Indeed, when he wrote, their successor kings in those kingdoms were Edward's clients, who would have been rebelling had they opposed the English king.[57] It is also clear from the disdain with which he notes their 'barbarous' traits that he regarded the Scots and Welsh as inferior peoples, a sentiment which, as an immigrant, he had absorbed at Edward's court. His assumptions aside, there is no evidence that Macbeth, king of Alba (i.e. Scotland), or Gruffudd of North Wales paid tribute to Edward or was in any other respect his client, although there were precedents for such relationships, and clientage in the 1040s and 1050s is by no means implausible.

The *Vita* moreover is correct that hostilities erupted almost at the same time, for after a decade of peaceful dealing with both rulers, Edward sent an army against Macbeth in 1054 and fought Gruffudd ap Llewelyn the following year. Though it is tempting to see a more martial persona in the Pointed Helmet coinage of *c*. 1053, and to speculate about Edward's growing appetite for insular dominion after recent political embarrassments, the causes of these wars must be sought in the poorly documented regions where they occurred. Mystery inevitably surrounds them, but Edward's determination to intervene with timely and effective violence remained as central to his strategy as its delegation to military commanders. In the 1040s, his deployment of Earl Swegn, transplanted housecarls, and Norman castellans bore witness to ingenuity and experimentation – the same traits discernible in his privatization of coastal defences, or rather their delegation to south-eastern ports. Recognized early by the encomiast as a quick learner, he had learned from the successes and failures that followed, becoming wiser in his operations, choosier in his commanders, and firmer in his resolve.[58]

There were various reasons for a client king to cast off his clientage. Maybe the tribute was becoming burdensome, an investment with too few benefits. Perhaps the politicking of internal agents, or external pressures, required a reconfiguration of alliances. Overlords too would seek to replace clients who were financing tribute payment by raiding the overlord's territory or committing other intolerable affronts. The outbreak of war in 1054 is a reminder of how little we know about diplomatic relations with Alba. Macbeth's activities are obscure because sources for the north are meagre. A few details, nevertheless, help set the scene. His pilgrimage to Rome in 1050 indicates he had a grasp on his kingdom, since he was confident enough to leave it and go abroad; while his lavish distribution of alms on that occasion might indicate he was canvassing support for

---

[57] *Vita*, pp. 65–7: 'they rose up' (*insurrexerunt*); cf. the poem, *The Death of Edward*, in ASC C, 1065 [1065–6]; D, 1065 [1065–6], which describes the late king as the ruler of Scots and Welsh.

[58] Keynes and Love, 'Earl Godwine's Ship', p. 196.

an ambitious scheme.[59] That Macbeth welcomed the castellans Osbern Pentecost and Hugh reveals he was recruiting warriors. They were skilled in marcher warfare and would fight for him in 1054. By welcoming them, he was exploiting English disunity and forging ties with Normandy.

If Macbeth was hoping to enlarge his dominion by occupying additional territory, there was Lothian – the disputed land between the Tweed and the Forth – to consider, and there was also the kingdom (or former kingdom) of the Cumbrians, which extended both north and south of the Solway. In 945 the English king Edmund had ceded it to Malcolm I of Alba on the condition of receiving his support by land and sea.[60] Later, after it came into the hands of an independent Cumbrian dynasty, Edward's father had campaigned there in the manner of an overlord exercising his authority. The absence of any record of a king of the Cumbrians after Owain in 1018, coupled with the fact that Earl Siward is recorded as having dominated territory 'formerly belonging to the Cumbrians', hints at the fragmentation of the polity at about this time.[61] In such an arena, different claimants could test their strength in battle.

Edward sent Siward north with a mighty force comprising a raiding land-army and a raiding ship-army. The nearest precedent for his action was Æthelred's campaign of 1000, in which the king had dispatched ships from Chester while harrying the Cumbrian kingdom with his land-army, hoping to rendezvous near the Clyde.[62] An entry in the *Annals of Ulster* against the year 1054, recording 'a battle between the men of Alba and the Saxons, in which there were slain 3000 of the men of Alba and 1500 of the Saxons, including Doilfinn son of Finntor', reveals the involvement of at least one military leader who was known across the Irish Sea.[63] C reports a battle on 27 July in which Siward fought the Scots and put Macbeth to flight, returning laden with booty. His son Osbern, his sister's son Siward, and some of his housecarls and the king's housecarls were killed there. John of Worcester adds that all the Normans who had fled to Macbeth's kingdom were killed too, meaning Osbern Pentecost, Hugh, and their followers.[64] Eliminating the Normans may have been a second objective.

John was one of three historians writing sixty or seventy years later who provided what he thought was another detail. Siward, he tells us, after defeating Macbeth, set up Malcolm, 'son of the king of the Cumbrians', as king in his place, acting on Edward's orders. William of Malmesbury uses

[59] Woolf, *Pictland to Alba*, p. 259.

[60] G. Molyneaux, *The Formation of the English Kingdom in the Tenth Century* (Oxford, 2015), p. 33.

[61] S 1243; F. Edmonds, 'The Emergence and Transformation of Medieval Cumbria', *SHR* 93 (2014), 195–216, at pp. 208–9, and see below, p. 181.

[62] ASC E, 1000; Woolf, *Pictland to Alba*, p. 222.

[63] *The Annals of Ulster (to A.D. 1131)*, ed. S. Mac Airt and G. Mac Niocaill (Dublin, 1983), U1054.6; Woolf, *Pictland to Alba*, p. 261.

[64] ASC C, D, 1054; *JW*, ii, p. 575.

similar words to say that Siward installed Malcolm, 'son of the king of the Cumbrians', though unlike John he indicates that Macbeth died in Siward's battle. That was certainly not true. Their contemporary, Simeon of Durham, noted in an annal for 1046 – a mistake for 1054 – that Siward 'expelled Macbeth and set another in his place; but after his departure Macbeth recovered the kingdom'. He does not tell us who the 'other' short-lived client ruler was.[65] It might therefore seem we have the testimony of three careful, though later, historians claiming Siward toppled Macbeth and installed a client ruler. The problem, however, is that their voices are not independent, for they drew on each other. We know at least that John and William compared notes, and Simeon borrowed from an early version of John's chronicle.[66] An error generated by one could have been taken up by all, and it is not in doubt in William's case that Malcolm, 'son of the king of the Cumbrians', is meant to be the Malcolm who, four years later, slew Macbeth in battle and claimed the Scottish throne.

Had John and William referred to Malcolm, 'son of the king of Alba', it would be easier to dismiss their story as a conflation of Siward's victory over Macbeth and Malcolm's victory over him in 1058. For it would be an unquestionable reference to Malcolm, Donnchad's son. Donnchad is better known to us as the good king Duncan, immortalized by Shakespeare and murdered by Macbeth. Whether he was king of the Cumbrians he was certainly king of Alba. And since his son recovered the Alban throne in battle at a date in the 1050s which they may not have known, it would have been tempting for twelfth-century historians to have assumed that he obtained it when Siward defeated Macbeth. Their reference to a Malcolm, 'son of the king of the Cumbrians', is confusing because Donnchad was, foremost, a king of Alba.[67] If he was also king of the Cumbrians, it would have been strange to refer to him by the title of his lesser kingdom. Still, there is no evidence that John or William knew that Donnchad was king of Alba, and they may not have known the identity of Malcolm's father. Neither in fact mentions Donnchad. Sometimes John and William made reasonable guesses and got things wrong.[68] Here we might conclude that they compared ideas and merged two victories over Macbeth into one, while supposing that Malcolm was the son of a Cumbrian king. Simeon's confusion is also explicable. If, for example, he knew that Macbeth retained the throne after 1054, it would account for his idea that 'Macbeth

[65] JW, ii, p. 575; GR, II, § 196 (p. 349); Woolf, Pictland to Alba, p. 262.

[66] M. Brett, 'John of Worcester and his Contemporaries', in R. H. C. Davis and J. M. Wallace-Hadrill, eds, The Writing of History in the Middle Ages: Essays presented to Richard William Southern (Oxford, 1981), 101–26, at pp. 113–17; JW, ii, pp. lxxi, lxxix–lxxx.

[67] Cf. most recently Alex Woolf, pursuing A. A. M. Duncan's argument that Malcolm, 'son of the king of the Cumbrians', was a different person: Pictland to Alba, pp. 261–3.

[68] R. R. Darlington and P. McGurk, 'The "Chronicon ex Chronicis" of "Florence" of Worcester and Its Uses of Sources for English History before 1066', ANS 5 (1983), 185–96, at pp. 186, 187, 190.

recovered the kingdom'. He was trying to make John and William's version fit with his own knowledge of northern affairs.

We may learn a little more about this matter from a writ issued by Gospatric, a senior member of the House of Bamburgh, granting titles and freedoms to his followers in territory 'formerly belonging to the Cumbrians'.[69] The lands in question may be roughly defined by the Derwent, the Eamont, the lakeland mountains, and the marshes at the head of the Solway.[70] A key clause for dating the writ is the order that no man should break the peace 'which Earl Siward and I have granted him'. Since a lord's peace expired at his death, there was no point referring to Siward's after his death in 1055. That Siward is placed before the issuer suggests Gospatric was his deputy in the territory lately annexed from the kingdom of the Cumbrians. A likely context for its acquisition was the defeat of Macbeth. Although the C/D record implies that the battle with Macbeth occurred in Alba, one could equally try out the idea that Macbeth was driven from the Cumbrian kingdom. This hypothesis is attractive because, while Edward had no obvious reason to topple an Alban king, he would have been forced to act if Macbeth occupied Cumbria with the aid of Norman castellans.

At this point, remembering that Siward's forces advanced by land and sea is important, because the uplands extending from Northumbria through central Scotland formed a barrier between the east coast plain and the west coast plain. Irish interest in the campaign, and the involvement of the western Northumbrian leader Doilfinn, son of Finntor, could relate to a conflict that took place in Clydesdale. In this scenario, we might imagine the English army advancing up the Roman road from York, via Carlisle, while the ship-army steered towards the Clyde estuary. Edward, like his father, was attacking in a pincer movement. The Irish in Ulster, who were concerned about Cumbrian affairs, paid attention to the conflict. Macbeth met Siward's forces somewhere in the western Lowlands, the Normans were killed, and the fortifications they had possibly erected were occupied or destroyed. If we treat Gospatric's writ as part of the outcome, we find him implanted defensively with vice-regal powers and autonomy in 1054–5. A son of Ealdorman Uhtred of Northumbria (d. 1016) and his second wife, Gospatric was in his forties.[71] Installing him near Carlisle was a way of securing the western approach to the Tyne Gap and the Stainmore Gap, both of which were historically attack routes into Siward's earldom. It was also a way of bringing the House of Bamburgh more securely into the pen of officialdom.

[69] S 1243; *Charters of Northern Houses*, ed. D. A. Woodman, Anglo-Saxon Charters 16 (Oxford, 2012), pp. 363–7, 70–8; text and translation at pp. 370–1 (no. 21).

[70] Harmer, *Writs*, no. 121 (pp. 419–24); cf. W. E. Kapelle, *The Norman Conquest of the North: The Region and its Transformation, 1000–1135* (London, 1979), pp. 43–4.

[71] A. Williams, *The English and the Norman Conquest* (Woodbridge, 1995), p. 28 for the family tree. Cf. Stafford, *Emma and Edith*, p. 270, picking up the same individual in 1064.

While English supremacy in the north remained precarious in the aftermath of Siward's death, Gruffudd ap Llewelyn was exploiting the weakness of his southern rival Gruffudd ap Rhydderch, which was in no small part the result of Edward's Welsh policy. For by allying with the northern Welsh king and punishing his southern namesake, Edward had tipped the balance of power in Wales. In 1055, ap Llewelyn found his chance to kill ap Rhydderch and extend his rule from Anglesey to the Severn estuary. He then turned against England, either to rally the warring Welsh by making the English their common enemy, or because the costs of an enlarged kingdom forced him to raid across the border, or because (like Macbeth?) he found an opportunity to exploit divisions at Edward's court. Folcard, who depicts Macbeth and Gruffudd as Edward's clients, says they rebelled 'almost at the same time', referring to conflicts that erupted in 1054 and 1055, and flared up intermittently thereafter.[72] Between one eruption and the other, when Macbeth was licking his wounds and Gruffudd seized his chance to conquer Wales, intrigue once again enveloped Edward's court, this time over who should replace Siward.

Edward was facing the challenge of replacing an earl established since Cnut's time in a remote and complex part of the realm. There is no indication he had visited the north or had much time to consider whom to appoint to the Northumbrian earldom. Death in battle had removed Siward's elder son from the running. His younger son, Waltheof, was still a child. Edward needed a man who could take the mantle of his predecessor and rally the Bernician nobility, the House of Bamburgh and its allies, if not himself of their number. The king also had to consider the balance of influence between the Leofwinesons and the Godwinsons and needed an earl who would be active at court and amenable to a southern command structure. Over the last few years, as Siward attended to the far north, the Leofwinesons had increased their influence in Lincolnshire and Nottinghamshire. Later in the reign, those counties were regarded as part of the earldom of Northumbria, and that may have been true in Siward's day – there is a gap in our knowledge. No doubt the Leofwinesons wished to retain influence in the zone, but a new earl might lay claim to it. Either way, the cubs of the two rival Houses would fight for every scrap of meat.

Folcard, an admirer of the Godwinsons, writing ten years later, inadvertently reveals the tension that had long existed. He does so mainly by omission, for his account merely praises Leofric in passing and says no more about his son Ælfgar than the fact that he was the father of two sons who are introduced as Tostig's long-standing enemies.[73] Tracing the progress of this rivalry between the Godwinsons and the Leofwinesons as

[72] *Vita*, p. 65.
[73] Ibid., pp. 35, 77. It is significant that Folcard on p. 35 lists Siward before Leofric, though the latter was the senior earl. His ordering is further evidence of his northern perspective.

it advanced through the second and third generations is key to interpreting the final decade of the reign. For it would fuel not only the
simmering of Edward's court, but also the breakdown of relations with
Gruffudd ap Llywelyn and the rise of northern opposition to Edward's
regime. Leofric and Godwine had sparred since the 1030s. In the 1040s,
Godwine had benefited more from Edward's largesse, while Leofric
bettered him at winning arguments in meetings of the witan. Ælfgar,
however, was falling behind Harold by the 1050s. And the appointment to
the Northumbrian earldom would determine which of the rival Houses
came out on top.

Folcard reports that Harold and Edith were lobbying for Tostig's
appointment – some indication that relations were still good between the
three of them.[74] Baldwin of Flanders might conceivably have lobbied for
it too. Without knowing Ælfgar's side of the story, we cannot be sure he
was in the running, but the sequel suggests he was. We do know that
at some point Ælfgar married his daughter Ealdgyth to Gruffudd ap
Llywelyn.[75] For Gruffudd, the marriage was a step towards extending his
dominion into Mercia. Whether the two were wed by 1055, Gruffudd may
have lobbied for Ælfgar's promotion to Northumbria, and it is possible
that Leofric, who had a track record of winning over the witan, lobbied
for him too. Since Edward's way of operating was to determine whom he
would appoint before presenting his candidate to the witan for approval,
it should have been plain that the witan was meant to be a rubber stamp.
Speaking publicly against a stitched-up appointment was an insult to the
king and may have breached a convention that objectors should extract
their concessions in advance.

A week before Mid-Lent (19 March 1055), the king summoned the
witan to discharge business that included Siward's replacement. He had
probably made up his mind to give the earldom to Tostig, but Tostig's
faction anticipated opposition and feared it would be strong enough to
sway the king. So they sprang a trap to remove their rival Ælfgar. E, which
gives the only report of the manoeuvre, says it was put to him that he was
a traitor to the king and all the people of the land. The nature of his
treachery is unspecified, but E does remark that he 'admitted this before
all the men who were gathered there, although the words shot out against
his will'.[76] Tostig may have accused him himself, for he stood to benefit
and was ready to charge even Harold with treachery before the witan on
a later occasion.[77] It was Tostig moreover, not Harold, who incurred the
enmity of Ælfgar's sons. The other accounts merely indicate that Ælfgar
was provoked to lose his temper. C, possibly a Mercian source, claims that

[74] Ibid., p. 49; ASC E, 1055.
[75] Baxter, *Earls of Mercia*, pp. 299–300.
[76] ASC E, 1055.
[77] *Vita*, p. 81.

he 'was outlawed without any fault' – the closest the writer comes to criti-cizing the king. D softens the criticism, changing the words to 'almost without fault'.[78] E follows its description of Ælfgar's outburst by saying that the king gave Siward's earldom to Tostig. The juxtaposition is our reason for thinking that Ælfgar was outlawed for opposing Tostig's promotion.

The complaint that Ælfgar was 'outlawed without fault' adds a chilly touch to the cultic atmosphere we earlier perceived to be intensifying around the jewelled figure on the throne. As in modern cults, where one or two fierce devotees have emerged as the gatekeepers of a figure of adoration, Edith and her brothers were installing themselves as guard-dogs around the unearthly king. Devouring the monopolies of exclusive proximity, they built their power around Edward's own narrative, loyally presenting him as the untouchable anointed,[79] and savaging the rivals who dared oppose his will. Probably Osgod in 1046, and Ælfgar in 1055, ran into the Godwinson hounds. Their symbiotic relationship with the king failed only when Edward's designs went against them. Between the last eruption of tensions (itself a result of that breakdown in 1051) and the Lenten gathering of 1055, other factions at court could still hang on to the hope of sharing dominion with Edward's in-laws. The events of 1055 finally demonstrated that their hopes were in vain. It may be that there was – unknown to us – a third, Bernician, candidate for the earldom of Northumbria. The Gospatric whom we encountered as Siward's deputy in Cumbria could have made a strong dynastic claim. If he did, Bernician ambitions were relegated too, though there is no sign of Gospatric falling out with Tostig at this stage.

Ælfgar's designs upon Northumbria may have related to the fact that his wife was of the old Northumbrian nobility – a kinswoman of the Northumbrian ealdorman murdered in 1006, on the orders of Edward's father.[80] Another consideration was the risk that would be posed by having Tostig and Harold to the north and south, conspiring to separate his East Anglian domain from his paternal earldom of Mercia. Driven from the realm, he had little choice but to play the game his rivals had played successfully a few years earlier. He therefore took his ships (maybe with Leofric's approval, from Chester), sailed into the Irish Sea, and recruited eighteen crews of pirates. He also went to Gruffudd, who received him under safe-conduct. Clearly their alliance – marital or not – was effective by that date. If Gruffudd was already Ælfgar's son-in-law, he risked sharing the ill-effects of Ælfgar's fall from grace, a prospect which may have firmed his decision to break the peace with Edward. We should remember, however, he had lately become king over all of Wales,

[78] ASC C, D, 1055.
[79] Cf. *Vita*, p. 46.
[80] Baxter, *Earls of Mercia*, p. 301.

so had nowhere left to raid but over the English border. By siding with Edward's new enemy, Ælfgar gave ammunition to his accusers. But he had decided that in the absence of justice he might as well be a traitor.

The alliance of opposition made its move in October 1055, five months after Ælfgar's banishment. C, D, and E give him a prominent role in the raid it mounted, but the *Vita* and the Welsh chronicle *Brut y Tywysogyon* name Gruffudd alone as the aggressor. The *Brut* states that Gruffudd advanced a host against the English and arrayed his troops at Hereford. Earl Ralph, who was back in command in the marches, met him with a large army but was forced to retreat.[81] C relates that his troops fled 'before a spear was thrown' because 'they were on horseback', and that four or five hundred men were slain in the rout. The twelfth-century chronicler John of Worcester took this to mean that the *English* were on horseback, explaining that the French earl had ordered them to fight in an unaccustomed way and was the first to flee when his experiment failed. The original report, reflected in C, makes better sense, however, if the phrase 'because they were on horseback' refers to the attacking army, charging Ralph's infantry. Caught by a cavalry manoeuvre with no time to hurl a spear, the fleeing English must have been rapidly overtaken and cut down. John of Worcester was so busy making sense of his misreading by coming up with a tale of foreign ineptitude that he failed to spot the absurdity of thinking that hundreds of fleeing horsemen were caught and slain by pursuing infantry.[82] Aided by Ælfgar, Gruffudd's mounted raiders next set fire to Hereford. They ransacked and burned the cathedral, killed the priests who were holding out inside, slaughtered some of the townspeople, and led away others for the slave markets.[83]

Switching commanders, Edward turned to Harold, who swiftly assembled the levies of neighbouring counties near Gloucester and marched them a little way into Wales, exposing Gruffudd's vulnerability. At the same time, he ordered a ditch and fortified embankment to be constructed around Hereford, which would keep out the cavalry. Harold, Gruffudd, and Ælfgar then negotiated a peace at Billingsley between Ludlow and Bridgnorth, where it was agreed that Ælfgar should receive back his earldom and all his possessions, after his hostile alliance 'had done maximum harm', as D remarks disapprovingly.[84] Though it is probable Leofric dissociated himself from his son's rebellion, he did not act as a peacebroker, and his sympathy with the rebel cause is indicated by the fact that Ælfgar sent his pirates to Chester, in his father's earldom, to collect their pay. Indeed, it is likely he had embarked from there, since the

---

[81] *Brut y Tywysogyon*, ed. Jones, p. 14; cf. *Vita*, p. 65 and ASC C, D, E, 1055.

[82] ASC C, D, 1055; *JW*, ii, pp. 577–9.

[83] ASC C, 1055. The chroniclers tend to distinguish between hostage-taking and slave-taking.

[84] ASC D, 1055.

alternative would have him sailing round the coast from his East Anglian earldom against the Channel current and into the Irish Sea.

The ruthlessness of 1055, which was exhibited in the manoeuvring that led to Ælfgar's banishment and raised a notch in his retaliation, erupted from old rivalries which were being renewed in the second generation. It marked a breakdown of the entente of 1052. For all the concern about English unity, the avoidance of civil war, and the danger of exposing the realm to foreign enemies, rivals at Edward's court were once again pushing each other to the limits. After the sack of Hereford on 24 October, the peace agreed at Billingsley was a way forward, but it was a pragmatic agreement inspired less by ideals of cooperative government than a realization, on both sides, of the harm they were willing to do. Each had felt the other's edge, and both recoiled. It remained to be seen whether the new heavyweights Harold and Ælfgar were doing no more than assuming their fathers' rivalry at court. Godwine and Leofric had begun it. They had also learned where to stop. Still, it is not clear who was responsible for Ælfgar's entrapment. If it was Tostig, it might explain Harold's role in brokering a peace.

Harold used the crisis in the march as an opportunity to extend his command into the void created by Ralph's incompetence and the withdrawal of Earl Odda. An old man who became a monk before dying the following year, Odda played no visible part in Harold's efforts around Gloucestershire, despite having a hall at Deerhurst and possibly holding the county within his earldom.[85] Harold asserted his lordship in Herefordshire by fortifying Hereford and, in 1056, after the death of its bishop, replacing him with his own chaplain, Leofgar. Edward must have approved the appointment, but sober men of religion frowned upon it as a further token of indulgence. Leofgar fancied himself as a warrior. Contrary to religious custom, he retained his long moustaches; and rather than trusting to the spiritual armour certified by St Paul, he 'abandoned his chrism and cross', took up earthly weapons and went to fight against Gruffudd. So much for the peace. Eight days before midsummer 1056 he was killed with his priests and Ælfnoth the sheriff and 'many other good men' – a formula used to signify disapproval.[86] It was an easy criticism to make after the outcome confirmed the chronicler's prejudices. Yet it was not the first time necessity demanded a fighting bishop in the marches, and Leofgar was the man to replace Ealdred in that role.

The punitive raids into Wales continued through 1056 until they achieved their aim of bringing Gruffudd to terms, though not without hardship, travail, and loss of men and horses, as C relates. The leaders of those campaigns, Leofric, Harold, and Ealdred (who had returned after a year in Germany), eventually effected a reconciliation in which Gruffudd

---

[85] *JW*, ii, p. 581; Williams, *Land, Power and Politics*.
[86] ASC C, 1055–6.

swore oaths to be a loyal and undeceiving client-king to Edward, who received his submission.[87] It was possibly on this occasion, but more likely after Gruffudd's second attack in 1058, that Edward ceded land to him between the Dee and Offa's Dyke, where the Welsh king acquired part of Atiscros hundred, with its iron mines, and Exestan hundred too.[88]

RESOLUTION AND SETBACK

William, meanwhile, who could not have been pleased at the expulsion of the Norman party (and may have been doubly offended at the killing of the Norman castellans), now had opportunities to put pressure on Edward, if he chose, by naming his own price for the return of the hostages and by championing the exiled archbishop, Robert of Jumièges. Stigand was the caretaker in Canterbury; Cynesige of York still required papal approval, and the absence of archiepiscopal authority was embarrassing. The conse-cration of a new pope in April 1055 provided Edward with a chance to ease the situation, for Victor II, the emperor's candidate, had belatedly been installed. Cynesige of York duly set off for Rome to collect the pallium, and Edward's relative Abbot Wulfric of Ely and Abbot Siward of Chertsey joined him: for they procured twin papal privileges for their monasteries, most probably on that occasion.[89] The privileges were addressed to Edward, as if the king were renewing an interest in papal affairs and sending ambassadors to forge ties with Victor.[90] The dispute over Canterbury ended in a virtual sense on 25 May, with Robert's death at Jumièges.[91] Whether the news reached either the pope or the English emissaries, the latter did not return with a pallium for Stigand. Cynesige, on the other hand, apparently did return with a pallium, for he exercised the dominion which Edward had re-established over the Welsh and Scots by consecrating a bishop of Llandaff, in 1056, and two Scottish bishops.[92]

---

[87] *JW*, ii, p. 581.

[88] F. C. Suppe, 'Who Was Rhys Sais? Some Comments on Anglo-Welsh Relations before 1066', *HSJ* 7 (1995), 63–73, at p. 70; *GDB* 263a; Charles-Edwards, *Wales and the Britons*, p. 565. For the campaign of 1058 see below, pp. 191–2.

[89] ASC D, 1055; *LE*, pp. 163–4, 418. Savill cautions that the dating of Wulfric and Siward's privileges to 1055 is insecure: 'Papal Privileges', p. 235.

[90] JL 4350 (Ely); *Charters of Chertsey Abbey*, ed. S. E. Kelly, Anglo-Saxon Charters 19 (Oxford, 2015), appendix I, C; Savill, 'Papal Privileges', pp. 89–91.

[91] See Licence, 'Robert', p. 327, for the day of Robert's death.

[92] Barlow, *English Church*, p. 232; Hugh the Chanter, *The History of the Church of York, 1066–1127*, ed. and tr. C. Johnson; rev. M. Brett, C. N. L. Brooke, and M. Winterbottom, OMT (Oxford, 1990), p. 53; Woolf, *Pictland to Alba*, p. 263. They may have been bishops of Orkney rather than Glasgow, as Hugh would have us believe. Cf. J. Traeger, 'Johannes I., Scotus, ca. 1062–66', in idem, *Die Bischöfe des mittelalterlichen Bistums Schwerin* (Leipzig, 1984), pp. 16–18.

Since the emperor Henry was present at the council of Florence in June 1055, Edward's ambassadors might have consulted him about Ealdred's mission to bring about the return of Edward the Exile. It is even possible that a rendezvous was arranged, since Ealdred returned to England about that time and may, conceivably, have returned with Cynesige's deputation. All of this is speculative, but we can be sure that Ealdred spent a year with the emperor and Archbishop Heriman of Cologne. During that time, he permitted himself to be distracted by his own interests, learning about the regulations for the communal life of clergy, collecting exquisite books, and delighting in Rhenish metalwork. Yet he made little progress with his mission and returned without the aetheling. When he returned to England, he was rewarded, or punished, with the administration of Ramsbury – a see so impoverished that its bishop had abandoned it to become a monk in Flanders after failing to remove his see to Malmesbury. In 1056, as icing on the cake, Edward gave him Hereford – the minster wrecked by the Welsh.[93] The emperor's death on 5 October 1056 either complicated or expedited the mission Ealdred had begun, and it is possible that Harold's presence in Flanders a month later had to do with last-minute practicalities of the Exile's return.[94]

Following in the footsteps of his uncle and namesake, Edward the Exile came to England in spring 1057 as the senior eligible aetheling and claimant. That he must have taken courage from Edward's example is proof of a protracted but successful mission and of his willingness to take on the burden of royal duty. It is also testimony to the absoluteness of the doctrine of blood-entitlement at Edward's court, for the Exile had been forty years in a foreign land and perhaps spoke no English. In one respect, the doctrine was an affirmation of the mystique of Cerdic's line. In another, it was a corollary of the impulse to preserve unity – the impulse we see again and again, whether in the witan's refusal to countenance civil war, or in the *Vita*'s warnings against discord. For any heir other than a blood-heir was certain to be contentious, not only at home but overseas. Even if it was conceivable that the throne might, in a case of necessity, pass to somebody who was not of the blood, legitimacy had become so vested in the mystique of royalty that opting for a successor who lacked that mystique would be like putting a sign on the throne stating 'anyone may now apply'.

So much for the best-laid plans. Almost as soon as he set foot in England, the Exile died, before the king could see him. D was uncertain which agency under heaven was to blame for such a disaster – and no more able to make sense of it in a world where things happened for a reason. 'Alas!', he mourned, 'that was a cruel fate, and harmful to all this

---

[93] Barlow, *English Church*, pp. 89–90, 87.

[94] Harold witnessed a charter issued by Count Baldwin at Saint-Omer on 13 November 1056: Rijksarchief te Gent, Sint-Pietersabdij, charters, no. 133; Bates, *William*, pp. 147–8.

nation, that he so quickly ended his life after he came to England, to the misfortune of this wretched nation.'[95] Though it may seem prescient, his lament reflected the despair of a polity frustrated in every attempt to procure a blood-heir.[96] It may convey Ealdred's sorrow at the failure of years of diplomacy – for D gives the impression that it speaks for him. The Exile's wife Agatha and their offspring Margaret, Christina, and Edgar either came with him or arrived later. If their arrival was not yet expected, D had all the more cause for despair. It was seeming more and more as though the future of the exiled dynasty was being thwarted by some latter-day Juno. The dead prince was laid to rest at St Paul's, with his grand-father Æthelred. Edward's plans to provide a blood-heir had suffered another almighty setback, and only the little boy Edgar possessed the legitimacy to deter opportunists from stealing the throne.

FEEDING THE WOLVES

Graves were filling quickly that year with young and old. After the Exile's death on 19 April, Leofric died in September and Ralph on 21 December. At least the question that was on everyone's minds had been answered by Edgar's arrival at court. Attention now focused on how the king would reassign the earldoms, and deals were done probably in time for the Christmas assembly of 1057–8. Ælfgar received his father's earldom, Mercia, out of respect for his line and to keep him cooperative, but Godwinson cubs – there was an inexhaustible supply of them – would take precedence over his three sons, Burgheard, Edwin, and Morcar. Leofwine, another son of Godwine, Edward's brother-in-law, was installed in the south-east midlands – a portion of Ralph's former earldom. Gyrth, his brother, received the apprentice earldom of East Anglia on Ælfgar's trans-lation to Mercia. Harold commanded Wessex with the south-west midlands, which he had added to his portfolio the previous year. This meant that his power extended from the Kent coast to the Welsh borders, and his younger brothers commanded the north, the east, and the home counties. In stark contrast, the Leofwinesons were down from two earl-doms to one and confined to a shrinking Mercia. Ælfgar probably dared to declare the injustice, for in 1058 he was expelled from the kingdom a second time. Though it seems that nobody criticized his banishment this time, the silence is misleading, because C, which was the source of criti-cism in 1055, lacks annals for the years 1057–64.

With Leofric dead and Ælfgar gone, Tostig seized the opportunity to extend his control over Nottinghamshire and Lincolnshire – formerly a

[95] ASC D, 1057 (Swanton's translation).

[96] The belief that the annal must have been written in hindsight of the Conquest, and that political agents (rather than, say, God or Fortune) kept the Exile from seeing Edward, began with Freeman, *NC*, II, p. 419.

Leofwineson corridor linking Leofric's Mercia to Ælfgar's East Anglia.[97] In Roman times, it had been the land of the Coritani, the northernmost point of the legions' advance under Claudius and Nero. It therefore contained an axis of the road system, where the route from York to Nottingham joined the Fosse Way, running south west or branching off to Watling Street, and where Ermine Street began its straight descent to London. In 1016 it had been hotly contested as the zone linking north and south. The more Tostig could do to dominate that region, the more readily he could attend to both northern and southern affairs. Yet his ambitions reduced the hopes of an earldom being created for one of Ælfgar's sons. The main beneficiary of Ælfgar's banishment in 1055 and 1058, he used those opportunities to build a power-base in the north, balancing the one his elder brother was building in the south.

Edward liked them both and approved the arrangement, for Tostig needed the resources of a larger earldom in order to carry out his brief of overseeing the north and Scottish affairs. Trouble in that zone had not abated since the English intervention in 1054, but such sources as we have reveal little about its dynamics. While we may speculate that Edward commanded Tostig to maintain pressure on Macbeth, Folcard provides no details of his 'cunning schemes' against the Scots.[98] He does remark, however, that Tostig wore them down 'with a military campaign that spared his own men'.[99] This could imply that Tostig turned to mercenaries or allies to combat Scottish raiding parties. It could mean he bankrolled Malcolm's invasion of Alba, which would soon proceed at a remarkable pace. Though Folcard is foggy on Scotland, he does seem to allude here to a specific campaign which converted the Scots into England's allies. An interpolation in the chronicle of Simeon of Durham implies that, by 1061, Tostig and Malcolm had become blood-brothers.[100] If it preserves an accurate memory, it points to an early and important alliance. Edward and Duke Robert had become blood-brothers before joining in a campaign to restore Edward to the throne, and since Malcolm too was an exiled prince seeking to reclaim his father's throne, Edward may have warmed to him and ordered Tostig to assist. By November 1057 the regime in Alba was cracking apart, with Macbeth's stepson Lulach emerging as a replacement king.[101] Now was the time to go on the attack.

[97] For evidence that Tostig's earldom included Lincolnshire and Nottinghamshire, see *Vita*, p. 77, and Baxter, *Earls of Mercia*, p. 308, citing S 1160 (a writ address) and *GDB* 280a (Nottinghamshire), for the third penny.

[98] *Vita*, p. 67.

[99] Ibid., p. 66: 'et hostili expeditione cum salute suorum' (as the ablative of instrument).

[100] Simeon of Durham, *Historia regum*, in *Symeonis monachi opera omnia*, ed. T. Arnold, RS 75, 2 vols (London, 1882–5), II, 3–283, at pp. 174–5.

[101] Cf. Woolf, *Pictland to Alba*, pp. 263–5. Lulach was, perhaps, no friend of Macbeth, who seems to have been involved in burning Lulach's father alive in a house-burning ambush (ibid., p. 247).

Malcolm assembled his forces in spring 1058. Who they were and where they began to advance are not at all clear; but external powers had eyes on the campaign.[102] On 17 March he defeated and killed Lulach, at Essie in Strathbogie. News of the king's death reached the Irish annalists and probably Norway, for it seems the most likely stimulus for the Norwegian king Harald's decision to dispatch a fleet to Scotland under his son Magnus. He may already have obtained the submission of the earl of Orkney, as Adam of Bremen claims.[103] Suffering a defeat at the hands of the relentless Malcolm,[104] and not wishing to pursue him deeper into Alba, Magnus turned west along the coast and down into the Irish Sea, enlarging his fleet *en route* with Orcadian recruits, men of the Hebrides, and pirates from Dublin. Having already recorded Lulach's death, the annalist at Clonmacnoise noted their arrival.[105] The flotilla was large and varied enough to affirm Norwegian maritime hegemony, so Magnus could at least impress his father in that. But now it had to scout for somewhere to raid and get its pay.

Ælfgar had fled again to Gruffudd, who was wondering about breaking his peace with the English king. The pair were debating how to repeat past victories when Magnus's ship-army arrived seeking plunder and glory. John of Worcester reports that the Norwegian fleet joined Gruffudd 'unexpectedly'.[106] D relays the mood at court – that the saga was becoming tedious.[107] In Ireland, the annalist at Clonmacnoise could imagine that the fleet had tried to seize England and been thwarted by God – an allusion, possibly, to ships gone astray in bad weather.[108] A likelier scenario is that Gruffudd, Ælfgar, and Magnus joined in a raid up the Dee to Chester, targeting the earldom which Edward had confiscated from the serial outlaw. Harold was probably out of the country, for he went to Rome before 1060, augmenting his relic collection at shrines on the way; and he was probably the agent who in 1058 brought a pallium from Rome for Stigand.[109] He might have left before Ælfgar's banishment, since it would be a risk for him to depart with Ælfgar at large. Malcolm, meanwhile, got on with the conquest of Alba. In August, at Lumphanon in Deeside, he vanquished and slew Macbeth.

---

[102] Woolf, building on A. A. M. Duncan, makes a good case for an invasion launched from Orkney, but much rests on the late and very unreliable *Orkneyinga saga*, which is the only source to claim that Malcolm's first wife was Ingibjorg, the widow of Earl Thorfinnr of Orkney: *Pictland to Alba*, pp. 265–70.

[103] *GHEP*, p. 159.

[104] Woolf, *Pictland to Alba*, p. 269.

[105] 'The Annals of Tigernach', ed. W. Stokes, *Revue Celtique* 17 (1896), 6–33, 119–263, and 337–420, at pp. 398 and 399. There is no reason to think the Norwegians allied with Lulach; but cf. Woolf, *Pictland to Alba*, p. 269.

[106] *JW*, ii, p. 585.

[107] ASC D, 1058: 'it is tedious to tell how it all happened'.

[108] Cf. Woolf, *Pictland to Alba*, p. 264; 'Annals of Tigernach', ed. Stokes, p. 399.

[109] *Vita*, p. 53; ASC E, 1058; Freeman, *NC*, II, pp. 441–3.

The D author found it too tedious or uncomfortable to reveal what Edward did on being faced with a hostile fleet and no time to summon an army. Still, he probably did the sensible thing by paying off Magnus, ceding the territory west of the Dee to Gruffudd, and reinstating Ælfgar in his earldom. Gruffudd now ruled north-east Wales, former Mercian territory, from the burgh at Rhuddlan almost to the gates of Chester.[110] The main loser was the bishop of the town, whose land was ceded to Gruffudd. Doubtless Edward was furious and dreaming up all kinds of revenge on the earl and his insatiable accomplice, but he knew when to bide his time and grant concessions. He had only to wait for his enemies to make a mistake. Malcolm, who had fought too many Scots to be making more enemies, was, meanwhile, negotiating with his ministers. In 1059, Tostig, Archbishop Cynesige, and Bishop Æthelwine of Durham escorted him to Edward at Gloucester, where he could only have gone in such fashion to acknowledge Edward as his lord.[111] Since Edward was at Gloucester on two other occasions over the Christmas festival, in 1052–3 and 1063–4, the visit may have occurred at Christmas 1058–9. By ordering Malcolm's submission at Gloucester, Edward was reminding the Welsh what he expected of his clients. As usual, he was sending them a strong message; and he could do so with greater confidence now that Harold was back at his side.

Folcard provides few details about Harold's trip to Rome, but he does say Harold went first to France, where he studied the strategies of unnamed princes.[112] The vagueness of his account possibly stems from the fact that he wrote several years later, with little knowledge. (When writing about Tostig's trip to Rome, he drew on a detailed source.)[113] The best guess is that the writer conflated Harold's travels of 1056 – when we glimpse him in the company of Baldwin of Flanders and Guy of Ponthieu – and an otherwise unrecorded trip to Rome in 1058. It is difficult to place Harold's journey to Rome any later because he was in England for some part of 1059, and by 1060 he had gathered relics from Rome and the Rhineland to install in his minster at Waltham. The nearing of its completion by 1058 could have been a stimulus for Harold to go relic collecting.[114] It was, in any case, the petitioner's role to lobby for papal privileges; popes did not dispatch them on their own initiative. The papacy was a petition-response institution.[115] E, in stating that Benedict X 'sent' a pallium to Stigand, is concealing the identity of an emissary who went to demand it. This was either because Benedict had been discredited by that

---

[110] Charles-Edwards, *Wales and the Britons*, p. 561.

[111] Simeon, *Historia regum*, p. 174.

[112] *Vita*, pp. 51–3.

[113] Licence, 'A New Source for the *Vita Ædwardi*'.

[114] Cf. N. Rogers, 'The Waltham Abbey Relic-list', in C. Hicks, ed., *England in the Eleventh Century: Proceedings of the 1990 Harlaxton Symposium* (Stamford, 1992), pp. 157–81. The date of 1060 for Waltham's foundation is to an extent still speculative.

[115] Savill, 'Papal Privileges', pp. 18, 258–9.

time, and the annalist wished to conceal the fact that the initiative in the affair came not from him but from England, or because Harold had been discredited by the time the annal was written or revised. Folcard's lack of detail about Harold's trip to Rome would be another attempt to conceal an awkward truth. Since Benedict only occupied Peter's throne from April 1058 to January 1059 – the most likely year of Harold's visit – the textual silences point to Harold.

Between 1055, when Cynesige's embassy went to Pope Victor, and 1058, the future of papal policy had become uncertain. Since the 1040s, the emperor had controlled the papacy, installing his German and Lotharingian candidates and excluding scions of the noble Italian families that had formerly controlled the papal office. In 1056, the emperor had died, and in 1057 his last nominee, Victor, followed him. Fearing the Tusculan family might reassert their power over the papal office, the cardinals of the reforming faction hurriedly selected a successor to Victor without consulting the emperor's heir, Henry IV, who was still a minor. When their latest pope died in 1058, and the reformers lacked the numbers to carry another election, representatives of the Tusculan family seized the opportunity to install one of their own as Benedict X. The reformers immediately anathematized him and decamped to find a candidate of their own. But without imperial muscle behind them their prospects were poor, and for a full eight months there was no pope but Benedict.

Back in 1055, there was no possibility of Victor granting a pallium for Stigand, because Robert of Jumièges was still alive. When Edward learned of Victor's death and his successor's election as Stephen IX in August 1057, he would have been acting in character if he decided again to send ambassadors to the new pope. Still, little could be arranged before spring 1058, when Harold's legation could be dispatched. Harold might well have arrived in Rome to find Stephen dead and Benedict enthroned, tractable, and needy of allies. He duly returned with a pallium, putting Stigand in his debt. Stigand responded graciously by using his new authority to raise and consecrate Æthelric – a monk of his own flock at Christ Church – as bishop of the Sussex bishopric of Selsey. Unless Christ Church had two Æthelrics with episcopal potential, he was the kinsman of Harold who had been elected to Canterbury and passed over in favour of Robert in 1051.[116] By promoting the man who had a better canonical claim to Canterbury than he or his predecessor, Stigand righted an old wrong and returned a favour. It was a sign of the close political relationship forming between Stigand and Harold.

On the way to Rome, Harold had stopped at various great churches to purchase relics to add to his collection. We may imagine him jumping at the chance when Edward ordered him to go in spring 1058, because it

[116] *Vita*, pp. 30/1. It is not clear whether the usual form of his name was *Ægelric* (i.e. 'Ailric') or *Æðelric*.

allowed him to augment the relic endowment he had planned for his minster at Waltham in Essex, which would have been nearing completion.[117] Edward, unlike his mother, who had left her relics to Winchester, was building a new church to house his relic collection, at Westminster.[118] Not only was Harold emulating the king by following his example and re-founding Waltham; he would complete his basilica first. Some observers might have detected a spot of rivalry; others would have concluded that Harold was trying to impress and to please. Though the diploma describing Waltham's foundation is a forgery, put together at a later date, the minster's dedication to the Holy Cross was not without resonance, since it was on the Feast of the Exaltation of the Holy Cross on 14 September 1052 that the late Earl Godwine had confronted the king, prior to the restoration of familial peace.

We know that symbolism was important to the pious of that age – no longer do we think of it as a primitive time inhabited by blunt minds; and yet the significance of symbols in any scenario is hard to apprehend. Though the Cross certainly presented an image of a heavenly king at the very point of being dethroned (before rising triumphant), it is an attractive guess rather than a certainty that the nobles attending the ceremony were prompted to think of the parallels of 1052. The possibility is appealing partly because Edward's choice of Easter Day for his coronation does suggest that he was aware of parallels between the Resurrection and the death and rebirth of his dynasty. The other thing that makes it attractive is the degree of attention paid to the cult of the Cross in Edward's reign. Stigand, for one, was promoting it vigorously, but so were lay nobles. Thought was being given to Christ's sacrifice and to its many meanings.[119] The Cross promised hope of everlasting life – and the hope of Edward's dynasty now lay in Edgar. Rather than supposing his absence on such occasions we should imagine him accompanying the king and queen; for he went with them to Winchester for a monastic ceremony, and attending dedications was part of a noble upbringing.[120]

An attraction of the location was that it lay by Epping Forest, near the site of a previous patron's hunting lodge; and Harold would not have disgraced himself by failing to schedule, amid the festivities, an opportunity for the assembled nobility to indulge in spring sports. As well as collecting relics, he had books on falconry and is depicted with birds of

[117] Rogers, 'Waltham Abbey Relic-list', and see S. Keynes, 'Earl Harold and the Foundation of Waltham Holy Cross (1062)', *ANS* 39 (2017), 81–111

[118] Jones, 'Emma's Greek *Scrine*'.

[119] T. Licence and T. A. Heslop, '1066 and the Church', in D. Bates, ed., *1066 in Perspective* (Leeds, 2018), 156–75, at pp. 164–70.

[120] See, for example, 'The Liber confortatorius of Goscelin of Saint Bertin', ed. C. H. Talbot, *Analecta monastica, textes et études sur la vie des moines au moyen age, troisième série, Studia Anselmiana*, 37 (Rome, 1955), 1–117, at pp. 28–9, on two dedication ceremonies attended by the child Eve during the 1060s. On the royal visit to Winchester, see below pp. 288–9.

prey on the Bayeux Tapestry, a keen student of the swooping of hawks.[121] May was a time for hawking, and our scene is some ancient glade of Epping Forest. Light filters through the canopy. The bird of prey hovers in eternity, poised, waiting. Time seems to have been suspended as long as the hawking party holds a breath. On the day of the ceremony itself, the king showed his approval and appropriate largesse by donating relics out of his own vast collection and also by granting an estate at Millow in Bedfordshire to the canons of Harold's new minster.[122]

After the dedication, the nobles possibly made their way to London for the Whitsuntide assembly of 14 May.[123] Edward, impressed by Waltham, now outdid Harold, by conferring excess freedom on Westminster. The diploma he issued at the assembly not only confirmed to the abbey a grant of land in Hertfordshire, it also took the exceptional step of freeing the land from the common burdens of military service, bridge-work, and fortress-work, and the exactions of kings, bishops, and earls. No monarch in the past had granted such immunities, which were a nod to what lay in store for Westminster's consecration – still several years into the future. Total immunity of this sort made continental monasteries fabulously wealthy. In his first known diploma for the abbey (S 1031), Edward was establishing Westminster on a co-equal footing to the grand continental houses. Harold was not at liberty to confer similar immunities on Waltham, for they were concessions only a king could bestow.

The gatherings at Waltham and Westminster in 1060 held out the hope that the quarrels which had periodically erupted and ramified might, finally, be abating. At least in the north and in the midlands, the Leofwinesons enjoyed the support of Archbishop Cynesige against the ambitions of the northern earl. In December 1060, however, Cynesige died, and Ealdred was chosen to replace him at the Christmas assembly. His appointment renewed an old link between the sees of Worcester and York, which several of his predecessors had held jointly. Ealdred was certainly magnificent, if not always effective. (He had failed to capture Harold when pursuing him in 1051, lost a battle with the Welsh, and failed to bring back the Exile.) He was, nevertheless, a successful empire builder – a wolf as hungry for ecclesiastical titles to add to his growing collection as Stigand was in the south. As well as grabbing Worcester, he had administered Ramsbury in Bishop Herman's absence (1055–8) and had been running Hereford since Bishop Leofgar's death in 1056. Just as

---

[121] C. H. Haskins, 'King Harold's Books', *EHR* 37 (1922), 398–400.

[122] Rogers, 'Waltham Abbey Relic-list'; *GDB* 210b (whether or not on the occasion of the dedication).

[123] The absence of the bishop of London, though the gift was in his diocese, may fix the assembly at which S 1031 was granted at Pentecost (14 May) 1060, for Bishop William is known to have been in Flanders the next day (15 May) attending an exhibition of relics: *Miracula s. Ursmari in itinere per Flandriam facta*, ed. O. Holder-Egger, in MGH Scriptores, 15, 2 (Hanover, 1888), 837–42, at p. 839.

Tostig's power in the north aped the aggrandizement of his older brother, Ealdred's empire was approaching that of his southern counterpart, Stigand.

Ealdred's appointment to York was a further setback for Ælfgar, for if the new primate of the north leaned towards anyone, it was Edith and Tostig.[124] Edward had never cared for Ælfgar, and it suited him more to balance the factions that may already have been emerging within the Godwinson camp. On one side Stigand was cosying up to Harold, as he had with his father, Godwine. On the other, Ealdred of York was dealing more with Tostig and Edith. Indeed, it was about this time or a little later that Edith committed Folcard to Ealdred's care. We should be careful to note, at this stage, that there is no sign of disagreement between the alliances that were coalescing. And they should not be demarcated too rigidly. What united them was their contempt for Ælfgar. As long as they could content themselves in trampling upon him, Harold's set and Edith and Tostig's would not come into conflict, nor too much displease the king.

Like Harold, Edith was at once subservient to Edward and keen to emulate or compete with him in a friendly way. Humbling herself by choosing to sit at his feet was not merely a stage direction for his kingship, drawing attention to his sacralized remoteness. Humble, she nevertheless competed with him as Harold did, in a contained way, by rebuilding a religous house – the nunnery of Wilton, where she had been schooled.[125] Friendly rivalry of this kind enabled courtiers to transmute their competitive energies, even if it was hard to contain them completely in a climate where nobody could bear being outdone. Edward was growing fond of Edith and was grateful for her solicitude; he would praise her virtues in little asides to his companions and was inclining to her requests.[126] On Ealdred's translation to York, Edward awarded the bishopric of Hereford, which Ealdred now vacated, to Edith's chaplain, Walter the Lotharingian; and given that an outgoing prelate usually exercised a say in the choice of his successor, we might guess that Edith and Ealdred lobbied the king together. It does not seem likely they did so without the consent of Harold, who was earl there; but it is possible that Harold's choice of Leofgar had lost him the right to present his candidate to the see – a privilege Edward had granted him on the previous occasion. Certainly, Walter was Edith's man, and it may be that on this occasion Harold lost out.

By now the wolves were feeding and growing bigger at every turn. When, for example, Duduc of Wells – the last of Cnut's bishops – followed Cynesige to the grave, early in 1061, Harold contested his will, seizing the estates he had left to his bishopric; and Stigand dived into the carcase too,

---

[124] *Vita*, pp. liv–v, 53–7.
[125] Ibid., pp. 65, 71.
[126] Ibid., p. 65.

pressing the king to give him a monastery in Gloucester, which Duduc had given to Wells.[127] Once they had what they wanted or what they argued pertained to the fisc, Edward handed the see to his chaplain Giso, who thought about anathematizing Harold but settled for rebuking him.[128] Edith saw a golden opportunity elsewhere. Cynesige had left a gold-covered gospel book, land, and ornaments worth £300 to Peterborough where he was buried. Contesting his will, Edith seized the lot.[129] Ælfgar would have had to bite his lip, for Peterborough was a Leofwineson house run by his cousin. A greater concern, however, was Ealdred's ambition to extend his dominion over Lindsey. His argument for annexing it went back to Cynesige's predecessor, who had tried to incorporate the diocese of Lindsey into his archbishopric. Cynesige, in contrast, had been content for its bishop, Wulfwig of Dorchester, to nurture projects with the Leofwinesons. They had collaborated in establishing a minster at Stow with Cynesige's approval. Cynesige had even donated the bell.[130] Since then, however, Lincolnshire had come under Tostig's command. And Tostig was content for Ealdred to feed on Leofwineson assets.

ROME AGAIN

Edward, as always, had business to consider, which turned his attentions to Rome. For a start, Ealdred needed a pallium, while the Lindsey dispute was an ecclesiastical matter which required a judgment from the pope. At least by referring the decision, Edward could avoid taking sides, which would only exacerbate the tensions at court. He may have wanted a papal privilege for Westminster too. Since his last delegation to Rome, the reform party had ousted Benedict X and installed Nicholas II, who proceeded to depose his vanquished predecessor. If Edward was waiting to see whether Nicholas would outlast his Tusculan opponents, he could not wait forever. In the meantime, Benedict's exit and the reformers' refusal to acknowledge his acts raised doubts over the validity of Stigand's pallium. Though Nicholas may have been too embattled to quibble over the matter, Edward's contact with Benedict meant he had to be placatory, now the bother of sending a new embassy to Rome could no longer be postponed.

In 1061 he dispatched the embassy, including the bishops Ealdred, Walter, and Giso, no doubt with members of their households. The earls

---

[127] Keynes, 'Giso', pp. 230–1, 264, 266.

[128] Ibid., pp. 255, 267.

[129] *The Peterborough Chronicle of Hugh Candidus*, ed. W. T. Mellows (Oxford, 1949), p. 73.

[130] S 1233, S 1478; S. Baxter, 'The Death of Burgheard Son of Ælfgar and Its Context', in P. Fouracre and D. Ganz, ed., *Frankland: The Franks and the World of the Early Middle Ages: Essays in honour of Dame Jinty Nelson* (Manchester and New York, 2008), 266–84, at pp. 281–3.

Tostig and Gyrth led the company, along with Tostig's wife Judith, his commander Gospatric, and his housecarls. A scion of the House of Bamburgh, Gospatric was a nephew of that Gospatric we met earlier, and the grandson of Ealdorman Uhtred and Æthelred's daughter.[131] A troop of Edward's housecarls made up the escort, including Ælfgar's son Burgheard.[132] Wulfwig or his delegates may have gone ahead, for it is known he did business in Rome, but the *Vita* fails to mention him. Alternatively, his omission might reflect chagrin on the part of Ealdred, Folcard's informant. Ealdred had been sent 'to plead the business which the king had entrusted to him'.[133] Since the business which arose involved the pallium and Lindsey, it is likely Edward advised him that the latter would be decided at the papal court, and that he should take his suit to Rome and come back with a pallium. The size of the escort implies the company brought great treasure for the pope. In a gesture designed to please Nicholas and dodge the bullet that was Stigand, Giso and Walter were to seek consecration at the hands of the pope himself.

By all these measures, Edward affirmed his desire to treat Nicholas and his faction with respect. The party nevertheless took a northern route via Saxony and the upper reaches of the Rhine, stopping to venerate the shrines of saints along the way.[134] Their detour suggests they had been instructed first to report to the imperial court, for Nicholas had lost the favour of the regency government of the young Henry IV by cutting a deal with his enemies, the Normans of southern Italy. Folcard claims that when the party arrived in Rome, the pope made a show of honouring Tostig by seating him next to himself in the synod. Though he may have made up the claim to flatter an earl he admired, it is possible Nicholas wished to present Tostig as an example, for braving such a journey, and for bringing cash to replenish the papal coffers.

Despite the promising start, sticklers for procedure – or enemies of Ealdred – were laying an ambush, and he was condemned on the technicality of having migrated from one bishopric to another without the pope's permission. This was enough for the Easter synod to decide that he should be deprived of both Worcester and York. When Ealdred appealed, claiming he had transferred to York not for profit but at the king's command, allies corroborated his story, the ruling was revised, and he was permitted to keep Worcester. It had been a harsh ruling in the first place, but the absence of a bishop-elect of Worcester would have raised suspicions. For Ealdred's plan was to profit by holding Worcester with York, as

---

[131] Williams, *The English*, pp. 28–30.

[132] Baxter, 'Burgheard', pp. 278, 280–1.

[133] *Vita*, p. 53.

[134] Ibid.; F. Barlow, *The Godwins: The Rise and Fall of a Noble Dynasty* (Harlow, 2002), p. 89.

a predecessor had done as recently as 1040.[135] By refusing him the pallium, Nicholas placed England in an impossible position that forced the issue of Stigand. He nevertheless consecrated the two Lotharingians, Walter and Giso, on Easter Day (15 April) and granted Giso a privilege for his see ten days later.[136] No doubt their lobbying was informed by the knowledge that Lotharingian muscle had enabled Nicholas to triumph over Benedict's faction – a fact they could have confirmed while passing through Lotharingia.[137] The bishops then departed with Tostig, who had sent his wife and part of the escort ahead, anticipating a delay caused by Ealdred's appeal.

It could hardly have escaped his chuckling critics that failing in royal missions was, for Ealdred, becoming something of a speciality. This time, however, it was not the provision of an heir so much as the legitimacy of the English Church that was at stake. The reformers who had recaptured the papacy had disavowed both archbishops. As if this was not enough, on the day of their departure, the English party were attacked by partisans of Benedict led by Count Gerard of Galeria, who robbed them of £1,000 in local money.[138] Folcard relates that a quick-witted Gospatric fooled the bandits into thinking he was the leader, enabling Tostig to avoid capture by riding away. A jolly anecdote, it conceals ugly details in Folcard's source, which he presumably omitted since they reflected less well on Tostig. The source, Nicholas's letter to Ealdred, reports that some of the English were injured or killed in the fighting. Burgheard, a house-carl tasked with defending against such attacks, may have been mortally wounded.[139] His death on a mission in Tostig's care can hardly have soothed the enmity between Tostig and the surviving sons of Ælfgar, Edwin and Morcar, especially if he had been injured in a fight while Tostig fled.

Shamed and distressed by his enemies' impunity, Nicholas now relented and granted Ealdred a pallium as a special dispensation. His letter credits Archdeacon Hildebrand for swaying the synod, and it is entirely believable that the future Gregory VII, who worked so astutely for the reformed papacy, emphasized the danger of alienating England at that time. Folcard, altering what the letter reports, credits Tostig's forcefulness and

[135] Above, p. 75; below, pp. 201–2. For Ealdred's suit, see the letter from Nicholas II, in *The Historians of the Church of York and its Archbishops*, ed. J. Raine, RS 71, 3 vols (1879–94), III, pp. 5–7; *Vita*, pp. 53–7.

[136] JL 4457; Savill, 'Papal Privileges', pp. 84–5.

[137] D. Hägermann, *Das Papsttum am Vorabend des Investiturstreits. Stephan IX. (1057–1058), Benedikt X. (1058) und Nikolaus II. (1058–61)*, Päpste und Papsttum, Bd 36 (Stuttgart, 2008), pp. 65, 85–6.

[138] *Die Briefe des Petrus Damiani*, ed. K. Reindel, MGH Die Briefe der Deutschen Kaiserzeit, 4 vols (Munich, 1983–93), II, no. 89, pp. 531–79, at p. 566.

[139] On reports of Burgheard's death, see Baxter, 'Burgheard', pp. 267–73. Nicholas's letter hints at injuries and fatalities: 'uulneratisque tuis et caesis'.

Ealdred's honesty for obtaining the dispensation. He makes no mention of Hildebrand's efforts and omits the inconvenient detail that the concession was granted upon the understanding Ealdred would relinquish Worcester and consecrate a bishop there.[140] When Folcard was writing, Ealdred still held estates of the Worcester bishopric. Gerard of Galeria was anathematized with the ceremonial snuffing of candles.[141] Unfinished business was concluded, and Wulfwig won against Ealdred. A privilege affirming his authority over Lindsey and protecting the assets belonging to the minster at Stow was issued for his benefit on 3 May.[142] Laden with gifts, bearing the pope's letter,[143] which had been granted begrudgingly, the embassy began the homeward journey, stopping to bury Burgheard at Rheims cathedral, as had been his wish.

A writ issued about the time of their return suggests that Edward remained superficially dutiful towards the clergy. Addressed in favour of Giso, it grants the canons of Wells land at Wedmore – part of the royal manor at Cheddar in Somerset. Giso tells us he had approached the king to request a gift, and Edward had responded positively when Giso raised the subject of the canons' impoverishment. Whether he pricked the king's conscience for letting Harold and Stigand plunder Giso's estates (and Æthelred's conscience could certainly be pricked in such a way), we have already observed earlier Edward's concern for the material support of God's servants, and again it found expression in the terms of the grant of Wedmore, 'for the sustenance of the clergy'.[144] Like Edward's diploma for Westminster, the writ expresses the hope that the donor's soul should benefit, exposing the king's wish to protect himself in the afterlife. Edward was also looking to the past, declaring that the benefaction was to benefit his soul, his father's soul, and the souls of 'his ancestors, who founded the see'. He did not include his mother's soul. The reference to his ancestors, who must have included King Ine of Wessex, and their role in establishing the bishopric of Wells recalls the writ of the 1040s referring to St Edmund of Bury as Edward's 'kinsman'.[145] Edward was taking pride in his ancestors, real or imagined; and he was making provision for his legacy and the afterlife.

Barely had Edward's legation returned from Rome when Nicholas II died in July 1061. Then in September the cardinals installed Alexander II. The regency council for Henry IV, however, had already nullified the late pope's decrees and chose now to uphold the imperial prerogative by nominating its own candidate Honorius II, on 28 October. Over the next

---

[140] *Historians*, ed. Raine, III, p. 7; Malmesbury, *Life of Wulfstan*, p. 43.
[141] *Die Briefe*, ed. Reindel, II, no. 89, pp. 531–79, at p. 567.
[142] JL 4461.
[143] JL 4463.
[144] S 1115; Keynes, 'Giso', p. 265.
[145] See above, p. 114.

few years until the schism resolved in Alexander's favour, German chroniclers saw Honorius as the lawful pope, and Alexander as the usurper.[146] Legates representing Alexander's faction were in England in 1062, where Edward received them. But the two accounts of their visit contain irreconcilable differences. The first, William of Malmesbury's version of a lost *Life* of Bishop Wulfstan, implies that Ealdred brought the two legates back from Rome and took them on a tour of England before placing them in the care of Wulfstan, who was his prior at Worcester. The second account, given by John of Worcester, whose credentials are no less authoritative, claims the legates had been sent by Alexander to obtain answers from Edward on unspecified matters. John implies they arrived in Lent 1062 and claims the king had them detained at Worcester for the duration of Lent, while he considered their demands.[147] There are grounds for preferring John's version. First, though John followed William's source, he chose in this instance to correct it.[148] Second, Nicholas's letter makes no mention of legates, nor is there any in the *Vita*'s account. It is clear therefore that Ealdred returned in 1061 with the pallium and written instructions, and that legates from Alexander arrived in 1062.

Part of the legates' business, no doubt, was to ensure that Ealdred had surrendered the see of Worcester as Nicholas had instructed, which he had failed to do in the eight months since his return. Edward, perhaps caught out by this, and cross with Ealdred for dragging his feet, obliged the bishop to entertain them at his own cost at Worcester, the see whose income he was reluctant to relinquish. As in 1051 and 1052, he was playing for time, considering his answers to the legates' inquiries and probably soliciting news on the progress of the contest between popes. Ealdred meanwhile satisfied the inspectors by preparing before their eyes a model election in which the ascetic Wulfstan defeated the hard-headed administrator Abbot Æthelwig of Evesham. Yet both were Ealdred's men, and he had every intention of treating the victor as his deputy while retaining command of Worcester and absorbing its assets into his new archbishopric.[149] Wulfstan's election was agreed at the Easter council, canonically confirmed in August and sealed, on 8 September, with his consecration by Ealdred, because that was what Nicholas II had mandated. It is doubtful, however, that Alexander was secure enough to act against Stigand. Indeed, the principal business of the legates was, presumably, to obtain English backing in the schism, and they would not have been pushing too

---

[146] *Eleventh-century Germany: The Swabian Chronicles*, tr. I. S. Robinson (Manchester, 2008), pp. 27, 104.

[147] Malmesbury, *Life of Wulfstan*, pp. 43–5; *JW*, ii, p. 591.

[148] Usually he was content to follow Coleman's account: *The Vita Wulfstani of William of Malmesbury*, ed. R. R. Darlington (Royal Historical Society, Camden 3rd ser., xl, 1928), pp. xi–xvi.

[149] Ibid., pp. 47, 49–51. Note, however, that Hemming has only praise for Ealdred: *Hemingi chartularium*, ed. Hearne, II, pp. 395–6, 405–7.

hard on other matters, for fear of pushing Edward into the arms of the schismatic Honorius.

Their weakness also strengthened Ealdred's defiance. Ealdred had given up Hereford on attaining York, had failed in his bid for Lindsey, and was not about to surrender Worcester's wealth to Wulfstan. Like Stigand, he was a courtly prelate whose munificence would not be funded from the income of one see. There may already have been the division at Worcester between the monks' lands and the bishop's. Ealdred delayed Wulfstan's installation to give himself time for legal arrangements that would allow him to retain the latter. Even after he had consecrated him, he left the obedient monk in York, 'to do him [i.e. Wulfstan] honour', while he appropriated almost all of Worcester's episcopal estates.[150] All that Nicholas II had put in writing was that Ealdred should consecrate a bishop, not that he should relinquish the bishop*ric* (the -*ric* being Old English for the bishop's assets and wealth). Whenever Edward installed a new bishop, he issued a writ instructing his ministers in the locality to ensure the bishop was deprived of nothing that was lawfully his; but it was no safeguard against empire-builders like Ealdred, Harold, and Stigand, who had the resources to deploy the law to justify their acquisitions.[151] The king was no doubt aware they were impoverishing the sort of godly men whose interests he cherished. But he satisfied himself by admonishing them or trusting the courts. Ælfgar may have assisted Wulfstan by granting him land, but Harold let Ealdred get on with the business of stripping Worcester, calculating that Wulfstan would pursue no complaint and that the king would therefore forget the matter.[152]

A SENSE OF UNEASE

Whether the king felt bad about the asset stripping of Wells and Worcester, we need to consider what evidence there is of his attitudes to the wolves. A diploma dated 1063, issued for St Olave's, Exeter, suggests his mind was troubled. But its authenticity cannot be tested because it lacks the boundary clause and witness list, which its copyist did not include. The proem departs from the distant tone of Edward's earlier diplomas, sounding a personal note:

> I Edward, ordained king and defender of the English realm, call upon God with a restless mind,[153] not only that I may invoke the name of

---

[150] E. Mason, *St Wulfstan of Worcester c. 1008–1095* (Oxford, 1990), pp. 212, 215 (on the *mensa*); p. 85.

[151] E.g. S 1102 (Walter of Hereford), S 1111 and S 1112 (Giso of Wells), S 1156 (Wulfstan of Worcester).

[152] *Chartularium*, ed. Hearne, II, p. 406.

[153] S 1037: 'insomni animo': 'restless' conveys the agitation described in the next sentence.

royal protection [i.e. the divine name],[154] but also, surrounded by divine power, that I may prevail against the counsel and actions of God's enemies, and deserve to lead my kingdom of peace forward in tranquillity. For the mutability of worldly affairs very often troubles, agitates, and confuses my mind: see, everywhere, law and justice are at risk of being toppled; all around, discord and rebellion brew; everywhere, wicked presumption rages; profit overrules duty and justice, and the love of earthly riches, which is the root of all evils, brings about all these things. Our [royal] duty is to resist these evils by setting a good example: that is, by enriching God's churches, punishing wrongdoers, supporting the servants of justice, and treating rich and poor as equals before the law. Such are the deeds that delight the Lord.

The diploma then describes the gift Edward had made, at the request of one of the clergy of St Olave's, 'for the healing of my soul'.

It is difficult to know whether these words reflect Edward's thoughts. The bishops drafting his diplomas, admittedly, were tasked with putting words into his mouth, but where the tone is different and personal, it may reflect a ruler's concerns, or at the least a change of mood at court. Æthelred's diplomas underwent a shift in the early 990s, addressing in newly intimate ways the king's rumination. In that instance the voice of anxiety was evidently authentic and can be linked to the king's concurrent attempt to rid himself of a curse by righting perceived wrongs.[155] In Edward's diploma of 1063, authentic anxieties may again be breaking through, since the tone fits the conscientious attitudes revealed by Edward's actions and remarked on by observers. His desire to treat the rich and poor as equals before the law was celebrated in an epigram, which declares that rich and poor were alike to him.[156] Many lords did not take such a view. The emperor Henry had been criticized for holding lowly folk in contempt, and there is no evidence Harold respected their interests when enlarging his estates.[157] A second reason to believe that these worries were Edward's is the appearance of similar themes two years later during the king's terminal illness.[158] As his mind sickened, he complained of the wickedness of his subordinates. The emperors Hadrian and Antoninus Pius had made dying complaints of a similar kind.[159]

---

[154] S 1037 wrongly has 'ut non habeam' for 'ut habeam'.

[155] See above, p. 18.

[156] Godfrey of Winchester, *Epigrammata*, III, p. 149: 'Et dives cunctis et sibi pauper erat'. Cf. *Vita*, p. 65, which makes a different point, about his mercy and support for the poor.

[157] Weinfurter, *Salian Century*, pp. 103–4.

[158] Below, p. 240.

[159] *Historia Augusta*, vol. I: *Hadrian. Aelius. Antoninus Pius. Marcus Aurelius. L Verus. Avidius Cassius. Commodus. Pertinax. Didius Julianus. Septimius Severus. Pescennius Niger. Clodius Albinus*, tr. D. Magie, Loeb Classical Library 139 (Cambridge, MA, 1921), pp. 71, 75, 131.

If we read the preamble as an expression of Edward's anxieties in 1063, we glimpse a king unable to oppose the dismal drift of his thinking. Seldom does the head that wears the crown cease to ruminate, but as Edward grew ever more dependent on deputies running his administration, his impulse to indulge them gave traction to his fears. At his coronation, he had promised to appoint righteous ministers. He had also been informed that he must give account on Judgment Day for whatever they did unjustly by means of his might.[160] Yet it seemed as if men at the heart of the regime took what they wanted for their service, just as lesser servants creamed off profits of the administration.[161] Discord was brewing, rebellion not far off, and 'iniquitous presumption' (opposition to authority) was a storm-cloud on the horizon.[162] Harold had been enlarging Hitchin, one of his Hertfordshire manors, by taking lands nearby. Wymondley was Edward's land, belonging to the royal demesne, but Harold appropriated it and placed it in Hitchin 'three years before King Edward's death'. Hexton, also in Hertfordshire, was held by a sokeman, a man of the abbot of St Albans, but Harold had placed it in Hitchin, 'wrongly and by force'.[163] Edward's diploma hints at the restless ambivalence of a monarch who felt he should take a stance and lacked the resolve to do so. Every tiresome thing that had happened in his life had taught him to value peace and quiet. Yet in realpolitik the price of those things meant conniving at the rapacity of the men who procured their simulacrum.

Writing around that time, Jumièges captured a view of Edward from Normandy. It is proof that the myth of Edward as an untainted king circulated in his lifetime.[164] Bloodied rulers might be likened to David, but a king whose hands were clean of bloodshed would rank as another Solomon; he could build the Temple, procure peace, touch the years with gold.[165] Jumièges merely nods in that direction, but he offsets this politeness by painting Edward's father as a coward who massacred innocents, treacherously attacked Normandy, and was beaten off by Norman women.[166] The subtext was that Norman women trumped Edward's rotten paternal line. Such opinions were evidently current at William's court in Normandy even as Edward was trying to continue that line in the descendants of Edmund Ironside. As its prospects of survival grew with

---

[160] Clayton, 'Promissio Regis', pp. 148–9.

[161] J. Campbell, The Anglo-Saxon State (London and New York, 2000), pp. 207, 211, 222–3.

[162] Cf. Cassiodorus, In Psalmos 126. 2: 'iniqua praesumptio' (of the Pelagian heresy), in Magni Aurelii Cassiodori expositio Psalmorum, ed. M. Adriaen, Corpus Christianorum Series Latina, xcvii-viii, 2 vols (Turnhout, 1958).

[163] P. A. Clarke, The English Nobility under Edward the Confessor (Oxford, 1994), pp. 175–6.

[164] GND, II, p. 79. Cf. Lambert, Law and Order, p. 224; and on bloodshed, H. E. J. Cowdrey, 'The Peace and Truce of God in the Eleventh Century', P&P 46 (1970), 42–67, at p. 53; Meens, 'Politics', pp. 346–8.

[165] Vita, p. 7.

[166] GND, II, p. 15; Licence, 'Succession Question', pp. 115–16.

Edgar, passive-aggressive responses were emerging in the duchy. They may have come from the duke, who had been raised on tales about Æthelred's indebtedness to his grandfather, and of Edward's indebtedness to Robert and to him. As Edward's moneyers continued reinventing the old king's image – a picture showing him enthroned, a facing bust, a naturalistic profile – William began to peer more into the mirrors of power. He too could construct a narrative. He too was a ravening wolf.

Chapter 6

BETRAYAL

Cum sua quisque regat diverso flamina tractu,
quin lanient mundum; tanta est discordia fratrum.
(Though each has his domain in which to bluster, still they
well-nigh tear apart the world, such is the brothers' discord.)

Ovid, *Metamorphoses* I. 59–60

Like the army of stonemasons slowly sculpting, chipping away at the
edifice that would become his mausoleum, Time, the mighty sculptor, has
aged our king. Cares have worn their furrows on his brow. Most of
Edward's friends and kin have crossed into that vastness where all of us
must one day go. Most of the counsellors around him were younger men,
and he was precious – a venerable elder, wise in years. We must picture a
man of sixty. Except for a few remarks by the encomiast, the descriptions
we have of him come from the end of his life and reflect the state of being
he had attained after most of his days were tallied. Folcard, who had
apparently seen the king, gives a generic impression of his appearance.
Parallels are found in the pen-portraits of saints and patriarchs, but it may
not be distant from the truth. Edward was a fine figure of a man – tall,
with milky-white hair and beard. His face was broad with a flush of
colour. The long fingers of his emaciated hands let light through the gaps
between them.[1] Personable, but ever dignified, he went about 'with eyes
of humility': a comment setting him apart from men with 'proud eyes',
which the Book of Proverbs identified as one of God's pet hates – a sure
sign of a tyrant.[2] He was gracious and affable to all, says Folcard. To this
we may add that early loss had not left him craving to indulge petty tyran-
nies in his later years.

Evidence for Edward's restraint is found in the *Vita*, and in the elegy
published in the Chronicle – an alliterative poem known as *The Death of
Edward*, and in the epigram penned by Godfrey of Winchester. In different
ways, all three describe a man who had learned self-control. Folcard
mentions that when Edward was angry, his anger was terrible, but he
never indulged in it by railing. He had learned to say no to petitioners but

---

[1] *Vita*, p. 19.
[2] Ibid., and see above, p. 87. Folcard references Prov. 6:16 at p. 59 (see below, Appendix
3, p. 297, n. 60).

said it so graciously they left feeling he had done them a favour.[3] The elegist says that, though he had lived in exile, he was always cheerful. It calls him baleless (*bealuleas*), meaning 'without ill intent', which is more about maintaining a good conscience than nurturing goodwill, though the latter is its corollary.[4] This is also the sense in which the poet regarded Edward as *clæne* (clean), and Folcard saw him as 'unblemished', thinking of Edward's chastity.[5] Sin manifested as the lack of self-mastery, leading to a desire for control of others. Godfrey of Winchester gets to the point by saying Edward ruled himself as well as ruling others.[6] An achievement never attributed to Alexander, this was the highest compliment to a ruler.[7] He adds that the king never abused his riches, and that rich and poor were alike to him.[8] This should be taken to indicate he was no respecter of persons. It accords with Folcard's acclamation of a gracious man, humble towards all. His willingness to touch the sick reinforced the impression.[9]

Though Edward had always been a peaceable man he had wrestled with himself in the past. His resentment of Emma and Harthacnut is discernible in his punishment of the former, and in the Chronicle's damning verdict on the latter. Though his indignation abated when he settled on the throne, it flared up again when rebels or client kings challenged his authority. Yet suffering and loss, coupled with the sharp intelligence soon observed by the encomiast, combined to transform Edward into a man who preferred kindness to cruelty. Humility and cheerfulness were fruits of his intelligence. Another was what the encomiast described at the beginning of his reign as 'the power of his mind and counsel', and what the Chronicle poem identified afterwards as his 'skilful counsel'.[10] The latter implies his judgement improved with age. Edward was also a conscientious man whose self-control and serenity were hard-won from a fractious mind. Darkening fears could overtake him to invade his inner peace.

Edith had come to resemble him, being dignified and reserved, and able to manage her feelings.[11] Folcard regarded the couple as inseparable. For him, Edith was Edward's 'other part, alike in probity'. He refers

---

[3] *Vita*, p. 19.

[4] ASC C, 1065 [1065–6] (ed. O'Brien O'Keeffe, p. 119); Barlow, *Edward*, p. 129 and 129, n. 3.

[5] ASC C, 1065 [1065–6] (ed. O'Brien O'Keeffe, p. 119); *Vita*, pp. 18/19, giving 'integer'.

[6] Godfrey of Winchester, *Epigrammata*, III, p. 149: 'Seque suosque regens'.

[7] Hincmar, *De ordine*, p. 518 (*Governance*, tr. Herlihy, p. 210).

[8] Godfrey of Winchester, *Epigrammata*, III, p. 149.

[9] *Vita*, pp. 19, 93.

[10] Keynes and Love, 'Earl Godwine's Ship', p. 196: 'uirtute animi consiliique'. *Virtus* can mean virtue or innate power – giftedness perhaps; ASC C, 1065 [1065–6] (ed. O'Brien O'Keeffe, p. 118): 'cræftig ræda'.

[11] *Vita*, p. 23.

to the two as 'one person dwelling in double form', and, in another work, expresses the view that she was 'divinely joined to the king's side' to benefit the kingdom'.[12] It is clear that Edith was devoted to her husband, for she attended to his wardrobe, adapted to his advice, and would be buried at his side.[13] Folcard knew her well enough to believe that 'no page of any book could please her more than one which tells of Edward's qualities'.[14] Harold loved him too, for in the years since 1052, he had risked his life on campaign and served him loyally. The bond between Edward and Tostig was closer. Folcard describes it as *amor* – the strongest word he could have chosen.[15] Herman of Bury wrote of the king with affection, and Abbot Baldwin of Bury honoured him by providing an annual fish supper for the monks on his anniversary, so they might remember him in their prayers.[16] Notes made at Bury in and after his reign call him Edward the Good, an epithet that might have stuck, had it not been uptitled to 'Confessor'.[17] The poem in the Chronicle calls him a very dear prince and emphasizes, as Folcard does, the loyalty he won in return.[18]

Folcard talks of Edward's interests in old age, which may be compared with similar lists for the Frankish emperor Charlemagne (d. 814) and for Edward's ancestor, Alfred the Great (d. 899). For all three, hunting was top of the list. Alfred and Edward hunted with dogs and birds.[19] Charlemagne was still hunting at the age of seventy, and Edward at sixty.[20] Harold shared Edward's passion for hunting; he owned illuminated books on falconry, and both men had another hobby in common, being enthusiastic collectors of saints' relics.[21] Second on Alfred's list of interests was instructing goldsmiths to make treasures for him. This is not on Edward's list – we are told that Edith took charge of the goldsmiths; but Edward did order a crown to be made earlier in the reign.[22] The next pursuit on Alfred's list, also prominent in Charlemagne's, is the king's love of reading.[23] What Folcard seems to indicate by praising Edith's skills in

[12] Ibid., p. 7; p. lv.

[13] Sulcard, *Prologus*, p. 91, mentions Edith's burial with Edward at Westminster.

[14] *Vita*, p. 91.

[15] Ibid., p. 76, and see below, pp. 234–5.

[16] *MSE*, pp. 46–8, 61; *Anglo-Saxon Charters*, ed. and tr. A. J. Robertson (Cambridge, 1956), no. CIV, pp. 193–201, at p. 197.

[17] Ibid., p. 194: 'cincg se goda Eadward'; p. 196: 'Eadwardes . . . þæs godan kynges'.

[18] ASC C, 1065 [1065–6].

[19] *Asser's Life of King Alfred*, ed. Stevenson, p. 59; *Vita*, p. 63.

[20] Einhard, *Vita Karoli Magni: The Life of Charlemagne*, Bibliotheca Germanica 3, text with translation by E. S. Firchow and E. H. Zeydel (Coral Gables, FL, 1972; repr. Dudweiler, 1985), p. 86; *Vita*, p. 79.

[21] Haskins, 'Harold's Books'; Rogers, 'Waltham Abbey Relic-list'; John Flete, *The History of Westminster Abbey*, ed. J. Armitage Robinson (Cambridge, 1909), pp. 69–72, lists the numerous relics Edward was supposed to have donated to Westminster.

[22] *Asser's Life of King Alfred*, ed. Stevenson, p. 59; *Vita*, p. 25.

[23] *Asser's Life of King Alfred*, ed. Stevenson, p. 59; Einhard, *Vita Karoli Magni*, p. 92.

the liberal arts and attributing none to her husband is that Edward was not a bookish man, though Herman's remark that 'his loving generosity attracted to the realm men learned in many arts' points us to his refined tastes as a patron.[24] As we have seen, he was attentive at Mass and admired foreign monks for their discipline – a trait he valued; but the variety of services he attended and the range of his religious interests compare less fully to Charlemagne's or Alfred's.[25] Indeed, the latter were exceptionally impressive individuals.

BROTHERLY MANOEUVRES

The *Vita* paints a picture of Edward enjoying peaceful pursuits while delegating military tasks to his commanders Harold and Tostig. It is a picture to flatter the brothers and highlight the relationship and shared purpose they maintained before their quarrel. But there is truth in it too. Edward liked to delegate, in accordance with contemporary guidance on kingship, and Harold and Tostig were his deputies. Edward's policy was to let them build their empires, so that they would take better care of his. (He evidently took a similar line with the archbishops whose grandeur fed his magnificence.) Tostig's dealings with the Scots had been effective in the eight years he had occupied the northern earldom. Aided by the northern bishops, he had negotiated a truce with Malcolm and brought him to submit to Edward. Only one raid seems to have been recorded subsequently – and it occurred during Tostig's absence in 1061, when Malcolm's men invaded Lothian and attacked the isle of Lindisfarne.[26] It demonstrated that the Scots preferred to attack when Tostig was absent. Folcard speaks obliquely of the earl's strategies, but whatever they were, they persuaded the Scottish king to honour Edward and deliver hostages to confirm the peace.[27]

The interpolation in Simeon of Durham's chronicle, moreover, indicates that by 1061 Tostig and Malcolm had become sworn brothers.[28] The entry should not be dismissed, for the earl and his wife were well remembered at Durham where it was made, and because the strategy of forming unions through blood-brotherhood, albeit uncommon, was one Edward used to strengthen his bonds with Duke Robert. The traction Tostig enjoyed with Malcolm, even as early as 1059, reminds us that Tostig may have supported Malcolm's campaign for the Scottish throne.

---

[24] *Vita*, p. 63; *MSE*, p. 47.

[25] *Vita*, p. 63; *Asser's Life of King Alfred*, ed. Stevenson, pp. 59–60; Einhard, *Vita Karoli Magni*, pp. 94–6.

[26] Simeon, *Historia regum*, pp. 174–5. It should be noted, however, that Folcard refers vaguely to raids and campaigns: *Vita*, p. 67.

[27] *Vita*, p. 67.

[28] Simeon, *Historia regum*, p. 175, and see above, p. 190.

Such support would be in keeping with English opposition to Macbeth and might help to explain the confusion of twelfth-century historians who believed that the English had helped to install Malcolm. The *Vita* represents Tostig as a worthy commander and successor to the courageous Siward.[29] As such, he would chip away what was left of Macbeth's power.

In the same eight years while Tostig contained the Scots, Harold had not contained the Welsh. Part of his problem was that he controlled only the southern march, with the northern portion remaining under the command of Ælfgar, who would not act against Gruffudd. The main difficulty, however, was Gruffudd himself, an unpredictable, belligerent monarch who kept pushing at the boundaries, even where he met resistance. Gruffudd was also sea-borne, capable of leading attacks from the northern coast into the Dee, or round the southern coast into the Severn. Cutting him off by sea would neccesitate combining Harold's ships and Ælfgar's; but Ælfgar had no intention of destroying his supportive son-in-law; and while he remained in Mercia, Gruffudd could exploit the divisions of the marcher earls. Since 1055, Harold had brokered treaties and fortified Gloucester, which controlled the crossing of the lower Severn. But Gruffudd had raided where he liked and annexed a lot of land. In 1063, Gruffudd may have embarrassed Harold again.

Though the Chronicle is silent for the years 1062 and 1063, a poem in the *Vita* recalls that Gruffudd attacked across the Severn, and that England suffered the blow until Edward compelled him to regret the crime by sending in combined forces under Harold and Tostig.[30] Folcard, careful with geography, cannot be referring to Gruffudd's campaigns of the 1050s around the Wye at Hereford and in the Dee basin in Cheshire. The only location Gruffudd might have crossed the Severn was either north-east of Rhyd-y-Groes where he had fought the English in 1039, or south of the royal town of Gloucester by leading ships upriver into Harold's earldom. We should therefore identify a new affront in 1063, which precipitated English retribution. As in 1055 and 1058, when he seized land from a king willing to cede territory, Gruffudd was pressing at the boundaries of the English kingdom. Perhaps a five-year treaty had expired, but so had the king's patience. At the Christmas assembly, where Edward's presence at Gloucester recalled the assassination of Rhys ap Rhydderch exactly eleven years earlier, the king resorted to a similar plan. On this occasion, however, no Welsh head arrived for him on Twelfth Night 1064. For when Harold and his mounted assassins swooped on Rhuddlan late in December, Gruffudd had been warned and had already fled in his ship.

---

[29] *Vita*, p. 48, n. 115.

[30] Ibid., p. 87. The context, as well as the use of *sceleris*, implies that Edward punished Gruffudd for a specific raid in 1063 and not for his general course of conduct. See also Freeman, *NC*, II, p. 475. On the chronicles' gaps for those years, and the consequent slippage of dates for the annals, see below, pp. 258-9.

Ælfgar is last on record in 1062, confirming Wulfstan's election to the see of Worcester and receiving Edward's writ establishing the bishop in office. His final attestation is found in a forged diploma for the see of York, but it appears to derive from an authentic witness list of 31 December 1062.[31] His death or final exile may therefore be placed in 1063, a year for which the Chronicle has no annal. There is a temporal link between his exit and Gruffudd's fateful raid across the Severn, but not, as far as we know, a causal one. Still, it is reasonable to speculate, given that Gruffudd's two previous campaigns followed on his father-in-law's expulsion. Perhaps in 1063, Ælfgar opposed Edward a third time, was outlawed again, and fled to Gruffudd. Fighting to recover his earldom, the earl might have been killed. Whether the shame of the episode led to it being omitted or erased from the Chronicle (or whether it was something else that happened in those years which caused them to be expunged), there was no resolve on the king's part to break the dynasty, for before May 1065 – albeit maybe not immediately – Edward strengthened its hereditary control of the earldom by appointing Ælfgar's son, Edwin, as earl of Mercia. Perhaps he felt guilty about the manner of Ælfgar's death. About the same time, or a little later, he carved out a midland earldom for Waltheof, the son of Earl Siward.[32] In both cases, he may have felt that their parentage entitled them; that their turn had now come.

Harold's raid upon Rhuddlan was an attempt to remove Gruffudd at minimum expense and loss of life. When that failed, Edward devised a different plan, determined not to allow the enemy time to regroup.[33] Assembling a fleet in the spring, and calling out an army, he now enlisted Tostig and ordered the brothers to get Gruffudd in a pincer movement. It was reminiscent of the manoeuvres of the land-army and ship-army he had sent in 1054 to flush out Macbeth. Gruffudd was already crippled because Harold had burned his fleet, but there was always the danger that he might hire pirates from the Irish Sea. Harold, who had done this sort of work in 1052 (albeit on the wrong side), was ordered to take the fleet round the southern Welsh coast and subdue the people there. Tostig, who had trained in the Scottish borders, was to advance with mounted troops via the uplands of north Wales. The brothers would meet in the middle. Preparations would have taken a number of months, but by May 1064 all

---

[31] S 1037a; Appendix 2, pp. 274–5.

[32] Both earls first attest in S 1042, of May 1065. S 1033, which Waltheof attests, may not be contemporary, and I have doubts about S 1237, which he also attests.

[33] For the chronology, see B. T. Hudson, 'The Destruction of Gruffudd ap Llywelyn', *Welsh History Review* 15 (1990–1), 331–50. The evidence gathered by Hudson shows that the raid on Rhuddlan, the May campaign, and the Welsh king's death in August occurred in the space of eight months from December 1063 to August 1064. It should stand as an argument against Harold's presence in Normandy that year: cf. Bates, *William*, pp. 191–2. There is no reason to favour 1064 over 1065 for Harold's dealings with William (Bates, pers. comm.).

was set. Harold sailed out of Bristol, compelling the southern Welsh to surrender. Tostig may have taken the route of the Roman legions, advancing west of Chester towards Rhuddlan and Bangor. He could not have avoided taking troops through Ælfgar's earldom, but Ælfgar was no longer part of the equation.

Gruffudd's realm suffered the invasion until the Welsh renounced their king. The scale and violence of the campaign became the stuff of legend, aided by stone pillars Harold had erected, inscribed with the words, 'Here was Harold the Conqueror'.[34] On 5 August 1064, eight months after the raid that failed to capture him, the fugitive Gruffudd was identified in Ireland. His head was hacked off and transported to Harold, who took it to Edward with the figurehead of Gruffudd's ship. His widow Ealdgyth, Ælfgar's daughter, should have fallen into Edward's charge about that time. Edward entrusted Wales to Gruffudd's half-brothers Bleddyn and Rhiwallon, who swore oaths to him and gave hostages to him and to Harold; and they promised to be undeceiving, to serve the English king, and pay him tribute.[35] E, curiously, implies that Harold alone received Gruffudd's head and nominated just the one replacement ruler, rather than two.[36] The narrative it promotes (unlike D's, which retains Edward's role) leaves us with the feeling that Harold was boasting to friends, like Stigand, that the triumph was his, whereas Ealdred (i.e. D) wanted to give proper credit to the king. Yet the arrangement was no different in Scotland, whose king had submitted to Tostig and Edward.[37] It is clear therefore that Edward expected client kings to submit to the adjacent commanders and through them to him. He was a distant and imperial figure indeed.

It may have been about this point, with Harold as Edward's overseer of the Welsh, that proposals were mooted for him to marry Gruffudd's widow. Harold, in any case, must have married her between August 1064 and his death in 1066. The matter was pressing, since the former queen might become a dangerous woman. Edward had to bind her into a marriage as soon as he could. Harold, still not officially married, was the obvious best match. Forging a union between them would not only miti-gate the Leofwineson–Godwinson rivalry (for let it be recalled that Ealdgyth was sister to Edwin and Morcar); it would also reinforce Harold's hold over Wales, strengthening Edward's imperium. Propriety and the law nevertheless expected widows to wait a year before remarrying.[38] Meanwhile, there was work for Harold to do in tidying Welsh affairs.

---

[34] Barlow, *Godwins*, p. 95; Gerald of Wales, *Opera*, ed. J. F. Dimock, RS 21, 8 vols (London, 1861–77), VI, p. 217.

[35] ASC D, 1063 [1063–4].

[36] ASC E, 1063 [1063–4].

[37] *Vita*, p. 67.

[38] C. Fell, *Women in Anglo-Saxon England*, and C. Clark and E. Williams, *and the impact of 1066* (Oxford, 1984), p. 61.

THE BUBBLE OF REPUTATION

Edward was now the undisputed overlord of Britain, with client kings in Scotland and in Wales. Though he had been forbearing, princes who forfeited his patience had forfeited their thrones and heads. Godfrey of Winchester wrote that Edward terrified his enemies not by war but with his peace, and that no one dared break it.[39] The terror lay in not knowing the limits of his tolerance. Dangerous as he was, however, he had earned respect by putting peace first, preferring to cede territory and placate aggressors to the alternative of sending in his generals. His policy was in keeping with models of good kingship which advocated peacekeeping over war. As Hincmar preached, citing St Augustine, 'it is beyond doubt a greater felicity to have concord with a good neighbour than to subdue a wicked neighbour by warfare'.[40] From that perspective, Gruffudd's demise was a disagreeable outcome, compared with the relationship Tostig cultivated with the Scottish king, Malcolm.

Pursuing his delicate business of balancing the brothers, Folcard honoured Harold by crediting victory in Wales to him, and the subjugation of the Scots to Tostig.[41] Though his desire to be even-handed furnished him with a motive for downplaying Tostig's role in the campaign of 1064 (for Harold had played no part in Scotland), it strengthens the impression that this was a campaign in which the brothers competed for renown. Like the author of the *Liðsmannaflokkr*, who carefully balanced the achievements of Cnut and Thorkell, the author of the *Vita* tried to pacify tensions.[42] His readiness to credit Harold, even though Tostig was his favourite, combines with the evidence of the stone pillars Harold had erected – none are attributed to Tostig – in suggesting Harold was the needier of glory. Tostig, whose military record may have been tidier, let him receive it. If he was beginning to outshine his brother, even taking his place as Edward's principal favourite, it was better for Tostig not to crow.

That Harold depended more on his reputation as a soldier is clear from its emphasis in the *Vita*. Writing a year or two after the Welsh campaign, Folcard devoted a section of his work to the brothers' qualities. Artless though it seems, it is not as even-handed as it claims to be, for the qualities it ascribes only to Tostig (lacking, by implication, in Harold) serve to expose Harold's demerits. Tostig, we are told, was admirably restrained and keen to oppose evil; he was generous and had a religious wife who inspired him to honour Christ; he was a man to be trusted, steadfast in word, deed, and promise; he was chaste, desiring no woman but his wife

---

[39] Godfrey of Winchester, *Epigrammata*, III, p. 149.

[40] Hincmar, *De regis persona*, col. 840, quoting Augustine, *De civitate Dei*, iv, 15 (translation from Augustine, *The City of God against the Pagans*, ed. and tr. R. W. Dyson (Cambridge, 1998), p. 162).

[41] *Vita*, pp. 65–7.

[42] See above, p. 44.

(unlike Harold perhaps), and he governed the use of his body and his tongue.[43] Harold's distinct qualities were that he was taller, wiser, tougher, and better at dealing with criticism.[44] His were qualities of mind and body. Tostig's were qualities of the soul.

In the section of the *Vita* he devoted to the brothers, Folcard filled ten lines of writing with the qualities they shared, seven lines with Harold's, and thirteen and a half lines with Tostig's – almost twice as many. Turning to their foreign travels, he allowed Harold eleven lines and Tostig fifty-eight.[45] His preference for Tostig may have rested solely on the latter having more of the virtues monks admired, or on Folcard's closer acquaintance with Tostig while serving Ealdred in the north, but given his near infatuation with Edith, his preference was doubtless hers. Edward likewise warmed to zealous spirits, and Tostig had that quality. Whereas Harold was like Godwine, amiable, dependable, and admirable, Tostig was more like Robert of Jumièges in his zeal to combat enemies. Edward may have liked that zeal all the more because the realities of ruling obliged him to dampen its spark in himself. Harold pleased the king by serving him, even bringing him Gruffudd's head like a dutiful mastiff, but service was no short-cut to Edward's heart.

Zeal nevertheless had its dark side, as Folcard's comments reveal. For one thing, Tostig could not handle criticism. This suggests built-up resentment; that people could not be frank with him; that they were obliged to whisper against him behind his back. Another difficulty was that Tostig bore grudges. Folcard mentions but does not explain a long-standing enmity between him and the sons of Ælfgar.[46] It is telling that he links it only to Tostig and not to his brother Harold. Edwin, the elder surviving son of Ælfgar, was appointed to the Mercian earldom before 24 May 1065.[47] Tostig would not have been pleased, but Harold may have been neutral. Concerted opposition from the pair of them would have given Folcard grounds to associate the feud with both. Tostig was making enemies in Northumbria too. Complaints about his rule revolved around the imposition of harsh laws, the inflexibility of his justice, and a tax he had levied on the Northumbrians, possibly to finance the Welsh campaign.[48] Edward's regime had been criticized in 1052 for passing bad

---

[43] *Vita*, pp. 48/9–50/1: on p. 48, 'sed acrior paulisper in persequenda malitia' is a comparison with Harold, not a criticism of Tostig, as Barlow believed (following Freeman, *NC*, II, p. 388, n. 3). Tostig, in fact, is 'keener' than Harold to prosecute wrongdoers – a compliment. On Harold's reputation for adultery, Barlow, *Godwins*, p. 77.

[44] *Vita*, p. 49.

[45] Ibid., p. 48, lines 18–20, 27–9; p. 50, lines 10–14 (qualities in common); p. 48, lines 20–7 (Harold's); p. 48, line 29–p. 50, line 10 (Tostig's); and p. 50, line 23–p. 52, line 5 (Harold's travels); p. 52, line 6–p. 56, line 29 (Tostig's travels).

[46] Ibid., p. 77.

[47] Baxter, *Earls of Mercia*, p. 48.

[48] *JW*, ii, p. 599; cf. *Vita*, pp. 77, 79.

laws, and the lack of any legislation from his reign adds to the impression of mercurial justice. Though Folcard claims it was the earl's readiness to punish evildoers which made him enemies in the north, his explanation whitewashes Tostig's very unpleasant methods.[49]

John of Worcester, apparently citing a lost northern chronicle, states that when a faction of Northumbrian nobles opposed Tostig in 1064, he invited two of their leaders, Gamel, son of Orm, and Ulf, son of Doilfinn, to come and agree a peace treaty in his private chamber in York. There he had them killed.[50] Though extant versions of contemporary chronicles omit the charge, C may allude to it in its statement that Tostig 'despoiled of life and land all those he had power over'.[51] It must have been with trepidation that the elder Gospatric, Uhtred's son, travelled south for Edward's Christmas court in 1064.[52] Whether he was intending to denounce Tostig for his crimes or challenge him for the control of the northern earldom, the queen arranged for him to be murdered during the festivities, to protect her brother. Such at least were the accusations levelled in 1065 – and it is unlikely charges of murder in Tostig's chamber and at court were totally unfounded. Folcard's tale of the younger Gospatric risking his life to save Tostig looks like an attempt to quell rumours of enmity between him and the House of Bamburgh, though Tostig's preference for the nephew could partly account for the envy of the uncle. Here we appear to be seeing the last desperate attempts to manage a crisis of misrule. By killing enemies in York, Tostig showed he was deadly. Killing them at court raised the possibility (which the king could deny) that it was done with the king's approval.

These were standard tactics of regime intimidation, a throwback to the early tyranny of Siward and Harthacnut, or the viziership of Eadric Streona. Killings at court removed ring-leaders of opposition and terror-ized the decapitated faction, which had no way of knowing Pharaoh's intentions. Edward's favourites had correctly judged he would let them get away with murder. His critics in 1051 had complained of this trait when he shielded Eustace and the Frenchmen in the castle. Now in 1065, northern eyes were upon Edward. But as winter melted into spring and spring blossomed into summer, no initiative was taken to punish the perpetrators. Tostig, rather, went about his royal business, and Edith was allowed to behave like a virtuous queen, rebuilding Wilton nunnery. There were courtiers not implicated in the murders whom aggrieved

[49] *Vita*, pp. 77, 79.

[50] *JW*, ii, p. 599. The murder at court (see below) occurred about 28 December 1064. The murder in York occurred 'in the preceding year', which could mean 1063 or the year ending at Christmas 1064.

[51] ASC C, 1065.

[52] On his identity, see Williams, *The English and the Norman Conquest*, p. 28; Stafford, *Emma and Edith*, p. 270.

parties in the north might lobby for redress. They surely included members of the clergy, and they may have included Harold, for the enmity between Harold and Tostig which pervades the *Vita* must have seeded by this point. If Harold already hated Tostig early in 1065, Tostig's enemies had a fault-line by which to divide the royal court.

WILLIAM'S AMBITION

By early 1065, dangerous, unpredictable figures were manoeuvring in the periphery of Edward's vision. In the north, allies of the House of Bamburgh were agitating against Tostig. South, across the Channel, William was emerging as the strong man in northern France. To the south of Normandy and Brittany, marching with both territories, lay the pivotal county of Maine – pivotal in that its allegiance could swing towards William or against him. For years it had been under the control of William's enemy Geoffrey Martel, count of Anjou, who was the guardian of the young count, Herbert II of Maine. It had also substituted as a battleground where Martel and William tested each other. Jumièges reveals that William's attacks on Le Mans, the capital city, were intended to punish Martel for the dishonour he had inflicted on him in the past. The attacks continued for several years, with Herbert caught in the middle.[53] When Martel died in 1060, Herbert was still a minor, no more than thirteen or fourteen.

If Poitiers is to be trusted, Herbert had appealed to William, seeking to replace the overbearing Martel with a new guardian. Poitiers claims Herbert negotiated an alliance with William, doing homage to the duke, asking for one of his daughters in marriage, and promising the succession of Maine to him should he die childless. The difficulty in believing these claims is that Poitiers was mounting a defence of William's actions. He was evidently unhappy with Jumièges' account, which he was rewriting and expanding, because the only explanation Jumièges gave for William's eventual conquest of Maine in 1063 was his desire to punish Martel, who had died in 1060. This left unanswered questions about William's decision to continue attacking Maine until he conquered it. Poitiers was trying to justify his actions by claiming that Herbert invited his assistance and promised him Maine if he died without an heir. But his framework of legitimation is modelled on the one assembled in the 1060s to justify William's conquest of England. The proof of this is found in the fact that Jumièges employed the latter but did not hit on the idea of employing it for Maine too.[54]

In March 1062, Herbert had died, unmarried and childless. Edward's nephew, Walter of the Vexin, then occupied Maine, claiming a right to do

---

[53] *GND*, II, pp. 150/1: 'per aliquot annos'. For Herbert, cf. *GG*, pp. 59–63.

[54] *GG*, pp. 59–65 (pp. 57–9 on his defensive motives in writing); cf. *GND*, II, p. 151 (Maine – no story about a promise), and pp. 159–61 (England – a story about a promise).

so as the husband of Biota, the sister of Herbert's late father, Count Hugh IV. William meanwhile oiled his alliances and began to gather an army. In spring 1063, he cautiously advanced, doing little more than destroying crops and attacking minor strongholds. None of this provoked Martel's successor, Geoffrey the Bearded, into coming to Walter's aid, so William increased the pressure, besieging the capital Le Mans, whereupon Walter capitulated. In August, he and his wife died in William's custody. Orderic, in this instance, may be right that William poisoned them. Though Poitiers later borrowed a promise-story to justify the conquest, William began by seeing a window of opportunity to extend his southern border before resolving to push onwards in the absence of serious opposition. The fact that he pushed and pushed until he had conquered the territory revealed a boundless and steely opportunism. Afterwards, William besieged the formidable castle of Mayenne, whose lord had withstood his earlier advance. Capturing and refortifying it may have run into late 1063 or 1064, given that Poitiers boasts that for anyone other than William, it would have been a year's work.[55]

HAROLD CROSSES THE CHANNEL

We do not know Edward's reaction to William's manoeuvres, which resulted in the death of his nephew and niece; but it is a fair guess Edward was not celebrating. Walter's mother Gode was living in Lambeth. News of the deaths can only have brought sorrow to the court. Still, Edward could ill afford to involve himself in continental politics at that juncture, for his attention in 1063 and 1064 was largely on Wales. Cross-Channel business would have to wait – which brings us to the contentious matter of Harold's trip to Normandy, in which the earl supposedly swore to promote William's interest in the English throne. The adventure, which is outlined by Jumièges, supplied the basis of a story that would be woven into the Bayeux Tapestry and elaborated by Poitiers. Those three sources agree in depicting Harold's capture by Count Guy of Ponthieu; and William pressuring Guy into handing him over; and Harold accompanying the duke on campaign in Brittany and swearing an oath to William. Incidental detail in the Tapestry, such as the inclusion in the narrative of minor figures with links to the abbey where it was commissioned, makes it doubtful the entire story is a fiction,[56] but with no pre-Conquest

---

[55] *GG*, p. 67; and, generally, for the detail in this paragraph, cf. Bates, *William*, pp. 178–85.

[56] Turold, for example, was apparently present in Ponthieu: H. Tsurushima, '"Hic Est Miles": Some Images of Three Knights: Turold, Wadard and Vital', in M. J. Lewis, G. R. Owen-Crocker, and D. Terkla, eds, *The Bayeux Tapestry: New Approaches: Proceedings of a Conference at the British Museum* (Oxford, 2011), 81–91, at p. 90.

evidence to confirm it, we cannot know which elements were invented in hindsight. To understand the context, we must fix the date of Harold's journey, and we can do so with reference to the Breton campaign.

Poitiers' outline of the campaign is trustworthy for the simple reason that the panegyrist attempts to cover up his hero's humiliation. His account revolves around the condition of the ripening crop, which had suffered adverse conditions and was late coming to harvest.[57] The duke had not foreseen this, to the embarrassment of his apologist. Ears of grain, when ripe, fall over to one side. Poitiers says that the 'unripe crops were standing', meaning the harvest was delayed.[58] William was obliged to withdraw for lack of supplies and feed his army on the provisions of Rivallon of Dol, the ally who had requested his support against Conan of Brittany in the first place. Eventually, Rivallon's crop was ripe enough for William's troops to consider helping themselves. Then Rivallon quarrelled with William, who agreed to depart without touching the crop and without obtaining Conan's submission.[59] Harvesting normally got under way about the beginning of August. Given that the duke was expecting to feed his army, his campaign must have occurred in August or September to have suffered this kind of setback.

As to the date, Poitiers places Harold's adventure with William after the duke's destruction and refortification of the castle of Mayenne, which followed his conquest of Maine, and he presents it as the last episode to have occurred in William's career prior to Edward's death.[60] The year could not have been 1063, when William was occupied in Maine until at least July before capturing Mayenne, a feat which Poitiers judged to be a year's work for any man other than William, who achieved it speedily (but not, one assumes, with the miraculous speed prerequisite for a Breton campaign that September).[61] Nor can Harold's adventure be placed in 1064, a large part of which was occupied with the Welsh campaign, which started in May and continued into August when Harold collected Gruffudd's head. Edward and Harold were then involved in setting up a

---

[57] Poitiers tells us that the region was 'very infertile and greatly exhausted': *GG*, p. 77.

[58] *GG*, p. 74: 'Stabant in aristis fruges immaturae.' (Poitiers, unusually, places the verb at the beginning of the sentence to emphasize its significance.) He means the annual harvest, for he refers to produce stored from the 'anno superiore' (p. 74) and calls the crop the 'anni laborem' (p. 76).

[59] Cf. F. Neveux, 'L'expédition de Guillaume le Bâtard en Bretagne (vers 1064)', in J. Quaghebeur and S. Soleil, eds, *Le Pouvoir et la foi au Moyen Âge en Bretagne et dans l'Europe de l'Ouest: Mélanges en mémoire du professeur Hubert Guillotel* (Rennes, 2010), 619–37, at pp. 629–30, and Keats-Rohan, 'L'expédition de Guillaume, duc de Normandie, et du comte Harold en Bretagne (1064): le témoinage de la *tapisserie de Bayeux* et des chroniqueurs anglo-normands', *MSHAB* 40 (2013), 203–24, at pp. 216–18, for Conan's tactical retreats.

[60] He places Harold's arrival 'about the same time' (as William's capture of Mayenne and successful return): *GG*, p. 69.

[61] Ibid., pp. 65–9.

client regime in Wales – no trifling process.[62] Harold may then have spent the best part of a year tidying Welsh affairs, for he was active in the area around Portskewett the following summer.

The C/D annal for that year, 1065, starts by mentioning that before Lammas (1 August) Harold 'ordered some building to be done in Wales – at Portskewett – when he had subdued it'.[63] By that point, he had settled affairs in Wales and wished to set his stamp upon the conquest by commissioning the construction of a hunting lodge in prime Welsh territory. After ordering the building work in July, he does not reappear in the annals until mid-late October. During that time, the lodge being built at Portskewett was destroyed by Welsh marauders, and the workers were killed. Then in early October a massive rebellion overran Northumbria and advanced south. Edward was hunting at Britford in Wiltshire with Tostig, but Harold is nowhere to be seen reacting to the affronts of that year, as we might expect if he was present in England. Indeed, the assault on his building works in recently subdued territory, coupled with the boldness of the rebels, suggest that enemies were taking advantage of a major absence. We know Harold went overseas in 1056, though the Chronicle fails to mention it – and almost certainly again in 1058.[64] Another unchronicled absence is possible in 1065. The best way of combining Poitiers' evidence with Harold's movements is to suppose he crossed the Channel about the beginning of August 1065, returning in October.

HAROLD'S REASONS FOR CROSSING

Although Harold's reasons for crossing the Channel in 1065 are no better understood than his reasons for being in Flanders in 1056, such is the impulse to see those crossings as consequential that both have been linked to Edward's plans for the succession.[65] In the case of the 1065 crossing, Jumièges is the first to report that Edward sent Harold to William to confirm his promise of the throne; that the earl fell into the hands of Guy of Ponthieu; that William pressured Guy into releasing him, and that Harold stayed with him for some time and swore fealty to him about the kingdom with many oaths.[66] His testimony, with that of the Tapestry and the *Gesta Guilelmi*, reflects an evolving narrative put about by William's supporters to strengthen his claim to the throne. We need not doubt that Harold landed at Ponthieu, where Jumièges, Poitiers, and the Tapestry

---

[62] See above, pp. 192–3. Hudson's convincing re-dating leaves no room for foreign adventures in 1064.

[63] ASC C, D, 1065.

[64] Above, pp. 192–3.

[65] E.g. P. Grierson, 'A Visit of Earl Harold to Flanders in 1056', *EHR* 51 (1936), 90–7, at pp. 94–6.

[66] *GND*, II, p. 159 (in the section added to his work *c.* 1069).

would have us believe Guy made him his captive. Yet the fact he landed in Ponthieu hardly supports the Norman claim that he was making for Normandy, and the possibility remains that he arrived as Guy's guest, and that Guy's mightier neighbour forced him to hand the visitor over. The Tapestry shows Harold embarking with hunting dogs and birds of prey, which could be interpreted as diplomatic gifts.[67] Hunting was on Harold's mind in August that year, as his builders got to work at Portskewett.

Expectations of marriage might also have been occupying Harold's thoughts, for a year had passed since Gruffudd's death, on 5 August 1064, and Ealdgyth, his widow, could now remarry without censure. If Edward had it mind for her to marry Harold, to nurture harmony between the two leading noble dynasties and strengthen his hold over Wales, it was the earl's last chance to investigate alternatives. On one hand, by marrying the former Welsh queen he might aspire to rule Wales himself one day, securing the march by allying with the House of Mercia. On the other hand, there were advantages in a cross-Channel marriage, like Tostig's union with Judith of Flanders. Marrying into the House of Ponthieu or even the ducal House of Normandy would stimulate trade to and from Wessex and secure it through cross-Channel collaboration in maritime defence. It would also confirm Harold's position on the European stage. Busy in Wales for the past year and faced with the prospect of having to make his big decision, Harold would have been wise to ask the king for respite – for one last chance to go on a 'fishing expedition'. Wherever he was angling, William reeled him in.

Post-Conquest accounts peddle various tales of what passed between Harold and William. The most persistent story is that Harold swore an oath to him, which the duke later used against him. Variations on this narrative report that Harold went to rescue the hostages whom William had held since 1052, or that he ended up sealing a marital alliance.[68] Detail aside, in all sources the emphasis is on deception. Guy of Amiens casts Harold and William as deceivers, trying to deceive each other.[69] The Tapestry is interested in predatory conduct. When we look to its margins, we see birds and beasts from the fable genre associated with Aesop, interacting in ways that reflect the pride, folly, trickery, ambition, and ruthlessness of men. The juxtaposition of fables and scenes invites the viewer to compare the worldly beasts and the protagonists depicted in the main frieze, but the fables overlap and lack the fixity for making specific

---

[67] BT, 4.

[68] E.g. HN, pp. 5–6 (rescue mission); Simon, Gesta abbatum sancti Bertini Sithiensium, ed. O. Holder-Egger, in MGH Scriptores 13 (Hanover, 1881), 635–62, at p. 641 (Harold's refusal to honour a marriage alliance); GR, II, § 228 (pp. 417–19). The stories about a proposed marriage alliance constitute slight evidence that Harold had not committed to Ealdgyth at that point.

[69] Carmen, pp. 17, 19.

comparisons.[70] Like the *Vita* and the *Carmen*, the Tapestry creates tension between the heroism of its protagonists and their wanton destructiveness. The *Vita* does so with allusions to shape-shifting, monstrosity, and bloody pagan conflict in its poetry.[71] The *Carmen* does so by presenting William and Harold's soldiers as thralls of bloodthirsty Mars, taking leave of their consciousness to perpetrate unchristian slaughter.[72] The Tapestry does so by reducing the arguments of great men to the squabbles of beasts, rendered marginal in the grander scheme. All three sources visualize a world of misplaced priorities; a nexus of scheming and manoeuvring, in which the elite were entangled in deceit and self-deception.

Folcard, writing *c.* 1066, makes no mention of Harold's adventure with William. He does explain that Harold and his spies had studied the capabilities and manoeuvres of unspecified French princes, to the extent that the latter were unable to deceive him with false intelligence, but he places that phase of intelligence gathering before Harold's pilgrimage to Rome.[73] Whatever the date of the pilgrimage, it was not 1065. Harold was in the company of Count Baldwin, Guy of Ponthieu, and other princes in Flanders in November 1056, and since 1058 is the most likely date of the pilgrimage, Folcard may refer to activities of the later 1050s.[74] If so, his vagueness is understandable. Nor should it surprise us that he omitted the debacle of Harold's escapade in Normandy in 1065, for he also omitted the uncomfortable detail of the Godwines' rebellion in 1051; and events of an altogether different magnitude had overtaken the narrative, in the form of the northern uprising and the rift between Harold and Tostig.

Guy of Amiens, who was Guy of Ponthieu's uncle, writing *c.* 1067, proffers something more solid. Without giving the date or circumstances, he communicates the Norman claim, that Edward had promised and decreed that William should succeed him and had sent Harold to William with a ring and sword as pledges. He also relays the claim that Harold had sworn oaths of 'friendship' to William and become his man, but as a secret perjurer, implying that the oaths concerned William's claim to the throne.[75] Two things are worth noting here, the first being that Guy takes no responsibility for claims made by his characters. In one instance, he states that William sent deceitful messages to match the deceit of his opponents. He alerts us to William's deceit before relaying a message from the

---

[70] E. C. Pastan and S. D. White, with K. Gilbert, *The Bayeux Tapestry and its Contexts: A Reassessment* (Woodbridge, 2014), pp. 35, 154–82; G. R. Owen-Crocker, 'The Bayeux Tapestry: The Voice from the Border', in S. L. Keefer and R. H. Bremner Jr, ed., *Signs on the Edge: Space, Text and Margin in Medieval Manuscripts* (Louvain, 2007), pp. 235–58.

[71] *Vita*, pp. 59–61, 85–9.

[72] *Carmen*, pp. 23–5, 33. Mars, however, is more in control of the English, it seems.

[73] *Vita*, pp. 51–3, and see above, p. 192.

[74] Rijksarchief te Gent, Sint-Pietersabdij, charters, no. 133; and see above, pp. 192–3.

[75] *Carmen*, pp. 21 and 17.

duke affirming Edward's promise of the throne, among other things.[76] Having warned his readers, he is inviting us to ponder whether William's character is deceiving us too. This draws attention to the fact that Guy is creating a drama, assigning speeches to actors without vouching for their content. More than that, he seems to undermine it. The second point is that the pledges in Guy's account are not hostages but a ring and a sword. Jumièges, writing his final part *c.* 1069, makes no mention of the hostages and evidently did not think them important. Both writers do, however, attest the early contention that Harold swore to promote William's claim to the throne.

Poitiers follows Jumièges here but adds the detail that William summoned a council at Bonneville-sur-Touques where Harold swore to be his man in the court of King Edward, to do his utmost to ensure that the throne should pass to William on Edward's death, and to fortify the castle of Dover and other castles for William's knights in the meantime. Citing unidentified witnesses, Poitiers assures us that those were his very words. Afterwards, he tells us, William took Harold on the Breton campaign because the earl was eager for glory, before releasing his nephew, the second hostage, out of respect for Harold's person.[77] The part of this which rings most true is the reference to Harold's eagerness for glory. Poitiers of course, writing in the mid-1070s, identifies the hostages as Edward's original pledges, but if William had been furious that Harold had tricked him into releasing a hostage who was a pledge for the English throne, Guy of Amiens would have had a much better storyline for his character than lame references to a ring and a sword, which were the sorts of gifts any prince might bestow on another. The real reason William had ended up with the hostages had to do with the fallout from 1052. He had clung on to them as pawns.

The Tapestry begins with a meeting involving Edward and Harold, which in the context may be taken to imply either that the king was sending him on a mission, or that Harold was requesting Edward's leave. It depicts Harold sailing to Ponthieu, falling into the hands of its count, Guy, and being conveyed by Guy to William after the arrival of messengers from the duke. At the duke's court, Harold is depicted addressing William about a man at whom he is pointing and whom he is leading by the hand. Then he appears campaigning with William in Brittany and finally swearing an oath or oaths on reliquaries, probably at Bayeux.[78] While it is hard to decide whether the design was completed nearer to 1066 or 1080, a more pressing difficulty in interpreting the Tapestry is its way of being both vivid and opaque. The paradox arises from its habit of combining theatrical scenes full of implicit meaning with text offering little

---

[76] Ibid., pp. 45–7.
[77] *GG*, pp. 69–77.
[78] *BT*, 1–26.

more than stage directions. The text is almost at pains to declare only what is necessary or obvious, limiting itself to names of characters and places, and to axiomatic explanations, such as 'these men wonder at the star', above a group of men pointing at Halley's Comet.[79] By dissolving meaning while inviting viewers to find it among shifting fragments of imagery and text, the designer was drawing inquirers towards a deeper understanding of the drama. That had to do with timeless truths of human behaviour and patterns of historical events.

If we accept that the scene in which Harold leads a man by the hand shows him pleading for the release of one of the hostages, it might confirm the reasonable assumption that Harold would have taken the opportunity to do so. Poitiers claims that the duke released one hostage out of respect for Harold's person, doubtless at his petition; but Eadmer's claim that he went abroad to obtain their overdue release smacks of an attempt to counter the Norman claim that he went to confirm the throne to William.[80] Like the Norman apologists, Eadmer, writing in the early twelfth century, had to get around the problem that Harold had gone to Ponthieu. He did so by maintaining he had been blown off-course, an idea to be teased from the Tapestry, which in a rare bit of narrative colour tells us that Harold crossed the Channel 'with his sails full of wind'.[81] Full sails are bad if the wind is blowing from the wrong direction. The joke may be that the wind in his sails took the wind out of his sails, as it were. Again, however, the Tapestry cultivates ambiguity, inviting viewers to make sense of it themselves. Eadmer may have been a viewer, for he grew up in the 1060s–70s in Canterbury where the Tapestry was conceived, party – perhaps – to early interpretations. His idea that Edward was displeased with Harold for falling into William's trap recalls a scene in which the king reprimands the returning earl,[82] as well as the Aesopian themes of entrapment and deceit. The Tapestry, however, could itself be accommodating a narrative crafted to counter the Norman version. For it accepts Harold swore an oath but challenges the idea that Edward was glad of it.[83]

If Harold did end up making promises and taking home a hostage, it is easy to see why some explanations extrapolated his motives from the

[79] Ibid., 32.

[80] *GG*, p. 77; *HN*, pp. 5–6.

[81] *BT*, 5; G. R. Owen-Crocker, ' " . . . *Velis vento plenis* . . .": Sea Crossings in the Bayeux Tapestry', in S. S. Klein, W. Schipper, and S. Lewis-Simpson, eds, *The Maritime World of the Anglo-Saxons* (Tempe, AZ, 2014), 131–56, at pp. 138–9.

[82] N. Brooks, 'The Authority and Interpretation of the Bayeux Tapestry', *ANS* 1 (1979), 1–34, 191–9; repr. in N. Brooks, *Communities and Warfare, 700–1400* (London and Rio Grande, 2000), 175–218, at pp. 187–9; and see S. Lewis, *The Rhetoric of Power in the Bayeux Tapestry* (Cambridge, 1999), pp. 104–6.

[83] As noted in Pastan and White, *The Bayeux Tapestry*, pp. 56–7, the work 'was intended to hint at different and conflicting stories . . . while conveying doubt and uncertainty about the truthfulness of any of them'.

outcomes. Harold was a secretive man who masked his intentions and, like everyone, put out false information. Yet his relationship with William was obviously complicated by the latter's long-term detention of his younger brother and nephew. (It is, of course, pertinent that the two things everyone knew about that relationship – the hostages and how it ended – were central to subsequent imaginings of the encounter.) Whether attempts had been made to recover the hostages and whether Harold or other relatives could visit them are things we cannot answer. We are also as ignorant as the authors we rely on about other, more covert aspects of Harold's dealings with William. It is not automatically true that William, because he prised Harold from Guy, had the earl in his power. Nor, given our blindness to the human behaviour accompanying the performance of ritual, can we assume that his oaths made comparable impressions upon each participant or witness.[84] Was a light-hearted piece of theatre later made out to be something very serious, just as the animal antics in the Tapestry's margins later give way to hewn limbs and severed heads? Harold rescued William's men from the quicksand of the Couesnon. Nobody could have foreseen they would soon be firing crossbow bolts into the faces of Harold's men.[85]

One conclusion that seems inescapable is that Harold had promised William something sufficiently concrete for the duke to release a hostage in return, though he retained the other hostage, Wulfnoth, as a pledge of Harold's good faith. It was not the English throne, even if William's apologists did a good job in circulating that rumour. It might, however, have been to marry into the ducal House, for the belief that Harold reneged on a marriage agreement is found in English and Flemish sources. Eadmer claims he swore to marry William's daughter, and William may have had an eleven- or twelve-year-old daughter in 1065, who would soon come of age.[86] Such an oath should have been substantial enough to secure the release of a hostage, and it represents the realistic maximum that William could have extracted from his prisoner, given that England was not Harold's, or Edward's, to promise away. It was also in keeping with long-term ducal aspirations to forge marital alliances with English royals.

As a soldier who liked to boast of his conquests by erecting stone pillars, Harold could boast to William that he had lately secured his king upon the throne. Like animals that puff themselves up when threatened, he could warn off the Norman predator by seeming larger. William in turn could

[84] See P. Hyams, 'Homage and Feudalism: A Judicious Separation', in N. Fryde, P. Monnet, and O. G. Oexle, eds, *Die Gegenwart des Feudalismus* (Göttingen, 2002), 13–49, at pp. 17–20.

[85] *Carmen*, p. 23.

[86] *HN*, p. 6; Bates, *William*, p. 128, and pp. 198–9 on the identity of the daughter, which remains uncertain. For the Flemish version, see Simon, *Gesta abbatum*, p. 641.

tell of how his ancestors had helped Edward and his forebears: how Rollo
had secured a king named Athelstan; how Richard had rescued Æthelred,
and how Robert and even he had assisted Edward to the throne. He
would have been telling Harold nothing not already set down by Dudo
and Jumièges, except the last claim, which found its way into Poitiers and
may already have been current. If Edward was in Harold's debt, he was
more in debt to William and his ancestors. The two had something in
common there and quite a lot to talk about. Privately, they might have
agreed that either of them would be a worthier successor to Edward than
the boy Edgar, who was nearing his majority. Perhaps they talked in ways
that flattered and encouraged each other's ambitions.

Although we may only speculate, one of the clearest links between the
creatures in the margins of the Tapestry and the actors in its main frieze
is the positioning of two peacocks, confronted above William and Harold
at their first encounter.[87] William's peacock, plumed in the same colour
as the duke, looks on passively like the duke below, while Harold's bird
looks down at it and fans his tail. Beneath the displaying peacock, Harold
addresses the duke about the hostage he is leading by the hand. Each
peacock has three bobbled plumes on its head, which resemble a miniature crown. But rather than alluding to the topic of discussion, they may
be prophetic, like the ghostly ships in a later margin, which forewarn of
William's invasion.[88] The peacocks might encourage us to think of
Harold and William as rivals who were keen to impress each other. Their
decision to go campaigning together, if Harold had any choice in it, puts
their relationship in a similar light.

WILLIAM AND HAROLD GO CAMPAIGNING

After settling affairs in Maine and capturing the castle of Mayenne,
William could have spent much of 1064 and 1065 planning an intervention
in Brittany. Having consolidated his alliances to the east and the south, he
looked west to the territory of Count Conan II, whom Poitiers charges
with being provocative and defying Norman lordship over Brittany – an
old excuse for bullying, which William now wished to use.[89] Among his
possible Breton allies was Eudo, Conan's uncle, whose relationship with
the count had been difficult. In the past, Conan had briefly imprisoned
him. Eudo, moreover, had detached himself from the count of Anjou,
William's enemy, and may have been leaning towards William. Rivallon
of Dol, a major landowner in eastern Brittany, had also been moving into
William's orbit. Marching into Brittany would test this support. According

---

[87] *BT*, 17; G. R. Owen-Crocker, 'Squawk Talk: Commentary by Birds in the Bayeux
Tapestry', *ASE* 34 (2005), 237–56, at p. 248.

[88] *BT*, 32.

[89] For what follows, see *GG*, pp. 73–7; *BT*, 18–24; Bates, *William*, pp. 200–4.

to Poitiers, Conan impudently announced a date 'on which he would attack the frontiers of Normandy'.[90] In reality, a plan had surely been hatched for Rivallon to rebel against Conan, prompting the latter to besiege his castle, providing a pretext for William to intervene. If a military manual had been written, with a section called 'pretexts for invasion', the trick would have been high on the list, along with alleging vassalage and claiming that a territory had been promised by a dead ruler. William's uncle, Count William of Arques, had laid such a trap in 1053, rebelling against his nephew whose subsequent siege of his castle elicited the requisite intervention by the king of France allied with the count of Anjou.[91] Conan doubtless knew what Rivallon and William were up to, and had laid his own plans with the new count of Anjou.[92] When he swiftly abandoned his siege of Dol on William's arrival, the duke probably thought he had caught him unawares.

Opportunistic as always, William decided to push and push, at what seemed like scant resistance. The Tapestry indicates that he turned south to capture Rennes, before advancing north to attack Dinan. Conan staged a series of tactical retreats, luring William deeper into Brittany. Buoyed by his success, and hoping to impress Harold, the duke probably thought his campaign in Maine was repeating itself, as one by one strongholds surrendered. Yet he was failing to find any stores of grain or cattle, as if his opponents had removed them; nor, owing to dry and barren conditions, was the harvest on time. Deep inside Brittany, unable to feed his army, William was forced to retreat; but as soon as he had crossed its frontiers, he learned that Conan and Geoffrey of Anjou were ready to face him in battle. Their timing was impeccable. Goaded to react, William led his army back to Rivallon's land, where supplies were available, or crops were nearly ready to harvest. But when his army pitched their tents, expecting to feed themselves at Rivallon's expense, Rivallon complained, and William was obliged to return to Normandy.

Poitiers gilds William's mishaps with all sorts of noble motives, saying he retreated in preference to plundering churches and because he assumed that Conan would come begging forgiveness; and that he withdrew from Rivallon's lands only when it was apparent that his enemies were fleeing again.[93] But Conan and Geoffrey had timed their challenge to make a response impossible. That it left William and Rivallon squabbling must have sent chuckles around their camp. Harold, meanwhile, had nobly rescued a couple of Norman soldiers from the quicksand of the Couesnon, which sometimes drowned scores of pilgrims to Mont-Saint-Michel.[94] This certainly

---

[90] *GG*, p. 73.
[91] Bates, *William*, p. 130.
[92] Neveux, 'L'expédition', pp. 629–30.
[93] *GG*, pp. 75–7.
[94] *BT*, 20; Katherine Keats-Rohan, pers. comm.

impressed the designer of the Tapestry, even if William's fortunes in the campaign were questionable. Harold was not a fool. He knew William was dangerous. Indeed, his conquest of Maine, hold on Guy of Ponthieu, and his deep advance into Brittany proved he was a contender who intervened in sovereign principalities at the first opportunity. Poitiers legitimized his aggression again and again: in Maine, Brittany, and England.[95] The duke's apologist claims that Harold swore his oaths to William before the campaign, though the Tapestry places them after. If the latter is correct, and not merely ordering events to tell a good story, Harold might have thought he had the measure of him and could outmanoeuvre the duke. The Tapestry shows Harold receiving armour from William after the campaign, implying he became William's man or agreed a bond of friendship, before swearing oaths and returning to England to make his excuses to Edward.[96]

Whatever the content of Harold's negotiations – and Harold, being secretive, is unlikely to have made them public unless William compelled him to swear public oaths – this was all fuel for suspicions in Edward's mind. Still, his offence could hardly have involved swearing away the kingdom; more likely it involved some other undertaking, such as committing to a marital union with the ducal dynasty. The Tapestry depicts Harold reporting to Edward with the placatory gestures of somebody in the wrong, while Edward reprimands him with a stern finger.[97] If marriage was the issue, Harold was doubly sworn without Edward's consent. He had been too free with his promises, and Normandy or Mercia would soon have to be jilted.

EDWARD ESTABLISHES HIS HEIR

Several royal children were being reared at court at that time.[98] Those we know of were Edgar, his two sisters, and Harold, the son of the late Earl Ralph, all of whom were Edward's great nieces or nephews. For a childless couple, Edward and Edith had quite a family around them. No onlooker could argue the bloodline was dead, but nor was it lineal, for Edward had built his dynastic narrative on his filial relationship to Æthelred. He had also built it around a subtle effort to bury the memory of Edmund Ironside, evidenced by the lack of references to him in Edwardian sources, the lack of royal patronage for Glastonbury, his burial place, and the *Vita*'s claim that the English swore an oath to acknowledge Edward as king while he was still in Emma's womb.[99] Edward had been peddling versions of this story since the 1030s to shore up his claim to the throne. The difficulty he

---

[95] As noted by Bates, *William*, pp. 177–8 (Maine), p. 200 (Brittany), p. 219 (England).
[96] *GG*, p. 71; *BT*, 24–6.
[97] Brooks, 'The Authority and Interpretation', pp. 187–9.
[98] *Vita*, pp. lxvi, 25.
[99] Ibid., p. 13.

may now have faced lay in the implication that Æthelred's sons by his first marriage had been disinherited. Though there is no record of Edward disinheriting rival claimants as Cnut had done, the possibility remains that he did so and reversed his policy after realizing he would never have a son of his own.[100]

Such was the web of dynastic fiction threatening to entangle Edward when he decided to recall the son of Edmund Ironside. Whether anybody cared is uncertain, but the narrative now had to link the Exile to Æthelred, lest he be snubbed as a collateral claimant descended from a royal half-brother of Edward whose line had been debarred. Two pieces of evidence suggest the narrative was indeed tweaked. The first is the fact that when death stole him away, along with the hope he represented, the Exile was buried at St Paul's with Æthelred, rather than at Glastonbury with his father Edmund, signifying his adoption into the reigning branch of the dynasty. Nothing is known about the ceremony, but the personage and location make it easy to envisage the contemporary equivalent of a state funeral. The second is Edward's decision to declare Edgar 'aetheling' ('throneworthy'), a title hitherto reserved for the sons of kings. Its assignation to Edgar, the grandson of a king, shows that he, like his father, was adopted into the reigning branch of the dynasty.

The context in which we find the title employed suggests it was used on ceremonial occasions. A series of names recorded in the Book of Life of New Minster, Winchester, includes relatives of a monk named Ælfwig, who was appointed abbot there in 1063 or 1064 and probably encouraged his relations to have their names enrolled.[101] Whether he was, as claimed, a brother of the late Earl Godwine or maybe another relative of his, the purpose of enlisting names in the book was to record the admission of honorary members to the prayers and benefits of the monastic commu-nity. The five consecutive entries are those of 'Eadgifu, daughter of Earl Godwine', an unidentified man called Ælfstan (who may or may not be Ælfwig's relative), and 'King Edward', 'Queen Edith', and 'Edgar Ætheling', as a group of three. The fact that a single scribe entered their three names together suggests they arrived and entered confraternity as a family unit. A parallel is found in another royal trio – Cnut, Emma, and Harthacnut, who entered confraternity with the church of Bremen, and whose names were similarly recorded in its Book of Life.[102] In that instance, it would have been clear to onlookers that Harthacnut was the

---

[100] On the strategy of disinheriting a rival branch, see R. Abels, 'Royal Succession and the Growth of Political Stability in Ninth-century Wessex', *HSJ* 12 (2002), 83–98.

[101] Licence, 'Succession Question', pp. 120–3; Stafford, *Emma and Edith*, p. 269, n. 61. See also *'Liber Vitae' of the New Minster*, ed. Keynes, pp. 91–2. A late-twelfth-century annotator identified him with an *Ælfwi*[g] *puer* whose name was added to the list of monks *c.* 1031, but he is unlikely to have had records to confirm such a minor detail, and the connexion he made was most probably conjectural.

[102] Licence, 'Succession Question', p. 123, n. 41.

prospective heir to Denmark, as it would have been clear to anybody attending the ceremony at Winchester that Edgar was being lined up for the throne. The entry of those names is a unique surviving reflection of the parading of Edgar. It shows him accompanying the king and queen in the manner of an adopted son.

Procedures of adoption seem not to have existed in England at that date. Poitiers' later claim that Edward adopted William as his son was probably intended to overwrite his actual adoption of Edgar.[103] By calling Edgar 'aetheling', Edward created a kind of adoption since the title aetheling in the past had been borne only by the sons of kings. Edith's 'mother-hood' of the royal boys she was fostering matched Edward's 'fatherhood' of Edgar.[104] Decrees of the time placed aethelings on a specific legal footing, equivalent to that of an archbishop and second only to the king.[105] In Æthelred's diplomas they sometimes witnessed second to the king in the witness lists, above the queen, although in most cases the queen came second, as in the entry in the New Minster Book of Life.[106] If it was decided after 1061 that aethelings should again be included among the signatories, we might be none the wiser, given that no witness list later than 1061 survives which is free of the charge of forgery or tampering.[107] Still, no convention decreed that aethelings should witness diplomas. Nor did witness lists identify everyone who was present at assemblies.[108]

Edward's decision to designate Edgar his heir in an entry in a Book of Life recalls the case of Henry the Fowler, king of East Francia (919–36). Though contemporary chroniclers mention no occasion on which Henry's son Otto was crowned, he is found as 'King Otto' in his father's lifetime in the Book of Life from the monastery of Reichenau, where the royal family stayed in 929. The enrolment can be dated to their visit and is a single, group entry for the living royal family, including Otto's father. In that respect it resembles the entry in the New Minster Book of Life and the one described by Adam of Bremen. Henry, the German king, was using the ceremony of enrolment in confraternity to designate his succes-sor.[109] Since there was no English precedent for crowning a prince in his

[103] *GG*, p. 115.

[104] Stafford, *Emma and Edith*, p. 76; *Vita*, p. 25. In 1066, Edith was guardian to Earl Ralph's son, Harold. See also Foot, *Athelstan*, p. 55, modelling Athelstan as a foster father.

[105] D. N. Dumville, 'The Aetheling: A Study in Anglo-Saxon Constitutional History', *ASE* 8 (1979), 1–33, at p. 32.

[106] Above, p. 24.

[107] The last witness lists associated with undoubtedly authentic diplomas are those of S 1027, S 1028, and S 1031. S 1034 is possibly authentic too. S 1033's witness list appears to have been created at a late date.

[108] Stafford, *Emma and Edith*, pp. 197–9; Roach, *Kingship and Consent*, pp. 40–2.

[109] K. Schmid, 'Die Thronfolge Ottos des Großen', *Zeitschrift der Savigny-Stiftung für Rechtsgeschichte: Germanistische Abteilung* 81.1 (1964), 80–163, at pp. 108–19. I'm grateful to Levi Roach for alerting me to the parallel.

father's lifetime, Edward could not go so far as to call Edgar 'king', but he could title him 'aetheling', which meant that he alone was throneworthy and ceremonially confirmed his adoption.[110] As in the case from tenth-century Germany, no ceremony is recorded in the chronicles – at least not in the extant versions (all of which lack annals for 1062 and 1063) – and yet the monarch is seen using confraternity enrolment to identify his chosen heir. As with many of his appointments to offices of state, he presented his candidate for approval with the expectation of consent.

Edward took more steps to strengthen Edgar's position. As well as parading him in the filial role, he was building alliances which strengthened Edgar's hand. Orderic reports that Edward arranged a treaty in which Edgar's sister Margaret was betrothed to Malcolm of the Scots, with Lothian as her dowry.[111] The claim is plausible since Edward is known to have used marriage to weave peace between kindred and neighbouring powers. More to the point, Margaret's marriage to Malcolm would not have been the brainchild of Harold or William, for it strengthened their rival Edgar. Whether it occurred in 1068 or 1070, we do find other instances where a considerable period of time elapsed between betrothal and cohabitation, particularly if one partner was a minor.[112] A precedent for the delay is found in the case of Gunnhilda (i.e. Cunegunda), whose marriage to the emperor's son Henry was arranged by Cnut but occurred in 1036, the year following Cnut's death.[113] Margaret's birth-date and so the year in which she reached a marriageable age at twelve or thirteen can only be estimated; but the arrangement presumably belongs to the final years of the reign. Malcolm's incursion of 1061 reminded Edward of the difficulty and cost of maintaining a claim to Lothian. In Gruffudd's case, he had allowed the client king to chip away at the frontiers, provided he recognized Edward's overlordship and did not push too far. Granting Lothian to Malcolm as Margaret's dowry reflects a similar strategy, for Edward was less concerned about small-scale shrinkage of his territories than building alliances to support his heir.

Edward's promotion of Edgar left little room for a situation in which Harold was sworn to William. As we noted earlier, however, that may well not have been the understanding in 1065. Indeed, it is just as likely – if not more so – that Harold had sworn an oath to Edward. For this, we turn to a new source which sets out the relevant story. Hariulf of Saint-Riquier was a monk writing in Ponthieu in the 1080s. His testimony merits attention because of its neutrality and because one of his chief sources was

---

[110] Edmund Ironside's seeming reference to himself as 'Eadmundus aetheling rex' (S 947) may represent an attempt at self-designation during his father's lifetime, but it could equally be a product of later tampering.

[111] OV, IV, pp. 270–1.

[112] Reynolds, *Marriage*, pp. 322–3.

[113] Above, p. 66.

Abbot Gervin I of Saint-Riquier (1045–75), a well-respected man and a visitor to Edward's court. Gervin was the monk who once recoiled when Edith offered him the kiss of peace. Hariulf claims that after Edward's death an earl named Harold seized the English throne in contravention of an oath he had sworn to Edward, that he would yield the kingdom without any impediment to Edward's *pronepos* (great-nephew) 'Elfgar'. The garbling of the name *Edgar* by a foreign writer is no cause for concern, given that the same two names, Elfgar and Edgar, are muddled in *Little Domesday*, where Earl Ælfgar is mistakenly called 'Earl Edgar' (*Comes Edgarus*).[114] Hariulf also says that when Harold seized the throne from 'Elfgar', God decreed that William should be king. In short, Edward wanted Edgar, but God intervened on William's behalf to punish Harold.

Edward knew better than anyone the importance of oaths in proving royal title. Early in his career, he put it about that the English had sworn an oath to have him as their king. His experience of negotiations around the succession in the 1030s and 1040s taught him that the extraction of oaths could be useful. The *Encomium* claims he insisted that an oath, or rather the lack of one, was a crucial factor in the succession debate, artfully inverting his assertion that an oath had been sworn to him.[115] The C/D text of the Chronicle says oaths were sworn to him in or before 1041, confirming his title as Harthacnut's heir.[116] Before Edgar arrived in England, the practice of swearing an oath in recognition of a child heir had been revived in the German empire, where in 1053 the princes swore to recognize Henry III's son as their future king.[117] Having gone to great lengths to recall the exiles from Hungary, Edward would have been responding strangely to his own experience, and to practice current in the empire, had he not secured a general oath on Edgar's behalf. It was not a sign he feared opposition, but a sensible, conventional measure to smooth Edgar's path to the throne.

What we glimpse in the New Minster Book of Life, in the incidental detail from Orderic, and in Hariulf's testimony is the tip of the iceberg. Most of our sources were completed after the Conquest by supporters of Harold or William and can be guaranteed to have done the job of airbrushing Edgar from the record. We should at least be willing to consider the maximum scenario in which Edgar accompanied Edward and Edith on grand occasions; was adopted in a public ceremony; was granted lands and titles, and the promise of the royal estate; and was sworn in as heir at the ceremony involving Harold (and other leading figures) which Hariulf implies took place. It might have occurred in 1062

---

[114] Licence, 'Succession Question', p. 123.

[115] Above, pp. 59–60.

[116] ASC C, D, 1041.

[117] Hermann of Reichenau, *Chronicon*, ed. G. Pertz, MGH Scriptores 5 (Hannover, 1844), 74–133, at p. 133.

or 1063, where the chronicles conspire in silence. The diploma for St Olave's, Exeter, refers to worries that stalked the king's thoughts. They included 'discord and rebellion', and 'wicked presumption'. So long as he commanded the wolves, he could bind them to Edgar by oaths. And for now those guard-dogs were tame enough. Edith sat at his feet. Harold ran around doing his bidding in most things, and Tostig ate from his hand.

Sure enough, the old king was labouring methodically to knit the little fatherless exile into a family. Just as he knew about oaths, he knew the importance of kinship; and he knew his duty to exiles, foreigners, and orphans. If anyone, he had his uncle Richard to thank for that. Twice he had built a new family for himself, first in Normandy, where he had tied his cousin Robert more tightly to him as a brother; and again in England, where he had quickly embraced Godwine's kin and kept them close to him despite fierce disagreements. Now he began to do the same for Edgar, first by adopting him; secondly, by uniting his House with that of another formerly exiled claimant, Malcolm. It was a link that tightened Edgar's ties with Tostig, as Malcolm's blood-brother. Though Edward liked to seem remote and grand, we know he formed close friendships and kept his family close at Lambeth; and we might regard him as a family man building surrogate families to replace the family he had lost. A paternal love of children would not be out of keeping, though Folcard would never relay it, for fear of calling to mind Edgar. And if Edward sympathized especially with a fatherless exile, he would not be the first or last to invest in a protégé who reminded him of himself.

INTO DARKNESS

Emanating from the royal court and colluding in its silences, the *Vita* leaves the end of the reign shrouded in considerable darkness. It does, however, cast a shadowy light on the quarrel between Harold and Tostig, which the author judged to be such a threat to the realm's stability that he compared it to the civil war between Caesar and Pompey, which had brought about the end of the Roman Republic, and the fratricidal war between the sons of Oedipus, which led to the downfall of the ruling dynasty of Thebes.[118] Those comparisons were a clue to the nature and magnitude of what was afoot. They warned the reader that primordial chaos might reassert itself – that the disorder of a kingdom at war with itself would be mirrored in the cosmos. Being pagan precedents, however, they lacked the prophetic import of Scripture. Pagan history, unlike the prophetic patterns in the Bible, was not bound to repeat itself. Yet an ill-defined evil menaced the ruling dynasty, taking the shape of discord between Harold and Tostig – brotherly discord that would blaze a trail for

---

[118] E. M. Tyler, *England in Europe: English Royal Women and Literary Patronage, c. 1000–c. 1150* (Toronto, 2017), pp. 144–6, 175–80.

every evil. It threatened not only familial harmony, the concord personified by Edith,[119] but also the dominion embodied by Edward and upheld
by the brothers. When they fought the Welsh and Scots, unity prevailed;
but when they turned on each other, viciousness descended and opened a
door to monsters.

In July 1065, Harold laid out plans for his hunting lodge, opposite
Bristol, on the Welsh side of the Bristol Channel. He ordered it to be
stocked with large supplies of food and drink, so that his lord, King Edward,
could stay there for the chase.[120] Then he went overseas and fell into the
hands of scheming men who detained him. The king was attending to his
usual business. An abbot was needed for Bury St Edmunds, to replace
Leofstan, who had died.[121] Edith and other courtiers were lobbying for him
to appoint his physician Baldwin, but, as he reminded them, he needed the
approval of Stigand, who was administering the abbey in the vacancy.
Summoning the prior and monks and the bishops with an interest, Edward
pushed for Baldwin but duly compensated Stigand by promising him the
revenue of the next great abbatial vacancy to arise. Agreed in this, they all
proceeded to the royal palace at Windsor, where Edward presented his
candidate to an assembly. He swore an oath too, affirming his devotion to
St Edmund's community. All of this was carefully staged to present and
enact consensus.[122] The deal, agreed beforehand, was sealed when Stigand
blessed Baldwin as abbot on 15 August. Four days later the archbishop
received Ely on the surely anticipated death of its abbot Wulfric, relin-
quishing Bury to Baldwin the same day.

By this point, news of Harold's detention may have leaked to the
Welsh, emboldening Caradog, son of the late southern king Gruffudd
(d. 1055), to attack Portskewett with a raiding band, kill nearly all the
workers and their overseers, and carry away the goods that had been
stockpiled there. The raid occurred on St Bartholomew's Day, 24 August.
D observes, 'We do not know who first suggested this folly',[123] as if to draw
attention away from the Welsh, and towards the English court. Whether
the court had been trying to keep Harold's plight a secret for security
reasons, news gets out. And divided regimes can leak secrets. Edward's
now had multiple fault-lines, one of which would soon come to light
between Harold and Tostig. The twelfth-century writer Henry of
Huntingdon tells a story set near the end of the reign in Hereford in the
Welsh borders. Harold's servants are preparing a feast for Edward. Tostig
is envious, so he dismembers the servants, putting body parts in each

[119] Ibid., p. 190.

[120] This and part of what follows is from *JW*, ii, p. 597.

[121] For the reconstruction that follows, see Licence, 'Herbert Losinga's Trip to Rome',
p. 166, and *MSE*, pp. xxx–xxxi, 61.

[122] Cf. Roach, *Kingship and Consent*, pp. 14–15, 44.

[123] ASC D, 1065 (ed. Cubbin, p. 77): 'Ne wisten we hwa þone unræd ærest gerædde'.

vessel for wine, mead, ale, and cider.[124] If this is a reworking of the Portskewett affair, it points a finger at Tostig. Henry is rarely useful for our period, but the darkness of his story recalls a poem in the *Vita* about discord arising between the two brothers. The poem hinges on a comparison between their rivalry and 'pagan plays', in which Atreus murders his brother's children and feeds them to him at a banquet.[125] It shows Henry was not alone in casting their rivalry in cannibalistic terms, for a contemporary observer did so too and found it most distressing.

None of this is to imply that Tostig encouraged the raid, far less that he pickled human flesh. Still, we may consider a scenario in which Harold had commissioned the lodge to be built for festivities connected to his wedding plans. If he was preparing to marry Ealdgyth, the sister of Tostig's enemies, Tostig might have vented his feelings by instrumentalizing a Welsh marauder. If, on the other hand, Harold was having doubts and sailed off in the hope of securing a different bride, Ealdgyth herself or her brothers might have planned the attack upon the venue. As for Harold and Tostig, sibling rivalry alone may account for the quarrel between them. Ambitious for his sons, Godwine taught them to compete. And in later years Edward, having learned the trick from his own parents, may have triangulated in an attempt to keep them competing. Sending Tostig into Wales in 1064 may be an example, for Wales was Harold's arena; and it cannot have salved his pride, on failing to capture Gruffudd, that Edward had ordered in his younger brother to help. Harold's response to the slight had been to erect stone pillars everywhere claiming the conquest as his. He and Tostig had both been trained in the business of bettering each other.

August ripened into September, and the day came for the dedication of Edith's church at Wilton. The next poem in the *Vita* after the cannibalism poem celebrates her re-foundation of the nunnery, which Folcard apostrophizes as the mother-to-be of countless spiritual offspring. Though she mothered the royal boys she had no children of her own, and Folcard hoped the metaphor might comfort her. Tostig was delayed at Edward's court by the king's 'love' and orders to conduct royal business.[126] This, significantly, is the only place in Folcard's extant text where he uses the noun *amor* and reveals that the king loved someone. It might refer to brotherly love or an attraction of the heart. Since his love of Tostig is presented as his prior motive for detaining him, the implication may be that the royal business was his excuse for having him by his side. The timing of this unique revelation that Edward loved someone is critical to

---

[124] Henry of Huntingdon, *Historia Anglorum: The History of the English People*, ed. and tr. D. Greenway, OMT (Oxford, 1996), p. 383.

[125] Tyler, *England in Europe*, p. 181 makes a connexion with Henry of Huntingdon. Folcard (*Vita*, p. 59, n. 146) seems to identify Thyestes as the murderer.

[126] *Vita*, pp. 73–5, 76: 'eius detentus amore et iussis in disponendis regalis palatii negotiis'.

Folcard's plot – because it was the last moment Edward and Tostig shared before their world fell apart. September is hunting season – but no one was hunting at Portskewett. Harold's lodge and invitation to the king lay in ashes. Meanwhile, Edward and Tostig were enjoying the chase near the royal manor of Britford.

All was set for rebellion as the thegns of Yorkshire and Northumbria gathered in a great assembly to outlaw their absent earl. A force of 200 men led by persons unknown to us – Gamelbeorn, Dunstan son of Æthelnoth, and Glonieorn son of Heardwulf – descended upon York on 3 October.[127] They broke into Tostig's house, captured two of his house-carls who were trying to flee, and made an example by killing them outside the city walls. The next day they captured and killed more than 200 of Tostig's men on the north side of the Humber. They broke into his treasury, carried away his treasure, and set fire to his buildings.[128] So far, spies might have regarded their initiative as spontaneous, but the extent of their preparations was clear from what they achieved next. Summoning Ælfgar's son, Morcar, they named him as their earl, sending word to his elder brother Edwin that the rebellion was advancing. With Morcar at its head, the army marched south, swelling with reinforcements from Derbyshire, Nottinghamshire, and Lincolnshire.[129] The rebels drew up lists of people they wanted to kill, 'and many were slaughtered in the cities of York and Lincoln, in the streets, on water, in woods and on roads'. Anyone associated with Tostig was put to death.[130] Folcard, who had links with the earl, probably fled south at this point. Gospatric's loyalty is shown by the fact that he was not among the rebel leadership, though a scion of the House of Bamburgh; and also by the fact that Folcard wrote of him warmly.

When the rebels reached Northampton, Edwin arrived to meet them with the men of Mercia and many Welshmen. They may have made the rendezvous within a week of the attack on York, for C reports that the assembly at Northampton came 'very quickly' after the outbreak of the rebellion.[131] When news reached the king, he played for time as in 1051 by sending messengers to the rebels with orders for them to desist. Promising to address their grievances, he summoned reinforcements. Wary of making straight for Britford, where his allies would assemble, he remained in the nearby forest with his entourage.[132] Harold had returned and made himself available. Whatever bargain he had struck with William, Edward was in no position to punish him. The chroniclers reveal that he

---

[127] See Clarke, *English Nobility*, p. 113 for references to these men in Domesday Book.
[128] ASC D, 1065; *JW*, ii, pp. 597–9.
[129] Baxter, *Earls of Mercia*, pp. 48–9.
[130] *Vita*, p. 77.
[131] ASC C, 1065.
[132] *Vita*, p. 79.

was the messenger sent to pacify the rebels at Northampton. John of Worcester adds that Edward sent him at Tostig's request.[133] If so, he either trusted Harold or expected him to show his hand and incriminate himself. Some to-ing and fro-ing of negotiations occurred. Folcard claims that Edward sent negotiators a second and third time, but he may have exaggerated, wanting to compare the king's reasonableness with the rebels' intransigence. The chroniclers corroborate Harold's presence at meetings at Northampton and Oxford.[134] Evidently the rebels were advancing, with Harold as the go-between, and Edward stalling with proposals.

The assembly-points they chose reflect the logic of the Roman road network, but they also raise questions about control of the midland corridor. In 1065 Siward's son Waltheof seems to have possessed an earldom, and Domesday Book suggests his command included Northamptonshire and Huntingdonshire.[135] The earl, who had barely attained his majority, would be caught up in rebellions in 1069 and 1075, but since the rebels were about to harry Northampton he may have remained loyal.[136] Either that, or the territory was still Tostig's and was given to Waltheof in the tidying-up. Oxfordshire was probably still part of Edwin's earldom of Mercia at the time of the rebellion, but there is reason to suppose Edward reacted in Harold's absence by granting the territory to Gyrth, who may have been with the king when rebellion broke out. Gyrth was serving as earl there in December 1065 but was not yet implanted either with land or commended men – an indication he had only recently received Oxfordshire.[137] This, and the strangeness of the county being given to an earl of East Anglia, suggests Edward put him in charge there at the time of the rebellion. It was a crucial county for the rebels, since Oxford was the gateway linking Wessex to Mercia and the north.[138] If an army of Northumbrians and Mercians took Oxford, their cause was likely to prevail.

C and John of Worcester insist that Harold laboured to broker peace between the rebels and Tostig, but they rejected all overtures. After parlaying at Northampton, they sent him back to Edward with the demand that Morcar be their earl.[139] Then they harried the territory around Northampton, killing the inhabitants, burning houses and grain supplies, and seizing many thousands of cattle. They also seized many hundreds of people as captives and slaves. When Harold returned, he agreed to their demand and renewed the law of Cnut for them in Edward's

---

[133] *JW*, ii, p. 599.

[134] The *Vita* and C place the second assembly at Oxford. D/E probably err in placing both at Northampton.

[135] Baxter, 'Succession Question', Maps 10–12.

[136] Ibid., Map 11, with references – S 1110, S 1160.

[137] Cf. Baxter, *Earls of Mercia*, p. 308; S 1139, S 1147, S 1148, and *Writs*, ed. Harmer, pp. 326–7, dating the writs.

[138] Baxter, 'The Earls of Mercia and their Commended Men', pp. 35–7.

[139] ASC D, E, 1065.

name – a token of assurance that they should now expect justice from the regime. The rebels, however, were adamant that Edward must banish Tostig or have the whole lot of them as his enemies.[140] Such was their demand at the assembly in Oxford on 28 October. It was about the time Edward advanced to Britford and met the support that had been arriving. Folcard is our only witness to the furious exchanges that ensued.

Moved by prior suspicions, or by opposition to the line Harold was taking as negotiator, some now accused Harold of artfully inciting the rebellion. Without contradicting the charge, Folcard scorns it and asserts that he dared not and would not believe Harold would do such a thing to his brother. Tostig, however, whom he also admired, testified before the king and the witan, charging Harold with the crime. Harold – 'alas, too generous with oaths', as Folcard interposes – quickly cleared himself with oaths.[141] The interjection laments his trait of giving his word lightly, implying that if his oaths had been credible, trust might have been restored. Folcard might be alluding to oaths Harold had sworn to William, but his despair arose from Harold's inability to prove his innocence – a naive reading of the situation. Whether Harold was complicit from the start, Tostig's accusation is a sure indication that Harold had come around to the rebels' way of thinking. Tostig expected nothing less than total loyalty of the sort Edith displayed when ordering the death of his enemy. To him, Harold's position was a betrayal, and he might as well have been complicit. Certainly, Harold could have fought to the death to protect his brother. But, having spoken with the rebels, he was better placed to judge the situation.

Edward, as in 1052, wanted to fight the conspirators who challenged his authority and threatened to deprive him of a favourite. He called out the fyrd, which failed to materialize. His commanders protested that changeable winter weather was setting in, and they repeated an argument from 1052: that no one had the appetite for civil war. As the king raged in anger, some tried to calm him and urged him not to go to war, but when they saw that Edward was determined to march, they deserted him, 'wrongfully' says Folcard, 'and against his will'.[142] He could hardly be exempting Harold, Leofwine, and Gyrth from the company of unnamed deserters. It might then have dawned upon Edward that Harold was with the rebels; that his third family was shattered and his line might come to an end. A neurological injury affected him, probably a stroke or the onset of a degenerative illness. Insensible, he began railing at God and cursing his disobedient subjects. Edith, who always relied on Edward's support in meetings of the witan, found that her counsels now fell upon deaf ears. Unable to reconcile her brothers, she began weeping inconsolably.[143]

[140] Ibid.; *Vita*, p. 79.
[141] *Vita*, pp. 79–81.
[142] Ibid., p. 81.
[143] Ibid.

Since neither C nor the *Vita* suggests Edward made any concessions, it is possible the king was already insensible when Harold declared that the rebels should have Morcar and confirmed Cnut's laws in Edward's name on 28 October. Alternatively, he might have had his stroke in the aftermath of that assembly. Folcard's statement, that 'from that day until the day of his death he bore a sickness of the mind', implies the king was no longer in charge of his faculties.[144] He could attend ceremonies and look like a king, but others governed for him. Early in November, to Edward's profound distress, Tostig was forced into exile. Laden with the king's gifts, he led his family and followers to Flanders, where Baldwin made him the custodian of the port of Saint-Omer. This was an aggressive move which set the earl up for making a comeback against his enemies. Meanwhile, as Edward's condition grew worse, it was decided to bring forward the consecration of Westminster, his mausoleum.[145] It is in the context of the end of Edward's reign, when the king was insensible, and not before, that John of Worcester refers to Harold as the 'under-king' (*subregulus*).[146] Even without a clue, we might infer that Harold had become regent. In that sense, the reign of Harold Godwinson began in November 1065. Edward remained, but he was fading into darkness.

While invitations were being sent out and preparations made for Westminster's consecration, Harold contemplated the possibility of Edward's death. Edith could nowise persuade him to reinstate Tostig,[147] and such a thing, besides, would damage the alliance he was forging with Edwin and Morcar. If doubt remained about his commitment to marrying their sister Ealdgyth, now was the time to provide the assurances and seal the crucial union between Wessex, Mercia, Wales, and Northumbria.[148] It is likely that Harold's approach in negotiating with the rebels in October had involved firming up that commitment and letting go any promise he had made to marry into the ducal House. This would help to explain the explosive response from Tostig, and Folcard's allusion to broken oaths. Having confirmed Gyrth in his possession of Oxfordshire, moreover, Harold had manoeuvred himself into a position where all the junior earls were in his debt, and the kingdom was broadly united. It was not something he could have foreseen, but he had his father's knack of perceiving and moving with the tide of events. Most rebellions do not succeed. William's first decade as king saw several failed rebellions. What is striking about that of 1065 is the total success of an army led by novices against a

---

[144] Ibid.

[145] *JW*, ii, p. 599.

[146] Ibid., pp. 600/1. The Tapestry's reference to Harold as 'dux Anglorum' is of no significance. It was how a foreigner might refer to 'an earl of the English' ('an English earl'). Peter Damian, in 1062, referred to Tostig as 'dux Anglorum': *Die Briefe*, ed. Reindel, II, no. 89, pp. 531–79, at p. 566.

[147] *Vita*, p. 81.

[148] Baxter, *Earls of Mercia*, pp. 48–52, 299–300.

dangerous and experienced regime. That it ended with Harold as a go-between was enough to persuade a paranoid Tostig that Harold was pulling the strings. Harold nevertheless had to factor in the aetheling, for Edgar was near the age of majority.

Because Edgar has often been written out of our accounts, or dismissed as a boy or an imbecile, it is easy to forget he had opinions on the dramatic events playing out around him. Whatever they were, they enabled others to predict what his actions might be if he inherited the power of the royal estate. It was in the interest of those around him to mould, steer, and manipulate his opinions, whether out of noble or personal motives. Edith had taken on the role of rearing the royal boys and might be expected to lead the regency government while Edgar made the transition to independent rule. Queens normally took on that role. In recent times the empress Agnes from 1056, and Anna of Kiev from 1060, had guided the regency governments for their sons Henry IV of Germany and Philip of France, and though neither remained in the role for more than a few years, it was quite enough to create an effect.[149] Edith's wishes for reconciliation with Tostig were opposite to Harold's. Edith and Edward had been fond of Tostig, moreover, and would have nurtured their love of him in Edgar or tried to. Unless Edgar reacted by forging contrary opinions, he was Tostig's potential ally. More to the point, young kings emerging from the chrysalis of minority rule were typically unpredictable and liked to cast aside their former guardians.[150] At best, Edgar's accession might undo Harold's designs. At worst, it could bring about his downfall.

The consecration of Westminster was scheduled for Christmas Day, it being free of worldly business.[151] Only the porch was unfinished, but there was no time to delay. Well in advance of festivities, temporary buildings were erected in the palace and abbey precincts as lodgings and banqueting halls for the guests. Much attention was given to their preparation. As Christmas approached, nobles and commoners began arriving from across the realm, but the king took a turn for the worse on Christmas Eve, and the consecration was delayed. All the following day, and for the next two, Edward hid his illness from his dining companions, putting on a cheerful face and bidding them be merry. Privately, his suffering intensified, as the queen took care of his every need. On 28 December, the Feast of the Holy Innocents, he summoned Stigand and the bishops and instructed them to proceed with the consecration in his absence, for he

---

[149] E. J. Ward, 'Anne of Kiev (c. 1024–c. 1075) and a Reassessment of Maternal Power in the Minority Kingship of Philip I of France', *Historical Research* 89 (2016), 435–53.

[150] Roach, *Æthelred*, pp. 110–11.

[151] What follows draws on a translation of a lost portion of the *Vita*, made by or for the antiquary John Stow in the late sixteenth century. Printed in Summerson, 'Tudor Antiquaries', at pp. 177–8, it is a better witness to the text than the extracts from Sulcard and Osbert substituted in Barlow's edition at pp. 111–12 (and was unknown in Barlow's lifetime).

was too ill to leave the palace. The queen and the earls attended, and the bishops performed the mournful ceremony.

As the old year ran with the new, the king took to his bed. Frail, drowsy, and weakened by illness, he became unintelligible. Memories of former days and long-dead friends vividly entered his mind. He dreamt of a green tree that was destiny, but the trunk was split apart and broken. When he did utter words, he continued railing against evildoers in the highest offices of the realm, or prophesied death and destruction. Alternately he seemed to entrust the affairs of the kingdom to those very same people, but despite lucid moments these were the ravings of a dying mind.[152] Edith was sitting on the floor and warming his feet in her lap. The detail is in the *Vita* and was captured for posterity in the Tapestry's deathbed scene.[153] Harold and Robert fitz Wimarc – the king's kinsman and steward of the palace – were also in attendance, with Stigand and a few others whom the king had summoned.[154] They probably included his physician Baldwin, Bury's new abbot. Members of the witan would have stayed near Westminster, involved in the manoeuverings. This was an extremely dangerous phase.

Writs may have been issued and diplomas drawn up – a flurry of activity in Edward's name, though most of the extant versions are post-Conquest forgeries which leave in doubt which grants were really made.[155] Edward's will, if he dictated one, would not long survive the king. Opponents were disposed of, among them Spirites, a mighty West-country cleric who had been promoted by Harthacnut. Domesday Book reveals that he lost his property at Christmas 1065, when it went to Robert fitz Wimarc.[156] The king's chamberlain Hugolin would be put to death in circumstances that elude us.[157] At the time of the revolt in October, no one had foreseen Edward's death. The elegist could describe it as 'sudden'.[158] But if the king's inner circle had been concealing his condition and issuing orders in his name, there was no hiding it now. As preparations were made for Edward's funeral, Harold planned his coup. He would agree a story with those present, that Edward had nominated him in a last-minute decision, and that the witan had chosen him. Some would oppose the move, but court dependants such as Robert fitz Wimarc may have been biddable. No doubt in the past week Harold had approached or leaned on enough of the witan to be sure of a favourable reaction.

---

[152] *Vita*, pp. 117–19.

[153] Ibid., p. 119; *BT*, 30.

[154] Ibid. (both).

[155] The consecration was the occasion for gifts to be confirmed. For Westminster, see *Writs*, ed. Harmer, pp. 286–339. Stow's notes confirm a reference to land grants being made: Summerson, 'Tudor Antiquaries', p. 178.

[156] *GDB* 252b.

[157] Barlow, *Edward*, pp. 165–6.

[158] ASC C, 1065 [1065–6].

Edward died on 5 January 1066, upon the eve of Epiphany. His body was wrapped in a shroud of Byzantine silk, with a circlet on his head and a reliquary of the Cross hung about his neck.[159] The following morning, the funeral procession made its way through the cold from the palace to the abbey, accompanied by clerics chanting dirges and a ringing of bells. In front of assembled mourners – the great and good of the realm – the coffin was lowered into the tomb near the high altar. Then at the Introit of the Mass, once Edward was safely in his grave, Harold was enthroned to the shouts of his cheerleaders, crowned, anointed, and invested with the regalia.[160] No king had been quicker to get the crown on his head.

EPIPHANY

The West Saxon line, which had reigned in Britain for 571 years since Cerdic and 261 since Ecgberht, came with him, as concerns the throne, entirely to an end; for while grief for the king's death was still fresh, on that same feast of Epiphany Harold, who had exacted an oath of loyalty from the chief nobles, seized the crown, though the English say that it was granted to him by the king. This claim, however, rests, I think, more on good will than judgement . . .[161]

So wrote William of Malmesbury sixty years later. He thought the English credulous in any case. The truth was that Edward's reign ended in disaster. Edith understood that, and her uncontrolled weeping for the loss of the two men she loved best, Edward and Tostig, opened Folcard's eyes. Others remained hopeful, not wanting to imagine that the peace Edward had woven for twenty-four years would soon lie in tatters. It is telling that the narratives around the end of the reign – the *Vita*, the *Carmen*, the Tapestry – explore themes of deceit and self-deception: for we may read some of the texts being spun at this time as weaving a literature of denial. Just as the *Encomium* was in denial about the shakiness of Emma's triumvirate, so the *Vita* and the poem known as *The Death of Edward* knit a blanket around the elephant in the room. The encomiast had concealed Harthacnut's unpopularity, the bitterness of feeling between Edward and his mother and half-brother, and the threat to them posed by his return.

---

[159] Taylour, *A true and perfect narrative*, pp. 12–14; K. Ciggaar, 'England and Byzantium on the Eve of the Norman Conquest (the Reign of Edward the Confessor)', *ANS* 5 (1983), 78–96, at pp. 90–5.

[160] *MSE*, pp. 61–3. Herman, who uses the verb 'inthronizo', can only be referring to the coronation on Baldwin's good authority. John of Worcester's claim that Ealdred crowned Harold is part of his defence of Harold's good reputation: *JW*, ii, p. 601. Stigand was evidently not disqualified from sacral duties, for, a week earlier, he had presided at the consecration of Westminster (Summerson, 'Tudor Antiquaries', p. 177).

[161] *GR*, II, § 228 (pp. 419–21).

Folcard and the poet concealed the supplanting of Edgar, which left the realm vulnerable to predators. Though some of the fears that were being suppressed do bubble over in the *Vita*'s poetry, its nightmares were of fratricidal civil war between Harold and Tostig. That was the worst outcome Edith foresaw at the start of Harold's reign. Ten months later, four more of her brothers were dead, and 'devils' had overrun the kingdom.[162]

At news of Edward's death, it was said that England mourned and all her neighbouring kingdoms.[163] A courtly elegist wrote a sombre *pièce d'occasion*, which begins like this:

> Here King Edward, England's ruler,
> sent a righteous soul to Christ,
> a holy spirit into God's keeping.
> Here in the world he lived for a while
> in majesty, skilful in counsel.
> For twenty-four years and a half,
> that glorious lord distributed riches,
> a most distinguished lord of heroes,
> Æthelred's son, ruling Welsh, Scots,
> and Britons too, Angles and Saxons,
> all alike his champions,
> so that cold sea waves encompass
> all steadfast and loyal liege men,
> who obeyed Edward, the noble king.[164]

It was as Æthelred's son that Edward had presented himself in 1042, and as such he was remembered. The poem, a product of Harold's era, forged links between Harold and Edward to legitimize Harold's rule. Depicting Edward as righteous, blameless, and wise, it concludes by claiming he entrusted the kingdom to Harold, a noble earl and a greatly distinguished man. To reinforce the point subliminally, the poet repeats the same words of praise for both rulers. By calling Harold 'noble' (*æþelum*, line 31) and 'highly distinguished' (*heahþungenum*, line 30), the poet subtly connects him to Edward, having described Edward as 'noble' (*æðele*) on three occasions, and once as 'well distinguished' (*wel geþungen*).[165] Nobility

---

[162] *Vita*, p. 117.

[163] Sulcard, *Prologus*, p. 91.

[164] ASC C, 1065 [1065–6] (ed. O'Brien O'Keeffe, pp. 118–19). The poem, known as *The Death of Edward*, continues for another twenty lines. My translation adapts those of Whitelock et al., *The Anglo-Saxon Chronicle*, p. 139, and Swanton, *The Anglo-Saxon Chronicles*, pp. 192–4. Note that it seems to date Edward's reign from 1041, perhaps on the grounds that he was sworn in as king in that year.

[165] ASC C, 1065 [1065–6] (ed. O'Brien O'Keeffe, pp. 118–19): line 12: *æðelum kinge*; line 24: *æðela*; line 27: *æðelne*, and line 9: *wel geþungen*.

and distinction were qualities of throneworthiness. By making them shared qualities of Edward and Harold, the poet diluted the uniqueness of the title 'aetheling', which Edgar alone possessed. Edgar is not only gaslighted by his omission; he is also silently diminished by the implication that the admittedly 'noble' teenager lacked the 'distinction' of Edward and Harold. In this, the poem and the *Vita* maintain a conspiracy, though the D chronicler would declare, once Harold was safely dead, that Edgar was the rightful heir. And this would be the verdict of the witan after Harold's demise.[166] The poem also connected Harold with Edward by describing Edward as true to his word (*soþfæste*) and Harold as faithful (*holdlice*) to Edward, in word and deed.[167] This was to pre-empt detractors who might accuse Harold of breaking faith with his late lord by usurping the throne of Cerdic.[168]

The *Vita*, which also colludes with Harold's regime and may be regarded as a product of it, repeats the official line by declaring that the dying Edward entrusted the realm to Harold, although it stops short of stating that Edward nominated him as his successor rather than his executor. The verb it gives, *commendo*, is equivalent to the poet's *befæstan*, suggesting that one author might have had the other's account in mind. Folcard adds that, as well as passing the realm to him, Edward had commended Edith to Harold's care, ordering him to serve and honour her as his lady (*domina*) and sister, and not to deprive her of any due honour she had obtained from him (i.e. Edward).[169] His comments developed the theme of Edith having no influence over Harold, emphasizing her vulnerability to his implied predation. This was the author's attempt to speak up for his marginalized queen, or distance her from Harold's coup. Folcard also invites us to query the idea that Harold was faithful (*holdlice*), by his comment that the earl was free with oaths. Yet he drops his hints without departing from the pretence that Edward designated Harold. He too airbrushes out the aetheling and credits Edward and Harold with most of the qualities attached to each by the elegist.

Another emanation of the desire to veneer Harold's regime and advertise his devotion to Edward was the reverence, bordering on cult, that attached to the dead king. It manifested in the treatment of his body – in life, robed in jewels like a Byzantine saint, and wrapped in silk in death and buried near the altar like a dedicatory relic. The last English king before Edward who is known to have been buried wearing a cross-reliquary was Edmund of East Anglia, the martyr whom Edward revered as his ancestor. Late in his reign, the saint's coffin was opened, his body was inspected, and it was confirmed that the pendant still hung around his

---

[166] ASC D, 1066.
[167] *The Death of Edward*, in ASC C, 1065 [1065–6], lines 2 and 32.
[168] E.g. *Carmen*, p. 21.
[169] *Vita*, p. 123.

neck.[170] Months before he died, in August 1065, Edward swore to honour Edmund's community.[171] His burial with a similar pendant was inviting comparisons. The poem, moreover, is clear in stating that Edward went straight to heaven.[172] When most Christians died they had to await the Judgment or purge their sins in the otherworld. Saints differed, in that they went straight to heaven; and only the purest monks, nuns, and solitaries joined them in the ascent. Saints' *Lives* refer to angels bearing their souls aloft.[173] That the poem, near its end, announces that Edward was borne to heaven by angels could be seen as an attempt to nurture a rumour that there were witnesses to his apotheosis.[174] Immediately after this statement, the poet reports that 'the wise man' (and proto-saint) committed the realm to Harold. It is obvious from this juxtaposition what narrative the usurper was constructing to legitimize his coup.

Harold's story was that the wise king – a saint in the making – had chosen him, a noble and distinguished man like himself, who at all times had served him loyally and seen to his every need.[175] This is exactly the story we have in the *Vita* (begun about the time Edward's power was waning in October 1065), and it is the poet's story too. As such, it found its way into C and D, while E and the Tapestry add to this that 'men chose him' to be king too. The scene in which Harold sits enthroned must surely represent his coronation, since one of the men standing to his right and pointing to Harold is offering him a sword, a way of showing that the electors are handing him power.[176] Stigand, an officiating prelate, stands to his left, and since there are good reasons for thinking he had a hand in shaping E and the Tapestry's narrative, the fact that both emphasize the role played by the 'men' who chose the new king suggests that Stigand may have been the person who orchestrated the coup – whether or not he was the prelate who put the crown on Harold's head.[177] His machinations would explain why Folcard turned keenly against Stigand between writing the first and second sections of the *Vita*, for in the interval the coup had gone horribly wrong.[178] This at least was the view held at Bury by *c.* 1070, where the monk Herman summed things up by stating that Harold had cunningly seized the throne, and that it was this which led to his down-

---

[170] *MSE*, p. 53.

[171] Ibid., p. 61.

[172] ASC C, 1065 [1065–6].

[173] See e.g. T. Licence, 'Goscelin of Saint-Bertin and the Hagiography of St Eadwold of Cerne', *Journal of Medieval Latin* 16 (2007), 182–207, at p. 207.

[174] ASC C, 1065 [1065–6].

[175] As we read at the end of the poem, ibid.

[176] ASC E, 1066; *BT*, 31. Since the image is framed, it should be taken as the same occasion.

[177] *JW*, ii, p. 601, reports that Ealdred crowned Harold, and see above, n. 160.

[178] Licence, 'Date and Authorship', p. 266.

fall.[179] And it is possible to detect criticism of the coup in D's remark that, after Harold's death, Edgar was chosen, 'as was his natural right'. We might even read it as Ealdred rounding on Stigand.

Propaganda aside, Harold's regime was in trouble. Within months, neighbouring powers had turned against him. In Edward's time they had been allies or peaceable neighbours. Now Flanders, Normandy, Boulogne, Norway, and Scotland were plotting Harold's downfall. The collective shift in foreign policy against England's new king is proof these powers regarded him as illegitimate. There is even a clue from Pope Alexander II that Harold managed to fall out with the reform party in Rome.[180] Flanders harboured Tostig; but by spring 1066, Count Baldwin knew that his son-in-law, William, was committed to invasion, and that he could no longer offer Tostig unalloyed support. In May Tostig took his fleet to raid the south coast of England. Chased from there by Harold, and from the Humber thereafter by Edwin, he sailed north to Scotland, where Malcolm received him and Harald of Norway and debated invasion plans. By that stage Harold's opponents were divided into a northern alliance and a southern one. The southern axis, comprising Normandy and lesser counties under its sway, along with Flanders and Boulogne, was backing William. The northern alliance may have backed Edgar. Whether or not Malcolm was already betrothed to his sister, he and Tostig's deputy Gospatric would emerge as Edgar's backers in 1068; and Harald of Norway – Edgar's uncle – could not rule two kingdoms while Sven Estrithsson was at large. If his invasion succeeded, he would need a client ruler in England. It is commonly assumed that Hardrada or Tostig wanted the English throne. But all we know of the plans of the northern alliance is C's claim that they wished 'to win this land'.[181] Invasion alliances were wise to keep their options open.

After seizing the throne, Harold had expelled Edgar from the realm.[182] In 1068 he would flee to Scotland, so it is possible he went north early in 1066 too. Before Easter, Harold went to York. He was fearing trouble, for kings did not venture that far north for any other reason. In one account, which is plausible, he took Bishop Wulfstan north with him to help win over the Northumbrians, who had not yet given him their allegiance.[183] Since one of their leaders was Tostig's commander, Gospatric, who would later join Malcolm in fighting for Edgar, it should come as no surprise that the remnant of the House of Bamburgh might have held off offering Harold its support. D says nothing of Edgar's whereabouts until after the

---

[179] *MSE*, p. 63.

[180] Alexander II, *Epistola* 139: PL 146, col. 1413. An 'evil head', probably Harold or Stigand, had decided to stop sending money to Rome (or rather to Alexander's faction).

[181] ASC C, 1066.

[182] *Chronique*, ed. Lot, p. 241.

[183] Malmesbury, *Life of Wulfstan*, p. 567.

Battle of Hastings, when the witan chose him as king, 'as was his natural right'.[184] The emphasis, as previously suggested, feels like a reaction to the smoke and mirrors of Harold's counterfeit legitimacy and its disastrous effects on England's relations with foreign powers. In October 1066, the witan realized too late that united support for Edgar was the only thing that might have safeguarded the realm. As in 'the year of the four emperors', when the Julio-Claudian dynasty ended, 1066 was turning into a free-for-all.[185] Harold's usurpation opened the way for similarly sized predators, and William and Harald Hardrada challenged him for the kill.

Folcard, writing the first part of the *Vita* in 1065–6, did not foresee William's conquest. The evil he anticipated and hoped could be averted was war between the queen's brothers.[186] In the climate of uncertainty, while trotting out the official narrative, Folcard dared not assert that Harold was Edward's rightful successor in the eyes of God. Rather, as authors often did in troubled times,[187] he hedged his bets with prophecies, which book-end his account of the reign. The first dodges the question of who was really meant to succeed Edward, which was never satisfactorily resolved. It describes how St Peter appeared to a venerable bishop and told him God alone knew who the heir would be.[188] The second prophecy, which comes at the end of Folcard's work, was written after the Conquest and claims to foretell the arrival of the Normans. Two long-dead monks visit the dying king to announce that God intended to hand the kingdom over to devils within a year and a day of his death. The prophecy – relayed apparently by dead friends from Normandy – was hardly flattering to the Normans, but it also marks a moment where the biographer gives up pretending that the regime could lay claim to virtue. In a last-ditch defence of Edward and Edith, he blames England's demise on the earls, bishops, abbots, and men in holy orders who were 'servants of the devil'.[189] By this defence, he further undermined the pro-Harold narrative which he was still, equivocally, upholding.

Despite Folcard's attempt to promote a cult by recording a small collection of miracles allegedly performed by Edward in his lifetime, and notwithstanding the general attempt on the part of Harold's regime to put the dead king in a saintly light, it is doubtful any cult was growing at Edward's tomb. Though there were tales of people cured by the touch of his holy hands, or by contact with water he washed them in, Folcard added no posthumous cures and refers to such evasively or obliquely.

---

[184] ASC D, 1066.
[185] AD 68/9. See K. Wellesley, *The Year of the Four Emperors*, 3rd edn (London; New York, 2000).
[186] Licence, 'Date and Authorship', p. 263.
[187] Given-Wilson, *Henry IV*, p. 138.
[188] *Vita*, p. 115.
[189] Ibid., p. 117.

Indeed, he adapts a standard formula from Matthew's Gospel, listing miracles attributable to Christ, which saints were meant to replicate: 'For at the tomb through him the blind receive their sight, the lame are made to walk, the sick are healed, the sorrowing refreshed . . .'.[190] Fleshing out this skeleton fell to the forger Osbert of Clare, who fabricated claims upon every pretext. We see an example of how he operated in his response to Sulcard's legend about how Edward sought absolution for his vow to go on pilgrimage, and how the pope replied that he should found an abbey in honour of St Peter. For the legend inspired Osbert, or an equally devious accomplice, to forge two papal letters, which he inserted into his *Life* of St Edward and into one of his several forged diplomas for Westminster.[191] Likewise, Folcard's half-specific claims which lent themselves to creative expansion – his generic comments that Edward cured the lame and gave sight to the blind – may have inspired the first two miracles supplied by Osbert, for he tells of a Norman called Ralf who recovered the ability to walk at Edward's tomb within eight days of his burial, and of a group of blind men who had gone there within thirty days and received their sight.[192] Osbert's fourth miracle relays the cure of another blind man.[193] To any critical investigator, Folcard's hackneyed formula could be referenced as evidence for stories Osbert cooked up.

Osbert was mendacious in other ways. He seems to have taken the Old English *Vision of Leofric*, relocated the action at Westminster, and made Edward the visionary, even though the original is set in Sandwich and only the earl sees the hand of God.[194] Osbert says he heard the miracle from Maurice, a subdeacon and monk of Westminster, who heard it read aloud from a sheet of parchment re-discovered at Worcester in the time of Bishop Wulfstan. Maurice had since died and could not be cross-examined. Another of Osbert's miracles, in which Edward prophesies Sven Estrithsson's death (as if it occurred in his lifetime), draws on the legend of how St Edmund had impaled Sven's predecessor and namesake, Sven Forkbeard. The third posthumous miracle which Osbert credits to Edward – a vision in which he instructs Abbot Ælfwine of Ramsey to urge

---

[190] *Vita*, pp. 92/3–96/7, and 126/7: 'ibi illuminatur caeci, in gressum solidantur claudi, infirmi curantur; merentes consolatione dei reparantur'. Cf. Matt. 11:5: 'Caeci uident, claudi ambulant, leprosi mundantur, surdi audiunt, mortui resurgunt', and Matt. 10:8: 'Infirmos curate'.

[191] 'La vie de s. Édouard', ed. Bloch, pp. 79–80 and 89–90; and cf. S 1041 and S 1043; P. Chaplais, 'The Original Charters of Herbert and Gervaise, Abbots of Westminster (1121–1157)', in P. M. Barnes and C. F. Slade, eds, *A Medieval Miscellany for Doris Mary Stenton* (London, 1962), 89–110, at pp. 90–5.

[192] 'La vie de S. Édouard', ed. Bloch, pp. 112–14.

[193] Ibid., p. 116.

[194] Ibid., pp. 91–2; P. Jackson, 'Osbert of Clare and the *Vision of Leofric*: The Transformation of an Old English Narrative', in K. O'Brien O'Keeffe and A. Orchard, ed., *Latin Learning and English Lore: Studies in Anglo-Saxon Literature for Michael Lapidge*, 2 vols (Toronto, 2005), II, 275–92, at pp. 282–4.

Harold to march on Hardrada – develops the idea of Edward as a saint who rescued England from Scandinavian invaders.[195] Since the miracle revolves around Edward assisting Harold at the battle of Stamford Bridge, the story may once have been part of the effort to legitimize Harold by linking him to Edward and showing he had his support. This impression is reinforced by the awkwardness with which Osbert twists it into use. For his message is that the saint got 'one tyrant to destroy another' – a conclusion which leaves us thinking Edward was at best disingenuous when he persuaded the doomed Harold that he had his back.[196]

In this instance, Osbert appears to have used a fossilized piece of Haroldian propaganda, albeit a miracle genuinely attributed to Edward, in a manner not dissimilar to that in which he deployed a vision associated with Earl Leofric but twisted it to lend support to Edward's cult. Finally, in pursuing his aim of equating Edward and Edmund, Osbert introduced the account of the opening of Edward's coffin and discovery of his bodily incorruption. Edmund's coffin had allegedly been opened and his incorruption confirmed in 1095.[197] Edward's body – or so Osbert says – was inspected in 1102, thirty-six years after his death. He credits the inspection to two venerable men, Abbot Gilbert of Westminster and Bishop Gundulf of Rochester, both conveniently dead. Next, we are told that when the coffin was opened the sweetest fragrance permeated the abbey (as it had done, allegedly, at the reopening of Edmund's coffin – Osbert pinched the idea and items of vocabulary).[198] They found a ring on his finger, sandals on his feet, a crown on his head, and a sceptre at his side. None of those grave goods were reported when the coffin was opened in 1685, but the rummager did discover a cross-reliquary around Edward's neck, which Osbert nowhere mentions, though the description we have indicates it was contemporary.[199] Like pretty much everything he adds to Edward's story, the opening of the coffin smells like fiction. The date 1102 may have been chosen for symmetry, being mid-way between Edward's death and 1138, the year of writing. Though his attempt to secure the papal canonization of his saint failed in Osbert's lifetime, the cause was revived successfully in 1161. Ailred's *Life of St Edward*, reworking Osbert's, laid the foundations for the legend, but long before then, even in Harold's time, Edward had faded into the image of a saint.[200]

---

[195] 'La vie de S. Édouard', ed. Bloch, pp. 114–15.
[196] Ibid., p. 115 (Edward is thus deployed indirectly to legitimize William).
[197] *MSE*, p. 281.
[198] 'La vie de S. Édouard', ed. Bloch, pp. 121–3.
[199] Taylour, *A true and perfect narrative*, pp. 12–14.
[200] See Barlow, *Edward*, pp. 256–85, and *Vita*, Appendix D.

CONCLUSION

Skeletons wrapped in silk; the lipless, gibbering dead; dragon's teeth, sown in evil ground and sprouting armies. Madness will arise, whether on the plains of Thessaly or the woody brows of Battle. Mars, that ancient devil, drives his thralls into the mincer while Christ and the saints look away.[1] Leaving 1066, we must fly to a plain where the tumult has subsided; where we who wander the cities of the dead can recreate their stories. There we can give voice to the silence, cupping in our hands the dust of centuries; breathing new life into a valley of dry bones; kneading and moulding the clay.

The historical biographer is like a traveller in ancient lands, assembling fragments of a fallen statue. Previous explorers have assembled a few, and at the outset I laid three upon the table for inspection. The first, that Edward never strived for the throne; the second, that he was ruled by his in-laws; the third, that he dangled the succession before multiple contenders. Ancient though they are, those three fragments no longer appear to fit. We now have a clearer idea of what the outline of this king should look like. We know that he regarded the throne as a birthright, and that he strived for and obtained it. We can see, furthermore, that the decades spent awaiting his inheritance translated into a conscientious ethic of service. Perhaps we can discern a man whose sufferings left him little appetite for harshness and with a need to cling to favourites. Edward worked for peace and built it with his neighbours. He implemented innovative systems for defending the coast and the Welsh march. He responded to the reform papacy with practical initiatives. He worked for the military and spiritual safeguarding of his subjects.

Statues aside, it is well to remember that time and events change us; that one man in his time plays many parts. Edward in 1016 was the boy penitent, hoping for redemption with the recovery of his throne. By 1025, the religious ethos of responsible rule in the France of Robert the Pious and Richard II of Normandy was shaping a conscientious twenty-year-old. By 1036, Edward had become the competitor, winning friends, pushing his side of the story, commanding a fleet. Before 1044, the dutiful

---

[1] Commentators on 1066 weave together allusions from Lucan, *Pharsalia*, VII, 551–4, 567–70 (tr. R. Graves, *Lucan Pharsalia: Dramatic Episodes of the Civil Wars*, London, 1956; new edn, 1961). See e.g. *Vita*, pp. 85–7; *Carmen*, pp. 23–5, 33.

king had emerged, guarding the coast, humble before God. Then in the 1050s, we see Edward the overlord dispatching his generals to crush upstart kings – a middle-aged ruler, partial to favourites, doing things his way, and brooking little opposition. Last comes the patriarch, holy and regal, letting his ministers use the perks of power; basking in their devotion. That is the likeness Folcard captured near the end of the reign when the elegist, writing the Chronicle poem, provided a portrait of the king as a ring-giver; a distinguished ruler of champions; a well-beloved lord.

Can we observe fixity in the motion of his being – something we might call character? Where habitual action comes into our view the answer may be yes. Edward's reputation was consistently that of a sincere and conscientious ruler, and there is little difficulty in matching that reputation to the policies he pursued. Often we glimpse him treating others with respect. Folcard's remark that the king said no to petitioners in a way that left them feeling gratified; the anecdote about how he mollified Edith when an abbot refused to kiss her; his intention to consult the relevant bishops before selecting an abbot for Bury all show him as a careful people manager. Winning over the disappointed; not only soothing Edith's anger but converting her into a champion of the no-kissing policy; building a lasting peace with neighbouring powers, including hostile Flanders – those were the fruits of a high emotional intelligence combined with winning smoothness. Here was a man very well practised in getting his way.

Neither quality is surprising. The emotional intelligence fits with the image of the boy exile, trained in a penitential climate (and subsequently forced by adversity) to divert his gaze inward to contemplate his sins; the same young man who befriended monks in Normandy and looked to Duke Richard II as a role model. So too the smoothness is what we might expect of a man who had learned to survive in exile and smooth his path to the throne by winning over others, either by personal allure or promise of future reward. We might go so far as to say that Edward cast a spell over people. At some level they seem to have understood and resented its effect, for that would explain why figures such as Godwine, Robert of Jumièges, Harold, and William resisted him from time to time, often in passive-aggressive ways, while at the same time abiding in their devotion towards him. Godwine thought about killing him in 1052 but could not bring himself to do so. Harold was continually trying to impress him – but he also pilfered his estates. William – if the ducal biographer Jumièges reflects his views – sniped at Edward's father but was a little in awe of the king. Opportunist though he was, his invasion was born of a real desire to be regarded as Edward's heir – a desire Harold shared of course.

The spell Edward cast was in part the consequence of his character traits (such as goodness, integrity, and sincerity), and partly a result of his skill in crafting his own narrative. It helped that he did so with royal conviction: a sense of his entitlement to rule. Even from his boyhood, his penitential tour of saints' shrines, the claims he made to the throne, his instant reversal of the political narrative in 1042 reveal a precocious concern with controlling how people perceived his story. By casting himself as England's redeemer, a prince of peace, the resurrected Christ, and as Solomon – untainted and resplendent – Edward gave his subjects a king they could believe in. Probably more than any king before, he exploited the mystique of royalty and his bloodline to capture their hearts. We who now abide under a constitutional monarchy underestimate the potency of that mystique in past societies, where royalty was next to divinity. Edward understood it, amplifying English and French precedents.

While Edward was usually patient and respectful, such was his belief in his right to rule, and his skill and determination in getting his way, that, once he had made his mind up, there was no room for opposition. The human and political insight that made him a skilled people manager aided him in this regard too, for it taught him the value of sending strong messages such as a massive fleet at harbour; a Welsh head on a spike (maybe at Gloucester, gazing towards Wales with unseeing eyes); the summoning of foreign allies such as Duke William; the order to harry Dover; the erection of castles; the dispatching of mere earls to overthrow Scottish and Welsh kings; the breaking of his own mother. Surrounding himself with the Godwinsons was a message too, in that a man who keeps wolves is not a man who fears being bitten. Wolves, indeed, fell under his spell. Edith, who was enough of a wolf to devour the assets of rivals and even have them killed, not only forgave Edward for packing her off to a nunnery; she actually came round to the opinion he was a saint. The contrast with Emma's desire to erase all vestiges of Æthelred could not be starker.

One aspect of the traditional portrait created by Edward's biographers (though Adam of Bremen, writing in the 1070s, is the first to present such a view) was the idea that the king was ruled by his in-laws – an idea that might seem plausible if we let the crises of 1052 and 1065 dominate our attention. On both occasions, however, the backlash to royal rule occurred after Edward had gone unusally far in securing his own way. The rebels, moreover, revealed their fear of the power Edward wielded through his proxies by targeting their envy at those who basked in his favour, not daring to take aim at the king himself. It is possible, therefore, that Edward himself put about the idea that he was encircled by wicked advisors, as a means of washing his hands of their misbehaviour, which was becoming more apparent in the closing years of the reign. We can imagine Edward lending a sympathetic ear when Bishop Giso or Wulfstan complained of predation; and we can imagine him telling them graciously that his hands, alas, were tied. A tendency at Edward's court to shift blame from the king is seen in Folcard's attempt to pin the blame for the crisis of 1051–2 on Robert of Jumièges (who was scapegoated by the court chroniclers), and to blame the revolt of 1065 on the rebels (rather than the siblings close to

Edward who had indulged in a spree of murders). The shifting of blame was crucial to the regime's perpetual effort to control the political narrative. It was a necessary adjunct to the apologetics of kingship too, for a king who claimed innocence and disempowerment could dodge Ælfric's rebuke, 'Hit is awriten on bocum þæt se byð ealswa scyldig se þe þæt yfel geþafað swa swa se þe hit deð, gif he hit gebetan mæg and embe þa bote ne hogað' ('It is written in books that he who permits evil is just as guilty as he who does it, if he can remedy it and does not busy himself about the remedy').[2]

Whether a man could succeed as a king and a saint is doubtful; yet Edward, more than other English kings, conjured that possibility. His cult is best explained as the culmination of the narrative he had been weaving around himself: a narrative of sacrality, in which his inner circle were deeply invested – not least when trying to transfer the glittering mantle to Harold. Edward's consistently clean reputation corroborated the narrative; any vices and lapses in his judgement were more easily occluded by its rose-coloured tint, which endured (in the eye of enrapt admirers) even upon the cheeks of his corpse.[3] The peace he had maintained would be taken as the seal of divine favour, affirming the truth of his sanctity; the more so after it was shattered by the wars of 1066.

Though his reign was not invulnerable to the upsets that occur when jockeying factions at court dislodge and trample opponents, civil war was avoided, and the temperament of his rule prioritized wise counsel and unity, consensual decision making (at least within the inner circle), and the weaving of peace at home and abroad. Reluctant to destroy insiders, he let tension cool and reaffirmed his authority by banishing his opponents, it seems with the understanding that an exile might attempt, and might be permitted, to make a comeback. This unwritten rule worked, provided everyone understood the game. Gone were the darker days when a king might cull the nobility. By the end of the reign, the semblance of civility was collapsing. Murderers were at work. Edward looked away. A younger generation was reinventing the rules, and they were neither so kind nor forgiving.

Whether from eagerness to impress or to mimic his power, the rivalries between the wolves portended a storm of destruction. Practised at balancing their appetites, the king had to ensure it did not imperil the future of his line. On one side were those whose loyalty would smooth Edgar's succession; he probably had Edith, Tostig, and Ealdred in that camp. On a different side possibly – though not in open opposition – were Harold, Stigand, and the sons of Ælfgar. The ousting of Tostig in 1065 was a military coup which tipped the balance decisively. There was no desire to topple Edward, and before 1065 there may have been no desire to

---

[2] Clayton, 'De Duodecim Abusiuis', p. 156 (Rom. 1:32).
[3] *Vita*, p. 125.

supplant the aetheling; but after the rebellion, the idea that the king was in Harold's hands was beginning to look more credible. Harold was flexible and amiable, but he lacked Edward's grasp on the fabric of legitimacy. He tried to fashion it with alliances, armies, and narratives connecting him to Edward. What he needed was the royal blood, indispensable to the myth of kingship which Edward had exploited so thoroughly for more than thirty years, ever since he first assumed the kingly title. By effectively removing the blood mystique from the qualifications a king should possess, Harold brought the office within William's grasp; and since William had never unlearned the infant's reflex of grasping whatever presented itself, he readied his army, charged up a hill, and bloodied his way to the throne.

THE SECTION OF THE E TEXT
COVERING EDWARD'S REIGN

It was Charles Plummer in 1892 who first proposed that the section of the E text covering Edward's reign was composed at St Augustine's, Canterbury: an argument accepted by later commentators and editors.[1] Apart from its interest in Kentish affairs, which might suggest only a Canterbury origin, the case for assigning it to St Augustine's depends on its notices of the deaths and appointments of abbots of that house – notices it always provides and for no other abbey. There were, however, two monasteries in Canterbury, the other being Christ Church cathedral priory. It has not been pointed out – since it is nothing exceptional – that E records deaths and appointments of heads of the cathedral priory too, that is, the archbishops. On this reasoning, E is just as likely to be a Christ Church chronicle, interested in changes of leadership at both monasteries. Its interest in the archbishops of Canterbury, moreover, is not limited to such notices. Whereas E tells us nothing of St Augustine's abbots besides obits and appointments (and the fact that one, with other named clergy, was sent to a papal synod), the detail it provides about the affairs of the archbishops exceeds that in any parallel chronicle. E records not only Robert of Jumièges' journey to Rome for the pallium, but the day of his return, and the (different) day of his installation. It details his encounter with Spearhafoc and his refusal to consecrate him. E's annal for 1052 uniquely records Stigand's role in resolving the stand-off between Edward and Godwine. It mentions his receipt of a pallium in 1058 and goes to the unusual length of telling us that he consecrated two bishops that year, and that he influenced Edward's choice of a new abbot for St Augustine's in 1061. The evidence tips the balance in favour of E's ancestor being a Christ Church chronicle, interested in the archbishops.

Past scholars have been thrown off the scent by E's support for Godwine (except when he plunders Kent),[2] coupled with the assumption that Christ Church was hostile to the earl. The assumption is based, if not on

---

[1] C. Plummer (revising an edition by J. Earle), *Two of the Saxon Chronicles Parallel, with supplementary extracts from the others*, 2 vols (Oxford, 1892–9), II, pp. xlviii–l; *The Anglo-Saxon Chronicle*, ed. Whitelock, with Douglas and Tucker, p. xvi; Dumville, 'Some Aspects', pp. 23–9; ASC, *MS E*, ed. Irvine, pp. lxxv–lxxxii; Baxter, 'MS C', pp. 1189–91.

[2] As noted by Baxter, 'MS C', p. 1206, n. 88.

Godwine's conflict with Robert of Jumièges, then upon the reputation Godwine acquired – in Lanfranc's time as archbishop (1070–89) – as a despoiler of Christ Church.[3] Prior to 1070, however, Godwine enjoyed favourable relations with the monastery. In 1050 the monks elected his kinsman Æthelric to head their community as archbishop. From 1052, the see was occupied by Stigand, a supporter of Godwine who wept at his flight into exile in 1051,[4] and who received Canterbury as part of the settlement brokered on his triumphant return. Before 1066, moreover, the rivalry between Christ Church and St Augustine's, which is discernible after the Conquest, had not caught hold.[5] In that period, Stigand regarded St Augustine's as a proprietary monastery. From 1061, its abbot was Stigand's man, Æthelsige, a monk imported from Stigand's other cathedral, in Winchester, and nominated by Edward on Stigand's advice (E 1061).[6] A Christ Church chronicle completed in Stigand's time should be expected to have taken an interest in the abbatial appointments to St Augustine's without following the abbots' affairs as closely as those of the archbishops.

The view of David Dumville, accepted by Stephen Baxter, was that C and E bear witness to a set of annals covering the years 1035–44, composed by a 'royalist ecclesiastic'.[7] Susan Irvine disputed the idea of a group of source annals beneath those years but agreed that C and E shared source annals for the years 1043 and 1044 (C 1043–4, E 1042–3ª).[8] Dumville also suggested that Abbot Siward of Abingdon brought a chronicle to Canterbury in 1044 when he was consecrated archbishop in place of the ailing Eadsige, a hypothesis which explained the fact that the source annal for 1044 is the last C and E had in common, and which accounted for C and E's continued interest in the abbots of Abingdon, to 1048 or 1050. As Dumville remarked, 'seeing Siward as an intermediary would not naturally get us to St Augustine's rather than Christ Church', but if E's ancestor is a Christ Church chronicle, his argument is strengthened; and E (or rather its ancestor) was certainly at Christ Church by the end of the century.[9] The extant manuscript was made and brought up to date at Peterborough *c.* 1121, a process that involved the interpolation of Peterborough material.[10] This is easily detected by its relevance to Peterborough and its omission from D and F, both of which drew on √E (i.e. a text recognizably ancestral to E). Somewhere along the line, groups

---

[3] Cf. *MS E*, ed. Irvine, pp. lxxv–lxxxii.

[4] *Vita*, pp. 35–7.

[5] P. Hayward, 'Gregory the Great as "Apostle of the English" in Post-Conquest Canterbury', *JEH* 55 (2004), 19–57.

[6] *MS E*, ed. Irvine, p. 85: 'folgode þa Stigande' (taking Edward as the subject).

[7] Dumville, 'Some Aspects', p. 25; Baxter, 'MS C', p. 1198.

[8] *MS E*, ed. Irvine, p. lxxxv.

[9] Dumville, 'Some Aspects', pp. 28–9, 52; Baxter, 'MS C', p. 1191.

[10] *MS E*, ed. Irvine, pp. xiii–xviii.

of annals from √E became chronologically dislocated in the copying, so that the annal for 1043 was assigned to 1042; 1044 to 1043, and so on, with greater disjuncture following (where events of 1048 and 1049, for example, are run together against the year 1046).[11]

As mentioned earlier, C and E shared a source for the annals for 1043–4. For the most part they bear identical witness to its content. Where they differ is in their notices of Stigand. C records that Stigand, in 1043, was consecrated bishop of the East Angles. E records the same. Then at the end of the annal, C records that Stigand was deprived of his bishopric. E lacks that detail alone. At the end of their otherwise identical annals for 1044 (C 1044, E 1043ᵃ), C alone has a notice of Edward's marriage ten nights before Candlemas (2 February), reflecting the fact that C or its source at that point commences the year from Lady Day (25 March). √E, which commences the year in January, removed the marriage of January 1045 into its 1045 annal (E 1043ᵇ) and replaced it with the statement 'and Stigand obtained his bishopric'. This statement concludes E's annal for 1044 (E 1043ᵃ). It can only be as a result of such tampering that E's annals for those years are the only annals in the Chronicle to mention the consecration and accession of a bishop in separate entries. The anomaly occurs because the compiler of Edwardian √E was suppressing the fact of Stigand's deposition, creating the impression of a mere delay prior to his installation.

√E's alteration of the source annals to Stigand's advantage appears the more significant when its claim that Stigand came into his bishopric in 1044 is tested against charter evidence. There are five plausibly authentic diplomas for 1044 (S 1001, S 1003, S 1004, S 1005, and S 1006) and four datable to 1045 (S 1007, S 1008, S 1010, and S 1012). Stigand attests none of them. He first attests as bishop in 1046 (S 1014 and S 1015) and regularly thereafter. Combined with the lack of writs addressed to Stigand in 1044–5, despite a profusion of early writs for Bury, that amounts to evidence that Stigand was reinstated in 1046 – not 1044 as E claims.[12] E's annals for 1043–4 (E 1042–3ᵃ) constitute a retrospective revision of the source annals by a compiler who laboured to conceal the fact that Stigand had been deposed for the best part of three years. By concluding what was supposed to be its annal for 1044 (E 1043ᵃ) with a notice of Stigand's accession, the compiler of √E also brought his career into focus.

The next manifestations of the chronicler's favour towards Stigand appear in the annal for 1052, where Stigand is cast as the mediator who resolves the conflict between Edward and Godwine. Stigand went out to

<hr/>

[11] Cf. ibid., pp. xxxi–xxxii.

[12] The dating termini Harmer assigns to her no. 13 and no. 14 (S 1073; S 1074) suppose that Stigand obtained his see in 1044 and left it in 1047. The first date depends on E; the second is incorrect (Barlow, *Edward*, p. 87, n. 1). The writs should be re-dated to 1046 × 1051/2.

Godwine 'with God's help' and arranged an exchange of hostages. Robert and his companions fled, and we learn that he 'left behind him his pallium and all the Church in this country. This was God's will, in that he had obtained the dignity when it was not God's will.' The striking thing about the passage is God's debut appearance in the narrative. He is for Stigand, against Robert, and He appears three times. The claim that God willed Robert's desertion is a plot point preparing the way for Stigand's succession to the archdiocese. The claim he abandoned his pallium pre-empts the objection that Stigand is a usurper. After describing the peaceful settlement wrought by Stigand's mediation, the annal ends – like the annal for 1044 – with his promotion, this time to Canterbury: 'And Bishop Stigand succeeded to the Archbishopric of Canterbury'. Again, the conclusion of an annal on a reference to his promotion makes the rise of Stigand central to the story. In this instance, it seems to be a reward for rescuing the realm (with God's help) from civil war. (In the extant manuscript, the point at which √E 1052 ended is occluded by a Peterborough interpolation concerning Abbot Earnwig, which was tacked on afterwards.)

Stigand now appears as the saviour of the realm, the restorer of unity, duly rewarded in his advancement to Canterbury. Moving forward to 1058, we are told that Pope Benedict X sent him a pallium. The annal for 1058 then goes to the unusual trouble of showing that Stigand exercised his rights, stating that Stigand (after receiving the pallium) 'consecrated Æthelric, a monk of Christ Church, as bishop of Sussex, and Abbot Siward (of Chertsey) as bishop of Rochester' (E 1058). At this point, the chronicler subtly reveals his allegiance to Benedict over the reform party of the papacy by the verbs he chooses to use when describing their succession. In 1057, the reformer Stephen was 'chosen' as pope (*gecoren*), and in 1059 another reformer, Nicholas, was also 'chosen' (*gecoren*); but in between, in 1058, Benedict was 'consecrated' as pope (*gehalgod*) – a nuance of allegiance.[13] The verb was a challenge to the reform party, who claimed that Benedict's consecration was illegitimate. When the √D chronicler rewrote the annal, he replaced *gehalgod* with the neutral *geset* ('installed').[14] The pride √E took in recording Stigand's episcopal consecrations and in signalling allegiance to Benedict echoes the pride seemingly detectable in Stigand's attestation in a diploma of 1059 (S 1028) as 'archbishop of Canterbury and bishop of Winchester too'.[15] The theme of his influence continues in E's annal for 1061, which says that on the death of Abbot Wulfric of St Augustine's, Edward 'followed [the advice

---

[13] For the text, see *MS E*, ed. Irvine, p. 85.

[14] *MS D*, ed. Cubbin, p. 76. I agree with Irvine and Baxter that Cubbin understates √D's reliance on √E through the later 1050s into the 1060s: Baxter, 'MS C', p. 1192, n. 16; *MS E*, ed. Irvine, p. lxxxi.

[15] S 1028: 'Ego Stigandus metropolitanus Christi ecclesie archiepiscopus, necne Wintoniensis ecclesie'.

of] Stigand' in appointing Æthelsige, a monk of Old Minster, Winchester – Stigand's other cathedral – as Wulfric's successor.[16] E's annal for 1061 is the last to mention Stigand, but E 1067 records the fire that destroyed Christ Church and is perhaps an indication that √E was still being compiled there at that date.[17]

One more detail relating to Stigand in E appears in the annal for 1047 (E 1045), where he is called 'bishop in the north'. This may be an eye-slip, for Eadnoth of Dorchester, who was the northernmost bishop in the arch-diocese, is called 'bishop of the north' below, in the annal for 1049 (E 1046), which may have appeared lower on or across the page. Alternatively, the title may be an attempt to aggrandize Stigand's office; or we may speculate whether Stigand was reinstated as bishop in Norfolk only, while Grimcytel of Selsey continued to hold Suffolk in plurality until his death in 1047 (a hypothesis not incompatible with the evidence of writs and diplomas).

E's annals from 1052 to 1061 inclusive bear correct dates. A new disloca-tion of dating begins with the annal labelled 1062. While √E was still at Christ Church in the late eleventh century a copy was made incorporating thirty-eight continental Latin annals, extending from AD 114 to 1063, which were inserted at the heads of vernacular annals or into gaps. Almost all were extracted from a Norman compilation known as the 'Annals of Rouen'.[18] Stigand's chronicle appears to have had no annals for the years 1062 and 1063. Into this gap the later compiler inserted the Latin annal reporting William's conquest of Maine. In the parent text, the annal is assigned correctly to the year 1063.[19] In E's evolution, however (because of a gap, one assumes), it became attached to 1062, initiating a chain-effect, in which the annal recording the Welsh campaign, which occurred in 1064, became attached to 1063, and the annal for the northern revolt of 1065 attached to 1064. E's annals for the events of 1063–5 (i.e. the conquest of Maine, Welsh campaign, and northern revolt) are all one year behind, because of √E's seeming hiatus. In 1066, correct dating resumes, no doubt because the date of the Conquest (unlike those of the Welsh campaign and the revolt) was universally known. √E's lack of annals for 1062 and 1063 is curious because, before this point, there is an annal for every year of Edward's reign.

---

[16] E 1061: 'folgode þa Stigande' (taking Edward as the subject): *MS E*, ed. Irvine, p. 85. Whitelock et al. take Æthelsige to be the subject: *The Anglo-Saxon Chronicle*, tr. Whitelock et al., p. 136. Swanton takes Edward as the subject: *The Anglo-Saxon Chronicles*, ed. and tr. Swanton, p. 190.

[17] Baxter too thinks that √E may have been compiled in Canterbury until at least 1066: 'MS C', p. 1190, n. 9. Irvine is inclined to see a new phase beginning at E 1064 (*MS E*, ed. Irvine, pp. lxxxii–lxxxviii). In this she follows Dumville, 'Some Aspects', pp. 30–1. It is relevant, perhaps, that Lanfranc's Christ Church seems to have erased Stigand's memory: cf. Keats-Rohan, 'Through the Eye of the Needle', p. 167.

[18] Dumville, 'Some Aspects', p. 32; *MS E*, ed. Irvine, p. lxxxviii–xc.

[19] Bates, *William*, p. 182.

Does this suggest Stigand's chronicle ended in 1061? Not necessarily. C lacks annals for the years 1057–64 but resumes in – as Baxter observes – a similar tone in 1065.[20] Perhaps the √E compiler preferred to omit the events of 1062–3. Alternatively, annals for those years may have been suppressed after the Conquest because of sensitive content. If so, the deletion was made before D was completed, for D draws on E up to 1061 and remains in dialogue with E until 1066/7. (The reason D records the death of an abbot of St Augustine's in 1061 is that the compiler was basing his annal on √E 1061. D takes no interest of its own in deaths of abbots, so it is too much of a coincidence that it should suddenly and independently record the death of Wulfric of St Augustine's.) D's annal for the Welsh campaign (D 1063, running into 1064) may be an expansion of √E 1063, and its annals for 1065 and 1066 are largely a conflation of C or √C and √E's annals.[21] E's annals for those years – and thus D's too – were compiled at some remove, for the DE annal for 1065 (E 1064, D 1065) says the rebels did damage around Northampton, 'so that that shire and other neighbouring shires were the worse for it for many years'. Even if the phrase is hyperbole, 'many years' could hardly be fewer than three years, so the annal must have been added to E and D in 1068 at the earliest. E 1067, recording the fire that destroyed Christ Church, is the last annal to reveal a special interest in Canterbury's affairs. Stigand's deposition in 1070 and death in 1072 are not noticed in the chronicle.[22]

In the past, the section of E spanning Edward's reign has been treated as a contemporary chronicle up to 1065.[23] That hypothesis must now be reviewed in the light of my arguments about Stigand. First, E 1043[a], stating that Stigand obtained his bishopric (in 1044), cannot be contemporary – he was not reinstated until 1046 – and must in any case date from Stigand's time at Canterbury after 1052. Second, E 1052's assertion that Stigand 'succeeded to the archbishopric' is problematic for obvious reasons. C reminds us that in the year 1053 'there was no archbishop in this land' (C 1053), but even C employs deception by placing Stigand on a level footing with Cynesige, as if both were archbishops-elect who had not yet obtained a pallium. Like E, it conceals the controversy of Robert's continuation in office, and it may be concealing the detail that the bishops who went overseas to be consecrated went to him.[24] E 1058 is interesting for its reference to Benedict's consecration. Normally popes were consecrated by

---

[20] Baxter, 'MS C', pp. 1212–14.

[21] *MS E*, ed. Irvine, p. xxxii.

[22] Nor was he subsequently commemorated at Christ Church, which (under Lanfranc) seems to have erased his memory: Keats-Rohan, 'Through the Eye of the Needle', p. 167.

[23] E.g. Baxter, 'MS C', p. 1190, but Stafford cautions us about the possibility of post-Conquest compiling and editing having occurred: P. Stafford, 'Archbishop Ealdred and the D Chronicle', in D. Crouch and K. Thompson, eds, *Normandy and its Neighbours 900–1250: Essays for David Bates* (Turnhout, 2011), 135–56, at p. 142.

[24] Licence, 'Robert', p. 327.

the cardinal-bishop of Ostia. In his absence, the task could be deputed to the archpriest of Ostia or the archpriest of Velletri.[25] Since the cardinal-bishop, Peter Damian, had refused to officiate, as one of Benedict's opponents, the reformers put about the rumour that a mere priest of Velletri (who could barely pronounce the rites) had been press-ganged into performing the consecration.[26] By arguing it was irregular, they implied the sacrament was invalid so that they could denounce his pontificate and nullify his acts. They also alleged he had intruded himself by violence and the simoniacal purchase of support.[27] In truth, Benedict may have undergone a legitimate consecration by the archpriest of Velletri, given that he was himself bishop of Velletri. The validity of Stigand's pallium depended on a point of debate.

Stigand's installation at Canterbury and acquisition of a pallium from Benedict would have been controversial at the time, if not soon afterwards, so there is no reason to interpret the defensiveness of E 1052 and E 1058 as the product of a post-Conquest climate in which Stigand faced the threat of deposition. That said, it may be. Either way, it is certain that √E was composed by a partisan of Stigand in 1052 × 1070. To find it sympathetic to Godwine and hostile to Robert is no surprise. The last annal of what we may call Stigand's chronicle could be E 1067. √E's allegiance to Stigand should strengthen the consensus linking √D, in those years, with the other archbishop, Ealdred.[28] Up to 1066/7, D and E are in dialogue, perhaps because the archbishops were collaborating. A context for this might have been the royal court or meetings of the witan.[29] D also drew on C. Its tendency to dilute partisan content in C and E has been noted in earlier studies, and we can now add other examples.[30] First, D resolves C and E's conflicting reports of Stigand's appointment and deposition in 1043–4 by simply omitting any reference to him at this juncture. Second, D replaces E's disputable claim that Benedict was 'consecrated' with the statement that he was 'installed' (E/D 1058). The annal D 1066 still represents Ealdred's chronicle, with its defensive claim that Ealdred extracted an oath from William before crowning him. (William promptly broke it.) √D (i.e. Ealdred's chronicle) may have concluded at the end of the annal for 1066, on the prayer 'May the end be good when God wills it'. After

[25] See in general N. Gussone, *Thron und Inthronisation des Papstes von den Anfängen bis zum 12. Jahrhundert*, Bonner historische Forschungen, 41 (Bonn, 1978).

[26] *Die Briefe*, ed. Reindel, II, no. 58, pp. 190–4, at p. 193.

[27] Ibid., p. 193.

[28] Baxter, 'MS C', pp. 1191–2; Stafford, 'Archbishop Ealdred', pp. 148, 156.

[29] For the idea that centrally produced annals were tweaked near the point of issue, see N. Brooks, 'Why Is the *Anglo-Saxon Chronicle* about Kings?', *ASE* 39 (2011), 43–70. Poems such as *The Death of Edward* may have been composed at court and disseminated, but Brooks' premise that kingly content means courtly content is belied by continental monastic annals, which display a similar interest in kings and affairs of the realm.

[30] E.g. Baxter, 'MS C', p. 1194.

this seeming terminus, it looks to the north and the children of Edward the Exile. As Stafford notes, however, the continuator may have interpolated northern material or references to the Exile and his progeny into Ealdred's chronicle, a caveat we must bear in mind when considering the annals for Edward's reign.[31]

C is a contemporary chronicle, compiled initially in 1045, then kept up to date annually or in stints until 1056. It lacks annals for the years 1057–64 and recommences in 1065 before breaking off mid-way through the aftermath of the battle of Stamford Bridge. C is difficult to place. Highly reputable scholars have suggested Abingdon, Canterbury, Ramsey, London or, most recently, the west midlands.[32] The difficulty stems from C's broad range of reference points. No individual or location emerges resolutely from its pages. Up to 1050 (like E), it records abbatial appointments to Abingdon, but its interests are already diverse at that point and assume no clear pattern. As Baxter observes, two of the most idiosyncratic entries relate to Evesham (C 1037: the death of Dean Æfic, and C 1054: the consecration of Evesham's church), but D – as Baxter also points out – contains references to Evesham not found in C, though they can, ingeniously, be fitted to the case for an Evesham origin for C regardless.[33]

The case for C's alignment with Leofric rests largely on its Mercian notices and hostility towards Godwine.[34] Certainly, C 1036 and C 1052–3 are anti-Godwine, and C 1056 criticizes Bishop Leofgar, who was Harold's man in Hereford (previously Mercian territory). Yet C's sympathy for Leofric's son Earl Ælfgar at the point of his banishment in 1055 quickly yields to an account of his priest-slaying, minster-torching reprisals, even if C appears satisfied at the witan's decision to reinstate him (C 1055). There is no discernible pattern in the reporting of the deaths of abbots (C 1049: Westminster and Thorney; C 1053: Coventry, Glastonbury, and Winchcombe) or in notices of burial places sometimes supplied for prelates and earls (C 1047: Grimcytel at Christ Church; C 1049: Beorn at Winchester 'with Cnut'; C 1050: Ælfric at Peterborough; C 1053: Godwine at Old Minster, Winchester; C 1055: Siward at Galmanho; Æthelstan at Hereford; C 1056: Odda at Pershore). The only identifiable theme in C is the chronicler's disapproval of improprieties and irreligious conduct. That, rather than any ostensible support for Leofric, underlies its treatment of Godwine (C 1036, 1052, 1053), raiding (C 1055), Leofgar – and by extension those responsible for his appointment (C 1056), Edward's appointment of Ulf (C 1049), and perhaps the lack of an archbishop (C 1053). The same tone of disapproval resumes in C 1065, which accuses Tostig of robbing God. Nowhere is the disapproval more political than

---

[31] Stafford, 'Archbishop Ealdred', pp. 135–42, 150–2.
[32] Dumville, 'Some Aspects', p. 27; Baxter, 'MS C', pp. 1216–23.
[33] Baxter, 'MS C', pp. 1214–15.
[34] Ibid., pp. 1194, 1198–1214.

religious (insofar as the two can be separated). Baxter is nevertheless right to observe that C's criticism tends to fall on Godwine's kin and allies, and that the chronicler excuses Ælfgar's outrage of 1055 by claiming that the earl of Mercia had been wronged. It is this differentiation in his treatment of the two Houses that upholds the argument that the C chronicler was loyal to the Mercian cause, even if his connexions and interests generally were wide-ranging.

A couple of points are worth making in conclusion. First, an examination of E combined with the consensus on D reinforces a link between the chronicles and the two archbishops.[35] This forces us to consider whether any seeming alignment of chronicles with putative secular factions at court (i.e. the affinities of different earls) might be incidental to an alignment with the prelate overseeing a chronicle's production. Second, no extant chronicle supplies annals for the years 1062 and 1063. Like the absence of diplomas for the years 1051–8, this is either a coincidence arising, for example, from the distractions of other business, or it represents an attempt by central agencies to suppress the memory of events, perhaps in the aftermath of the Conquest. Hariulf of Saint-Riquier indicates that Edward extracted an oath in recognition of Edgar's right to succeed.[36] A notice such as this against the year 1062 or 1063 would surely have been erased after William's accession, if not after Harold's. Third, E's use of deceit is now more apparent. It bends the truth to Stigand's advantage where necessary and perhaps in ways we cannot detect, while concealing Godwine's misdemeanours in 1036 and 1051/2.

[35] On which, P. Stafford, 'The Making of Chronicles and the Making of England: The Anglo-Saxon Chronicles after Alfred', *TRHS*, 6th ser. 27 (2017), 65–86, at pp. 75–6.
[36] *Chronique*, ed. Lot, p. 241.

APPENDIX 2

EDWARD'S DIPLOMAS

PART I: 1042–61

Sixty-two items have been catalogued which purport to be diplomas issued by Edward during his reign.[1] For the period 1042–61, twenty-four are dated or can be dated on internal evidence to within a year or two of issue and have a reasonable claim to authenticity, whether as 'original' single-sheets (e.g. S 1028, S 1031) or as copies of originals.[2] Several diplomas datable to the years 1061–6 will be considered separately in Part II, as it has been suggested diploma production became regulated under a 'chancellor' about that time.[3] Of the twenty-four possibly authentic diplomas from 1042–61, twenty can be dated between 1042 and 1050, and four between 1059 and 1061. The seeming hiatus in diploma production between 1051 and 1058 could be explained in various ways. It may be a trick of the evidence, in that diplomas may have been issued in those years before being lost or written over by forgers in later contexts. Lacunae in the run of diplomas are found in the latter part of Æthelred's reign, the reigns of Cnut and his sons, and the, admittedly brief, reign of Harold II. In those cases, regime change may have ushered in large-scale upheavals in land ownership and rendered heaps of existing landbooks obsolete. In some cases, existing landbooks might have been handed over to new owners as symbols of ownership, without the need to draw up new ones. Oral testimony was at least as important as documentation in the process of land conveyance, and it is worth noting that many archives have been lost, including the episcopal archives of Lichfield and East Anglia, as well as any

---

[1] S 998–S 1053 (including S 1037a), S 1055, S 1056, S 1058, S 1060 = 62. S 1054 is an Old English note, S 1057 is more a note with a witness list, S1059 is a confirmation of a land agreement, S 1061 belongs to the period of his unofficial reign (i.e. *c.* 1033–41), and S 1062 is a note in Old English.

[2] I treat as possessing a reasonable claim to authenticity S 998, S 999, S 1001, S 1003–S 1009, S 1012–S 1015, S 1017, S 1018, S 1019, s 1021, S 1022, S 1027, S 1028, S 1031, S 1034 and S 1044. I reject S 1000, S 1002, S 1010, S 1011, S 1020, S 1023, S 1024, S 1025, S 1026, S 1029 and all the undatable diplomas, S 1045–S 1053, S 1055, S 1056, S 1058 and S 1060. I discuss S 1033 in Part II, concerning diplomas from the years 1061–6.

[3] S. D. Keynes, 'Regenbald the Chancellor (*sic*)', *ANS* 10 (1988), 185–222; idem, 'Church Councils, Royal Assemblies, and Anglo-Saxon Royal Diplomas', in G. R. Owen-Crocker and B. W. Schneider, eds, *Kingship, Legislation and Power in Anglo-Saxon England* (Woodbridge, 2013), 17–182, at pp. 130–4; Keynes, 'Earl Harold', p. 101.

number of monastic archives. A writ, datable 1053 × 1057, ordering Bishop Wulfwig of Dorchester to draw up a diploma, demonstrates that the production of diplomas was conceivable in the years 1051–8, although the diploma was not issued until 1059.[4] It may be significant that even among the forgeries only five suggest a date of issue between 1051 and 1058.[5]

Another possibility is that the gaps in the run of diplomas have a historical explanation, such as a scaling back of royal business in periods of insecurity.[6] We could apply such a hypothesis to the period covering the crises of 1051–2, the Scottish and Welsh wars of 1054–6, and the invasion of 1058, with interim reshuffles of earldoms. One possible explanation has to do with the growing use of the writ-charter in Edward's reign as a supplementary and more convenient instrument for putting the recipient in possession of estates and titles. The writ-charter, or writs generally, allowed a swift transfer to take place and may have required less involvement on the part of the Church, since the diploma traditionally invoked God and divine sanctions to protect land rights in eternity, whereas a writ expired when the king who issued it died or revoked it.[7] The first confirmable use of a pendent seal is in the 1050s, in association with the sealing of a writ. If this was an innovation of that time, it may account for the abatement in diploma production, at least until reasons were found for reviving the issuing of diplomas about the end of the decade.[8] (The sequence recommences in 1059.)

As to the agents or agencies responsible for producing Anglo-Saxon diplomas, debates between proponents of a central secretariat and proponents of the farming-out of production to local agents such as bishops or abbots are beginning to resolve into synthesis. Simon Keynes posits local and central production occurring side by side and has advanced such views since 1980, while Levi Roach reminds us that local agents could be central agents too, given that bishops and abbots were frequently at court.[9] He also maintains, in the case of Æthelred's diplomas (and contrary to other scholars), that both elements of the diploma – the substantive part and the witness list – were produced at the assembly where the diploma was to be issued. A key question is whether production of one or both elements was

---

[4] S 1105; S 1028.

[5] S 1023; S 1024; S 1025; S 1026, and S 1060.

[6] Roach, *Kingship and Consent*, p. 212.

[7] Bishop and Chaplais, *Facsimiles*, pp. ix–xii; R. Sharpe, 'The Use of Writs in the Eleventh Century', *ASE* 32 (2003), 247–91, at pp. 248, 284. On defining the writ-charter against any other writ, see pp. 249–50.

[8] Keynes regards the introduction of the double-sided pendent seal as a development 'probably of the early 1050s': S. Keynes, 'The Use of Seals in Anglo-Saxon England', in J. Cherry, J. Berenbeim, and L. de Beer, eds, *Seals and Status: The Power of Objects* (London, 2018), 73–83, at p. 79.

[9] Keynes, *The Diplomas*, pp. 26–8; idem, 'Church Councils', p. 137; Roach, *Kingship and Consent*, pp. 77–89; idem, *Æthelred*, p. 11.

in the hands of the king's priests, that is, the royal chaplains.[10] In any case one must allow that the drafter of the diploma may not have been the scribe, and that a draft is different to a final 'display' text, copied out with an integrated dating clause and witness list.

The debate I have crudely outlined revolves around the long tenth century. Less attention has been paid to Edward's diplomas as a group, though inroads have been made. Keynes has recently reinforced his argument that 'there is reason to suppose' that some of the 'finest and grandest' diplomas 'were being produced in the early 1060s by an agency which might well have been dignified by contemporaries as a royal chancery'.[11] He envisages a central agency under the 'chancellor' Regenbald, assisted by notaries, drafting and scribing diplomas.[12] We will examine that hypothesis in Part II. While I cannot comment on conventions of production in previous reigns, an argument can be built for how diplomas were produced in the first two decades of Edward's reign.

In the period 1042–61, there is reason to think that the overseeing of diploma production conventionally fell to the bishop in whose diocese the land-gift was. Three kinds of evidence point to that conclusion. The first is a group of writs in which the king instructs the diocesan bishop to draw up a diploma. The second consists of attestations of diocesans telling us they were responsible for drafting the diploma they are attesting. The third is a pattern in which the diocesan attests at the end of the senior group of witnesses – usually the king, queen (if present), and two archbishops – before the rest of the witnesses. The pattern at least draws our attention to the importance of the diocesan in relation to diplomas. While his position may simply reflect the relative importance of his testimony in transactions which involved estates in his diocese, it also tends to underline the writ evidence indicating that he was the official charged with overseeing production of the relevant landbooks. Charles Insley has connected the production of Crediton/ Exeter diplomas to the diocesan through the period 960–1069.[13] Keynes discovered evidence for the role of the diocesan in drafting diplomas in the tenth and early eleventh centuries, but he was wary of developing a model on such lines, observing that the diocesan sometimes happened to be the recipient, and preferring to refer to production in those instances being tasked to an 'interested ecclesiastic' (inverted commas his). He is cautious about the verb *dicto* which appears to refer to drafting or dictation, casting doubt on how we should translate it.[14]

---

[10] Roach, *Kingship and Consent*, 79–89, at pp. 88–9 on royal priests, and Keynes, 'Regenbald', pp. 185–97.

[11] Keynes, 'Church Councils', p. 137.

[12] Keynes, 'Earl Harold', passim.

[13] C. Insley, 'Charters and Episcopal Scriptoria in the Anglo-Saxon South-West', *EME* 7 (1998), 173–97.

[14] Keynes, 'Church Councils', pp. 97–8; *The Diplomas*, 19–28, at p. 28; 'Church Councils', p. 137.

Caveats aside for a moment, let us consider each of the three kinds of
evidence I have outlined above. The writ evidence consists of a writ in
which Edward orders the diocesan Wulfwig of Dorchester to draw up a
diploma (*boc*) for a grant of land in Oxfordshire to the French abbey of
Saint-Denis (1053 × 1057: S 1105); a writ ordering the diocesan Giso of
Wells to draw up a diploma (*priuilegium*) for a gift of land in Somerset to his
canons at St Andrew's, Wells (1061 × 1065: S 1115), and a writ ordering
Ealdred to draw up a diploma (*priuilegium*) for lands belonging to Beverley
minster, mostly or all within his diocese one imagines (1061 × 1065: S 1067).
We therefore have three writs in which Edward delegates diploma production to the diocesan bishop – and no examples of him delegating the task
to anyone else – in the period 1042–61. I include the last two writs as
possibly dating to 1061, although they may be later, because they are the
sort of writs prelates acquired on coming into office.[15]

The second kind of evidence consists of statements in which the diocesan claims to have composed the diploma. In a diploma of 1044 granting
land in Devon to the king's chaplain Leofric, the diocesan, Bishop Lyfing
of Crediton, attests with the words 'I Lyfing, bishop of the church of
Crediton, have written [this] with my pen at the king's request' ('Ego
Lyfingus Crydianensis aecclesiae pontifex rogatus a rege calomo scripsi':
S 1003). It makes no sense to take this as a reference to the king asking him
to add the normal subscription. Rather, the bishop refers to a writ of the
kind described above, or to a verbal command, asking him to write the
diploma. In another diploma, of 1049, granting land in Cornwall to one of
Edward's thegns, the diocesan, Bishop Leofric, attests with the words 'I
Bishop Leofric, drafting [this], have added my name' ('Ego Leofricus episcopus dictando titulaui': S 1019). In a third diploma, of 1061, granting land
to an abbot in Somerset, the diocesan, Bishop Giso of Wells, appears at the
head of the witness list with the words 'I Giso, bishop by God's grace,
composed this diploma' ('Ego Giso Dei gratia episcopus hanc cartam
dictaui': S 1034). We therefore have six examples of a bishop drawing up a
diploma for a land-gift in his diocese. The dates are 1044, 1049, 1053 ×
1057, and 1061 × 1065 (2 examples). The one example of a bishop who is
not the diocesan claiming to have drafted a diploma is S 998 (1042), which
concerns a land grant in Devon, where Bishop Brihtwold of Ramsbury
attests 'dictando titulaui'. But its witness list was modelled on examples
from Cnut's reign and seems to be inauthentic.[16] In four of the six cases in

---

[15] As shown by Sharpe, 'The Use of Writs', p. 248.

[16] The witness lists to S 962, S 963, S 971, and S 998 (all pertaining to the see of Devon)
show clear evidence of cross-fertilization. Edward's formula of attestation in S 998 'crucis
taumate' derives from Cnut's in S 962, S 963, and S 971 ('crucis taumate'). Archbishop
Eadsige's 'principatum et beniuolentium' is modelled on Archbishop Æthelnoth's 'principatum et beneuolentium' in S 962 and S 971. Emma attests in all the charters and no other
as 'Ælfgyfo [*sic*, or Ælfgyfu] regina humillima adiuui' (S 962, S 963, S 971, S 998), and all
four attach 'dictando titulaui' to one of the attesting bishops. In S 998 it is Brihtwold, but

which the diocesan is the draftsman, he was not the beneficiary of the land-gift. The only sense in which he was an 'interested ecclesiastic' in such cases was in his capacity as the diocesan. This implies the diocesan drafted diplomas chiefly in that capacity.

As noted above, some have argued that *dictando titulaui* (as in S 1019) cannot be taken as evidence of authorship. Two Exeter diplomas, both dated 1031 and preserved as single sheets of the first half of the eleventh century, have a bishop attesting with the form *dictando titulaui* and both, as Pierre Chaplais observed, were copied out by the same scribe. But this is compatible with the bishop having overseen the drafting, or even having done it himself.[17] Simon Keynes was also wary of taking *dictaui* (as in S 1034) to mean that the bishop employing it drafted the diploma, but in the parallel environment of epistolography the meaning of the verb *dicto* was clear enough, having changed from 'dictate' in Antiquity to 'compose' in the Middle Ages.[18] There are, in fact, twenty-four diplomas in Sawyer's catalogue that attach the formula *dictaui* to one of the witnesses in the witness list, and in no instance is it attached to more than one witness in the same list, unlike verbs of attestation, which are often repeated in a list. As a random example, the witness list for S 597 (of 956) has *consensi* three times, *roboraui* five times, *subscripsi* once, *signum crucis impressi* once, *confirmaui* twice, and *dictaui* once. Moreover, of all the verbs commonly occurring in witness lists, *dictaui* is the only one which never occurs in the same list more than once, and the same is true of its participle *dictando*.[19] In a few cases *dictaui* can be shown to mean something different to *subscripsi* (e.g. S 1632 and S 914, which both have the formula 'dictaui et subscripsi'). A differentiation between *dicto* and *scribo* occurs in epistolography.[20] This is all evidence for taking *dicto* as meaning 'composed'; *scribo* as meaning 'scribed', and *subscribo* as 'attested'.

Further proof of the importance of the diocesan in activities associated with Edward's diplomas is the position he normally occupies in the list of signatories. In most diplomas, the diocesan concludes what we might call the senior group of witnesses who comprise the king, queen (if present), the

---

this is lifted from S 963, which also has 'Byrhtwold dictando titulaui'. S 1019 uses this formula too but in other respects sits apart from this quartet.

[17] S 963 and S 971 (which belong to the quartet mentioned above). Cf. P. Chaplais, 'The Authenticity of the Royal Anglo-Saxon Diplomas of Exeter', *Bulletin of the Institute of Historical Research* 39 (1966), 1–34, at p. 24, and Keynes, *The Diplomas*, p. 27, n. 43. For discussion of these diplomas, see Insley, 'Charters and Episcopal Scriptoria', pp. 191–2.

[18] Keynes, *The Diplomas*, p. 63, n. 113. Cf. G. Constable, 'Forged Letters in the Middle Ages', in *Fälschungen im Mittelalter: Internationaler Kongreß der Monumenta Germaniae Historica München, 16.–19. September 1986*, MGH Schriften 33, 5 vols (Hanover, 1988), V, 11–37, at p. 27.

[19] Assuming the reliability of the search engine: http://www.esawyer.org.uk/searchfiles/index.html (accessed 9 March 2018).

[20] Constable, 'Forged Letters', p. 27.

two archbishops, and the diocesan. Other witnesses follow, sometimes in order of seniority by date of appointment (as in S 1027, S 1028, S 1031). Below I supply details of grants in different dioceses and the position of the diocesan in the witness list:[21]

> Ramsbury, S 999, diocesan Brihtwold concludes the senior group;
> Dorchester, S 1014, diocesan Eadnoth II concludes the senior group;
> Dorchester, S 1022, diocesan Ulf concludes the senior group;
> Dorchester, S 1028, diocesan Wulfwig concludes the senior group;
> Crediton, S 1003 and S 1005, diocesan Lyfing concludes the senior group in both, but not in S 998;
> Crediton/ Exeter, S 1019 and S 1027, diocesan Leofric concludes the senior group, but not in S 1021 (diocesan omitted);
> Wells, S 1006, diocesan Duduc in no special position;
> Wells, S 1034, diocesan Giso heads the witness list with a *dictaui* titulus;
> London, S 1015, diocesan Robert concludes the senior group;
> London, S 1031, diocesan omitted;
> Winchester, S 1007, S 1008, S 1009, S 1012, and S 1013, diocesan Ælfwine concludes the senior group in all five;
> Winchester, S 1018, diocesan Stigand concludes the senior group (he was not yet archbishop of Canterbury);
> Canterbury, S 1044, the diocesan is already in the senior group, being the archbishop; and S 1017 is of an uncertain diocese.[22]

These details permit the following observations. Of the twenty-four diplomas datable to between 1042 and 1061 possessing reasonable claims to authenticity, twenty-three allow us to identify the diocese where the land-gift or privileges lay. Out of those, one has the diocesan at the head of the senior group of witnesses, one within the senior group (as the archbishop of Canterbury), and fifteen have him concluding the senior group. If Giso's elevated protocol at the top of the senior group in S 1034 is an aggrandizement upon the principle of the diocesan signing at the end of the senior group, he – and the archbishop in S 1044 – can be considered as occupying a proper place in the list. Of the six remaining diplomas which do not conform to the pattern, two omit the diocesan (S 1021 and S 1031) so neither confirm the pattern nor contradict it. That leaves four diplomas which do not conform to the pattern (S 998, S 1001, S 1004, and S 1006). All are from early in the reign: S 998 is of 1042; S 1001, S 1004, and S 1006 are of 1044. They have two other features in common. All

---

[21] The positions are based on the best lists provided in the Electronic Sawyer database, checked when possible against editions and/or single sheets or other 'best' witnesses.

[22] The same pattern is found in the two possibly authentic diplomas of Harthacnut: S 993 (diocesan Brihtwold of Ramsbury concludes the senior group); S 994 (diocesan Ælfwine of Winchester concludes the senior group). I omit S 1001 and S 1004 (see below).

include, after the boundary clause, a dating clause introducing the witness list, and all conclude the senior group with Bishop Ælfwine of Winchester. They also overlap with another group (S 1001, S 1006, S 1007, and S 1008)[23] which are connected by the fact that they all contain the same clause introducing the witness list (though the date varies): 'Anno dominicae incarnationis ... sub astipulatione primatum quorum nomine hic caraxata sunt.' In those diplomas too, Ælfwine concludes the senior group; in the last two of them he is also the diocesan.

It follows that in every one of our twenty-three diplomas where the diocese of the land-gift is identifiable the bishop concluding the senior group is either the diocesan or Ælfwine. In five cases he is both. In nine he is Ælfwine. The fact that four of those diplomas (two in which he is diocesan, two in which he is not) share a dating clause which introduces the witness list gives us reason to think they may have been drafted by the same person, or at least that the circumstantial parts (i.e. the dating clause and witness list) were drafted by the same person and appended to the substantive text of the diploma. In six other cases we have evidence in writs or attestations that the diocesan drafted the diploma, or at least that he was tasked with overseeing its creation, and in the four noted above, which share a dating clause, the identical clauses support the hypothesis that Ælfwine or one of his clergy drafted at least the circumstantial parts. One diploma in which Ælfwine concludes the senior group (S 998) claims to have been dictated by Brihtwold of Ramsbury, but it lifts that detail from a diploma of Cnut (S 963), which was one of the models for its witness list. Taken all together, the evidence suggests that the person responsible for the contents of the diploma attested at the end of the senior group of witnesses. Early in Edward's reign, that person was sometimes the diocesan (as in S 999, of 1043) and sometimes Ælfwine. In a run of charters, it was both, and after Ælfwine's death in 1047 it was invariably the diocesan. Whether Ælfwine drafted the substantive text or just the circumstantial clauses of the diplomas in which he concludes the senior group, that position was the preserve thereafter of the composer/overseer-diocesan. The single diploma that cannot be localized (S 1017, of 1048) is in the cartulary of Burton, a Mercian monastery, and the bishop concluding the senior group is Æthelstan of Hereford (d. 1056), whose presence there suggests that the land at *Berghe* may have lain in the Welsh marches. He was blind for the last thirteen years of his life,[24] but that need not have prevented him from overseeing the production of a diploma.

Spurious diplomas from the years 1042–61 can be tested against that pattern. S 1060, for example, purports to be a confirmation of land to Peterborough. Though the text is forged, the witness list may be authentic,

---

[23] I am grateful to Alex Rumble for pointing out that S 994 and S 1008 were written by the same scribe.

[24] *JW*, ii, p. 579.

since it is acceptable for 1055 × 1060 and has the diocesan Wulfwig of Dorchester concluding the senior group. Other forged diplomas with the diocesan in the correct place are S 1002 (Ælfweard of London), S 1020 and S 1023 (Herman of Ramsbury), S 1025 (Ulf of Dorchester), and S 1029 (Wulfwig of Dorchester), though S 1010, S 1011, S 1024, and S 1026 do not conform to the pattern, as might be expected of forgeries. In S 1058 the diocesan Ealdred of Worcester is absent, as in S 1021 and S 1031. The remarkable thing is that a slight majority of the forgeries – six against four – have the diocesan in the correct place too. This merely confirms the pattern. It follows also that any list that does not position the diocesan last in the senior group gives grounds for suspicion.

In the light of the evidence outlined above, it may now be possible to propose a model of diploma production in Edward's first two decades as king. When a diploma was required, the need for one would come to the attention of the diocesan (by the king's writ or other means), and the diocesan would supervise its production. He might delegate the archival work of modelling the text and ascertaining estate boundaries to clerics at his disposal; alternatively, he might himself have had a hand in drafting substantive elements. The relationship between diploma production and assemblies is unclear.[25] It is hard to argue for the existence of any convention stipulating that finished diplomas should always be handed over to the recipients formally at assemblies. Sometimes that may have occurred, and in such instances the dating clause and witness list might have been added to the draft text and the whole landbook have been written up by a skilled calligrapher on that occasion. In other instances, however, receipt of the diploma may not have occurred in a significant setting; and it is worth remembering in this regard that the writ was the royal instrument by which a recipient was put in possession of assets. In any event, these processes of production distanced the king from the contents of diplomas issued in his name. We should not expect to see his sentiments in them, and indeed the tone of Edward's diplomas is generally formal and impersonal.

In the case of S 1028, a single-sheet original confirming land in Oxfordshire to the royal abbey of Saint-Denis outside Paris, we happen to know that the scribe of the diploma was the king's physician Baldwin. The evidence for the attribution is twofold. First, he appends what appears to be a notarial inscription in the form of a final protocol at the end of the witness list. Second, I identified the scribal hand as the last of a series of continental hands that added recipes to a medical book, prior to the addition of more recipes by hands associated with the abbey of Bury St

---

[25] Though the argument is often put for post-assembly production, the model espoused by Chaplais, Insley, 'Charters and Episcopal Scriptoria', pp. 181–4, 195, would also allow for pre-assembly drafting of diplomas.

Edmunds.[26] Baldwin became abbot of Bury in 1065. The medical book is almost certainly one he brought from the Continent, and since the last hand to insert a recipe before the Bury hands is the hand that wrote the single-sheet S 1028 and appended the final protocol, beginning 'I Baldwin', it is safe to regard it as Baldwin's hand. That the surviving single sheet is in portrait rather than landscape format shows also that the scribe adhered to Capetian rather than English conventions of layout. About the time the diploma was issued, Baldwin became a monk at Saint-Denis and was thus a suitable recipient for conveying the document to the brethren. It is possible that he was copying a text drafted by Wulfwig or an agent of his (as Wulfwig had been instructed to draft one in the writ, S 1105), for the layout of his exemplar did not fit into the portrait format – other English single-sheets are landscape format. He was therefore obliged to insert the last five words of Edward's long *signum*, and a fourth column of witnesses, into spaces on the right of the page. He identified the insertions with para-graph marks.[27] All of this shows that in the case of S 1028, the scribe was not the draftsman and was re-formatting a hypothesized exemplar that was in landscape format.[28]

A question remains why the diocesan is sometimes absent as in S 1021, S 1031, and the spurious S 1058 (which has an acceptable witness list). In the case of S 1031, a single-sheet original recording a gift to Westminster in 1060, I have suggested the assembly was held at Pentecost when William of London was in Flanders. An assembly was held in London at Pentecost the previous year.[29] Similarly, S 1058 may have been issued when the diocesan Ealdred was absent at the council of Rome in 1050, an idea strengthened by the absence of Earl Swegn, who was in exile at that time. S 1021 is peculiar in many respects and existed in more than one version. The absence of the diocesan Leofric of Exeter is not easily explained, since he was a participant in the ceremony described in the diploma, but since the latter is a foundation charter of sorts, it should perhaps be treated as an exceptional document. Insley's forthcoming edition of the Exeter charters will hopefully shed light on its complexi-ties.[30] S 1105, the writ to Wulfwig of 1053 × 1057, confirms that instructions to produce diplomas could be issued well in advance of the occasion on which the physical document was presented to the recipient (in this

[26] M. Gullick, 'An Eleventh-century Bury Medical Manuscript', in Licence, ed., *Bury St Edmunds*, 190–226, at pp. 207–10. Gullick considers whether the hand might be that of an amanuensis, but it appears unlikely that Baldwin would have employed a scribe of mediocre quality.

[27] *Facsimiles of Anglo-Saxon Charters*, ed. S. Keynes, Anglo-Saxon Charters, Supplementary Volume I (Oxford, 1991), 21a (S 1028) (hereafter *BAFacs*).

[28] I merely reinforce a point made by Chaplais and Insley: Insley, 'Charters and Episcopal Scriptoria', p. 184.

[29] Keynes, 'Church Councils', p. 152. See above, p. 195, n. 123.

[30] For now, see Insley, 'Charters and Episcopal Scriptoria', pp. 192–3.

instance in 1059). Early warning was clearly necessary where details such as estate boundaries had to be surveyed or confirmed by the shire court.

PART II: 1061–6

In 1061 or afterwards we begin to see evidence of Edward authorizing the production of pancartes, a category of diploma which confirmed a religious institution in all its possessions. Pancartes were becoming more common about this time in the French kingdom. Usually they contain lists of the estates and, sometimes, consolidated boundary clauses. Evidence of their introduction is twofold. First, we have the writ authorizing Archbishop Ealdred of York to draw up a pancarte (*priuilegium*) for the lands pertaining to St John's minster at Beverley (S 1067). The writ is datable 1061 × 1065. Second, we have a pancarte for the estates of Wells bishopric drawn up by Giso in 1065 (S 1042). His notarial protocol and his subscription are found after the witness list: 'This charter was written by the same Bishop Giso on my orders [i.e. Edward's] . . . in the royal town of Windsor. The hand of Bishop Giso attests.' ('Scripta est haec karta ab eodem Gisone episcopo iussu meo. . . . Signum manu Gisonis.') As in S 1034, where Giso's positioning as the 'drafter' of the diploma broke with convention, so here his position as the 'draftsman' breaks with convention, as we might expect. This is Giso 'being Giso'. Other diplomas purporting to date from these years are pancartes too, notably the Waltham diploma (S 1036) and First and Third charters of Westminster (S 1043, S 1041). In the two instances where the 'draftsman' of a pancarte can be identified (S 1067, S 1042) it is again the diocesan, a fact which suggests that the arrival of pancartes did not accompany a change in the agency overseeing production.[31]

The several diplomas from these years need to be considered individually and in relation to the patterns and conventions already observed. S 1033, dated 1061, purports to be a grant of land in Devon to St Mary's, Rouen. The best text is a thirteenth-century facsimile transcript made in Rouen and preserved in the Christ Church archive.[32] It is not a pancarte. The diplomas chronologically either side of it list bishops and earls in order of seniority by date of appointment. This is true of S 1027 (1059, Exeter diocese), S 1028 (1059, Dorchester diocese), S 1031 (1060, London diocese), S 1034 (1061, Wells diocese), and S 1036 (1062, London diocese). S 1033's arrangement is haphazard. The bishops in the order given are Æthelric (of Selsey, 1057/8), Leofric (of Exeter, 1046), and Siward (of Rochester, 1058). The earls are Harold (1045), Tostig (1055), Ælfgar (1051/3, but also after Tostig in the authentic S 1031 and S 1034), Gyrth (1057/8), Waltheof (?), and Leofwine (1057/8). It is concerning that an

---

[31] S 1038, which claims to have been dictated by the abbot, is a forgery: see below, p. 275.

[32] Canterbury, Dean and Chapter, R. 51; *BAFacs*, 42.

Exeter diocese diploma of 1059 is correct in its episcopal hierarchy while this one is not. A second problem is that the witness list fails to place the diocesan at the end of the senior group, an anomaly hitherto characteristic of forgeries. Another anomaly is Waltheof, who is certainly misplaced in the hierarchy of earls and whose occupancy of an earldom as early as 1061 is uncorroborated.[33]

There is, moreover, a suggestion that the witness list at least was compiled after the gathering at which the diploma was allegedly issued. It is introduced by the clause, 'Here are given the names of witnesses who were in attendance when I presented the charter of this donation' ('Hic sunt designata nomina testium qui fuerunt in praesentia quando exhibui donationis cartulam'). The irregularities in the witness list can therefore be understood as the result of its unauthorized creation at some point after 1061, possibly after 1066 when St Mary's needed to firm up any claim it had upon the land. Perhaps a diploma had been drawn up but not issued, or perhaps the text was fabricated at St Mary's. That St Mary's had come into possession of the land by 1066 is indicated in Domesday Book, though we might wonder whether its entry reflects the canons' success in staking a claim to the land after 1066. Alternatively, they may have been put in possession by a writ without having received a diploma. Saint-Denis had to wait at least two years between the issue of the writ and the diploma granting it Taynton.

S 1036 is the famous diploma for Waltham, dated 1062. Keynes has drawn our attention to elements that seem authentic.[34] The most compelling is the witness list, which includes eleven bishops – more than normal – ranked in seniority by date of appointment. (Æthelmær of Elmham is not misplaced as Keynes supposes, for he was appointed in 1051/2.)[35] This is impressive, and it is likely eleven bishops would have attended the assembly in Gloucester at Easter 1062 in the presence of the papal legates, as Keynes suggests. As in S 1033, however, the diocesan does not conclude the senior group – an anomaly hitherto seen only in forgeries. William of London appears in his rank place in the hierarchy. There are two other suspicious features. The first is the immunity granted to Waltham and its possessions from all pleas outside the court of its jurisdiction, paralleled only in the forged Malmesbury pancarte of 1065 (S 1038, discussed below). It goes far beyond Edward's immunity for Westminster's estate at Wheathampstead, which he freed from the three common burdens (S 1031). S 1036's claim that Waltham was immune to all pleas outside its own court and from all gelds is typical of excessive immunities claimed by post-Conquest forgers. Apart from the anachronism, it is hard to imagine any upholder of justice agreeing to such a thing.

---

[33] As Oleson pointed out: *The Witenagemot*, p. 153. Cf. S 1237, possibly another late creation.

[34] Keynes, 'Earl Harold', passim.

[35] Barlow, *Edward*, p. 87.

There is also a problem with the witness list, with the titles appended to many names – titles such as 'the king's kinsman', 'steward of the royal palace', 'the king's chancellor', etc. Tabulated by Keynes alongside titles found in other diplomas, as a group they stick out like a sore thumb.[36] As Keynes observes, individual parallels can be found in other witness lists and in Domesday Book, but it is the number and variety of ornate titles that stand out – eight in total. The Wells pancarte of 1065 has only four (*procurator, pincerna, cubicularius,* and *princeps*), and Osbert's forged First and Third charters for Westminster (S 1043 and S 1041) have only one (*regis cancellarius*). A different problem in the use of titles is the presence of 'Baldwin *capellanus*'. As Keynes points out, he is probably the king's physician, for no other Baldwin is known to have served the king, and the name was uncommon in England at that time. Yet we have it from a reliable contemporary that Baldwin was ordained priest by Pope Alexander in 1071, so he could hardly have been a royal chaplain in 1062, as he would not have been qualified to celebrate Mass.[37] The multiple elaborate titles look like the work of a knowledgeable forger keen to embellish a list already at his disposal. Which are his invention and which were in the original is a matter for speculation.[38]

The golden diploma of Waltham (paralleled by Crowland forgeries which also employed golden crosses) may have been the source for details Osbert of Clare included when forging the First and Third charters for nearby Westminster.[39] They have in common Regenbald 'the chancellor' and Swithgar 'the notary', though the formula Osbert used to describe Regenbald ('regiae dignitatis cancellarius') was the same he used for the fictitious chancellor Wulfwig in his Second charter, allegedly of 1045 (S 1011), and copied a form of words used to describe Philip I's chancellor in the French charter Osbert was using as a model.[40] Osbert was not so adept a forger as to rank his bishops and earls in the correct order, a convention we see used consistently in authentic charters from 1059 onwards, and occasionally before that date.

S 1037a is a forgery conferring on Archbishop Ealdred the right to ordain the bishops of Worcester. It implies Worcester should be part of the northern archdiocese and fits a context in which Wulfstan was trying

[36] Keynes, 'Regenbald', p. 206. Cf. Barlow, *Edward*, pp. 164–5.

[37] *MSE*, p. 69; J. Barrow, 'Grades of Ordination and Clerical Careers, c. 900–c. 1200', *ANS* 32 (2010), 41–61, at p. 46. Edward did also have a godson called Baldwin, who was a monk at Westminster: Barlow, *Edward*, p. 191.

[38] The forger may have conflated names from more than one witness list: Clarke, *English Nobility*, p. 128.

[39] For Crowland's golden diplomas, see A. Hiatt, *The Making of Medieval Forgeries: False Documents in Fifteenth-century England* (London, 2004), pp. 44–5.

[40] S 1043; S 1011; *Receuil des actes de Philippe Ier*, ed. M. Prou (Paris, 1908), no. 40; B. W. Scholz, 'Two Forged Charters from the Abbey of Westminster and Their Relationship with St. Denis', *EHR* 76 (1961), 466–78, at p. 468.

to break free of York after 1066. Though the diploma – if it can be called such – is dated 1065, this is apparently an error for 1062. The date MLXII ends with two minims which in many later scribal hands would have been nearly joined by serifs at the base. They could therefore be mistaken for a U, that is a V, the numeral 5, and since the earliest copy of the text dates from the fourteenth century, there is a chance this may have happened. The regnal date given is 21st Edward, that is 1062–3, and the witness list is acceptable for 1062 (31 December). It includes two archbishops, three bishops (not in order of accession), Robert the Staller, three chaplains (Osbern, Regenbald, and Peter), five earls in a correct order (with Tostig ahead of Ælfgar, as in S 1031 and S 1033), four thegns, and a certain Walter. Three abbots and a subdeacon named Ealdred have been added after the (terminal) dating clause. The last is possibly the Ealdred who became the archbishop's deacon.[41] Problems with the witness list may be explained as disruptions arising in copying – that is, the placing of Bishop Leofric after Bishop William, and a decision to include the abbots and Ealdred at the end after initially planning to omit them. The draftsman-archbishop is already included in the senior group. The list may reflect a genuine list of December 1062, possibly from a lost pancarte Archbishop Ealdred may have drawn up for Beverley, as instructed in S 1067.

S 1037 is a diploma dated 1063 granting land in Devon to St Olave's, Exeter. The only extant copy terminates at the incipit of the boundary clause. Without a witness list we cannot test its claims to authenticity, but the proem is noteworthy for the unusual insights it purports to offer into Edward's fears and concerns. Though this is a departure from the conventional, more distant proems of his earlier diplomas, such departures were not unprecedented.[42] Still, it is necessary to reserve judgement in this case. S 1042, Giso's pancarte for Wells, has been mentioned. There are indications of post-Conquest tampering in the substantive part of the diploma, where the list of estates has been updated, and in forms of attestation in the witness list.[43] The nine bishops attest in the correct order of seniority, apart from Æthelric of Selsey, who is misplaced. This could be a copyist's glitch. The earls are in the right order too, and the witness list is acceptable for the date, May 1065. S 1038, dated 1065 for Malmesbury, is the only diploma which purports to have been dictated by an agent other than the diocesan, namely Abbot Brihtric of Malmesbury. It is a forgery, as Susan Kelly has demonstrated.[44]

---

[41] Cf. *Charters of Northern Houses*, ed. Woodman, nos 11, 10.

[42] Roach, *Æthelred*, pp. 137–43 (discussing S 993).

[43] S. Keynes, *Giso*, pp. 232–8; *Charters of Bath and Wells*, ed. S. E. Kelly, Anglo-Saxon Charters 13 (Oxford, 2007), pp. 238–47 (no. 40).

[44] *Charters of Malmesbury Abbey*, ed. S. E. Kelly, Anglo-Saxon Charters 11 (Oxford, 2005), pp. 244–50 (no. 33).

A few of the late diplomas bear the *signum* of the king's priest Regenbald. In S 1037a, reflecting a witness list of December 1062, he attests as the second of three royal chaplains with no special title (Osbern, Regenbald, and Peter). In S 1033's list, drawn up at some date after the alleged issuing of the diploma in 1061, he is *regis sigillarius*, 'the king's seal-bearer'. In S 1036, which interpolates titles, he is *regis cancellarius*, the king's chancellor. In S 1043 he is *cancellarius* and *regiae dignitatis cancellarius* (a formula the forger borrowed from a charter of Saint-Denis); and in S 1041, by the same forger, he appears with the same titles. A writ of Edward survives declaring that Regenbald his priest is to have judicial and financial rights over his land and men and the same fine payable to him as to any bishop.[45] The date of the writ is unknown, and it assigns no special title to Regenbald. No other grant of its nature exists, and Regenbald himself had an obvious motive to forge such a writ after Edward's death. A writ of William datable to 1076 × 1085 indicates that Bishop Wulfstan of Worcester, Abbot Æthelwig of Evesham, and Regenbald 'the chancellor' (*cancellarius*) had established which lands in Worcestershire belonged to the abbey of Westminster.[46] Two writs of William datable to 1066 × 1067 grant land to Regenbald 'my priest', and by May 1068 William's Norman priest Herfast was attesting charters as chancellor (*cancellarius*).[47]

On that evidence, Regenbald was involved as a representative of 'central government' with ecclesiastical officials of the Worcestershire shire court in confirming Westminster's holdings in Worcestershire at a date between 1062 (Wulfstan's appointment) and 1068 (the latest date for Herfast's appointment). In that capacity, he occupied a role which by the late 1070s could be referred to as 'chancellor'. Yet the first appearance of that title occurs in May 1068. Edward's writ and William's two writs of 1066 × 1067 refer to Regenbald as 'my priest', and he has no special rank or title among the chaplains in the witness list of S 1037a, probably of December 1062. He was, however, in William's favour soon after the Conquest. The likeliest scenario is that William appointed him chancellor before crossing to Normandy in March or April 1067. Regenbald would then have been tasked with touring the shire courts to assess the multitude of claims that were being made.[48] He would either confirm them or not. This could explain his presence in Worcestershire with Wulfstan and Æthelwig, who were also quick to offer a hand to the new regime. Regenbald's task was an unenviable one. William returned to England in December 1067 and by May 1068 had replaced Regenbald with Herfast.

The only evidence Regenbald held office in Edward's reign comes from witness lists which show indications either of being late compilations

---

[45] S 1097; Keynes, 'Regenbald', p. 197.

[46] *Regesta*, no. 311.

[47] Ibid., nos 223 and 224, 181, 138.

[48] Cf. Williams, *The English*, pp. 7–11.

(S 1033) or being embellished at a later date (S 1036) or forged (S 1030, S 1043, and S 1041). S 1033 is the most interesting, as it titles him *sigillarius*, and Edward presumably needed one or more seal-bearers for sealing writs, overseeing writ production, or proving title.[49] It is in that capacity we see him acting (probably in 1067) as an intermediary between a central government agency and the shires. That office could also explain why Edward enriched or elevated him by granting him rights over his land and men and a bishop's fine (S 1097). The attraction of Regenbald to a forger lay in the collective memory that he was the individual who had been tasked with proving title after the Conquest. To append his name to a forgery was to authenticate it. Alternatively, the knowledge he had served as chancellor about that date may have influenced the forgers who created historical detail by appending titles to names in witness lists. Edward, however, had no need of a chancellor or central agency for diploma production. As the seven examples of diocesan bishops overseeing production demonstrate, he had a perfectly adequate system in place. The last example (Giso's, S 1042) confirms that it operated all the way through from the early years to the end of the reign.

PART III: EDWARD'S SEAL AND WRITS

Uncertainty surrounds the early use of the writ in Anglo-Saxon England. Florence Harmer traced it back to Alfred's reign,[50] but no writ appears before Æthelred's; and of the 112 preserved mostly as copies in cartularies but occasionally as originals, 99 are from Edward's reign.[51] By the mid-1050s, writs were authenticated by the king's double-sided seal (the 'Great Seal'), which was affixed to one of usually two very narrow strips of parchment cut horizontally parallel to the lower edge to within a short distance of the left-hand edge. The upper strip (or single strip in one case) was a tongue for the pendent seal, which hung below the writ. The lower strip has been interpreted as a wrapping tie.[52] Three different matrices purporting to be Edward's are witnessed by the corpus of seals. One of those matrices, witnessed by the three examples of the so-called Second Seal, is thought to be genuine.[53] The earliest seal created from this matrix was attached to a writ of Edward for Saint-Denis issued in 1053 × 1057

---

[49] See Part III of this appendix.

[50] *Writs*, ed. Harmer, pp. 10–13; G. A. Barraclough, 'The Anglo-Saxon Writ', *History* 39 (1954), 193–215, at pp. 204–5.

[51] Bishop and Chaplais, *Facsimiles*, p. ix. This number does not include writs or references to writs discovered since the publication of their edition, but nothing has appeared which alters the general picture.

[52] The exception, which seems to have had one strip only, is S 1105: see the commentary on *BAFacs*, 20.

[53] Bishop and Chaplais, *Facsimiles*, pp. xi–xiii, xxii–iv, and no. 3 (plate III), no. 20 (plate XVIII), and no. 25 (plate XXIII (b) and (c)).

(S 1105). The writ survives as Archives Nationales, Paris, K. 19, no. 6, but the seal (which had become detached) is missing, though it is shown in photographs.[54] Arguments for the use of a pendent seal to authenticate writ-charters, prior to the earliest example, are necessarily speculative and have taken three approaches. The first is to seek references to a king's seal being used at an earlier date. The second is to look for clues pointing to earlier origins in the design of Edward's seal. The third is to suppose that writs were always sealed that way, and that earlier examples have been lost.

The use of seals by elites in England prior to Edward's reign is attested by occasional references and the survival of matrices.[55] There are, for example, references to Æthelred's seal (*insegel*), but since no impressions survive, it is impossible to establish whether such references relate to a signet (a seal stamped on wax applied to parchment), or to a double-sided pendent seal.[56] Moving to the second approach, Harmer and others cited evidence from sagas and other late sources that present Cnut as using a seal.[57] Few scholars today, however, would trust details supplied by those sources. Harmer and others also claimed to have found clues in the design of Edward's seal which pointed to earlier origins. First, it resembled the seal of Conrad II of Germany which must – they suggested – have inspired Cnut when he attended Conrad's imperial coronation in Rome. Second, that the seal was double-sided pointed to Cnut as being its originator on the grounds that the two sides were intended to denote his rule over two kingdoms. Edward, it was proposed, merely kept the design.[58] Geoffrey Barraclough believed there were such close resemblances between the earliest Danish seal – of Cnut IV (1080–6) – and the Conqueror's seal that the shared model must have been a lost seal of Cnut (d. 1035).[59] This kind of 'evolutionary' theory, positing a missing link, does not allow for the cross-fertilization of images from visual media which were known via multiple channels of contact. We should also imagine multiple possible reasons for the seal being double-sided. There is no reason to conclude that its double sidedness must signify command over two kingdoms. Since a seal was a guard against forgery, a double-sided seal may have been created because it would be harder to forge.

Pierre Chaplais accepted the hypothesis that Cnut introduced the double-sided Great Seal, and he came to the opinion that Cnut had introduced the writ. (He doubted the authenticity of the two writs attributed to

[54] Ibid., no. 20 (plate XVIII); *BAFacs*, 20.

[55] T. A. Heslop, 'Seals', in M. Lapidge, J. Blair, S. Keynes, and D. Scragg, eds, *The Blackwell Encyclopaedia of Anglo-Saxon England* (London, 1999), pp. 413–14.

[56] Cf. Harmer, *Writs*, pp. 10, 92–3.

[57] E.g. ibid., pp. 17–18; Barraclough, 'The Anglo-Saxon Writ', pp. 208–9.

[58] Harmer, *Writs*, pp. 98–101; Barraclough, 'The Anglo-Saxon Writ', pp. 208–11.

[59] Barraclough, 'The Anglo-Saxon Writ', pp. 208–11.

Æthelred.) He therefore posited that 'the seal pendent affixed to a tongue was presumably introduced at the same time as the "writ-charter", during the reign of Cnut'.[60] His use of the word 'presumably' reveals his assumption that writ and pendent seal came into use together. In his discussion of the earliest original writ, thought to date from 1044, which is a writ of Edward confirming Abbot Leofstan of Bury in his possessions, Chaplais noted that because the parchment had been trimmed, 'any evidence of former sealing has thus been destroyed, but a ragged tear in the bottom left-hand corner may indicate that the document was once sealed'.[61] What he describes as a 'ragged tear' could equally be an initial mis-cut in the attempt at slicing off the lower edge of parchment when the writ was trimmed. Whether the trimming of the writ is evidence of an attempt to remove a seal is a matter of speculation, and we would have no way of knowing whether the seal that might have been removed was genuine. The date 1044 derives from the assumption that a confirmation would most probably have been issued when Leofstan came into his abbacy in that year. This is indeed likely, since it was the practice at Bury – and no doubt at other houses, where fewer or no writs have survived in the extant muniments – to renew its titles by obtaining writs of possession on the arrival of each new abbot or monarch.[62] Yet we cannot exclude the possibility that Leofstan was obliged to obtain or renew such a writ later in his abbacy (1044–65). Moreover, if the sealing of writs with a pendent seal was an innovation of *c.* 1050, earlier writs might have had to be renewed or sealed anew about that time.

The idea that the writ was invented complete with its appendant means of authentication (as Chaplais supposed) has nothing to recommend it per se. If the statistics show the gradual introduction of the writ through Cnut's reign, the earliest means of authentication may have been its hand-writing, or the identity of the bearer, both being standard means of confirming the genuineness of letters at that time – and it should be remembered here that the writ was conceived as an epistolary mandate.[63] The decision to authenticate writs by attaching a seal pendent may have come later, in response to growing concerns about forgery. Indeed, few instruments of administration – or anything else for that matter – emerge fully formed; normally, they evolve by adaptation to unanticipated obstacles. Whether or not Cnut introduced the writ, Edward may have introduced the Great Seal.[64] Given the massive loss of ephemeral documents such as writs (which were valid only in the shared lifetime of giver and

---

[60] Bishop and Chaplais, *Facsimiles*, p. xii.

[61] Ibid., no. 1 (plate 1).

[62] Sharpe, 'The Use of Writs', pp. 248, 284.

[63] Constable, 'Forged Letters', pp. 11–13, 33–4, and for an example of bearer authentication, *EER*, p. 43.

[64] Keynes, 'Use of Seals', p. 79.

recipient), it is nonetheless improbable that the writ-charter for Saint-Denis (of 1053 × 1057) happened to preserve the first ever example of its use, even if Edward introduced the Great Seal about that time. ASC E records that in 1050 Spearhafoc came to Archbishop Robert with the king's 'writ and seal' ('mid þæs cynges gewrite and insegle'), a reference to a sealed writ, which put him in possession of the see of London.[65] Again, however, we cannot be certain that this was a pendent seal rather than a signet. We must also consider the possibility of anachronism, since the text was composed at some point after 1052 by a partisan of Stigand, and his opposition to Archbishop Robert provided the author with an incentive to bolster the case for Spearhafoc's formal authorization. It is worth considering whether there might be a connexion between the Sovereign/ Eagles coin issue of the mid-1050s, in which the king – in a radical departure – is shown enthroned in majesty, holding a staff (or sceptre) and orb, and the introduction of the Great Seal, which also shows the king enthroned in majesty, holding an orb and sceptre. Perhaps the majesty portrait on that coinage was substituted for the bust to familiarize monied elites with the image on the Great Seal which they were increasingly seeing appended to writs in the shire court.

It is also worth considering whether the introduction of the Great Seal, perhaps c. 1050, gave fresh impetus to the use of writs, which might account for the abeyance of the diploma for the next several years. As previously observed, there is a break in the series of diplomas between 1050 and 1059, when the sequence recommences. During those years the king may have found it convenient to switch to the writ as his preferred executive instrument, newly authenticated as it was by his seal, though the complication here is that the writ was not an instrument (unlike the diploma) for establishing title in a fashion that was permanent and in principle inalienable. As such – at least, in the Edwardian phase of its evolution – the writ-charter could not replace the diploma, nor are there signs that it was meant to, for the writ-charter for Saint-Denis awaited the creation of a diploma by the diocesan Wulfwig. In the meantime – at least two years in that instance – it served to put the abbey in possession of Taynton in Oxfordshire. Writs permanently alienating royal prerogatives and possessions may have been necessary where it was thought the diploma might take a while to draw up, though for such cases Keynes's general point also applies: that the writ's audience was the shire court, whereas diplomas addressed posterity.[66] Last, we might consider whether the introduction of the Great Seal led to the designation of an official or unofficial seal-bearer. This may have been a still later evolution of the apparatus surrounding the issuing of writs. Slight support is given to the idea

[65] ASC E, 1048 [1051] (ed. Irvine, p. 80).
[66] S. Keynes, 'Charters and Writs', in Lapidge et al., ed., *The Blackwell Encyclopaedia*, 99–100, at p. 100.

by the reference to Regenbald as *sigillarius* ('seal-bearer') in S 1033, and by the privilege he seems to have enjoyed in receiving quasi-episcopal status; possibly his task was to prove title by confirming the genuineness of writs, with the help of the Great Seal – a hypothesis in accord with arguments proposed in Part II of this appendix.

APPENDIX 3

FOLCARD AND *PSYCHOMACHIA*

A peine un mot a-t-il surgi sous sa plume, qu'il évoque deux, trois idées différentes; et comme il ne veut rien sacrificier de cette richesse, la phrase devient touffue.

(A word has scarcely appeared under the pen when it begins to call up two or three different ideas; and, as the writer does not at all want to sacrifice any of this richness, the sentence becomes dense with meaning.)[1]

PART I: THE *VITA*

Psychomachia is a poem of nearly one thousand lines by the Christian Latin poet Prudentius (d. after 405). It begins with Abraham, 'who first showed us the way of believing' by his willingness to sacrifice Isaac. By his example, we learn, he 'has counselled us to war against the unbelieving peoples' and shown that we beget no 'child' that is pleasing to God until our battling spirit has overcome the monsters of the enslaved heart.[2] The 'child' in this sense means the soul purified by spiritual struggle and obedient to Christ. The 'childless' woman, allegorically, is the soul not yet made fertile by the eternal seed of the Spirit (*Psy*. Pref. 64–8). Every soul, however, is contested between forces of light and darkness. This is the meaning of *Psychomachia*: 'the soul's contest'. In the contest, which occupies the rest of the poem, Christ sends Virtues to fight against the monsters that are the Vices.[3] Both are personified. Faith is first on the battlefield, to fight a monster called Worship of the Old Gods (*Fidem Veterum Cultura Deorum*); then Chastity overcomes Lust, Patience defeats Wrath, and so on. As victory seems at hand, Concord starts to lead the triumphant Virtues home. But Discord sneaks up on her and injures her, whereupon Faith, her sister, comes to her aid, Discord is forced to reveal herself, and the Virtues tear her apart.[4] Faith, 'the queen of the Virtues', and

---

[1] A. Blaise, *Manuel du latin chrétien* (Strasbourg, 1955), p. 26 (*A Handbook of Christian Latin: Style, Morphology, and Syntax*, tr. G. C. Roti (Washington DC, 1994), p. 11).

[2] *Psy.* Pref. 1–14.

[3] *Psy.* 11–20.

[4] Ibid. 644–5 (Concord gives the signal), 672 (she is injured by a dagger thrust), 683 (Discord is the culprit), 708–14 (she reveals herself), 715–25 (she is torn apart). On Faith coming to her aid, ibid., 800–1.

her sister Concord, the 'greatest' of the Virtues, then deliver victory speeches.[5]

Concord addresses the Virtues first, and after congratulating them on the glory they have won by their struggle, she reminds them that the nation's peace depends on goodwill between its citizens and warns them, as soldiers, to be on guard lest discordant thought arise among their tenets: 'for a divided will creates disorder in our inmost nature, making two parties in a heart at variance' (*Psy.* 755–61). She then addresses the theme of hating one's brother. If one holds any hatred for one's brother, one's sacrifice to God is unacceptable. Faith now delivers her speech, explaining how she aided her sister, her partner in the fight against the monsters; and that after bloodshed they must follow Solomon's example and build a Temple for Christ to indwell. The two of them then lay out the soul's Temple, where Wisdom sits enthroned in the inner chamber (*Psy.* 823–40). Finally, the moral of the poem is summarized: 'Light and darkness with their opposing spirits are at war, and our twofold being inspires powers at variance with each other, until Christ Our God comes to our aid' (*Psy.* 908–10).

Like the Classical poems of Virgil, Ovid, Lucan, and Statius, Christian Latin poems by authors such as Caelius Sedulius, Arator, and Prudentius were classroom texts familiar to Folcard and his readers. What has not hitherto been noticed is the use of *Psychomachia* as a model for the struggle described in the *Vita Ædwardi*. This is clearest in Poem VI of the *Vita* (which Tyler numbers Poem V).[6] Poem VI is the poem treating the theme of civil war between brothers. It begins by presenting Harold and Tostig as two mighty oaks holding up the kingdom while peace unites them. But Ill Fortune menaces them (VI. 1–12). Discord then arrives and inflicts a hidden wound – an allusion to her stealth and hidden dagger (*Psy.* 689, 694).[7] Poem VI then proceeds for a while in apostrophe to Discord, deploring her crimes (VI. 13–25). At line 23, mention is made of Discord's seventh, most deadly crime, a reference to Proverbs 6:16–19, where it is identified as the crime of stirring up discord between brothers. The poet then turns to pagan poetry to show that Discord was abhorred even by the pagans. Here, Faith is introduced to the stage. We learn that even before Faith Herself (*Ipsa Fides*) came down to Earth, Error (i.e. pagan belief) knew that discord was a crime, while Concord tried to repair the damage Discord inflicted (VI. 25–37). A defence is being made of pagan poetry, for the truth to which it bears witness: 'Would Pagan Error

---

[5] Ibid. 750–822. Faith is queen of the Virtues at line 37; Concord the greatest ('maxima Virtus') at 689.

[6] Poem VI appears in the *Vita* at pp. 58/8–60/1. Tyler's numbering does not include the introductory and concluding poetic dialogues between the poet and his muse. For her comments on the poem, see *England in Europe*, pp. 171–90.

[7] *Psy.* 689: 'sicam sub ueste tegit'; 694: 'quae manus hic inimica latet . . .?' ('what enemy hand lurks here?').

without fact declare thus?' (VI. 43). Finally, the poet invokes the sister powers who overcome Discord and conclude the combat in *Psychomachia*. First, he prays to 'the guardian spirit, Holy Faith' ('deifica custos, Sancta Fides'); then he prays to 'mother, Holy Concord' ('mater, Concordia Sancta') for peace lest the brothers become stubble for the eternal fire (VI. 48–56). As Concord explains in her speech in *Psychomachia*, hatred between brothers is an unacceptable offering of the soul, whereas peace is the best offering to God (*Psy.* 772–4, 784–6).

The prayer that concludes Poem VI, invoking Faith and Concord, is summoning the sisters who lead the Virtues to victory in *Psychomachia* after they defeat Discord, who is identified in both poems as discord between brothers. Folcard, like Prudentius, personifies Virtues and Vices. He also refers us back to the opening line of *Psychomachia* by addressing Faith as 'the first way of salvation' ('uia prima salutis': VI. 51). For this must be an allusion to Abraham showing us 'the first way of believing' ('prima credendi uia': *Psy.* Pref. 1). That 'way of believing' was faith in God, hence the address to Faith in similar terms. In eleventh-century classrooms, *Psychomachia* was read with prosodic, lexical, grammatical, syntactical, and commentary glosses.[8] Studying the lexical and commentary glosses lets us see how Folcard was using *Psychomachia* for reference points. The gloss to *Psy.* Pref. 2 notes that Abraham's seed, Isaac, is the seed of Christ.[9] His readiness to sacrifice his son earns him the blessing of becoming the father of many. In *Psy.* Pref. 5, Isaac is a 'pledge' (*pignus*), since he is the son God promised – a pledge of His faithfulness. The gloss to *Psy.* Pref. 5 explains that children are called pledges because the hope of posterity is placed in them ('pignora filii nuncupatur, eo quod in eis futurae posteritatis spes habeatur').[10] The noun *proles* (offspring/ progeny) is also used early in *Psychomachia* to describe the 'child' who is allegorically the progeny of the soul. *Psy.* Pref. 11 declares that we can beget no progeny pleasing to God ('prolem . . . Deo placentem') without having triumphed in the soul's contest.

This leads us to the next poem, Poem VII (Tyler's Poem VI), where we might expect (after the prayer to Faith and Concord against Discord at the end of VI) to find reference to the soul's progeny.[11] Sure enough, the poem begins with an apostrophe to the Virgin Mary, hailing her for

---

[8] G. R. Wieland, *The Latin Glosses on Arator and Prudentius, in Cambridge University Library MS Gg 5. 35* (Toronto, 1983). Prudentius became a very popular classroom author in England during the tenth century: J. D. A. Ogilvy, *Books Known to the English, 597–1066* (Cambridge, MA, 1967), pp. 10, 231.

[9] S. O'Sullivan, *Early Medieval Glosses on Prudentius' Psychomachia: The Weitz Tradition*, Mittellateinische Studien und Texte, ed. P. G. Schmidt, Bd 31 (Leiden, 2004), p. 141: 'seminis = Christ uel Isaac'; Wieland, *Latin Glosses*, p. 10: 'seminis: illius per quod nasciturus erat Christus' (from BL, Cotton Cleopatra C viii (*s.* xi)). There were also standard illustrations as a visual aid to interpretation.

[10] O'Sullivan, *Early Medieval Glosses*, p. 142.

[11] Poem VII: *Vita*, pp. 72/3–4/5.

bearing 'blessed offspring' ('prolem ... beatam': VII. 1). Her child is of course Christ – the seed of Abraham – but her progeny is Christ's faithful. Where Prudentius refers to the Spirit making a childless soul fertile by the eternal seed, readers would naturally think of the insemination of the Virgin with Abraham's seed, Christ (*Psy.* Pref. 64–7). Indeed, the relevant lines from *Psychomachia* use two key words – *semen* (seed) and *serus* (late) – used at the start of Poem VII: ('Abram beati seminis serus Pater': 'Abram, late in life, the father of a blessed progeny': *Psy.* Pref. 2). In Poem VII, the 'celebrated mother' bearing blessed offspring is Edith's newly re-founded nunnery at Wilton, which was dedicated to the Virgin Mary and is person-ified and apostrophized as Mary in the poem. At line 11 we learn that her (spiritual) progeny (*proles*) will number a hundred thousand – a rhetorical token of infinity (VII. 11, cf. Gen. 22:17–18). The personification of Wilton as Mary is important because, elsewhere in the *Vita*, Folcard employs slip-page to present Edith as Mary and as Concord.[12] At the end of the previous poem, Poem VI, Concord is apostrophized as 'mother Concord', equating her with mother Mary, whose triumph in the soul's contest is proclaimed by the *proles* she bears at the beginning of Poem VII.

Folcard was interested in the double meaning of *pignus* as 'child' and as 'hope of future posterity', as developed in the *Psychomachian* gloss. He plays upon it in the *Life* of St Bertin. There he tells us that Bertin was born of 'a heroic line' ('generosa progenitorum stirpe') and that the child (*pignus*) was carefully reared, so that he became 'a great one in the Lord' (with an implied reference back to *pignus*, but evidently no longer to a child but rather to a hope of future posterity, for Bertin went on to win many souls for Christ).[13] The play on the double meaning of *pignus* is clearer in the *Vita*'s Poem III (Tyler's Poem II).[14] The poem begins by acclaiming Earl Godwine, who is blessed with offspring ('prole ... beatus': III. 1). As we have seen, the theme is picked up later in Poem VII (cf. 'prolem ... beatam': VII. 1). Godwine's four children (abl. *natis*) are pledges of hope for England's peace ('his quattuor natis dans Anglis pignora pacis': III. 1–2). Leaving aside whether Godwine's four offspring should be identified literally as four of his children or allegorically as the four rivers of paradise, signifying the hope of his progeny generally, we read in this poem that all will be well if they keep the pact of peace ('federe seruato': III. 24), but that Wicked Envy (*Liuor Iniquus*) threatens to break it, and that if such a thing occurs Primordial Chaos (*Antiquumque Chaos*) will again capture the world

---

[12] E. Tyler, 'The *Vita Ædwardi*: The Politics of Poetry at Wilton Abbey', *ANS* 31 (2009), 135–56, pp. 146–7; eadem, *England in Europe*, p. 155; cf. pp. 208–12.

[13] Folcard, *Vita s. Bertini*: PL 147, cols 1089–98, at col. 1089: 'Hic itaque suis pignus admodum dilectus progenitoribus nutriebatur diligenter infantulus, uti tantus in Domino post futurus' ('And so this very dear child was carefully raised by his parents, so that he became a great [*pignus*] in the Lord afterwards'). *Infantulus* here is an example of a noun used as an adjective: cf. Blaise, *Handbook*, p. 7 (§12, 2.4).

[14] Poem III: *Vita*, pp. 26/7–8/9. For Tyler's discussion, see *England in Europe*, pp. 160–6.

(III. 35). Though the final observation envisages a return to the shapeless-ness and darkness preceding the world's creation – the chaos described by Ovid at the beginning of *Metamorphoses* – the poem may also be antici-pating Poem VI, where Godwine's offspring Harold and Tostig, initially united in peace ('unito federe pacis': VI. 3, echoing the 'federe' of III. 24), are attacked by Discord.

The morphing of Envy, unchecked, into Discord accords with the Ovidian backdrop, in which shape-shifting monsters emerge from primor-dial chaos. As in *Psychomachia*, Virtues have to contend with those monsters. In Poem VI, Harold and Tostig combat them, aided by Faith and by Concord (who is Edith and Mary). At the end of the poem, the prayer for their deliverance from the flames of hell seems to have been effective, for in the next poem Edith/ Mary is promised an infinite progeny after building the temple of her soul (Wilton), which the devil's flames were unable to destroy.[15] The next and final poem, however, Poem VIII, reveals what has become of the earthly progeny begotten of Godwine.[16] Inimical Deceit (*Fraus* – a monster from *Psychomachia*) has tricked the poet and stolen his subject matter.[17] He had hoped to weave a glittering account of the brothers, as the streams of Paradise, but Hostile Sin (*Hostile Nefas*: VIII. 15) is the burning torrent engulfing their hearts. Envy had turned into Discord, and – in another Prudentian conceit – Discord has given rise to Sin.[18] History's course of events (personified in Clio) no longer recalls the streams of Paradise, but Infernal Chaos (*Infernale Chaos*: VIII. 21–2), the monster anticipated in Poem III, where she appears as Ancient Chaos (*Antiquumque Chaos*: III. 35). The poet had intended to tell of a holy progeny ('sanctam . . . progeniem': VIII. 24), but now he sings of a stock born to sudden death ('stirps, nata neci subite': VIIII. 26–7). The use here of *stirps* and *nata* recalls the introduction of Godwine's progeny at the start of Poem III ('stirpe beatus auita, his quattuor natis': III. 1–2). That progeny is now consumed by the fire of its self-destructive sin.

When Faith and Concord, at the end of *Psychomachia*, construct a new temple, they adorn it with precious jewels. This may inform our reading of the prose passage of the *Vita* where Edith adorns Edward with gems.[19] She is, by analogy, adorning her soul. In Poem VIII, Deceit (*Fraus*) has robbed the poet of the ornaments he planned to weave into his account of the brothers. Harold, Tostig, and perhaps other offspring have fallen in the contest of the soul. Slain by Vices, they lie among the 'dead' at the beginning of Poem VIII (VIII. 1–2). Edith, however, receives God's promise of an infi-nite blessed progeny (Poem VII) in the children begotten of Wilton – many

---

[15] *Vita*, pp. 72/3.

[16] Poem VIII: *Vita*, pp. 84/5–90/1.

[17] VIII. 6; cf. *Psy.* 258–9: 'Fraus . . . furtim'.

[18] Cf. Lapidge, 'A Stoic Metaphor', p. 829, citing Prudentius, *Hamartigenia*, 236–46.

[19] *Vita*, pp. 22/3–24/5.

future generations of nuns; and Edward triumphs in the contest too. It is important to note that the depiction of Edith/ Mary as Concord building the temple that is Wilton finds its parallel in Edward's construction of Westminster. Edward is likened twice to Solomon – the builder of the First Temple; and Westminster is referred to as a temple and described with similar attention to detail as found in the description of the First Temple, and of the temple constructed by Faith and Concord at the end of *Pyschomachia*.[20] Poem I recalls that Solomon signifies peace, so it follows that Edward/ Solomon's temple is the temple of peace – the peace that pervades his reign, which Concord/ Edith declares to be the best offering to God. The fact that Solomon signified peace and was allowed to build the Temple for having no blood on his hands is found in the commentary glosses.[21]

After Concord's speech on the subject of preserving peace by unity, Faith speaks of the need to build a purified temple that Christ may indwell. This, she says, is the task Solomon set on foot.[22] When Edward is likened to peaceful Solomon, whose reign followed David's wars (in Poem I), the reference is to Faith's speech (*Psy.* 805–6).[23] Edward not only builds the temple of peace; he stands for Faith, with the miracles that ensue. Edward is Faith. Edith is Concord. Both build their temples (Wilton and Westminster). There Wisdom is enshrined, and it is Edith's love of wisdom that inspires her in the soul's contest – she appears as Lady Philosophy, the lover of wisdom as personified by Boethius.[24] In *Psychomachia*, Abraham points the way to Faith; and his story in Genesis begins with a promise of offspring (Gen. 12:2). In the *Vita*, however, in the vision granted to a holy bishop, St Peter declares that Edward will lead a chaste life; that God has already provided for an heir to succeed him.[25] We are meant to infer that Edward, like Abraham, trusted to God to furnish

[20] Ibid., pp. 6/7, 18/19, 68/9.

[21] *Psy.* 755, 785–7. Isidore of Seville declared that Solomon signified peace, and his etymology found its way into the commentary gloss on Arator, which likened Solomon to Christ also: Wieland, *Latin Glosses*, p. 176: 'pacificum – Salomon pacificus interpretatur et quis pacificus nisi Christus'. The commentary on *Psychomachia* remarks (*Psy.* 806): 'Dauid rex uoluit aedificare templum Domino sed quia uir sanguinii erat, id est bellicosus a Domino prohibetur est . . . Filius ergo eius id est Salomon qui interpretatur pacificus eo quod in diebus suis pacem habuit adeo ut et reges munera transmitterent, templum Domino in Ierusalem construxit' ('King David wished to build a temple to the Lord, but because he was a bloody man, or rather a warlike man, the Lord forbade it him. . . . His son, i.e. Solomon, who signifies peace because he enjoyed peace in his reign, to the extent that kings sent him gifts, built a temple to the Lord in Jerusalem'): J. M. Burnam, *Commentaire anonyme sur Prudence, d'après le manuscrit 413 de Valenciennes* (Paris, 1910), p. 113 (translation mine).

[22] *Psy.* 803–8.

[23] Compare *Psy.* 805–6 ('regni quod tandem pacifer heres/ belligeri armatae successor inermus . . . Solomon': 'the peaceful successor to a warlike throne, the unarmed successor to an armed court') and *Vita*, p. 6 ('ut post bella David pax succedens Salomonis': 'how after David's wars came Solomon's peace').

[24] Tyler, *England in Europe*, pp. 147–9.

[25] *Vita*, pp. 14/15.

his progeny. The theme is later pursued in Virgilian forays into whether Edward is a new Æneas, siring new Trojans.

In these forays in Poem II (Tyler's Poem I), Tyler believed that phrases borrowed from the *Æneid* take on a sinister meaning. Godwine, soon to be cast as the founder of a progeny himself (Poem III) arrives, like the Greeks, 'bearing gifts' ('dona ferentes') and with a dragon on his sails – a snake that links him to Pyrrhus and the destruction of Troy.[26] Tyler once believed the tags were insignificant – convenient formulae that fitted into a hexameter and suited the Virgilian theme of this part of the poem.[27] Though she later changed her mind, it is hard to see what bearing they might have on our interpretation of the text.[28] Godwine is not a menacing figure. He is praised throughout the work, and he remains loyal to the king when monsters from *Psychomachia* attack. In Poem V, Deceit and Envy ('Fraudem . . . Liuor': V. 16) threaten him, but he abhors the temptation of regicide (V. 42–3) and restores peace to the realm.[29] The menace in Poem III comes from Robert of Jumièges – a Scylla sitting at the edge of Charybdis, muddying the font of Paradise (i.e. Godwine) and the clear streams flowing forth, which Poem VIII identifies as 'the boys of the royal line'.[30] The two parts cum factions, one reaching the heavens, the other plunging to Hades, are Godwine's party and Robert's. Such is the fundamental division of the warring soul of *Psychomachia*. The heavenward part tends the hope of the soul's progeny.

---

[26] Tyler, 'Politics of Poetry'; *England in Europe*, p. 154. The *ore trisulcis* combination is not, however, rare.

[27] E. M. Tyler, '"When Wings Incarnadine with Gold are Spread": The *Vita Ædwardi Regis* and the Display of Treasure at the Court of Edward the Confessor', in eadem, ed., *Treasure in the Medieval West* (York, 2000), 83–107, at p. 96, on finding applied to Godwine the turn of phrase Virgil employed of Greeks bearing gifts ('dona ferentes'): 'Should we see Godwine as a Pyrrhus figure?' 'No', says Tyler, 'we should attribute these allusions, as well as the others . . . to the general Vergilian framework.'

[28] Tyler, 'Politics of Poetry', p. 144: 'Should we see Godwine as a Pyrrhus figure?' This time the answer is 'yes'. Tyler would have us read the *Vita* as hostile to Godwine: *England in Europe*, p. 187: 'it can in no way be read as a Godwinist account' (cf. p. 137). Cf. *Vita*, pp. 30/1 (sympathy for Godwine who is likened to Christ, as sinless but suffering earthly punishment; like Joseph); pp. 38/9 (Godwine is a man of God – the stream of Paradise); pp. 40/1 (he is father to the English; for the people his flight was a disaster and 'the ruin of the English'; the 'destruction of the country'); pp. 42/3 (he is 'loyal and devoted to God' and would rather die than act against the king); pp. 46/7 (he spares God's anointed, and is another David; he is 'of happy memory'). It is hard to find anything negative about Godwine unless one counts two common tags from the *Æneid*.

[29] *Vita*, pp. 44/5–46/7.

[30] VIII. 9: 'pueros, regum de stirpe . . . Elisii quattuor fluminibus similes' (*Vita*, p. 84). The monster in Poem III, *inimica uoratrix*, recalls the Charybdis of Prudentius, *Cathamerinon*, VI. 105–11, which 'imam petit gehennam' (cf. III. 17: 'profunda petit'). *Cathamerinon*, VI is referenced in Poem VI (below). The riddling image is explained at the beginning of Poem IV (IV. 2–4: *Vita*, p. 39), where we learn that Godwine, the font of Paradise, has been muddied by Scylla's (i.e. Robert's) poison. Scylla and Charybdis often morphed into each other in this way.

The darker part devours its own parent.[31] The pact the brothers must keep, to avoid disaster, as stated in Poem III ('federe seruato') and Poem VI ('federe pacis'), is the holy pact ('sacro federe') sworn by Faith and Concord in sisterly love, to triumph over the Vices.[32] It is the love which Envy/ Discord threatens later to destroy (VI. 23–4) – the very bond that binds the cosmos.[33]

Near the beginning of the *Vita*, we learn that God cut down Cnut's stock ('eius totam stirpem ille . . . succidit') because he had preserved among his seed one to whom he planned to give the sceptre ('quia in eius semine reseruauit, cui Anglia regni annuerat uirgam': *Vita*, p. 10). This is a reference to Edward as Wisdom, who sits enthroned in Christ's temple at the end of *Psychomachia*, holding a sceptre. Wisdom's sceptre is described as 'a living rod of green wood; severed from its stock ("stirpe recisum"), it draws no nurture from moist earthly soil, yet puts forth perfect foliage and with blooms of blood-red roses intermingles white lilies that never droop on withering stems' (*Psy.* 879–83). After cutting down Cnut's line, God shows the English a flower kept from the stock of their ancient kings ('de antiquorum regum stirpe seruatum florem ostendit': *Vita*, p. 12), and He gives them strength of mind to seek the flower for their kingdom as well as their salvation. Then comes the vision in which St Peter tells Edward (the flower) that God will provide a king of His choosing to succeed him (*Vita*, p. 14). At the end of the *Vita*, in the dying Edward's vision, the theme is resumed in the green tree: 'when a green tree, if cut down in the middle of its trunk, and the part cut off carried the space of three furlongs from the stock, shall be joined again to its trunk, by itself and without the hand of man or any sort of stake, and begin once more to push leaves and bear fruit from the old love of its uniting sap, then first can a remission of these great sins be hoped for'.[34] We should consider this severed, flowering tree in relation to Wisdom's severed, flowering sceptre at the end of *Psychomachia*: 'the sceptre that was prefigured by the flowering rod that Aaron carried, which, pushing buds out of its dry bark, unfolded a tender grace with burgeoning hope, and the parched twig suddenly swelled into new fruits' (*Psy.* 884–7).

Here we may recall the tree in Poem III, into which the four streams of Paradise flow. One part of the soul reaches to heaven, tending the hope of its progeny ('spemque sui generis nido fouet', III. 16; cf. 'explicuit tenerum

---

[31] Poem III, pp. 26/7.

[32] *Psy.* 734–5: 'hunc sincera Fides simul et Concordia, sacro/ foedere iuratae Christi sub amore sorores' ('honest Faith and, with her, Concord, sisters sworn in holy alliance in the love of Christ').

[33] Lapidge, 'A Stoic Metaphor', pp. 834–6 (with reference to Boethius).

[34] *Vita*, p. 118/19: 'si arbor uiridis a medio sui succidatur corpore, at pars abscisa trium iugerum spatio a suo deportetur stipite, cum per se et absque humana manu uel quouis amminiculo suo connectetur trunco, ceperitque denuo uirescere, et fructificare ex coales-centis sui amore pristino, tunc primum tantorum malorum sperari remissio'.

spe pubescente decorem': *Psy.* 886); the other part tears at the trunk. The tree in this poem, and in the vision of the green tree, is the kingdom of the English, and it is the soul, both of which are contested by light and dark powers. In the vision, we discover that the tree has finally been ruptured. Forgiveness and healing can only come when the kingdom/ soul is restored to its pristine unity. A clue as to how this may yet happen is found in the allusion to Aaron's rod in *Psychomachia*, for in the Book of Numbers, God orders the twelve tribes of Israel each to place a rod in the Tabernacle, with the leader's name on the rod of each tribe. His intention in this is to make known whom he favoured to lead and bear the sins of the people. Aaron's rod was the one that flowered, and by this sign God's will was made known.[35]

The other reference point is Lucan's *Pharsalia*, the epic telling of the civil wars fought between Caesar and Pompey. In Book V, the senators who had refused to go over to Caesar assemble and vote to place Pompey in charge of Rome: 'A reign of uninterrupted peace,' the senators agree, 'had made us grow ignorant of what civil war implied, and the sudden fury of revolt consequently scattered us in all directions. Yet behold us again – lopped limbs, as it were magically assembling and being reunited to the parent trunk.'[36] In both sources, that is, *Psychomachia* and *Pharsalia*, the model Folcard deploys is of the nation coming together to choose a new leader who will unite them under God. Harold is dead, we must understand, and the Normans are 'devils' (*Vita*, pp. 116/17) sent by the Lord to punish the English for their sins. It is possible, however, that the longed-for ruler is Edgar Ætheling.

After relaying the vision and providing for Edith and the realm, Edward reposes in death and displays in his countenance the glory of a soul departing to God. Like Wisdom's sceptre, his face blooms with roses intermingled with lilies ('caro faciei ut rosa ruberet, subiecta barba ut lilium canderet': *Vita*, p. 124/ 'tum sanguine tinctis/ intertexta rosis candentia lilia miscet': *Psy.* 881–2). The bloom of Christ's wisdom is on his face. His body is borne to the completed Westminster abbey, which signifies the temple of his soul. His death and the glorification of his soul coincide with its completion. Miracles at his tomb prove that he dwells with God in heaven (*Vita*, p. 126). He has triumphed in the contest.

PART II: *VIGOR*

The chronicle of Hariulf of Saint-Riquier, in the part completed in 1088, preserves under the name 'Folcard' a poem of twenty-seven hexameters on St Vigor, an early bishop and evangelist of Bayeux.[37] Saint-Riquier claimed to possess the bulk of Vigor's relics, and the narrative into which

---

[35] Num. 17:6–8.

[36] Lucan, *Pharsalia*, v. 35–7: 'ignaros scelerum longaque in pace quietos/ bellorum primus sparsit furor: omnia rursus/ membra loco redeunt' (tr. R. Graves, p. 84).

[37] *Chronique*, ed. Lot, p. 227 (*BHL* 8614).

the poem is inserted describes the circumstances that prompted Abbot Gervin II (1045–75) to upgrade the status of the saint's feast. In doing so, he commissioned a new reliquary, which took a few years to construct; and when it was completed, he gathered ecclesiastical dignitaries to celebrate the translation of Vigor's remains into the new shrine.[38] Apart from what may seem to be implied by its context, nothing is said about the poem, the reason for its composition, or the Folcard who wrote it. To an extent, however, the poem speaks for itself. As now, Vigor was known from his legendary early eleventh-century *Life*, which tells of his birth in Arras, departure to preach, repeated banishment of an enormous fire-breathing snake, his acquisition of territories (including Cerisy) from grateful lords as a result; his promotion to the bishopric of Bayeux, his conversion of the idol-worshippers of Mount Phanus (renamed Mount Chrismat) at Bayeux, his construction of a monastery on the Mount, and his death and burial there.[39]

Below, I provide the text and a translation of the first six lines of the poem by 'Folcard':

Festa dies patris rutilat celebranda Vigoris	The day dawns of our worshipful father Vigor,
Patrem Baiocas, quem fratrem gaudet Atrebas	Whom Bayeux celebrates as a father, Arras as a brother.
Huius grata Deo genitrix, generosa uirago	His mother, pleasing to God, a noble heroine,
Pignore de tanto capit assertore superno	Wins, by a relic of heaven's great champion,
Natum, quem gestat; benedixit Diua Potestas	A son, whom she bears;[40] whom Divine Power blessed
Sacrauitque sibi, cuncto sacrauit et orbi.	And consecrated to Herself, and consecrated to the whole world.

---

[38] Ibid., pp. 225–9.

[39] *De sancto Vigore episcopo Baiocensi in Gallia*, in *Acta SS.*, Nov., I (1 Nov.), 297–304. On the context and likely date of composition (*c.* 1030–45), see J. Howe, 'The Date of the "Life" of St. Vigor of Bayeux', *AB* 102 (1984), 302–12; and S. K. Herrick, *Imagining the Sacred Past: Hagiography and Power in Early Normandy* (Cambridge, MA, 2007), pp. 38–44, 74–93.

[40] Lewis and Short: *Capio*, definition I. 1. B, 'to win', with the ablative of means. Here the object is *natum*, and the ablative of means is *pignore* (relic/ pledge). http://www.perseus.tufts.edu/hopper/text?doc=Perseus%3Atext%3A1999.04.0059%3Aentry%3Dcapio1 (accessed 1 November 2019).

Several aspects of those opening lines are important. First is the use of personification, including the personified Bayeux, who celebrates her 'father' Vigor. Second is the slippage between Bayeux and the Virgin Mary. This is understandable, given that Bayeux cathedral was dedicated to the Virgin, who could in that sense personify Bayeux. But there is much artistry in the slippage. It is suggested initially by the words 'grata Deo genitrix' ('mother pleasing to God'), which immediately prompt the reader to think of the Blessed Virgin. The epithet that follows, however, 'generosa uirago', has been adapted for Bayeux. Its source is a Responsory in the Mass for the feast of the Conception: 'Abrahae stirpe generosa uirgo prodit gloriosa quae nullius per exemplum se sacrauit Deo templum'.[41] The poet's audience, after hearing 'grata Deo genitrix', would expect the word *uirgo* to follow *generosa*, but instead we have *uirago* ('heroine') – an epithet more suited to a city personified in the Classical tradition (cf. Britannia). The play on *uirgo/ uirago* (paronomasia) is a joke, and we can be confident it is no transcription error because the same joke appears in the *Vita Ædwardi*. There we come upon Edith hurrying to finish Wilton, her temple: 'Ad cuius dedicationem propere agendam moras non patitur benedicta uirago' ('In having a speedy dedication performed the blessed heroine would suffer no delay').[42] After *benedicta* we might wonder whether the subject is the Blessed Virgin, since it is her temple as well as Edith's; but the use of *uirago* ('heroine') points to Edith. The Responsory explains that the peerless virgin consecrated herself to God as a living temple for Him to indwell. Mary/ Edith are hurrying to consecrate herself/ themselves as a temple of the soul. The slippage between Mary and Edith, heralded by a play on *uirgo/ uirago* which alludes to this Responsory from the Marian Mass, is identical to the slippage between Mary and Bayeux, heralded by a play on *uirgo/ uirago* which alludes to the same Marian Responsory.

Such a complex play is iron-clad evidence that the same mind was at work on the *Vita* and the *Vigor* poem. Folcard might as well have signed his name on both. It is an author's personal joke, tied up in an interlace of word-play and allusions that no one else could have thought to replicate. The parallels, however, do not end there. We should also examine the slippage in both between the Virgin and her apostrophized church. Wilton, in Poem VII, is addressed as the Virgin, as 'inclita mater' ('celebrated mother': VII. 1). Bayeux likewise is addressed as the Virgin, as

[41] 'The noble virgin conceives [a child] from the glorious stock of Abraham; the peerless [woman] consecrated herself as a [living] temple to God': D. Lacoste (Project Manager and Principal Researcher) and J. Koláček (Web Developer), *Cantus: A Database for Latin Ecclesiastical Chant – Inventories of Chant Sources*, available from http://cantus.uwaterloo.ca/ (accessed 16 May 2018), Can 600016. The Feasts of the Conception and Presentation were introduced to England, possibly via Winchester, *c*. 1030: M. Clayton, *The Cult of the Virgin Mary in Anglo-Saxon England* (New York, 1990; new edn, Cambridge, 2010), pp. 42–7.

[42] *Vita*, p. 72.

'grata Deo genitrix' ('mother pleasing to God': *Vigor*, 3). We then have the – by now familiar – play on the word *pignus*. In the Vigor poem, *pignus* assumes its other meaning, 'relic'.[43] Folcard is describing an occasion when Bayeux obtained a relic of Vigor. As already noted, however, *pignus* also meant a child or a son. By obtaining a relic, Bayeux had won a son (*natum*). The use of *natus* in association with *pignus* to elicit multiple meanings is seen in the *Vita*, Poem III ('his quattuor natis dans Anglis pignora pacis': III. 2). In *Vigor*, the play effects slippage between Vigor, son of Bayeux, and Christ, son of Mary – which is appropriate, given the prior slippage between Mary and Bayeux.

The slippage of course extends to the verb *gesto* (bears). Just as Bayeux now 'bears' the relic in a celebratory procession, so Mary bears – in her womb – her son. We then encounter the personified female agency Divine Power, who has consecrated that son, Vigor/ Christ, to herself and to the whole world. This is a reference to Mary's Presentation of the infant Jesus at the Temple, but also to her offering of herself as a temple to God, because the 'sacrauitque sibi' of the Vigor poem (*Vigor*, 6) recalls the 'se sacrauit' of the Responsory in which Mary consecrated herself to the divine power.[44] The Responsory, as we have seen, is drawn into play three lines earlier (*Vigor*, 3) with paronomasia on 'generosa uirgo/ uirago'. It should be noted, this is not the only antiphon Folcard deploys to herald slippage between his heroine/s and the Virgin. In the preface to his *Life* of St John of Beverley, he explains that a woman, 'like the star of the sea' ('uelut maris stella'), rescued him from allegorical shipwreck, and that the woman was the queen.[45] 'Aue maris stella' ('Hail [Mary], star of the sea'), is of course a Responsory associated with the feasts of the Conception and the Annunciation.[46] Folcard's habit of effecting slippage by using Responsories associated with the Conception was not limited to one Responsory. In liturgical use, Responsories were begun by the cantor and taken up by the choir. To adapt or alter a Responsory was to tease one's audience in a playful manner that drew their attention to the conceit. We are reminded of the opening of Bertin's *Life*, where he is said to have been born of a 'generosa ... stirpe'.[47] This is another reference to the Responsory 'Abrahae stirpe generosa uirgo' and precedes a play upon the multiple meanings of *pignus*, such as we found in the *Vita* and the *Vigor* poem.[48]

---

[43] As used by Folcard, e.g. in *Vita s. Bertini*, col. 1096C: 'et numero pignerum sanctorum'.

[44] Can 600016. The Feast of the Presentation was introduced to England about the same time as the Feast of the Conception: Clayton, *Cult of the Virgin*, pp. 42–7. Liturgical usages for the relevant feasts are attested in twelfth-century and later manuscripts.

[45] *Vita s. Iohannis Beuerlacensis* (*BHL* 4339), in *Historians*, ed. Raine, I, 239–60, at p. 240.

[46] Can 008272.

[47] Folcard, *Vita s. Bertini*, col. 1089: 'generosa ... stirpe ... Hic itaque suis pignus ...'.

[48] Can 600016, and see above, pp. 284, 285.

With all those references, in the first seven lines of *Vigor*, to *pignora nata*, the Virgin bearing a child, and a Responsory associating her with Abraham's stock ('Abrahae stirpe'), we could be forgiven for thinking we might be back in the world of *Psychomachia*. Yet at line 14 we learn that Vigor became an exile from his native land, 'like the patriarch' ('Fiat ut a patria peregrinus cum patriarcha'). Word-play on *patria/ patriarcha* aside, this is a reference to the *Life* of Vigor, which states that its protagonist emulated the blessed patriarch Abraham, to whom it was said: 'Leave your country, and your kindred, and your father's house . . . and I will make of you a great nation.'[49] Vigor sets out, sowing (i.e. preaching) the word. At line 15, he is called *seminiuerbius* ('word-sowing'). He has just been likened to Abraham, so it is well to remember that Abraham's seed ('beati seminis': *Psy*. Pref. 2) is Christ.[50] Christ is also the Word, so by sowing the word, Vigor sowed Abraham's seed and expected offspring in the form of converts to Christ. The verses remind us of a reference to Mary in Poem VII's address to her, '[God's] heavenly seed [is] implanted in your womb' ('cuius fusa tua sata celica germen in aluo': VII. 8). This is not dissimilar to the Vigor poem's treatment of the 'word-sower', wending his way towards the people 'placed in his bosom by heaven' ('tendens ad populam sibi caelitus insinuatum': *Vigor*, 16). The joke is that they will be his progeny. Vigor is sowing the seed (Christ/ the W/word) to the seed already placed in his bosom by God.

As Vigor reaches Bayeux, the poet remarks that he is going there to preach to those held captive by Wicked Error ('Hanc adit ut doceat quos impius Error habebat': *Vigor*, 18). Error per se is not one of the personified Vices in *Psychomachia*. She is closest to Worship of the Old Gods (*Fidem Veterum Cultura Deorum*), who is the first of the Vices to challenge Faith. Error may simply be Folcard's avatar of that monster, whose name is too long for convenient use in a hexameter. We met her before in Poem VI as Error and Pagan Error (*Gentilis . . . Error*: VI, 30, 43), and her implied opposition to Faith Herself (*Ipsa Fides*: VI, 28–30) identifies her as Worship of the Old Gods, who stands against Faith in *Psychomachia* (*Psy*. 28–9). Yet it is not Vigor ('Christi . . . alumnum': *Vigor*, 19) but the Virtues sent by Christ ('Gratia Virtutum': *Vigor*, 19) who are going forth to confront Error. This is a reference to *Psychomachia* 11–20, where Christ's followers are told that Christ will aid them by sending the Virtues against the monsters. The first monster is Worship of the Old Gods, who in the Vigor poem appears as Wicked Error.[51] The contest of the soul has begun. Victory in this contest should result in blessed progeny, and sure enough the pagan inhabitants submit to baptism, and Vigor begets a progeny for God

---

[49] *De s. Vigore*, p. 298E; cf. Gen. 12:1–2.

[50] O'Sullivan, *Early Medieval Glosses*, p. 141.

[51] *Psy*. 29. In the commentary gloss, she is Idolatry (*Idolatria*): Burnam, *Commentaire*, p. 89; cf. Gg. 5. 35, f. 149v: 'ignara Idolatria'.

through the holy font of baptism ('Hancque Deo prolem per sacri fontis honorem,/ Sancte Vigor, generas': *Vigor*, 24–5). The *proles* he begets 'for God' is evidently the progeny pleasing to God ('prolem . . . Deo placentem') from *Psychomachia* line 11. And it is akin to the blessed progeny ('prolem . . . beatam') born of Wilton/ Mary/ Edith at the start of Poem VII (VII. 1). Just as Wilton/ Mary/ Edith is apostrophized and congratulated on her *prolem*, so Vigor/ Christ is apostrophized and congratulated on the same. Compare: 'Inclita mater, aue, prolem . . . beatam . . . concipies' (VII. 1–2) and 'Deo prolem . . . Sancte Vigor, generas' (*Vigor*, 24–5).

In Poem VI, the contest of the soul concludes, as we have seen, with a prayerful petition to the sisters Faith and Concord to rescue the brothers, Harold and Tostig, from eternal fire (VI. 48–56). The Vigor poem likewise concludes with a prayer to Vigor to rescue us – the petitioners – from the eternal flames. It even shares the 'ne . . .' clause with Poem VI, line 54. Compare 'ne de pignore regali seu stirpe fideli/ ignis perpetuam . . . hostis/ collegisse suis incendia longa fauillis' (VI. 54–6) and 'Flammarum domitor, qui mundi comprimis ignis, ne nos exurant, flammas compesce gehennae' (*Vigor*, 26–7). The prayer to Vigor as the Tamer of Flames refers to his taming of the fire-breathing serpent.[52] Its verb 'exuro' is used in the *Life* of Vigor to describe how the serpent burned people with its fiery breath ('exurit flatu suo').[53] The hostile fire (*ignis*) is in the prayer in Poem VI and the Vigor prayer. In both prayers, the poet beseeches the baptized progeny's deliverance from the eternal flames (cf. 'lotis baptismate': VI. 49).[54] The prayer at the end of Poem VI asks Faith to inflict the sign of the cross upon the enemy ('infer signa crucis': VI. 50). It then asks, 'let Erinys be driven into hell' ('Herebique fugetur Erynis': VI. 50). Erinys is a monster in *Psychomachia*, but in the gloss, we learn that she is the goddess of conflict; and in *Excidium Troiae*, she is named as Discord.[55] Faith is therefore summoned to banish Discord, as in *Psychomachia*.

Not only are the parallels between Poem VI and the Vigor poem striking; it is clear that Folcard employed *Psychomachia* as a framework for both. By apostrophizing the Virgin (as Bayeux), moreover, and by heralding Vigor as 'Father' – his relationship to Bayeux; and by placing himself at the end of the poem as a petitioner among the offspring praying to Bayeux for deliverance, Folcard indicates that the poem was written for

---

[52] *De s. Vigore*, p. 300E.

[53] Ibid.

[54] The tag is from Arator, *De actibus apostolorum*, I. 849 ('quicquid baptismate lotis'), I. 864 ('quibus in baptismate lotis'), but the idea of combining the baptized and chrismed with making the sign of the cross to expel the fiends of hell is from Prudentius, *Cathamerinon*, VI. 125–35.

[55] Wieland, *Latin Glosses*, p. 174 (*Psy.* 566): 'Erynis = lis uel tristitia, inde Erinis dicitur litis dea uel tristitia'; cf. *Excidium Troiae*, ed. A. K. Bate (Frankfurt, 1986), 2: 'Discordia uero, dea litis, ad ipsas nuptias uocata non est' ('Discord, the goddess of conflict, was not invited to the feast').

St Mary's cathedral, Bayeux. His use of *pignus* to mean relic must refer to an occasion when Bayeux acquired a relic of St Vigor. In doing so, he tells us, the Virgin (i.e. Bayeux cathedral) won and bore a child.

Those clues point towards the context of the poem's composition, for by 1073 Bishop Odo of Bayeux (1049/50–97) had founded an abbey upon Mount Chrismat, the site of Vigor's monastery. The foundation was under way in the late 1060s or early 1070s.[56] To consecrate an altar to Vigor, Odo required a relic of the saint and could have obtained one from Saint-Riquier or Cerisy. In 1066, Odo joined his half-brother, Duke William of Normandy, in his expedition to England and in 1067 was left in charge of the newly conquered country with William Fitz Osbern. Odo therefore became central to the English court when the courtly writer Folcard was finishing the *Vita Ædwardi*. It is about that time we first see Odo as the patron of poets such as Marbod of Rennes, whose refined play of allusions and word-play seem to have been much to the educated prelate's taste. Finding Folcard at court, he might have invited him to compose a poem on the acquisition of a relic of Vigor. Indeed, it was probably about the time he encountered Folcard that he acquired the relic. That a copy of Folcard's poem reached Saint-Riquier may indicate that the abbey had supplied the relic to Bayeux. The coyness Hariulf displays about the context of its composition reflects the fact that it was written to promote Vigor's cult at a different establishment. Abbot Gervin II of Saint-Riquier may have taken the opportunity to upgrade the cult of Vigor at his monastery. In preparing the new shrine, he borrowed verses from the poem to incorporate into Vigor's epitaph.[57] Since Gervin died in 1075, Folcard's poem must have been written before that date; and a date in the late 1060s or early 1070s is likely, for the reasons given above. This makes Folcard one of the earliest poets Odo is known to have patronized – a forerunner of the 'Loire poets' who were also Odo's protégés, notably Marbod of Rennes.[58]

Folcard's use of *Psychomachia* as a framework in the *Vita*, and as a framework for his poem on Vigor, reveals an interest in the contest of the soul, which determined the outcome of earthly struggle. The original title of his

[56] V. Gazeau, 'De part et d'autre de la Manche, réformateur et/ou stratège: l'évêque Odon de Bayeux, patron des moines et commanditaire de la Tapisserie de Bayeux', unpublished paper, 2018, pp. 7–13. On Odo's career, see D. Bates, 'The Character and Career of Odo, Bishop of Bayeux (1049/50–1097)', *Speculum* 50 (1975), 1–20. I am grateful to Prof. Gazeau for letting me read a draft of her paper.

[57] *De s. Vigore*, p. 292F: 'Mundi uictorem, lector, cognosce Vigorem/ Qui Victor es dictus, aufers discriminis ictus./ Flammarum domitor, qui mundi comprimis ignes,/ Ne nos exurant, flammas compesce gehennae.'

[58] W. Bulst, *Studien zu Marbods Carmina varia und Liber decem capitulorum*, Nachrichten von der Gesellschaft der Wissenschaften zu Göttingen, phil.-hist. Klasse IV, n. F. ii, Nr. 10 (Göttingen, 1939), pp. 180–5; and see pp. 227–8 for a poem to Marbod from Baudri of Bourgeuil, another 'Loire poet'.

work may have been something like 'A Song of Blessed Progeny' (*Carmen sanctae progeniei/ prolis*). It is clear, at least, that his intention was to tell not only of Edward but also of Edith, Godwine, and Godwine's male offspring.[59] Yet the figuring of Edith as Mary consecrating herself to God as a living temple is central to the overarching conceit. Harold and Tostig might have triumphed over the Welsh and Scots, but in the battle that mattered they succumbed first to Envy, then Discord, and finally to Sin. Their defeat in that battle brought about their spiritual demise. *Psychomachia* was a suitable framework in which Classical and Christian allusions might combine. Its protagonists could be found in both storyworlds. Discord, for example, in Poem VI, emerges from the Book of Proverbs, while Concord arrives from the pages of Lucan's *Pharsalia*.[60] Limbering up from their multiple storyworlds, the contestants prepare for battle. Ornamenting the battlefield, like banners all around, are Responsories associated with the Blessed Virgin, which flutter in the breeze of word-play, sometimes showing their protagonists to be heavenly (as Mary herself), sometimes earthly, as the heroines Edith and Bayeux. The *stirps* of the blessed progeny is the seed of Abraham ('Abrahae stirpe generosa uirgo') and Edward's royal line ('regum . . . stirpe': *Vita*, p. 12), and the stock of Godwine ('Felix prole pia dux stirpe beatus auita': III. 1). It is therefore both a royal progeny and the *stirps* of the Faithful ('pignore regali seu stirpe fideli': VI. 54). They are, of course, the seed of Abraham which would bring forth nations and kings according to God's covenant (Gen. 17:6), but Godwine's sons tragically become the 'stubble people' ('horrida stirps': VIII. 26) born to the flames. Godwine, who never let Deceit or Envy ('Fraudem . . . Liuor': V. 16) seduce him, triumphed in the contest of the soul and duly restored peace to the realm.[61] Edward and Edith happily triumph too. Christian and Classical texts, meanwhile, point us to the same moral. The path to salvation is that of the undivided soul.

---

[59] Cf. *Vita*, p. 84 (VIII. 24) 'rebamur sanctam dicere progeniem'. In Poem I (at pp. 6/7–8/9) it is clear that the poet intends to sing not only Edward's song but also Edith's, Godwine's, and that of the earl's offspring.

[60] Prov. 6:16–19 (above, p. 283); Tyler, 'Politcs of Poetry', p. 146.

[61] *Vita*, pp. 44–6.

THE DATE OF THE *GESTA NORMANNORUM DUCUM* BY WILLIAM OF JUMIÈGES[1]

The first seven books of Jumièges' *Gesta Normannorum Ducum*, to Book vii, chapter 12, concern affairs in the duchy of Normandy before 1066. The final chapters of that book (Book vii, chapters 13–21, and the Epilogue) address the conquest of England, to *c.* 1069. Elisabeth van Houts, who edited the work, regarded the 'Norman' portion as a product of the mid-1050s, and the 'English' portion as an addition of the late 1060s. She argued that the author had returned to his work a decade or so after finishing it, to add an account of the Conquest. A difficulty she nevertheless encountered in making that argument was the content of Book vii, chapter 11. Sandwiched between a chapter on the battle of Mortemer in 1054 (chapter 10) and a chapter on the battle of Varaville in 1057 (chapter 12), the intervening chapter seemed to relate to events of the mid-1050s. Its subject, however, was William's conquest of Maine, which began in the 1050s and ran on to 1063, when Maine surrendered to the duke and he captured the final bastion, the castle of Mayenne. Since the fall of Mayenne is mentioned in the last sentence of chapter 11, van Houts – believing the rest of chapter 11 and chapter 12 to be an account written in the 1050s – concluded that the sentence must have been added after 1063, perhaps when Jumièges returned to his work to add an account of England's conquest. She duly placed the last sentence in asterisks in the Latin text of her edition, signalling her opinion that it was an addition. She also concluded that the last sentence of chapter 12 must have been added later, because it records the death of King Henry of France in 1060, three years after Varaville.[2]

Chapter 11 troubled van Houts because it defied a chronological reading of Jumièges' narrative. 'One would expect the intervening chapter [between the ones on Mortemer and Varaville] to cover the years [between] 1054 and 1057, and so almost all of it does,' she wrote.[3] On careful inspection, however, it appears that most of the chapter concerns

---

[1] With thanks to Liam Draycott.
[2] *GND*, I, pp. xxxii–xxxiii.
[3] Ibid., p. xxxii.

the capitulation of Maine in 1063, for the reference – a third of the way down – to the defeated inhabitants surrendering their strongholds throughout the county and pledging fidelity to the duke cannot refer to anything else.[4] Jumièges, moreover, shows his readiness to dispense with chronology by stating in the chapter's opening sentence that William made attempts to capture Le Mans, Maine's capital, 'over several years'.[5] This remark seems to anticipate the outcome. At least, it pushes the narrative beyond the mid-1050s. Jumièges, as he often did, was telescoping events, collapsing several years of campaigning into one chapter.[6] If we accept the view that the last sentence of the chapter was added after 1063, we must also accept that the reference to the capitulation of Maine (a third of the way down) was added after 1063, and we should take the opening sentence as having been written in or after 1063, because it refers to several years of campaigning in Maine. In short, the whole chapter was written in or after 1063. It follows that chapter 12 can also be dated, like its predecessor, to 1063 or later.

Reading those chapters sympathetically means reading them – and the whole work – as literature, rather than expecting everything to be arranged in chronological order and every historical event to be mentioned in the text. Jumièges is telling a story, and it goes like this. Henry of France and Geoffrey Martel attacked Normandy, but William beat them off (vii. 10). William then punished Martel by attacking and capturing Maine (vii. 11). After Henry tried a second time to invade, William defeated him and cowed him into submission. Finally Henry died (vii. 12). It is a story of how William came to dominate northern France, just as the next nine chapters are a story about how he came to dominate England. As such, it takes certain liberties with the facts. Jumièges, in telescoping events, neglects to mention Martel's death in 1060 and replacement by Count Geoffrey the Bearded. He did so probably because it would be hard to present Maine's conquest as the punishment of Martel while pointing out that he died three years before it took place. Jumièges also writes of Maine as though it were Martel's, omitting the awkward detail that it had a count, who was a minor, to whom Martel stood guardian. Neither fact suited his narrative design of presenting the conquest of Maine as William's punishment of Martel, before adding his punishment of Henry in the climax.

In the 1070s, Poitiers rewrote Jumièges' *Gesta Normannorum ducum* and expanded it. More concerned with chronology, he took the troublesome chapter 11 and split it in two, keeping the first section between Mortemer and Varaville, but moving most of it forward to the early 1060s. Poitiers' Book 1, chapters 30–1 are an expansion of Jumièges' account of Mortemer (vii. 10). Chapters 32–3 embellish Jumièges' notice of early warfare in

---

[4] Ibid., II, pp. 150/1.
[5] Ibid., p. 150: 'per aliquot annos'.
[6] On his habit of telescoping, see ibid., I, p. li.

Maine (vii. 11). Chapter 34 is an expansion of his account of Varaville, also ending with the flight of Henry (vii. 12). Chapter 35 is an enlargement of the last sentence in Jumièges' chapter 12, reporting Henry's death (with Poitiers adding a notice of the death of Martel). Chapter 36 furnishes a defence for rewriting the conquest of Maine. Poitiers then rewrites it in chapters 37–41, which are a much-expanded re-telling of Jumièges' account of the conquest in his chapter 11. Here and there, Poitiers borrows phrases from Jumièges which confirm his interpretation of Jumièges' chronology. When rewriting his remarks upon the surrender of castles throughout Maine, Poitiers took them as referring to Maine's surrender in 1063. We can be sure he did so because he used the same words but moved the event forward to the early 1060s: Jumièges gives 'iam castellis per cunctum comitatum subactis' (*GND*, II, p. 150); Poitiers has 'castellis iam per totum comitatum subactis' (*GG*, p. 60). He also borrowed Jumièges' words for the burning of Mayenne. Jumièges has 'cepit igneque iniecto flammis combussit' (*GND*, II, p. 150). Poitiers has 'iniecti ignes castrum corripiunt' (*GG*, p. 66).

Poitiers' decision, in rewriting and expanding Jumièges, to push the bulk of his chapter on Maine forward to the 1060s corroborates the view that it mostly describes events of 1063. Rather than reading Jumièges' *Gesta Normannorum Ducum*, Books i–vii, chapter 12, as a work of the 1050s therefore, we must take it as a work of the 1060s. Indeed, the bulk of it must have been completed in or after 1063, and we cannot know how much of it was edited at that date, even if parts must have been written earlier. None of the arguments van Houts advanced for dating it to the 1050s prevents the re-dating, but we must be wary of thinking that because Jumièges did not mention this event or that event, he must have been writing before said events occurred.[7] This is demonstrably false in the case of chapter 11, written in 1063 but without reference to the death of Martel. We cannot be absolutely certain that the first seven books (up to vii. 12) were completed before 1066. That said, the last nine chapters do feel like an addition. The main reason for thinking so is Jumièges' failure to anticipate Edward's alleged promise to William earlier in his work. Poitiers, in rewriting it, made sure to go back and insert an early reference to it, so that the case for the conquest of England seemed less like a bolt from the blue.[8] On this evidence, we can date the completion of Books i–vii. 12 to 1063 or shortly after, and Book vii. 13–21, and the Epilogue, to *c*. 1069.

---

[7] Cf. ibid., I, p. xxxiii.
[8] *GG*, pp. 19, 69.

BIBLIOGRAPHY

THESES

O'Brien, E. L., 'The Cult of St Edward the Confessor, 1066–1399', D.Phil. dissertation (Oxford, 2001)

Plumtree, J., '"How the Corpse of a Most Mighty King . . ." The Use of Death and Burial of the English Monarch (from Edward to Henry I)', Ph.D. dissertation (Central European University, Budapest, 2014)

Savill, B., 'Papal Privileges in Early Medieval England, c. 680–1073', D.Phil. dissertation (Oxford, 2017)

PRIMARY SOURCES

Abbo of Fleury, *Collectio canonum*, PL 139, cols 473–508

Adam of Bremen, *Gesta Hammaburgensis ecclesiae pontificum*, ed. B. Schmeidler, MGH Scriptores (Hanover and Leipzig, 1917)

Ademari Cabannensis Chronicon, ed. P. Bourgain, assisted by R. Landes and G. Pon, CCCM 129 (Turnhout, 1999)

Ælfric, *Catholic Homilies: The First Series*, ed. P. Clemoes, EETS s.s. 17 (Oxford, 1997)

—— W. Braekman, ed., 'Wyrdwriteras: An Unpublished Ælfrician Text in Manuscript Hatton 115', *Revue belge de philologie et d'histoire* 44 (1966), 959–70

Aesop (via Romulus): *Der Lateinische Äsop des Romulus und die Prosa-Fassungen des Phädrus*, ed. G. Thiele (Heidelberg, 1910)

Ailred of Rievaulx, *Vita s. Edwardi regis*, PL 195, cols 737–90

André de Fleury: Vie de Gauzlin, abbé de Fleury, ed. R.-H. Bautier and G. Labory (Paris 1969)

Anglo-Saxon Charters, ed. and tr. A. J. Robertson (Cambridge, 1956)

Anglo-Saxon Chronicle: *The Anglo-Saxon Chronicle, a Collaborative Edition*, vol. 5: *MS C, a Semi-diplomatic Edition with Introduction and Indices*, ed. K. O'Brien O'Keeffe (Cambridge, 2001)

—— vol. 6: *MS D, a Semi-diplomatic Edition with Introduction and Indices*, ed. G. P. Cubbin (Cambridge, 1996)

—— vol. 7: *MS E, a Semi-diplomatic Edition with Introduction and Indices*, ed. S. Irvine (Cambridge, 2004)

—— C. Plummer (revising an edition by J. Earle), *Two of the Saxon Chronicles Parallel, with supplementary extracts from the others*, 2 vols (Oxford, 1892–9)

Anglo-Saxon Writs, ed. F. E. Harmer (Manchester, 1952; new edn, 1989)

Les Annales de Saint-Pierre de Gand et de Saint-Amand, ed. P. Grierson (Brussels, 1937)

'The Annals of Tigernach', ed. W. Stokes, *Revue Celtique* 17 (1896), 6–33, 119–263, and 337–420

The Annals of Ulster (to A. D. 1131), ed. S. Mac Airt and G. Mac Niocaill (Dublin, 1983)

Anselm: *S. Anselmi Cantuariensis archiepiscopi opera omnia*, ed. F. S. Schmitt, 6 vols (Edinburgh, 1946–61)

Anselme de Saint-Rémy, Histoire de la dédicace de Saint-Rémy, ed. and tr. J. Hourlier, in *La Champagne bénédictine: contribution à l'année saint Benoît*, Travaux de l'Academie nationale de Reims, vol. clx (Rheims, 1981), 181–297

Ashdown, M., *English and Norse documents relating to the reign of Ethelred the Unready* (Cambridge, 1930)

Asser's Life of King Alfred, Together with the Annals of St Neots, Erroneously Ascribed to Asser, ed. W. H. Stevenson, new impression with an article by D. Whitelock (Oxford, 1959)

Baldricus Burgulianus, *Carmina*, ed. K. Hilbert (Heidelberg, 1979)

Bayeux Tapestry: *The Bayeux Tapestry: The Complete Tapestry in Colour*, ed. D. M. Wilson (London, 1985)

Bishop, T. A. M., and P. Chaplais, eds, *Facsimiles of English Royal Writs to A.D. 1100, Presented to Vivian Hunter Galbraith* (Oxford, 1957)

Book of Llan Dav: *The Text of the Book of Llan Dav*, ed. J. G. Evans and J. Rhys (Oxford, 1893)

Brut y Tywysogyon, or The Chronicle of the Princes, Peniarth MS. 20 version, ed. and tr. T. Jones (Cardiff, 1952)

Byrhtferth of Ramsey, *The Lives of St Oswald and St Ecgwine*, ed. and tr. M. Lapidge, OMT (Oxford, 2009)

Canterbury Professions, ed. M. Richter, Canterbury and York Society, vol. 67 (Torquay, 1973)

The Cartulary of the Abbey of Mont-Saint-Michel, ed. K. S. B. Keats-Rohan (Donington, 2006)

Charters of Bath and Wells, ed. S. E. Kelly, Anglo-Saxon Charters 13 (Oxford, 2007)

Charters of Chertsey Abbey, ed. S. E. Kelly, Anglo-Saxon Charters 19 (Oxford, 2015)

Charters of Malmesbury Abbey, ed. S. E. Kelly, Anglo-Saxon Charters 11 (Oxford, 2005)

Charters of the New Minster, Winchester, ed. S. Miller, Anglo-Saxon Charters 9 (Oxford, 2001)

Charters of Northern Houses, ed. D. A. Woodman, Anglo-Saxon Charters 16 (Oxford, 2012)

Chronicon Abbatiae Rameseiensis, ed. W. Dunn Macray, RS 83 (London, 1886)

Dodsworth, R., and W. Dugdale, *Monasticon Anglicanum*, 3 vols (London, 1655–73)

Domesday Book: *Great Domesday Book: Library Edition*, ed. A. Williams and R. W. H. Erskine (London, 1986–92)

—— F. Barlow, M. Biddle, O. von Feilitzen and D. J. Keene, with various contributors, *Winchester in the Early Middle Ages: An Edition and Discussion of the Winton Domesday*, ed. M. Biddle, Winchester Studies 1 (Oxford, 1976)

Dudo of Saint-Quentin, *De gestis Normannie ducum seu de moribus et actis primorum Normanniae ducum*, ed. J. Lair, *Mémoires de la Société des Antiquaires de Normandie*, vol. xxiii (Caen, 1865)

Eadmer, *Historia nouorum in Anglia*, ed. M. Rule, RS 81 (London, 1884)

Einhard, *Vita Karoli Magni: The Life of Charlemagne*, Bibliotheca Germanica 3, text with translation by E. Scherabon Firchow and E. H. Zeydel (Coral Gables, FL, 1972; repr. Dudweiler, 1985)

Encomium Emmae Reginae, ed. A. Campbell, Camden 3rd ser. 72 (London, 1949)/ Camden Classic Reprints 4 (Cambridge, 1998), with a supplementary introduction by S. Keynes

Facsimiles of Anglo-Saxon Charters, ed. S. Keynes, Anglo-Saxon Charters, Supplementary Volume I (Oxford, 1991)

Flete, John, *The History of Westminster Abbey*, ed. J. Armitage Robinson (Cambridge, 1909)

Folcard: *The Life of King Edward who rests at Westminster*, ed. and tr. F. Barlow (London, 1962)

—— *The Life of King Edward who rests at Westminster, attributed to a monk of Saint-Bertin*, ed. and tr. F. Barlow, OMT (Oxford, 2nd edn, 1992)

—— *Vita s. Bertini*: PL 147, cols 1089–98

—— *Vita s. Iohannis Beuerlacensis* (*BHL* 4339), in *Historians of the Church of York*, ed. J. Raine the younger, RS 71, 3 vols (1879–94), I, 239–60

Fulbert of Chartres: *The Letters and Poems of Fulbert of Chartres*, ed. and tr. F. Behrends, OMT (Oxford, 1976)

Gerald of Wales, *Opera*, ed. J. F. Dimock, RS 21, 8 vols (London, 1861–77)

Die Gesetze der Angelsachsen, ed. F. Liebermann, 3 vols (Halle, 1903–16)

Godfrey of Winchester, *Epigrammata Historica*, in *The Anglo-Latin Satirical Poets and Epigrammatists of the Twelfth Century*, ed. T. Wright, RS 59, 2 vols (London, 1872)

Goscelin: A. Wilmart, 'La légende de sainte Édithe en prose et vers par le moine Goscelin', *AB* 56 (1938), 5–101, 265–307

—— T. Licence, 'Goscelin of Saint-Bertin and the Hagiography of St Eadwold of Cerne', *Journal of Medieval Latin* 16 (2007), 182–207

—— Herman the Archdeacon and Goscelin of Saint-Bertin, *Miracles of St Edmund*, ed. and tr. T. Licence, with the assistance of L. Lockyer, OMT (Oxford, 2014)

Guy of Amiens: *The Carmen de Hastingae Proelio of Guy Bishop of Amiens*, ed. C. Morton and H. Muntz, OMT (Oxford, 1972)

—— *The Carmen de Hastingae Proelio of Guy Bishop of Amiens*, ed. and tr. F. Barlow, OMT (Oxford, 1999)

Hariulf, *Chronique de l'abbaye de Saint-Riquier (Ve siècle–1104)*, ed. F. Lot (Paris, 1894)

Helgaud of Fleury, *Epitoma uitae Rotberti Pii*, ed. R. H. Bautier and G. Labory, Sources d'histoire médiévale (Paris 1965)

Hemingi chartularium ecclesiae Wigornensis, ed. T. Hearne, 2 vols (Oxford, 1723)

Henry of Huntingdon, *Historia Anglorum: The History of the English People*, ed. and tr. D. Greenway, OMT (Oxford, 1996)

Herman the Archdeacon and Goscelin of Saint-Bertin, *Miracles of St Edmund*, ed. and tr. T. Licence, with the assistance of L. Lockyer, OMT (Oxford, 2014)

Hermann of Reichenau, *Chronicon*, ed. G. Pertz, MGH Scriptores 5 (Hanover, 1844), 74–133

Hincmar of Rheims, *De regis persona et regio ministerio, ad Carolum Calvum regem*, PL 125, cols 833–56

—— *De ordine palatii*, ed. A. Boretius, MGH Capitularia regum Francorum 2 (Hanover, 1897), 518–30

Historia Ecclesie Abbendonensis: The History of the Church of Abingdon, ed. and tr. J. Hudson, OMT, 2 vols (Oxford, 2002–7)

The Historians of the Church of York and its Archbishops, ed. J. Raine, RS 71, 3 vols (1879–94)

Hugh the Chanter, *The History of the Church of York, 1066–1127*, ed. and tr. C. Johnson; revised M. Brett, C. N. L. Brooke, and M. Winterbottom, OMT (Oxford, 1990)

Inventio et miracula sancti Wulfranni, ed. J. Laporte, Société de Histoire de Normandie, *Mélanges: Documents publiés et annotés*, 14e série (Rouen and Paris, 1938), 1–87

John of Worcester: *The Chronicle of John of Worcester*, ed. R. R. Darlington and P. McGurk, OMT, 2 vols (vols ii and iii) (Oxford, 1995–8)

—— *The Chronicle of John of Worcester, Volume III*, ed. and tr. P. McGurk, OMT (Oxford, 1998)

The Laws of the Kings of England from Edmund to Henry I, ed. and tr. A. J. Robertson (Cambridge, 1925)

The Leofric Missal, ed. F. E. Warren (Oxford, 1883)

Letters: *Die ältere Wormser Briefsammlung*, MGH Epistolae. Die Briefe der deutschen Kaiserzeit 3 (Weimar, 1949)

Liber Eliensis, ed. E. O. Blake Camden 3rd ser., 92 (London, 1962)

Liber historiae Francorum, ed. B. Krusch, MGH Scriptores rerum Merovingicarum 2 (Hanover, 1888), 215–328

Liber Traditionum sancti Petri Blandiniensis: Livre des donations faites à l'Abbaye de Saint-Pierre de Gand, ed. A. Fayen, Cartulaire de la ville de Gand (Oorkondenboek der Stad Gent), 2e série, Chartes et Documents, I (Ghent, 1906)

The 'Liber Vitae' of the New Minster and Hyde Abbey, Winchester, British Library Stowe 944 [etc], ed. S. Keynes, Early English Manuscripts in Facsimile 26 (Copenhagen, 1996)

Matthew Paris (att.), *La Estoire de Seint Aedward le Rei*, ed. K. Y. Wallace, Anglo-Norman Text Society (London, 1983)

Miracula s. Ursmari in itinere per Flandriam facta, ed. O. Holder-Egger, in MGH Scriptores 15, 2 (Hanover, 1888), 837–42

Neustria Pia, ed. A. du Monstier (Rouen, 1633)

Orderic Vitalis: *The Gesta Normannorum Ducum of William of Jumièges, Orderic Vitalis, and Robert of Torigni*, ed. and tr. E. M. C. van Houts, OMT, 2 vols (Oxford, 1992–5)

—— *The Ecclesiastical History of Orderic Vitalis*, ed. and tr. M. Chibnall, OMT, 6 vols (Oxford, 1969–80)

Osbern, *Translatio sancti Ælfegi*, ed. A. R. Rumble, tr. R. Morris and A. R. Rumble, in Rumble, ed., *The Reign of Cnut, King of England, Denmark and Norway* (London and New York, 1994), 283–315

Osbert of Clare: 'La vie de s. Édouard le Confesseur par Osbert de Clare', ed. M. Bloch, *AB* 41 (1923), 5–131

Peter Damian: *Die Briefe des Petrus Damiani*, ed. K. Reindel, MGH Die Briefe der Deutschen Kaiserzeit, 4 vols (Munich, 1983–93)

The Peterborough Chronicle of Hugh Candidus, ed. W. T. Mellows (Oxford, 1949)

Prudentius, *Psychomachia*: H. J. Thompson, tr., *Prudentius, with an English Translation*, Loeb Classical Library 387, 2 vols (London, 1949–53), I, 274–343

—— J. M. Burnam, *Commentaire anonyme sur Prudence, d'après le manuscrit 413 de Valenciennes* (Paris, 1910)

Pseudo-Ecgbert: *Das altenglische Bussbuch: (sog. Confessionale pseudo-Egberti) ein Beitrag zu den kirchlichen Gesetzen der Angelsachsen*, ed. R. Spindler (Leipzig, 1934)

Recueil des actes des ducs de Normandie de 911 à 1066, ed. M. Fauroux, *Mémoires de la Société des Antiquaires de Normandie*, vol. xxxvi (Caen, 1961)

Receuil des actes de Philippe Ier, ed. M. Prou (Paris, 1908)

Regesta Regum Anglo-Normannorum: The Acta of William I (1066–1087), ed. D. Bates (Oxford, 1998)

Rodulfus Glaber, *Historiarum libri quinque*, ed. J. France, in *Rodulfus Glaber Opera*, ed. J. France, N. Bulst and P. Reynolds, OMT (Oxford, 1989)

Sedulius Scottus, *De Rectoribus Christianis (On Christian Rulers)*, ed. and tr. R. W. Dyson (Woodbridge, 2010)

Simeon of Durham, *Historia regum*, in *Symeonis monachi opera omnia*, ed. T. Arnold, RS 75, 2 vols (London, 1882–5), II, 3–283

Simon of Saint-Bertin, *Gesta abbatum sancti Bertini Sithiensium*, ed. O. Holder-Egger, in *MGH Scriptores* 13 (Hanover, 1881), 635–62

Smaragdus of Saint-Mihiel, *Via regia*, PL 102, cols 933–70

Sulcard: 'Sulcard of Westminster: *Prologus de Constructione Westmonasterii*', ed. B. W. Scholz, *Traditio* 20 (1964), 59–91

Thietmar of Merseburg, *Chronicon*, ed. R. Holtzmann, MGH Scriptores rerum Germanicarum n.s. 9 (Berlin, 1935)

The Thorney 'Liber Vitae': London, British Library, Additional MS 40,000, fols 1–12r, ed. L. Rollason (Woodbridge, 2015)

Van Lokeren, A., *Chartes et documents de l'abbaye de Saint Pierre au mont Blandin a Gant* (Ghent, 1868)

La Vie d'Edouard le Confesseur: poème Anglo-Normand du XIIe siècle, ed. Ö. Södergård (Uppsala, 1948)

De sancto Vigore episcopo Baiocensi in Gallia, in *Acta SS*, Nov., I (1 Nov.), 297–304

Vision of Leofric: P. A. Stokes, 'The Vision of Leofric: Manuscript, Text and Context', *Review of English Studies* 63 (2012), 529–50

Wace: *History of the Norman People: Wace's Roman de Rou*, tr. G. S. Burgess (Woodbridge, 2004)

Westminster Abbey Charters 1066–c. 1214, ed. E. Mason, assisted by the late Jennifer Bray, continuing the work of the late Desmond J. Murphy, London Record Society (London, 1988)

William of Jumièges: *The Gesta Normannorum Ducum of William of Jumièges, Orderic Vitalis, and Robert of Torigni*, ed. and tr. E. M. C. van Houts, OMT, 2 vols (Oxford, 1992–5)

William of Malmesbury, *Gesta regum Anglorum: The History of the English Kings*, ed. and tr. R. A. B. Mynors, M. Winterbottom, and R. M. Thomson, OMT, 2 vols (Oxford, 1998–9)

—— *Gesta Pontificum Anglorum*, ed. and tr. M. Winterbottom, with the assistance of R. M. Thomson, OMT, 2 vols (Oxford, 2007)

—— *Life of Wulfstan*, in idem, *Saints' Lives*, ed. and tr. M. Winterbottom and R. M. Thomson, OMT (Oxford, 2002)

—— *The Vita Wulfstani of William of Malmesbury*, ed. R. R. Darlington RHS Camden 3rd ser., 40 (London, 1928)

—— *The Early History of Glastonbury: An Edition, Translation and Study of William of Malmesbury's De Antiquitate Glastonie Ecclesie*, ed. and tr. J. Scott (Woodbridge, 1981)

William of Poitiers: *The Gesta Guillelmi of William of Poitiers*, ed. and tr. R. H. C. Davis and M. Chibnall, OMT (Oxford, 1998)

Wipo, *Gesta Chuonradi II. imperatoris*, in *Die Werke Wipos*, ed. H. Bresslau, MGH Scriptores, 59 (Hanover and Leipzig, 1915), 3–62

Wulfstan of Winchester, *Life of St. Æthelwold*, ed. and tr. M. Lapidge and M. Winterbottom, OMT (Oxford, 1991)

Wulfstan of York: *The Homilies of Wulfstan*, ed. D. Bethurum (Oxford, 1957)

—— *Sermo Lupi ad Anglos*, ed. D. Whitelock, 3rd edn (Exeter, 1976)

—— *The Political Writings of Archbishop Wulfstan of York*, ed. and tr. A. Rabin (Manchester, 2015)

SECONDARY SOURCES

Abels, R. P., *Lordship and Military Obligation in Anglo-Saxon England* (Berkeley and Los Angeles, CA, and London, 1988)

—— 'Royal Succession and the Growth of Political Stability in Ninth-century Wessex', *HSJ* 12 (2002), 83–98

Abrams, L., 'The Anglo-Saxons and the Christianization of Scandinavia', *ASE* 24 (1995), 213–49

Aird, W. M., 'Siward, earl of Northumbria (d. 1055)', *ODNB*

Albu, E., *The Normans in their Histories: Propaganda, Myth and Subversion* (Woodbridge, 2001)

Allen, M., 'The Volume of the English Currency c. 973–1158', in B. J. Cook and G. Williams, eds, *Coinage and History in the North Sea World, c. AD 500–1250: Essays in Honour of Marion Archibald* (Leiden and Boston, MA, 2006), 487–523

Ammon, M., ' "Ge mid wedde ge mid aðe": The Functions of Oath and Pledge in Anglo-Saxon Legal Culture', *Historical Research* 86 (2013), 515–35

Ayre, J., and R. Wroe-Brown, 'The Post-Roman Foreshore and the Origins of the Late Anglo-Saxon Waterfront and Dock of Æthelred's Hithe: Excavations at Bull Wharf, City of London', *Archaeological Journal* 172 (2015)

Banham, D., 'A Millennium in Medicine: New Medical Texts and Ideas in England in the Eleventh Century', in S. Keynes and A. P. Smyth, eds, *Anglo-Saxons: Studies Presented to Cyril Roy Hart* (Dublin, 2006), 230–42

—— 'Medicine at Bury in the Time of Abbot Baldwin', in T. Licence, ed., *Bury St Edmunds and the Norman Conquest* (Woodbridge, 2014), 226–46

Barlow, F., 'Edward the Confessor's Early Life, Character and Attitudes', *EHR* 80 (1965), 225–51; repr. in idem, *Norman Conquest and Beyond*, 57–83

—— 'Edward the Confessor and the Norman Conquest', Hastings and Bexhill Branch of the Historical Association Pamphlet, 1971; repr. in idem, *Norman Conquest and Beyond*, 99–111

—— 'Leofric and his Times', in idem, K. M. Dexter, A. M. Erskine and L. J. Lloyd, *Leofric of Exeter: Essays in Commemoration of the Foundation of Exeter Cathedral Library in A.D. 1072* (Exeter, 1972), 1–16

—— *The English Church 1000–1066* (London and New York, 2nd edn, 1979)

—— 'The King's Evil', *EHR* 95 (1980), 3–27

—— *The Norman Conquest and Beyond* (London, 1983)

—— *Edward the Confessor* (London, 1970; new edn, 1997)

—— *The Godwins: The Rise and Fall of a Noble Dynasty* (Harlow, 2002)

Barraclough, G. A., 'The Anglo-Saxon Writ', *History* 39 (1954), 193–215

Barrow, J., 'Grades of Ordination and Clerical Careers, c. 900–c. 1200', *ANS* 32 (2010), 41–61

Bates, D., 'The Character and Career of Odo, Bishop of Bayeux (1049/50–1097)', *Speculum* 50 (1975), 1–20

—— *Normandy before 1066* (London and New York, 1982)

—— 'Frank Barlow 1911–2009', *Proceedings of the British Academy* 172 (2011), 3–24

—— 'Anger, Emotion and a Biography of William the Conqueror', in Nelson et al., eds, *Gender and Historiography*, 21–33

—— *William the Conqueror* (New Haven and London, 2016)

Bates, D., J. Crick, and S. Hamilton, ed., *Writing Medieval Biography, 750–1250: Essays in Honour of Professor Frank Barlow* (Woodbridge, 2006)

Bauduin, P., *La première Normandie (Xe–XIe siècle): sur les frontières de la haute Normandie: identité et construction d'une principauté* (Caen, 2004)

—— 'Richard II de Normandie: figure princière et transferts culturels (fin dixième–début onzième siècle)', *ANS* 37 (2015), 53–82

Bauduin, P., and A. E. Musin, ed., *Vers l'Orient et vers l'Occident: regards croisés sur les dynamiques et les transferts culturels des Vikings à la Rous ancienne* (Caen, 2014)

Baxter, S., 'The Earls of Mercia and their Commended Men in the Mid Eleventh Century', *ANS* 23 (2001), 23–46

—— *The Earls of Mercia: Lordship and Power in Late Anglo-Saxon England* (Oxford, 2007)

—— 'MS C of the Anglo-Saxon Chronicle and the Politics of Mid-eleventh-century England', *EHR* 122 (2007), 1189–227

—— 'The Death of Burgheard Son of Ælfgar and Its Context', in P. Fouracre and D. Ganz, ed., *Frankland: The Franks and the World of the Early Middle Ages: Essays in honour of Dame Jinty Nelson* (Manchester and New York, 2008), 266–84

—— 'The Limits of the Late Anglo-Saxon State', in W. Pohl and V. Wieser, eds, *Der frühmittelalterliche Staat – europäische Perspektiven*, Forschungen zur Geschichte des Mittelalters 16 (Vienna, 2009), 503–13

—— 'Edward the Confessor and the Succession Question', in Mortimer, ed., *Edward*, 76–118

Biddle, M., 'Seasonal Festivals and Residence: Winchester, Westminster and Gloucester in the Tenth to Twelfth Centuries', *ANS* 8 (1986), 51–72

Bihrer, A., *Begegnungen zwischen dem ostfränkisch-deutschen Reich und England (850–1100). Kontakte – Konstellationen – Funktionalisierungen – Wirkungen* (Ostfildern, 2012)

Bischoff, G. and B.-M. Tock, eds, *Léon IX et son temps: actes du colloque international organisé par l'Institut d'histoire médiévale de l'Université Marc-Bloch, Strasbourg-Eguisheim, 20–22 juin 2002* (Turnhout, 2006)

Bloch, M., *Les rois thaumaturges. Étude sur le caractère surnaturel attribué à la puissance royale particulièrement en France et en Angleterre* (Strasbourg and Paris, 1924)

Bolton, T., 'English Political Refugees at the Court of Sven Estrithsson', *Medieval Scandinavia* 15 (2005), 17–26

—— 'Ælfgifu of Northampton: Cnut the Great's Other Woman', *Nottingham Medieval Studies* 51 (2007), 247–68

—— 'A Newly Emergent Mediaeval Manuscript Containing *Encomium Emmae Reginae* with the Only Known Complete Text of the Recension Prepared for King Edward the Confessor', *Mediaeval Studies* 19 (2009), 205–12

—— *The Empire of Cnut the Great: Conquest and the Consolidation of Power in Northern Europe in the Early Eleventh Century* (Leiden and Boston, MA, 2009)

—— *Cnut the Great* (New Haven, CT and London, 2017)

Bond, F., *Westminster Abbey* (Oxford, 1909)

Boshof, E., 'Lothringen, Frankreich und das Reich in der Regierungszeit Heinrichs III', *Rheinische Vierteljahrsblätter* 43 (1978), 63–127

Bouet, P., *Guilluame le Conquérant et les Normands au XIe siècle* (Condé-sur-Noireau, 2000)

—— 'Le Mont-Saint-Michel entre Bretagne et Normandie de 960 à 1060', in J. Quaghebeur and B. Medrignac, eds, *Bretons et Normands au Moyen Age: Rivalités, malentendus, convergences* (Rennes, 2008), 165–200

Bouet, P., and F. Neveux, 'Edward the Confessor's Succession According to the Bayeux Tapestry', in Lewis et al., eds, *The Bayeux Tapestry*, 59–65

Bouet, P., B. Levy, and F. Neveux, eds, *The Bayeux Tapestry: Embroidering the Facts of History* (Caen, 2004)

Bozóky, E., 'La construction de la sainteté d'Edouard le Confesseur et les rois d'Angleterre', in F. Laurent, L. Mathey-Maille, and M. Szkilnik, eds, *Des Saints et des rois: l'Hagiographie au service de l'histoire* (Paris, 2014), 159–73

—— 'The Sanctity and Canonisation of Edward the Confessor', in Mortimer, ed., *Edward*, 173–86

Bredehoft, T. A., '*Malcolm and Margaret*: The Poem in Annal 1067D', in A. Jorgensen, ed., *Reading the Anglo-Saxon Chronicle: Language, Literature, History* (Turnhout, 2010), 31–48

Brett, M., 'John of Worcester and his Contemporaries', in R. H. C. Davis and J. M. Wallace-Hadrill, eds, *The Writing of History in the Middle Ages: Essays presented to Richard William Southern* (Oxford, 1981), 101–26

Brooks, N., 'The Authority and Interpretation of the Bayeux Tapestry', *ANS* 1 (1979), 1–34, 191–9; repr. in N. Brooks, *Communities and Warfare, 700–1400* (London and Rio Grande, 2000), 175–218

—— 'Why Is the *Anglo-Saxon Chronicle* about Kings?', *ASE* 39 (2011), 43–70

Buc, P., *L'ambiguïté de livre: Prince, pouvoir et peuple dans les commentaires de la Bible au Moyen Age* (Paris, 1994)

Buckton, D., ed., *Byzantium: Treasures of Byzantine Art and Culture from British Collections* (London, 1994)

Bühler, A., 'Kaiser Heinrich IV. und Bertha von Turin – Eine schwierige Ehe im Spiegel der Urkunden', *Archiv für Kulturgeschichte* 83 (2001), 37–61

Bulst, W., *Studien zu Marbods Carmina varia und Liber decem capitulorum*, Nachrichten von der Gesellschaft der Wissenschaften zu Göttingen, phil.-hist. Klasse IV, n. F. ii, Nr. 10 (Göttingen, 1939)

Camp, C. T., *Anglo-Saxon Saints' Lives as History Writing in Late Medieval England* (Woodbridge, 2015)

Campbell, J., *The Anglo-Saxon State* (London and New York, 2000)

Campbell, M. W., 'Earl Godwin of Wessex and Edward the Confessor's Promise of the Throne to William of Normandy', *Traditio* 28 (1972), 141–58

Capitani, O., 'Benedetto X, antipapa', *Dizionario biografico degli Italiani* 8 (Rome, 1966), 366–70

Carpenter, D. A., 'King Henry III and Saint Edward the Confessor: The Origins of the Cult', *EHR* 102 (2007), 865–91

Chaney, W. A., *The Cult of Kingship in Anglo-Saxon England: The Transition from Paganism to Christianity* (Berkeley, CA, 1970)

Chaplais, P., 'The Original Charters of Herbert and Gervaise, Abbots of Westminster (1121–1157)', in P. M. Barnes and C. F. Slade, ed, *A Medieval Miscellany for Doris Mary Stenton* (London, 1962), 89–110

—— 'The Authenticity of the Royal Anglo-Saxon Diplomas of Exeter', *Bulletin of the Institute of Historical Research* 39 (1966), 1–34

Charles-Edwards, T. M., *Wales and the Britons 350–1064* (Oxford, 2013)

Chédeville, A., *Chartes et ses campaignes (XIe–XIIIe siècles)* (Paris, 1973)

Chédeville, A., and N. Y. Tonnerre, *La Bretagne Féodale, XIe–XIIIe siècle* (Rennes, 1987)

Chefneux, H., 'Les fables dans la Tapisserie de Bayeux', *Romania* 60 (1934), 1–35, 153–94

Ciggaar, K., 'England and Byzantium on the Eve of the Norman Conquest (the Reign of Edward the Confessor)', *ANS* 5 (1983), 78–96

Clarke, H. B., 'The Identity of the Designer of the Bayeux Tapestry', *ANS* 35 (2013), 120–39

Clarke, P. A., *The English Nobility under Edward the Confessor* (Oxford, 1994)

Clarkson, T., *The Men of the North: The Britons of Southern Scotland* (Edinburgh, 2010)

Clayton, M., 'The Old English *Promissio Regis*', *ASE* 37 (2008), 91–150

—— *The Cult of the Virgin Mary in Anglo-Saxon England* (New York, 1990; new edn, Cambridge, 2010)

—— 'De Duodecim Abusiuis, Lordship and Kingship in Anglo-Saxon England', in S. McWilliams, ed., *Saints and Scholars: New Perspectives on Anglo-Saxon Literature and Culture in Honour of Hugh Magennis* (Woodbridge, 2012), 141–63

—— *Two Ælfric Texts: 'The Twelve Abuses' and 'The Vices and Virtues': An Edition and Translation of Ælfric's Old English Version of 'De duodecim abusiuis' and 'De octo uitiis et de duodecim abusiuis'* (Cambridge, 2013)

Crick, J., 'Edgar, Albion and Insular Dominion', in Scragg, ed., *Edgar*, 158–70

Cohen, A. S., ed., *Eye and Mind: Collected Essays in Anglo-Saxon and Early Medieval Art by Robert Deshman* (Kalamazoo, 2010)

Constable, G., 'Forgery and Plagiarism in the Middle Ages', *Archiv für Diplomatik* 29 (1983), 1–41

—— 'Forged Letters in the Middle Ages', in *Fälschungen im Mittelalter: Internationaler Kongreß der Monumenta Germaniae Historica München, 16.–19. September 1986*, MGH Schriften 33, 5 vols (Hanover, 1988), V, 11–37

Cooper, J., 'The Last Four Anglo-Saxon Archbishops of York', *Borthwick Papers* 38 (York, 1970)

—— 'Cynesige [St Cynesige, Kynsige] (d. 1060), archbishop of York', *ODNB*

Cormack, R., *Byzantine Art*, Oxford History of Art (Oxford, 2000)

Cowdrey, H. E. J., 'The Peace and Truce of God in the Eleventh Century', *P&P* 46 (1970), 42–67

—— 'King Harold II and the Bayeux Tapestry: A Critical Introduction', in Owen-Crocker, ed., *King Harold II*, 1–15

Crawford, B. E., *Scandinavian Scotland* (Leicester, 1987)

—— *The Northern Earldoms: Orkney and Caithness from AD 870 to 1470* (Edinburgh, 2013)

—— 'The Kingdom of Man and the Earldom of Orkney – Some Comparisons', in J. V. Sigurðsson and T. Bolton, eds, *Celtic–Norse Relationships in the Irish Sea in the Middle Ages 800–1200* (Leiden and Boston, MA, 2014), 65–80

Crook, J., 'An Introduction to the Topography of the Medieval Palace at Westminster', in Rodwell and Tatton-Brown, eds, *Westminster*, II (Royal Palace), 1–21

Cubitt, C., 'Bishops and Succession Crises in Tenth- and Eleventh-century England', in Körntgen and Waßenhoven, eds, *Patterns of Episcopal Power*, 111–26

—— 'Apocalyptic and Eschatological Thought in England around the Year 1000', *TRHS*, 6th ser. 25 (2015), 27–52

Currie, C. R. J., 'Odda's Chapel, Ealdred's Inscriptions? The Deerhurst Inscriptions in Some Continental Contexts', *Historical Research* 83 (2010), 1–45

Cutler, K. E., 'The Godwinist Hostages: The Case for 1051', *Annuale Mediaevale* 12 (1972), 70–7

—— 'Edith, Queen of England, 1045–1066', *Mediaeval Studies* 35 (1973), 222–31

Darlington, R. R., and P. McGurk, 'The "Chronicon ex Chronicis" of "Florence" of Worcester and Its Use of Sources for English History before 1066', *ANS* 5 (1988), 185–96

Deshman, R., 'Christus Rex et Magi Reges: Kingship and Christology in Ottonian and Anglo-Saxon Art', *Frühmittelalterliche Studien* 10 (1976), 367–405; repr. in Cohen, ed., *Eye and Mind*, 137–70

—— '*Benedictus Monarcha et Monachus*: Early Medieval Ruler Theology and the Anglo-Saxon Reform', *Frühmittelalterliche Studien* 22 (1988), 204–40, repr. in Cohen, ed., *Eye and Mind*, 104–35

Douglas, D. C., 'Some Problems of Early Norman Chronology', *EHR* 65 (1950), 289–303

—— 'Edward the Confessor, Duke Willliam of Normandy, and the English Succession', *EHR* 68 (1953), 526–45

—— *William the Conqueror: The Norman Impact on England* (London, 1964; new edn, New Haven, CT, and London, 1999)

Downham, C., 'England and the Irish-Sea Zone in the Eleventh-Century', *ANS* 26 (2004), 55–73

Dumville, D. N., 'The Aetheling: A Study in Anglo-Saxon Constitutional History', *ASE* 8 (1979), 1–33

—— 'Some Aspects of Annalistic Writing at Canterbury in the Eleventh and Twelfth Centuries', *Peritia: Journal of the Medieval Academy of Ireland* 2 (1983), 23–57

Duncan, A. A. M., 'The Battle of Carham, 1018', *SHR* 55 (1976), 20–8

—— *The Kingship of the Scots, 842–1292: Succession and Independence* (Edinburgh, 2002)

Edmonds, F., 'The Emergence and Transformation of Medieval Cumbria', *SHR* 93 (2014), 195–216

Elliott, D., *Spiritual Marriage: Sexual Abstinence in Medieval Wedlock* (Princeton, NJ, 1993)

Engels, O., 'Der Dom zu Speyer im Spiegel des salischen und staufischen Selbstverständnisses', *Archiv für mittelrheinische Kirchengeschichte* 32 (1980), 27–40

Fernie, E., 'Edward the Confessor's Westminster Abbey', in Mortimer, ed., *Edward*, 139–50

Fleming, R., 'Domesday Estates of the King and the Godwines: A Study in Late Saxon Politics', *Speculum* 58 (1983), 987–1007

—— *Kings and Lords in Conquest England* (Cambridge, 1991)

—— 'Rural Elites and Urban Communities in Late Saxon England', *P&P* 141 (1993), 3–37

—— 'Acquiring, Flaunting and Destroying Silk in Late Anglo-Saxon England', *EME* 15 (2007), 127–58

Folz, R., *The Concept of Empire in Western Europe from the Fifth to the Fourteenth Century*, tr. S. A. Ogilvie (Frome and London, 1969)

Foot, S., 'The Making of Angelcynn: English Identity before the Norman Conquest', *TRHS*, 6th ser., 6 (1996), 25–49

—— *Æthelstan: The First King of England* (New Haven, CT and London, 2011)

Foys, M., K. E. Overbey, and D. Terkla, ed., *The Bayeux Tapestry: New Interpretations* (Woodbridge, 2009)

Freeman, A., *The Moneyer and the Mint in the Reign of Edward the Confessor 1042–1066*, BAR British Series 145 (1985)

Freeman, E. A., *The History of the Norman Conquest of England*, 6 vols (i–ii, 3rd edn, Oxford, 1877; iii–iv, 2nd edn, Oxford, 1875; v–vi, 1st edn, Oxford 1876–9)

Frey, L. H., 'Exile and Christian Elegy in Anglo-Saxon Epic Poetry', *Journal of English and German Philology* 62 (1963), 293–302

Gardiner, M., 'Shipping and Trade between England and the Continent during the Eleventh Century', *ANS* 22 (1999), 71–93

Garnett, G., 'Coronation and Propaganda: Some Implications of the Norman claim to the Throne of England in 1066', *TRHS*, 5th ser., 36 (1986), 91–116

—— '"Ducal" Succession in Early Normandy', in G. Garnett and J. Hudson, eds, *Law and Government in Medieval England and Normandy: Essays in honour of Sir James Holt* (Cambridge, 1994), 80–110

—— *Conquered England: Kingship, Succession and Tenure, 1066–1166* (Oxford, 2007)

Gazeau, V., *Normannia Monastica (Xe–XIIe siècle): Princes normands et abbés bénédictins; Prosopographie des abbés bénédictins*, 2 vols (Caen, 2007)

Gem, R. D. H., 'The Romanesque Rebuilding of Westminster Abbey (with a reconstruction by W. T. Ball)', *ANS* 3 (1981), 33–60

—— 'Craftsmen and Administrators in the Building of the Confessor's Abbey', in Mortimer, ed., *Edward*, 168–72

Giandrea, M. F. (see Smith, M. F.)

Glaesener, H., 'Un mariage fertile en conséquences (Godefroid le Barbu et Béatrice de Toscane'), *Revue d'histoire ecclésiastique* 42 (1947), 379–416

Golding, B., *Conquest and Colonisation: The Normans in Britain* (Basingstoke, 2nd edn, 2013)

Gouttebroze, J.-G., 'Deux modèles de sainteté royale: Edouard le Confesseur et saint Louis', *Cahiers de civilisation médiévale, Xe–XIIe siècles* 42 (1999), 243–58

Grassi, J., 'The Lands and Revenues of Edward the Confessor', *EHR* 117 (2002), 251–83

Green, J., 'Kingship, Lordship and Community in Eleventh-century England', *ANS* 31 (2009), 1–16

Greenfield, S. B., 'The Formulaic Expression of the Theme of "Exile" in Anglo-Saxon Poetry', *Speculum* 30 (1955), 200–6

Grierson, P., 'A Visit of Earl Harold to Flanders in 1056', *EHR* 51 (1936), 90–7

—— 'The Relations between England and Flanders before the Norman Conquest', *TRHS*, 4th ser., 23 (1941), 71–112

Guillot, O., *Le comte d'Anjou et son entourage au XIe siècle*, 2 vols (Paris, 1972)

Gullick, M., 'An Eleventh-century Bury Medical Manuscript', in Licence, ed., *Bury St Edmunds*, 190–226

Gussone, N., *Thron und Inthronisation des Papstes von den Anfängen bis zum 12. Jahrhundert*, Bonner historische Forschungen, 41 (Bonn, 1978)

Hadley, D., *The Northern Danelaw: Its Social Structure, c. 800–1100* (London, 2000)

Hägermann, D., *Das Papsttum am Vorabend des Investiturstreits. Stephan IX. (1057–1058), Benedikt X. (1058) und Nikolaus II. (1058–61)*, Päpste und Päpsttum, Bd 36 (Stuttgart, 2008)

Hamilton, S., 'A New Model for Royal Penance? Helgaud of Fleury's *Life of Robert the Pious*', *EME* 6 (1997), 189–200

Hare, M., 'Kings, Crowns and Festivals: The Origins of Gloucester as a Royal Ceremonial Centre', *Transactions of the Bristol and Gloucestershire Archaeological Society* 115 (1997), 41–78

Harrison, S., and J. McNeill, 'The Romanesque Monastic Buildings at Westminster Abbey', in Rodwell and Tatton-Brown, ed., *Westminster*, I (Royal Abbey), 69–103

Hart, C., 'The Mersea Charter of Edward the Confessor', *Essex Archaeology and History* 12 (1980), 94–102; repr. in idem, *The Danelaw* (London and Rio Grande, 1992), 495–508

Harvey, S., 'Eustace II of Boulogne and the English Coinage', in Roffe, ed., *The English*, 149–57

Haskins, C. H., 'King Harold's Books', *EHR* 37 (1922), 398–400

Hayward, P., 'Gregory the Great as "Apostle of the English" in Post-Conquest Canterbury', *JEH* 55 (2004)

Heikkilä, T., *Vita s. Symeonis Treverensis: Ein hochmittelalterlicher Heiligenkult im Kontext* (Helsinki, 2002)

Herrick, S. K., *Imagining the Sacred Past: Hagiography and Power in Early Normandy* (Cambridge, MA, 2007)

Hill, D., ed., *Ethelred the Unready: Papers from the Millenary Conference* (Oxford, 1978)

—— *An Atlas of Anglo-Saxon England* (Oxford, new edn, 1984)

Heslop, T. A., 'Seals', in Lapidge et al., eds, *The Blackwell Encyclopaedia*, 413–14

Higham, N. J., *The Death of Anglo-Saxon England* (Stroud, 1997)

—— 'Harold Godwinson: The Construction of Kingship', in Owen-Crocker, ed., *King Harold II*, 19–34

Hooper, N., 'Anglo-Saxon Warfare on the Eve of the Conquest: A Brief Survey', *ANS* 1 (1979), 84–93

—— 'Edgar the Ætheling: Anglo-Saxon Prince, Rebel and Crusader', *ASE* 14 (1985), 197–214

—— 'The Housecarls of England in the Eleventh Century', *ANS* 7 (1985), 161–76

—— 'Some Observations on the Navy in late Anglo-Saxon England', in C. Harper-Bill, C. J. Holdsworth, and J. L. Nelson, eds, *Studies in Medieval History presented to R. Allen Brown* (Woodbridge, 1989), 203–13

Howe, J., 'The Date of the "Life" of St. Vigor of Bayeux', *AB* 102 (1984), 302–12

Hudson, B. T., 'The Family of Harold Godwinson and the Irish Sea Province', *Journal of the Royal Society of Antiquaries of Ireland* 109 (1979), 92–100

—— 'The Destruction of Gruffudd ap Llywelyn', *Welsh History Review* 15 (1990–1), 331–50

—— 'Historical Literature of Early Scotland', *Studies in Scottish Literature* 26 (1991), 141–55

—— 'Cnut and the Scottish Kings', *EHR* 107 (1992), 350–60

—— 'The Scottish Chronicle', *SHR* 77 (1998), 129–61

Hudson, J., *The Oxford History of the Laws of England*, vol. 2: *871–1216* (Oxford, 2012)

Huntingdon, J., 'Edward the Celibate, Edward the Saint: Virginity in the Construction of Edward the Confessor', in A. Bernau, R. Evans, and S. Salih, eds, *Medieval Virginities* (Toronto, 2003), 119–39

—— 'Saintly Power as a Model of Royal Authority: The "Royal Touch" and Other Miracles in the Early Vitae of Edward the Confessor', in B. Bolton and C. Meeks, eds, *Aspects of Power and Authority in the Middle Ages* (Turnhout, 2007), 327–43

Hyams, P., 'Homage and Feudalism: A Judicious Separation', in N. Fryde, P. Monnet, and O. G. Oexle, eds, *Die Gegenwart des Feudalismus* (Göttingen, 2002), 13–49

Ingham, N., 'Has a Missing Daughter of Iaroslav Mudryi been Found?', *Russian History* 25 (1999), 231–70

Insley, C., 'Charters and Episcopal Scriptoria in the Anglo-Saxon South-west', *EME* 7 (1998), 173–97

—— 'Where Did All the Charters Go? Anglo-Saxon Charters and the New Politics of the Eleventh-century', *ANS* 24 (2002), 109–27

—— 'Charters, Ritual and Late Tenth-century Kingship', in Nelson et al., eds, *Gender and Historiography*, 75–89

Jackson, P., 'Osbert of Clare and the *Vision of Leofric*: The Transformation of an Old English Narrative', in K. O'Brien O'Keeffe and A. Orchard, eds, *Latin Learning and English Lore: Studies in Anglo-Saxon Literature for Michael Lapidge*, 2 vols (Toronto, 2005), II, 275–92

Jesch, J., *Ships and Men in the Late Viking Age: The Vocabulary of Runic Inscriptions* (Woodbridge, 2001)

Jetté, R., 'Is the Mystery of the Origins of Agatha, Wife of Edward the Exile, Finally Solved?', *New England Historical and Genealogical Register* 150 (1996), 417–32

John, E., 'Edward the Confessor and the Norman Succession', *EHR* 94 (1979), 241–67

Jones, L., 'The Enkolpion of Edward the Confessor: Byzantium and Anglo-Saxon Concepts of Rulership', in S. L. Keefer, K. L. Jolly, and C. E. Karkov, eds, *Cross and Cruciform in the Anglo-Saxon World: Studies to Honour the Memory of Timothy Reuter* (Morgantown, W. Va, 2010), 369–85

—— 'From *Anglorum Basileus* to Norman Saint: The Transformation of Edward the Confessor', *HSJ* 14 (2003), 71–90

—— 'Emma's Greek *Scrine*', in S. Baxter, C. Karkov, J. L. Nelson, and D. Pelteret, eds, *Early Medieval Studies in Memory of Patrick Wormald* (Farnham, 2009), 499–507

Jonsson, K., and G. van der Meer, 'Mints and Moneyers c. 973–1066', in K. Jonsson, ed., *Studies in Late Anglo-Saxon Coinage in Memory of Bror Emil Hildebrand*, Numismatic Essays No. 35 (Stockholm, 1990), 47–136

Kapelle, W. E., *The Norman Conquest of the North: The Region and its Transformation, 1000–1135* (London, 1979)

Karkov, C. E., *The Ruler Portraits of Anglo-Saxon England* (Woodbridge, 2004)

Keats-Rohan, K. S. B., 'William I and the Breton Contingent in the Non-Norman Conquest', *ANS* 13 (1990), 157–72

—— 'Le rôle des Bretons dans la politique de la colonisation normande d'Angleterre (c. 1042–1135)', *MSHAB* 74 (1996), 181–215

—— 'Testimonies of the Living Dead: The Martyrology-Necrology and Necrology in the Chapter Book of Mont-Saint-Michel (Avranches, Bibliothèque municipale,

MS 214)', in D. Rollason, A. J. Piper and M. Harvey, eds, *The Durham Liber Vitae and its Context* (Woodbridge, 2004), 165–90

—— 'Through the Eye of the Needle: Stigand, the Bayeux Tapestry and the Beginning of the *Historia Anglorum*', in Roffe, ed., *The English*, 159–74

—— 'L'expédition de Guillaume, duc de Normandie, et du comte Harold en Bretagne (1064): le témoinage de la *tapisserie de Bayeux* et des chroniqueurs anglo-normands', *MSHAB* 40 (2013), 203–24

—— 'Raoul *Anglicus* et Raoul de Gaël: un réexamen des données anglaises et bretonnes', *MSHAB* 94 (2016), 63–93

Kempshall, M., 'No Bishop, No King: The Ministerial Ideology of Kingship in Asser's *Res Gestae Aelfredi*', in R. Gameson and H. Leyser, eds, *Belief and Culture in the Early Middle Ages: Studies Presented to Henry Mayr-Harting* (Oxford, 2001), 106–27

Kershaw, P. J. E., *Peaceful Kings: Peace, Power, and the Early Medieval Political Imagination* (Oxford, 2011)

Keynes, S., *The Diplomas of King Æthelred 'The Unready', 978–1016: A Study in Their Use as Historical Evidence* (Cambridge, 1980)

—— 'The Crowland Psalter and the Sons of King Edmund Ironside', *Bodleian Library Record* 11 (1985), 359–70

—— 'Regenbald the Chancellor (*sic*)', *ANS* 10 (1988), 185–222

—— 'The Æthelings in Normandy', *ANS* 13 (1991), 173–205

—— 'Cnut's Earls', in Rumble, ed., *The Reign of Cnut*, 43–88

—— 'Giso, Bishop of Wells (1061–88)', *ANS* 19 (1997), 203–71

—— 'Charters and Writs', in Lapidge et al., eds, *The Blackwell Encyclopaedia*, 99–100

—— 'An Abbot, an Archbishop and the Viking Raids of 1006–7 and 1009–12', *ASE* 36 (2007), 151–220

—— 'Edward the Ætheling (*c.* 1005–16)', in Mortimer, ed., *Edward*, 41–62

—— 'The Cult of King Edward the Martyr during the Reign of King Æthelred the Unready', in Nelson et al., eds, *Gender and Historiography*, 115–25

—— 'Church Councils, Royal Assemblies, and Anglo-Saxon Royal Diplomas', in G. R. Owen-Crocker and B. W. Schneider, eds, *Kingship, Legislation and Power in Anglo-Saxon England* (Woodbridge, 2013), 17–182

—— 'King Æthelred the Unready and the Church of Rochester', in B. O'Brien and B. Bombi, eds, *Textus Roffensis: Law, Language, and Libraries in Early Medieval England* (Turnhout, 2015)

—— 'Earl Harold and the Foundation of Waltham Holy Cross (1062)', *ANS* 39 (2017), 81–111

—— 'The Use of Seals in Anglo-Saxon England', in J. Cherry, J. Berenbeim, and L. de Beer, ed., *Seals and Status: The Power of Objects* (London, 2018), 73–83

Keynes, S., and R. Love, 'Earl Godwine's Ship', *ASE* 38 (2009), 185–223

Keynes, S., and R. Naismith, 'The *Agnus Dei* Pennies of King Æthelred the Unready', *ASE* 40 (2011), 175–223

King, V. J., 'Ealdred, Archbishop of York: The Worcester Years', *ANS* 18 (1996), 123–37

Klein, S. S., W. Schipper, and S. Lewis-Simpson, eds, *The Maritime World of the Anglo-Saxons* (Tempe, AZ, 2014)

Knödler, J., 'Rhetorik mit Todesfolge. Diversitätskonstruktionen in mittelalterlichen Feldherrenreden am Beispiel der Rede Wilhelms des Eroberers vor der Schlacht bei Hastings', in G. Strack and J. Knödler, eds, *Rhetorik in Mittelalter und Renaissance. Konzepte – Praxis – Diversität*, Münchener Beiträge zur Geschichtswissenschaft 6 (Munich, 2011), 167–90

Konshuh, C., '*Anraed* in their *Unraed*: The Æthelredian Annals (983–1016) and Their Presentation of King and Advisors', *English Studies* 97 (2016), 140–62

Körner, S., *The Battle of Hastings, England and Europe 1035–1066*, Bibliotheca Historica Lundensis 14 (Lund, 1964)

Körntgen, L., and D. Waßenhoven, eds, *Patterns of Episcopal Power: Bishops in Tenth- and Eleventh-century Western Europe* (Bayreuth, 2011)

Kosto, A. J., *Hostages in the Middle Ages* (Oxford, 2012)

Lambert, T., *Law and Order in Anglo-Saxon England* (Oxford, 2017)

Lapidge, M., 'A Stoic Metaphor in Late Latin Poetry: The Binding of the Cosmos', *Latomus* 39 (1980), 817–37

Lapidge, M., and J. Mann, 'Reconstructing the Anglo-Latin Aesop: The Literary Tradition of the "Hexametrical Romulus"', in M. W. Herren, C. J. Mc Donough, and R. G. Arthur, eds, *Latin Culture in the Eleventh Century: Proceedings of the Third International Conference of Medieval Latin Studies, Cambridge, September 9–12 1998*, 2 vols (Turnhout, 2002), II, 1–33

Lapidge, M., J. Blair, S. Keynes, and D. Scragg, eds, *The Blackwell Encyclopaedia of Anglo-Saxon England* (London, 1999)

Larson, L. M., *The King's Household in England before the Norman Conquest* (Madison, WI, 1904)

—— *Canute the Great* (London, 1912)

Laurent, V., 'Byzance et l'Angleterre au lendemain de la conquête Normande', *Numismatic Circular* 71 (1963), 93–6

Lavelle, R., *Aethelred II: King of the English 987–1016* (Stroud, 2002)

—— 'The Use and Abuse of Hostages in Late Anglo-Saxon England', *EME* 14 (2006), 269–96

Lawson, M. K., *Cnut: England's Viking King* (Stroud, 1993; new edn, 2004)

Leclercq, J., and J.-P. Bonnes, *Un maître de la vie spirituelle au XIe siècle* (Paris, 1946)

Lemagnen, S., ed., *La Tapisserie de Bayeux: Une chronique des temps Vikings?* (Rouen, 2009)

Lethaby, W., 'The Palace of Westminster in the Eleventh and Twelfth Centuries', *Archaeologia* 60 (1906), 131–48

Lewis, A. W., 'Anticipatory Association of the Heir in Early Capetian France', *American Historical Review* 83 (1978), 906–27

Lewis, C. P., 'The French in England before the Conquest', *ANS* 17 (1995), 123–44

—— 'Waltheof, earl of Northumbria (c. 1050–1076), magnate', *ODNB*

Lewis, M. J., G. R. Owen-Crocker, and D. Terkla, ed., *The Bayeux Tapestry: New Approaches: Proceedings of a Conference at the British Museum* (Oxford, 2011)

Lewis, S., *The Rhetoric of Power in the Bayeux Tapestry* (Cambridge, 1999)

Licence, T., 'Goscelin of Saint-Bertin and the Hagiography of St Eadwold of Cerne', *Journal of Medieval Latin* 16 (2007), 182–207

—— *Hermits and Recluses in English Society, 970–1220* (Oxford, 2011)

—— 'Herbert Losinga's Trip to Rome and the Bishopric of Bury St Edmunds', *ANS* 34 (2012), 151–68

—— 'Robert of Jumièges, Archbishop in Exile (1052–5)', *ASE* 42 (2013), 313–29

—— ed., *Bury St Edmunds and the Norman Conquest* (Woodbridge, 2014)

—— 'The Date and Authorship of the *Vita Ædwardi Regis*', *ASE* 44 (2016), 259–85

—— 'Edward the Confessor and the Succession Question: A Fresh Look at the Sources', *ANS* 39 (2017), 113–27

—— 'A New Source for the *Vita Ædwardi Regis*', *Journal of Medieval Latin* 29 (2019), 1–19

Licence, T., and T. A. Heslop, '1066 and the Church', in D. Bates, ed., *1066 in Perspective* (Leeds, 2018), 156–75

Lionarons, J. T., *The Homiletic Writings of Archbishop Wulfstan: A Critical Study* (Woodbridge, 2010)

Loyn, H. R., *The Governance of Anglo-Saxon England 500–1087* (London, 1984)

Lund, N., 'Cnut's Danish Kingdom', in Rumble, ed., *The Reign of Cnut*, 27–42

Lynch, J. H., *Godparents and Kinship in Early Medieval Europe* (Princeton, NJ, 1986)

—— *Christianizing Kinship: Ritual Sponsorship in Anglo-Saxon England* (Ithaca, NY, 1998)

Lyon, S., 'The "Expanding Cross" Type of Edward the Confessor and the Appledore (1997) Hoard', *Numismatic Circular* 106 (1998), 426–8

Mack, K., 'Changing Thegns: Cnut's Conquest and the English Aristocracy', *Albion* 16 (1984), 375–87

—— 'The Stallers: Administrative Innovation in the Reign of King Edward the Confessor', *Journal of Medieval History* 12 (1986), 123–34

Maddicott, J. R., 'Edward the Confessor's Return to England in 1041', *EHR* 119 (2004), 650–66

—— *The Origins of the English Parliament, 924–1327* (Oxford, 2010)

Mann, J., *From Aesop to Reynard: Beast Literature in Medieval Britain* (Oxford, 2009)

Marafioti, N., *The King's Body: Burial and Succession in Late Anglo-Saxon England* (Toronto, 2014)

Margary, I. D., *Roman Roads in Britain* (London, 1955; rev. edn, 1967)

Martinet, S., 'Élinand, évêque de Laon méconnu (1052–1098)', in *Mémoires de la Fédération des sociétés d'histoire et d'archéologie de l'Aisne* 36 (1991), 58–78

Mason, E., *St Wulfstan of Worcester c. 1008–1095* (Oxford, 1990)

—— *The House of Godwine: The History of a Dynasty* (London and New York, 2004)

Maund, K., 'The Welsh Alliances of Earl Ælfgar of Mercia and his Family in the Mid-eleventh Century', *ANS* 11 (1989), 181–90

—— *Ireland, Wales, and England in the Eleventh Century* (Woodbridge, 1991)

McDonald, R. A., *The Kingdom of the Isles: Scotland's Western Seaboard, c. 1100–c. 1336* (East Linton, 1997)

McCready, W. D., *'Odiosa Sanctitas': St Peter Damian, Simony, and Reform* (Toronto, 2011)

Melnikova, E., 'The Baltic Policy of Jaroslav the Wise', in U. Fransson, M. Svedin, S. Bergerbrant, and F. Androshchuk, eds, *Cultural Interaction between East and West: Archaeology, Artefacts and Human Contacts in Northern Europe* (Stockholm, 2007), 73–77

Meens, R., 'Politics, Mirrors of Princes and the Bible: Sins, Kings and the Well-being of the realm', *EME* 7 (1998), 345–57

Molyneaux, G., *The Formation of the English Kingdom in the Tenth Century* (Oxford, 2015)

Mortimer, R., ed., *Edward the Confessor: The Man and the Legend* (Woodbridge, 2009)

—— 'Edward the Confessor: The Man and the Legend', in idem, ed., *Edward*, 1–40

Mostert, M., *The Political Theology of Abbo of Fleury: A Study of the Ideas about Society and Law of the Tenth-century Monastic Reform Movement* (Hilversum, 1987)

Muresan, D. I., '"Ego Wilhelmus victoriosus Anglorum basileus": Les circonstances de la synthèse impériale anglo-normande', *Annales de Normandie* 69 (2019), 107–64

Musset, L., 'Notules fécampoises', *Bulletin de la Société des Antiquaires de Normandie* 54 (1957–8), 584–98

—— 'Les relations extérieures de la Normandie du IXe au XIe siècle, d'après quelques trouvailles monétaires récentes', repr. from *Annales de Normandie* 4 (1958), 31–8, in idem, *Nordica et Normannica. Recueil d'études sur la Scandinavie ancienne et médiévale, les expéditions des Vikings et la fondation de la Normandie* (Paris, 1997), 297–306

Naismith, R., 'Payments for Land and Privilege in Anglo-Saxon England', *ASE* 41 (2012), 277–342

—— *Medieval European Coinage, with a catalogue of the coins in the Fitzwilliam Museum, Cambridge: 8 Britain and Ireland c. 400–1066* (Cambridge, 2017)

Naismith, R., and F. Tinti, 'The Origins of Peter's Pence', *EHR* 134 (2019), 521–52

Nelson, J. L., 'Coronation Rituals and Related Materials', in J. T. Rosenthal, ed., *Understanding Medieval Primary Sources: Using Historical Sources to Discover Medieval Europe* (London, 2012), 114–30

Nelson, J. L., S. Reynolds, and S. M. Johns, eds, *Gender and Historiography: Studies in the Earlier Middle Ages in Honour of Pauline Stafford* (London, 2012)

Neveux, F., 'L'expédition de Guillaume le Bâtard en Bretagne (vers 1064)', in J. Quaghebeur and S. Soleil, eds, *Le pouvoir et la foi au Moyen Âge en Bretagne et dans l'Europe de l'Ouest: Mélanges en mémoire du professeur Hubert Guillotel* (Rennes, 2010), 619–37

Oakley, F., *Empty Bottles of Gentilism: Kingship and the Divine in Late Antiquity and the Early Middle Ages (to 1050)* (New Haven, CT and London, 2010)

O' Brien, B., *God's Peace and King's Peace: The Laws of Edward the Confessor* (Philadelphia, PA, 1999)

—— 'Pre-Conquest Laws and Legislators in the Twelfth Century', in M. Brett and D. A. Woodman, eds, *The Long Twelfth-century View of the Anglo-Saxon Past* (Farnham, 2015), 229–72

Ogilvy, A., *Books Known to the English, 597–1066* (Cambridge, MA, 1967)

Oleson, T. J., *The Witenagemot in the Reign of Edward the Confessor: A Study in the Constitutional History of Eleventh-century England* (Oxford, 1955)

Orchard, A., 'Literary Background to the Encomium', *Journal of Medieval Latin* 11 (2001), 156–83

Ordnance Survey, *Britain before the Norman Conquest* (Southampton, 1973)

O'Sullivan, S., *Early Medieval Glosses on Prudentius' Psychomachia: The Weitz Tradition*, Mittellateinische Studien und Texte, ed. P. G. Schmidt, Bd. 31 (Leiden, 2004)

Otter, M., 'Closed Doors: An Epithalamium for Queen Edith, Widow and Virgin', in A. J. Weisl and C. Carlson, eds, *Constructions of Widowhood and Virginity in the Middle Ages* (New York, 1999), 63–92

—— '1066: The Moment of Transition in Two Narratives of the Norman Conquest', *Speculum* 74 (1999), 565–86

Owen-Crocker, G. R., 'Squawk Talk: Commentary by Birds in the Bayeux Tapestry', *ASE* 34 (2005), 237–56

—— ed., *King Harold II and the Bayeux Tapestry* (Woodbridge, 2005)

—— 'The Embroidered Word: Text in the Bayeux Tapestry', *Medieval Clothing and Textiles* 2 (2006), 35–59

—— 'The Interpretation of Gesture in the Bayeux Tapestry', *ANS* 29 (2007), 145–78

—— 'The Bayeux Tapestry: The Voice from the Border', in S. L. Keefer and R. H. Bremner Jr, eds, *Signs on the Edge: Space, Text and Margin in Medieval Manuscripts* (Louvain, 2007), 235–58

—— *The Bayeux Tapestry: Collected Papers* (Farnham, 2012)

—— '". . . Velis Vento Plenis . . .": Sea Crossings in the Bayeux Tapestry', in Klein et al., eds, *Maritime World*, 131–56

Pagan, H., 'The *PACX* Type of Edward the Confessor', *British Numismatic Journal* 81 (2011), 9–106

Parisse, M., P. Pégeot, and B.-M. Tock, ed., *Pancartes monastiques* (Turnhout, 1998)

Pastan, E. C., 'Building Stories: The Representation of Architecture in the Bayeux Embroidery', *ANS* 33 (2011), 151–85

—— 'A Feast for the Eyes: Representing Odo at the Banquet in the Bayeux Embroidery', *HSJ* 22 (2012), 83–121

Pastan, E. C., and S. D. White, 'Problematizing Patronage: Odo of Bayeux and the Bayeux Tapestry', in Foys et al., ed., *The Bayeux Tapestry: New Interpretations*, 1–24

Pastan, E. C., and S. D. White, with K. Gilbert, *The Bayeux Tapestry and its Contexts: A Reassessment* (Woodbridge, 2014)

Pelteret, D. A. E., *Slavery in Early Medieval England from the Reign of Alfred until the Twelfth Century* (Woodbridge, 1995)

—— 'Eleventh-century Anglo-Saxon Long-haul Travelers: Jerusalem, Constantinople, and Beyond', in Klein et al., eds, *Maritime World*, 75–129

Peltzer, J., *1066: Der Kampf um Englands Krone* (Munich, 2016)

Pohl, B., *Dudo of Saint-Quentin's 'Historia Normannorum': Tradition, Innovation and Memory* (Woodbridge and Rochester, NY, 2015)

Poole, R. G., *Viking Poems on War and Peace: A Study in Skaldic Narrative* (Toronto, 1991)

Potts, C., 'Normandy or Brittany? A Conflict of Interests at Mont Saint-Michel (966–1035)', *ANS* 12 (1990), 135–56

Pounds, N. J. G., *An Historical Geography of Europe 450 B.C.–A.D. 1330* (Cambridge, 1973)

Pratt, D., 'Demesne Exemption from Royal Taxation in Anglo-Saxon and Anglo-Norman England', *EHR* 123 (2013), 1–34

Raraty, D. G. J., 'Earl Godwine of Wessex: The Origins of his Power and his Political Loyalties', *History* 74 (1989), 3–19

Raw, B. C., *Anglo-Saxon Crucifixion Iconography and the Art of the Monastic Revival* (Cambridge, 1990)

Reynolds, P. L., *Marriage in the Western Church: The Christianization of Marriage during the Patristic and Early Medieval Periods* (new edn, Boston; Leiden, 2001)

Roach, L., 'Public Rites and Public Wrongs: Ritual Aspects of Diplomas in Tenth- and Eleventh-century England', *EME* 19 (2011), 182–203

—— *Kingship and Consent in Anglo-Saxon England, 871–978: Assemblies and the State in the Early Middle Ages* (Cambridge, 2013)

—— 'Penitential Discourse in the Diplomas of King Æthelred "the Unready"', *JEH* 64 (2013), 258–76

—— 'Apocalypse and Atonement in the Politics of Later Æthelredian England', *English Studies* 95 (2014), 733–57

—— *Æthelred the Unready* (New Haven, CT and London, 2016)

Robinson, I. S., *Henry IV of Germany, 1056–1106* (Cambridge, 1999)

Rodwell, W., 'New Glimpses of Edward the Confessor's Abbey at Westminster', in Mortimer, ed., *Edward*, 151–67

—— 'The Archaeology of Westminster Abbey: An Historiographical Overview', in Rodwell and Tatton-Brown, ed., *Westminster*, I (Royal Abbey), 34–60

Rodwell, W., and T. Tatton-Brown, ed., *Westminster: The Art, Architecture and Archaeology of the Royal Abbey and Palace*, BAA Conference Transactions 39, 2 pts (Leeds, 2015)

Roffe, D., ed., *The English and their Legacy, 900–122: Essays in Honour of Ann Williams* (Woodbridge, 2012)

Rogers, N., 'The Waltham Abbey Relic-list', in C. Hicks, ed., *England in the Eleventh Century: Proceedings of the 1990 Harlaxton Symposium* (Stamford, 1992), 157–81

Rollason, D. W., 'The Cults of Murdered Royal Saints in Anglo-Saxon England', *ASE* 11 (1982), 1–22

Rumble, A. R., ed., *The Reign of Cnut, King of England, Denmark and Norway* (London and New York, 1994)

Sawyer, P., *The Wealth of Anglo-Saxon England* (Oxford, 2013)

Schenk, G. J., *Zeremoniell und Politik. Herrschereinzüge im spätmittelalterlichen Reich*, Forschungen zur Kaiser- und Papstgeschichte des Mittelalters 21 (Cologne, 2003)

Schmid, K., 'Die Thronfolge Ottos des Großen', *Zeitschrift der Savigny-Stiftung für Rechtsgeschichte: Germanistische Abteilung* 81.1 (1964), 80–163

Schmidt, T., *Alexander II. und die römische Reformgruppe seiner Zeit*, Päpste und Päpsttum, Bd 11 (Stuttgart, 1977)

Scholz, B. W., 'Two Forged Charters from the Abbey of Westminster and Their Relationship with St. Denis', *EHR* 76 (1961), 466–78

Schramm, P. E., *Kaiser, Könige und Päpste: Gesammelte Aufsätze zur Geschichte des Mittelalters*, 4 vols (Stuttgart, 1968–71)

Scragg, D., ed., *Edgar, King of the English, 959–975* (Woodbridge, 2008)

Searle, E., *Predatory Kinship and the Creation of Norman Power, 840–1066* (Berkeley, CA, 1988)

Sharpe, R., 'The Use of Writs in the Eleventh Century', *ASE* 32 (2003), 247–91

Sheppard, A., *Families of the King: Writing Identity in the Anglo-Saxon Chronicle* (Toronto and London, 2004)

Smith, M. F., 'Archbishop Stigand and the Eye of the Needle', *ANS* 16 (1994), 199–219

Smith, M. F., R. Fleming, and P. Halpin, 'Court and Piety in Late Anglo-Saxon England', *Catholic Historical Review* 87 (2001), 569–602

Stafford, P., 'The "Farm of One Night" and the Organization of King Edward's Estates in Domesday', *Economic History Review*, 2nd ser. 33 (1980), 491–502

—— 'The Laws of Cnut and the History of the Anglo-Saxon Royal Promise', *ASE* 10 (1982), 173–90

—— *Unification and Conquest: A Political and Social History of England in the Tenth and Eleventh Centuries* (London, 1989)

—— *Queen Emma and Queen Edith: Queenship and Women's Power in Eleventh-century England* (Oxford, 1997)

—— 'Edith, Edward's Wife and Queen', in Mortimer, ed., *Edward*, 119–38

—— 'Archbishop Ealdred and the D Chronicle', in D. Crouch and K. Thompson, eds, *Normandy and its Neighbours 900–1250: Essays for David Bates* (Turnhout, 2011), 135–56

—— 'Royal Women and Transitions: Emma and Ælfgifu in 1035–1042/3', in Körntgen and Waßenhoven, eds, *Patterns of Episcopal Power*, 127–44

—— 'The Making of Chronicles and the Making of England: The Anglo-Saxon Chronicles after Alfred', *TRHS*, 6th ser. 27 (2017), 65–86

Stanley, A. P., *Historical Memorials of Westminster Abbey* (London, 5th edn, 1882)

Stenton, F. M., *Anglo-Saxon England* (Oxford, 3rd edn, 1971)

Stevenson, W. H., 'An Alleged Son of King Harold Harefoot', *EHR* 28 (1913), 112–17

Storey, J. E., 'Symeon as Annalist', in D. Rollason, ed., *Symeon of Durham: Historian of Durham and the North* (Stamford, 1998), 202–13

Summerson, H., 'Tudor Antiquaries and the *Vita Ædwardi Regis*', *ASE* 38 (2009), 157–84

Suppe, F. C., 'Who was Rhys Sais? Some Comments on Anglo-Welsh Relations before 1066', *HSJ* 7 (1995), 63–73

Talvio, T., 'Harold I and Harthacnut's Jewel Cross Type Reconsidered', in M. Blackburn, ed., *Anglo-Saxon Monetary History: Essays in Memory of Michael Dolley* (Leicester, 1986), 273–90

—— 'The Design of Edward the Confessor's Coins', in Jonsson, ed., *Studies in Late Anglo-Saxon Coinage*, 487–99

—— 'The Stylistic Structure of Edward the Confessor's Coinage', in R. Naismith, M. Allen, and E. Screen, eds, *Early Medieval Monetary History: Studies in Memory of Mark Blackburn* (Farnham, 2014), 173–86

Tanner, H. J., 'The Expansion of the Power and Influence of the Counts of Boulogne under Eustace II', *ANS* 14 (1992), 251–86

—— *Families, Friends and Allies: Boulogne and Politics in Northern France and England, c. 879–1160* (Leiden and Boston, 2004)

Taylour, C. [Henry Keepe], *A true and perfect narrative of the strange and unexpected finding the crucifix & gold-chain of that most pious prince, St Edward the Confessor* [etc] (London, 1688)

Tinti, F., 'The Pallium Privilege of Pope Nicholas II for Archbishop Ealdred of York', *JEH* 70 (2019), 708–30

Townend, M., 'Contextualizing the *Knútsdrápur*: Skaldic Praise-poetry at the Court of Cnut', *ASE* 30 (2001), 145–79

Tsurushima, H., '"*Hic Est Miles*": Some Images of Three Knights: Turold, Wadard and Vital', in Lewis et al., eds, *The Bayeux Tapestry*, 81–91

Tyler, E. M., '"When Wings Incarnadine with Gold are Spread": The *Vita Ædwardi Regis* and the Display of Treasure at the Court of Edward the Confessor', in eadem, ed., *Treasure in the Medieval West* (York, 2000), 83–107

—— 'Talking about History in Eleventh-century England: The *Encomium Emmae Reginae* and the Court of Harthacnut', *EME* 13 (2005), 359–83

—— 'Fictions of Family: The *Encomium Emmae Reginae* and Virgil's *Aeneid*', *Viator* 36 (2008), 149–79

—— 'The *Vita Ædwardi*: The Politics of Poetry at Wilton Abbey', *ANS* 31 (2009), 135–56

—— 'Trojans in Anglo-Saxon England: Precedent without Descent', *Review of English Studies* 64 (2013), 1–20

—— *England in Europe: English Royal Women and Literary Patronage, c. 1000– c. 1150* (Toronto, 2017)

Ubl, K., 'Der kinderlose König. Ein Testfall für die Ausdifferenzierung des Politischen im 11. Jahrhundert', *Historische Zeitschrift* 292 (2011), 323–63

Van Houts, E. M. C., 'The Political Relations between Normandy and England before
      1066 According to the *Gesta Normannorum Ducum*', in R. Foreville, ed., *Les mutations socio-
      culturelles au tournant des XIe–XIIe siècles* (Paris, 1984), 85–97
—— 'A Note on *Jezebel* and *Semiramis*, Two Latin Norman Poems from the Early Eleventh
      Century', *Journal of Medieval Latin* 2 (1992), 18–24
—— 'The Norman Conquest through European Eyes', *EHR* 110 (1995), 832–53
—— 'History and Hagiography at Saint-Wandrille: The "Inventio et Miracula sancti
      Vulfranni"', *ANS* 12 (1989), 233–51
—— 'Edward and Normandy', in Mortimer, ed., *Edward*, 63–76
—— 'Qui étaient les Normands?', in D. Bates and P. Bauduin, eds, *Penser les mondes
      normands médiévaux (911–2011)* (Caen, 2016), 129–46
Van Kempen, A. F. J., 'The Mercian Connection, Harold Godwineson's Ambitions,
      Diplomacy and Channel-crossing, 1056–1066', *History* 94 (2009), 2–19
Vince, A., *Saxon London: An Archaeological Investigation* (London, 1990)
—— ed., *Aspects of Saxo-Norman London*: 2: *Finds and Environmental Evidence*, London and
      Middlesex Archaeological Society, Special Paper 12 (Over Wallop, Hants., 1991)
Walker, D., 'Gruffudd ap Llywelyn (*d.* 1063)', *ODNB*
Walker, I. W., *Harold, the Last Anglo-Saxon King* (Stroud, 1997)
Ward, E. J., 'Anne of Kiev (*c.* 1024–*c.* 1075) and a Reassessment of Maternal Power in the
      Minority Kingship of Philip I of France', *Historical Research* 89 (2016), 435–53
Weinfurter, S., *The Salian Century: Main Currents in an Age of Transition*, tr. B. M. Bowlus
      (Philadelphia, PA, 1999)
Wickham, C., *Medieval Rome: Stability and Crisis of a City, 900–1150* (Oxford, 2014)
Wieland, G. R., *The Latin Glosses on Arator and Prudentius, in Cambridge University Library MS
      Gg. 5. 35* (Toronto, 1983)
Williams, A., 'Some Notes and Considerations on Problems Connected with the English
      Royal Succession, 860–1066', *ANS* 1 (1979), 144–67
—— 'Land and Power in the Eleventh Century: The Estates of Harold Godwineson', *ANS*
      3 (1981), 170–87
—— '"Cockles amongst the Wheat": Danes and English in the Western Midlands in the
      First Half of the Eleventh Century', *Midland History* 11 (1986), 1–22
—— 'The King's Nephew: The Family and Career of Ralph, Earl of Hereford', in
      C. Harper-Bill, C. J. Holdsworth, and J. L. Nelson, eds, *Studies in Medieval History presented
      to R. Allen Brown* (Woodbridge, 1989), 327–40
—— *The English and the Norman Conquest* (Woodbridge, 1995)
—— *Land, Power and Politics: The Family and Career of Odda of Deerhurst* (Deerhurst: The
      Deerhurst Lecture, 1997)
—— *Kingship and Government in Pre-Conquest England c. 500–1066* (Basingstoke and London,
      1999)
—— *Æthelred the Unready: The Ill-counselled King* (London, 2003)
—— 'A Bell-house and a Burh-geat: Lordly Residences in England before the Norman
      Conquest', in R. Liddiard, ed., *Anglo-Norman Castles* (Woodbridge, 2003)
—— 'Ælfgar, earl of Mercia', *ODNB*
—— 'Leofric, earl of Mercia', *ODNB*
—— 'Ralph the Staller, earl of East Anglia (d. 1068 × 70)', *ODNB*
—— 'Robert fitz Wimarc [*called* Robert the Staller] (*d. c.* 1070)', *ODNB*
—— *The World before Domesday: The English Aristocracy, 900–1066* (London, 2008)
—— 'The Piety of Earl Godwine', *ANS* 34 (2012), 237–56
—— 'Regional Communities and Royal Authority in the Late Old English Kingdom: The
      Crisis of 1051–1052 Revisited', *History* 98 (2013), 23–40
Williams, G., 'A Hoard of "Expanding Cross" Pennies from Appledore: Preliminary
      Report', *Numismatic Circular* 106 (1998), 152–3
Winkler, E. A., '1074 in the Twelfth Century', *ANS* 36 (2014), 241–58

—— *Royal Responsibility in Anglo-Norman Historical Writing* (Oxford, 2017)

Winterbottom, M., 'Notes on the Life of Edward the Confessor', *Medium Ævum* 56 (1987), 82–4

Woodman, F., 'Edward the Confessor's Church at Westminster: An Alternative View', in Rodwell and Tatton-Brown, eds, *Westminster*, I (Royal Abbey), 61–8

Woods, D., 'The *Agnus Dei* Penny of King Æthelred II: A Call to Hope in the Lord (Isaiah XL)?', *ASE* 42 (2013), 299–309

Woolf, A., *From Pictland to Alba, 789–1070* (Edinburgh, 2007)

Wormald, P., 'How Do We Know So Much about Anglo-Saxon Deerhurst?', in idem, *The Times of Bede: Studies in Early English Christian Society and its Historian*, ed. S. Baxter (Oxford, 2006), 229–48

Wyatt, D., *Slaves and Warriors in Medieval Britain and Ireland, 800–1200* (Leiden and Boston, 2009)

Zajac, T., 'Gloriosa Regina or "Alien Queen"? Some Reconsiderations on Anna Yaroslavna's Queenship (r. 1050–1075)', *Royal Studies Journal* 3 (2016), 23–70

INDEX